BASIC ECONOMICS

BASIC ECONOMICS

A Citizen's Guide to the Economy

REVISED AND EXPANDED EDITION

THOMAS SOWELL

Basic Books
A Member of the Perseus Books Group
New York

Books published by Basic Books are available at special discounts for bulk purchases in the United States by corporations, institutions, and other organizations. For more information, please contact the Special Markets Department at the Perseus Books Group, 11 Cambridge Center, Cambridge MA 02142, or call (617) 252-5298, (800) 255-1514 or e-mail j.mccrary@perseusbooks.com.

Sowell, Thomas, 1930–
    Basic economics : a citizens guide to the economy / Thomas Sowell.—
Rev. and expanded ed.
        p.   cm.
    Includes bibliographical references and index.
    ISBN 0-465-08145-2 (alk. paper)
    1. Economics.   I. Title.

HB171.S713 2003
330—dc21   2003013778

04 05 06 / 10 9 8 7 6 5 4

A few lines of reasoning can change the way we see the world.
Steven E. Landsburg

CONTENTS

Preface   ix

1   What is Economics?   1

PART I: PRICES AND MARKETS

2   The Role of Prices   7

3   Price Controls   21

4   An Overview   41

PART II: INDUSTRY AND COMMERCE

5   The Rise and Fall of Businesses   63

6   The Role of Profits—and Losses   78

7   Big Business and Government   99

8   An Overview   119

PART III: WORK AND PAY

9   Productivity and Pay   141

10 Controlled Labor Markets   159

11 An Overview   176

PART IV: TIME AND RISK

12 Investment and Speculation   191

13 Risks and Insurance   210

14 An Overview   229

PART V: THE NATIONAL ECONOMY

15 National Output   245

16 Money and the Banking System   257

17 The Role of Government   271

18 An Overview   295

PART VI: THE INTERNATIONAL ECONOMY

19 International Trade   307

20 International Transfers of Wealth   327

21 An Overview   346

PART VII: SPECIAL ECONOMIC ISSUES

22 "Non-Economic" Values   359

23 Myths About Markets   372

24 Parting Thoughts   390

Questions   397
Sources   407
Index   433

PREFACE

This is the revised and enlarged edition of an introduction to economics for the general public. In addition to being updated, *Basic Economics* has also become more internationalized by including information from more countries around the world, because the basic principles of economics are not confined by national borders. The fact that the first edition of this book has already been translated into Japanese and Polish suggests that others recognize this as well. While most chapter titles remain the same, their contents have changed considerably, reflecting the experiences of many different peoples and cultures.

Basic Economics has two main purposes. The first is to show certain general principles which apply in any economy—whether capitalist, socialist, feudal, or whatever. Another equally important purpose is to get the reader to look at economic policies and economic systems in terms of the incentives they create, rather than simply the goals that they proclaim. This means that consequences matter more than intentions—and not just the immediate consequences. The longer run repercussions of any economic policy need to be considered by the public, especially because so many public officials may not look beyond the next election.

This book was written both for the general public and for students in introductory economics courses. It has none of the graphs, equations, or statistical tables usually found in economics books. Nor does it use the technical jargon of economists. What I have learned after many years of teaching and writing about economics is that there are highly intelligent people who want to understand more about the way the economy works, but who have no interest in the paraphernalia of the economics profession. This book is written for such people.

Many other kinds of people may also find *Basic Economics* useful, including journalists who often comment on economic issues without having any background in the subject. Even scholars with Ph.D.s in other fields are often uninformed or misinformed about economics, though that seldom deters them from having and voicing opinions on economic issues.

Most of us are necessarily ignorant of many complex fields, from botany to brain surgery. As a result, we simply do not attempt to operate in, or comment on, those fields. However, every voter and every politician that they vote for affects economic policies. They cannot opt out of economic issues. Their only options are to be informed or not informed when making their choices. *Basic Economics* is intended to make it easy for them to be informed. The basic principles of economics are not hard to understand but they are easy to forget, especially amid the heady rhetoric of politics and the media. The vivid examples used throughout this book make these principles indelible, in a way that graphs and equations may not.

In keeping with the nature of *Basic Economic* as an introduction to economics for the general public, the usual footnotes or end-notes are left out. However, those who wish to check up on some of the surprising facts they will learn about here can find the sources listed at the end of the book.[1] That will also be a place for those who simply wish to find other books and articles to read, in order to explore further on some subject that they find intriguing. For instructors who are using *Basic Economics* as a textbook in their courses, some essay questions have been added at the back of the book. These questions may also be useful to parents who are homeschooling their children.

While it is advisable to understand the role of prices in a market economy before going on to other subjects, each chapter of this book has been written to stand alone, so that these chapters may be read in whatever order your own interest leads you to prefer. Whether you are reading *Basic Economics* for a course or just for your own understanding of the economy, it has been written with the thought that it should be not only a relaxed experience, but also an enjoyable one.

THOMAS SOWELL
Hoover Institution
Stanford University

---

[1]Much as I might like to take credit for all this information, I must admit that my research assistant, Na Liu, did most of the hard work.

Chapter 1

What Is Economics?

You can't have it all. Where would you put it?

—ANN LANDERS

Virtually everyone agrees on the importance of economics, but there is far less agreement on just what economics is. Among the many misconceptions of economics is that it is something that tells you how to make money or run a business or predict the ups and downs of the stock market. But economics is not personal finance or business administration, and predicting the ups and downs of the stock market has yet to be reduced to a set of dependable principles.

To know what economics is, we must first know what an economy is. Perhaps most of us think of an economy as a system for the production and distribution of the goods and services we use in everyday life. That is true as far as it goes, but it does not go far enough. The Garden of Eden was a system for the production and distribution of goods and services, but it was not an economy, because everything was available in unlimited abundance. Without scarcity, there is no need to economize—and therefore no economics. A distinguished British economist named Lionel Robbins gave the classic definition of economics:

> *Economics is the study of the use of scarce resources which have alternative uses.*

Some optimists have said that we now live in "an era of abundance" and some pessimists have said that we are entering "an era of scarcity." Both are wrong. The wide range of goods and services available to us vastly exceeds what past generations and past centuries had to offer. But every era has always been an era of scarcity.

What does "scarce" mean? It means that what everybody wants adds up to more than there is. This may seem like a simple thing, but its implications are often grossly misunderstood, even by highly educated people. For example, a feature article in the *New York Times* laid out the economic woes and worries of middle-class Americans—one of the most affluent groups of human beings ever to inhabit this planet. Although the story included a picture of a middle-class American family in their own swimming pool, the main headline read: "The American Middle, Just Getting By." Other headings in the article included:

Wishes Deferred and Plans Unmet

Goals That Remain Just Out of Sight

Dogged Saving and Some Luxuries

In short, middle-class Americans' desires exceed what they can comfortably afford, even though what they already have would be considered unbelievable prosperity by people in many other countries around the world—or even by earlier generations of Americans. Yet both they and the reporter regard them as "just getting by" and a Harvard sociologist spoke of "how budget-constrained these people really are." However, it is not something as man-made as a budget that constrains them: Reality constrains them. There has never been enough to satisfy everyone completely. That is the real constraint. That is what scarcity means.

Although per capita real income in the United States increased 50 percent in just one generation, these middle-class families "have had to work hard for their modest gains," according to a Fordham professor quoted in the same article. (Were they expecting manna from heaven?) As for how hard they worked and the modesty of their gains, it is doubtful whether most other people in the world would regard Americans' work in air-conditioned offices with coffee breaks as "hard" or their standard of living as "just getting by." However, as someone once said: "Just as soon as people make enough money to live comfortably, they want to live extravagantly." Even millionaires can have a hard time making ends meet if they try to live like billionaires.

The *New York Times* reporter wrote of one of these middle-class families:

After getting in over their heads in credit card spending years ago, their finances are now in order. "But if we make a wrong move," Geraldine Frazier said, "the pressure we had from the bills will come back, and that is painful."

To all these people—from academia and journalism, as well as the middle-class people themselves—it apparently seemed strange somehow that there should be such a thing as scarcity and that this should imply a need for both productive efforts on their part and personal responsibility in spending. Yet nothing has been more pervasive in the history of the human race than scarcity and all the requirements for economizing that go with scarcity.

Not only scarcity but also "alternative uses" are at the heart of economics. If each resource had only one use, economics would be much simpler. But water can be used to produce ice or steam by itself or innumerable mixtures and compounds in combination with other things. A virtually limitless number of products can also be produced from wood or from petroleum, iron ore, etc. How much of each resource should be allocated to each of its many uses? Every economy has to answer that question, and each one does, in one way or another, efficiently or inefficiently. Doing so efficiently is what economics is all about.

Whether the people in a given economy will be prosperous or poverty-stricken depends in large part on how well their resources are allocated. Rich resources often exist in very poor countries, simply because the country lacks the economic mechanisms, as well as specific skills, for efficiently turning those resources into abundant output. Conversely, countries with relatively few natural resources—Japan or Switzerland, for example—can have very high standards of living, if their people and their economy are well adapted for allocating and using whatever resources they have or can purchase from other countries.

Economics is not about the financial fate of individuals. It is about the material well-being of society as a whole. It shows cause and effect relationships involving prices, industry and commerce, work and pay, or the international balance of trade—all from the standpoint of how this affects the allocation of scarce resources in a way that raises or lowers the material standard of living of the people as a whole.

Money doesn't even have to be involved to make a decision be economic. When a military medical team arrives on a battlefield where soldiers have a variety of wounds, they are confronted with the classic economic problem of allocating scarce resources which have alternative uses. Almost never are there enough doctors, nurses, or paramedics to go around, nor enough medication. Some of the wounded are near death and have little chance of being saved, while others have a fighting chance if they get immediate care, and still others are only slightly wounded and will probably recover whether they get immediate medical care or not.

If the medical team does not allocate its time and medications efficiently, some wounded soldiers will die needlessly, while time is being spent attending to others not as urgently in need of care or still others whose wounds are so devastating that they will probably die in spite of anything that can be done for them. It is an economic problem, though not a dime changes hands.

Most of us hate even to think of having to make such choices. Indeed, as we have already seen, some middle-class Americans are distressed at having to make much milder choices and trade-offs. But life does not ask what we want. It presents us with options. Economics is just one of the ways of trying to make the most of those options.

While there are controversies in economics, as there are in science, this does not mean that economics is just a matter of opinion. There are basic propositions and procedures in economics on which a Marxist economist like Oskar Lange did not differ in any fundamental way from a conservative economist like Milton Friedman. It is these basic economic principles that this book is about.

Much of what follows in the chapters ahead is an analysis of what happens in an economy coordinated by prices and by the resulting flows of money and goods in a competitive market. But it also considers what happens when markets are not permitted to operate in that way, whether because of business, labor unions, or government.

One of the best ways of understanding the role of prices, for example, is by understanding what happens when they are not permitted to play their role in the market. How does an economy respond when prices are set or controlled by the government, rather than being allowed to fluctuate with supply and demand? What happens in an economy that is centrally planned, as distinguished from one in which decisions about how to use resources and distribute goods and services are made by millions of separate individuals, whose decisions are coordinated only by their responses to price movements?

All sorts of economies—capitalist, socialist, feudal, etc.—must determine in one way or another how the available resources are directed toward their various uses. But how well they do it can lead to poverty or affluence for a whole country. That is what the study of economics is all about and that is what makes it important.

PART I:
PRICES AND MARKETS

Chapter 2

The Role of Prices

Now that we know that the key task facing any economy is the allocation of scarce resources which have alternative uses, the next question is: How does an economy do that?

Different kinds of economies obviously do it differently. In a feudal economy, the lord of the manor simply told the people under him what to do and where he wanted resources put. It was much the same story in twentieth century Communist societies. In a market economy, however, there is no one to issue such orders to anyone else. The last premier of the Soviet Union, Mikhail Gorbachev, is said to have asked British Prime Minister Margaret Thatcher: How do you see to it that people get food? The answer was that she didn't. Prices did that. And the British people were better fed than those in the Soviet Union, even though the British have never grown enough food to feed themselves in more than a century. Prices bring them food from other countries.

Prices play a crucial role in determining how much of each resource gets used where. Yet this role is seldom understood by the public and it is often disregarded entirely by politicians.

Many people see prices as simply obstacles to their getting the things they want. Those who would like to live in a beach-front home, for example, may abandon such plans when they discover how expensive beach-front property is. But high prices are not the reason we cannot all live on the beach front. On the contrary, the inherent reality is that there are not nearly enough beach-front homes to go around and prices simply convey that underlying reality. When many people bid for a relatively few homes, those homes become very expensive because of supply and demand. But it is not the prices that cause the scarcity, which would exist under whatever other economic or social arrangements might be used instead of prices.

If the government were to come up with a "plan" for "universal access" to beach-front homes and put "caps" on the prices that could be charged for such property, that would not change the underlying reality of the high ratio of people to beach-front land. With a given population and a given amount of beach-front property, rationing without prices would now have to take place by bureaucratic fiat, political favoritism or random chance—but the rationing would still have to take place. Even if the government were to decree that beach-front homes were a "basic right" of all citizens, that would still not change the underlying reality in the slightest.

Prices are like messengers conveying news—sometimes bad news, in the case of beach-front property desired by far more people than can possibly live at the beach, but often also good news. For example, computers have been getting both cheaper and better at a very rapid rate, as a result of the development of technological ingenuity. Yet the vast majority of beneficiaries of these high-tech advances, insights, and talents have not the foggiest idea of what these technical changes are specifically. But prices convey to them the end results—which are all that matter for their own decision-making and their own enhanced productivity and well-being from using computers.

Similarly, if vast new rich iron ore deposits were discovered, perhaps no more than one percent of the population would be likely to be aware of it, but everyone would discover that things made of steel were becoming cheaper. People thinking of buying desks, for example, would discover that steel desks had become more of a bargain compared to wooden desks and some would undoubtedly change their minds as to which kind of desk to purchase because of that. The same would be true when comparing various other products made of steel to competing products made of wood, aluminum, plastic or other materials. In short, price changes would enable a whole society—indeed, consumers around the world—to adjust automatically to a greater abundance of iron ore, even if 99 percent of those consumers were wholly unaware of the new discovery.

Prices not only guide consumers, they guide producers as well. When all is said and done, producers cannot possibly know what millions of different consumers want. All that automobile manufacturers, for example, know is that when they produce cars with a certain combination of features they can sell those cars for a price that covers their production costs and leaves them a profit, but when they manufacture cars with a different combination of features, they don't sell as well. In order to get rid of the unsold cars, they must cut the prices to whatever level is necessary to get them off the dealers' lots, even if that means taking a loss. The alternative would be to take a bigger loss by not selling them at all.

While a free market economic system is sometimes called a profit system, it is really a profit-and-loss system—and the losses are equally important for the efficiency of the economy, because they tell the manufacturers what to stop producing. Without really knowing why consumers like one set of features rather than another, producers automatically produce more of what earns a profit and less of what is losing money. That amounts to producing what the consumers want and stopping the production of what they don't want. Although the producers are only looking out for themselves and their companies' bottom line, nevertheless from the standpoint of the economy as a whole the society is using its scarce resources more efficiently because decisions are guided by prices.

PRICES AND COSTS

The situation we have just examined—where the consumers want A and don't want B—is the simplest example of how prices lead to efficiency in the use of scarce resources. But prices are at least equally important in situation where consumers want both A and B, as well as many other things, some of which require the same ingredients in their production. For example, consumers not only want cheese, they want ice cream and yogurt, as well as other products made from milk. How do prices help the economy to determine how much milk should go to each of these products?

In bidding for cheese, ice cream, and yogurt, consumers are in effect also bidding for the milk that produces them. The money than comes in from the sales of these products is what enables the producers to buy more milk to use to continue producing their respective products. When the demand for cheese goes up, cheese-makers bid away some of the milk that before went into making ice cream or yogurt, in order to increase the output of their own product to meet the rising demand. In other words, the cost of milk rises to everyone when cheese-makers demand more. As other producers then raise the prices of ice cream and yogurt to cover the higher price of the milk that goes into them, consumers are likely to buy less of these other products at these higher prices.

How will each producer know just how much milk to buy? Obviously they will buy only as much milk as will repay its higher costs from the higher prices of ice cream and yogurt. If consumers who buy ice cream are not as discouraged by rising prices as consumers who buy yogurt are, then very little of the additional milk that goes into making more cheese will come at the expense of ice cream and more will come at the expense of yogurt.

What this all means as a general principle is that the price that one producer is willing to pay for milk (or any other ingredient) is the price that other producers are forced to pay for that same ingredient. Since scarce resources have alternative uses, the value placed on one of these uses by one individual or company becomes a cost that has to be paid by others who want to bid some of these resources away for their own use. From the standpoint of the economy as a whole, this means that *resources tend to flow to their most valued uses.*

This does not mean that one use categorically precludes all other uses. On the contrary, adjustments are incremental. Only that amount of milk which is as valuable to ice cream consumers or consumers of yogurt as it is to cheese purchasers will be used to make ice cream or yogurt. Whether considering consumers of cheese, ice cream, or yogurt, some will be anxious to have a certain amount, less anxious to have additional amounts, and finally—beyond some point—indifferent to having any more, or even unwilling to consume any more after becoming satiated.

Prices coordinate the use of resources, so that only that amount is used for one thing which is equal in value to what it is worth to others in other uses. That way, a price-coordinated economy does not flood people with cheese to the point where they are sick of it, while others are crying out in vain for more yogurt or ice cream. Absurd as such a situation would be, it has happened many times in economies where prices do not allocate scarce resources. The Soviet economy, for example, often had unsalable goods piling up in warehouses while people were waiting in long lines trying to get other things that they wanted.[1] The efficient allocation of scarce resources which have alternative uses is not just an abstract notion of economists. It determines how well or how badly millions of people live.

Again, as in the example of beach-front property, prices convey an underlying reality: *From the standpoint of society as a whole, the "cost" of anything is the*

---

[1]A visitor to the Soviet Union in 1987 reported "long lines of people still stood patiently for hours to buy things: on one street corner people were waiting to buy tomatoes from a cardboard box, one to a customer, and outside a shop next to our hotel there was a line for three days, about which we learned that on the day of our arrival that shop had received a new shipment of men's undershirts." Midge Decter, *An Old Wife's Tale,* p. 169.

value that it has in alternative uses. That cost is reflected in the market when the price that one individual is willing to pay becomes a cost that others are forced to pay, in order to get a share of the same scarce resource or the products made from it. But, no matter whether a particular society has a capitalist price system or a socialist economy or a feudal or other system, the real cost of anything is still its value in alternative uses. The real cost of building a bridge are the other things that could have been built with that same labor and material. This is also true at the level of a given individual, even when no money is involved. The cost of watching a television sitcom or soap opera is the value of the other things that could have been done with that same time.

Different economic systems deal with this underlying reality in different ways and with different degrees of efficiency, but the underlying reality exists independently of whatever particular economic system is used. Once we recognize that, we can then compare how economic systems which use prices to force people to share scarce resources among themselves differ in efficiency from economic systems which determine such things by having kings, politicians or bureaucrats issues orders saying who can get how much of what.

During the brief era of *glasnost* (openness) and *perestroika* (restructuring) in the last years of the Soviet Union, two Soviet economists named Nikolai Shmelev and Vladimir Popov wrote a book giving a very candid account of how their economy worked and this book was later translated into English. As Shmelev and Popov put it, production enterprises in the U.S.S.R. "always ask for more than they need" in the way of raw materials, equipment, and other resources used in production. "They take everything they can get, regardless of how much they actually need, and don't worry about economizing on materials," according to these economists. "After all, nobody 'at the top' knows exactly what the real requirements are," so "squandering" makes sense. Among the resources that get squandered are workers. These economists reported that "from 5 to 15 percent of the workers in the majority of enterprises are surplus and are kept 'just in case.'"

The consequence was that far more resources were used to produce a given amount of output in the Soviet economy as compared to a price-coordinated economic system, such as that in the United States. Citing official Soviet statistics, the Soviet economists lamented:

According to the calculations of the Soviet Institute of World Economy and International Relations, we use 1.5 times more materials and 2.1 times more energy per unit of national income than the United States. . . . We use 2.4 times more metal per unit of national income than the U.S. This correlation is apparent even without special calculations: we produce and consume 1.5 to 2 times more steel and cement than the United States, but we lag behind by at least half in production of items derived from them. . . . Recently, in Soviet industry the consumption of electrical energy exceeded the American level, but the volume of industrial output in the U.S.S.R. is—by the most generous estimates—only 80 percent of the American level.

The Soviet Union did not lack for resources, but was in fact one of the most richly endowed nations on earth—if not *the* most richly endowed. What it lacked was an economic system that made efficient use of scarce resources. Because Soviet enterprises were not under the same financial constraints as capitalist enterprises, they acquired more machines than they needed, "which then gather dust in warehouses or rust out of doors," as the Soviet economists put it. In short, Soviet enterprises were not forced to economize—that is, to treat their resources as both scarce and valuable in alternative uses. While such waste cost these enterprises little or nothing, they cost the Soviet people dearly, in the form of a lower standard of living than their resources and technology were capable of producing.

Such a waste of inputs as these economists described could not of course continue in the kind of economy where these inputs would have to be purchased and where the enterprise itself could survive only by keeping its costs lower than its sales receipts. In such a price-coordinated capitalist system, the amount of inputs ordered would be based on the enterprise's most accurate estimate of what was really needed, not on how much its managers could make sound plausible to higher government officials, who cannot possibly be experts on all the wide range of industries and products they oversee.

The contrast between the American and the Soviet economies is just one of many that can be made between economic systems which use prices to allocate resources and those which have relied on government control. In other regions of the world as well, and in other political systems, there have been similar contrasts between places that used prices to ration goods and allocate resources versus places that have relied on hereditary rulers, elected officials or appointed planning commissions.

When many African nations achieved independence in the 1960s, a famous bet was made between the president of Ghana and the president of the neighboring Ivory Coast as to which country would be more prosperous in the years ahead. At that time, Ghana was not only more prosperous than the Ivory Coast, it had more natural resources, so the bet might have seemed reckless on the part of the president of the Ivory Coast. However, he knew that Ghana was committed to a government-run economy and the Ivory Coast to a freer market. By 1982, the Ivory Coast had so surpassed Ghana that the poorest 20 percent of its people had a higher real income per capita than most of the people in Ghana.

This could not be attributed to any superiority of the country or its people. In fact, in later years, when Ivory Coast politicians eventually succumbed to the temptation to have the government control more of their country's economy, while Ghana finally learned from its mistakes and began to loosen government controls, these two countries' roles reversed—and now Ghana's economy began to grow, while that of the Ivory Coast declined.

Similar comparisons could be made between Burma and Thailand, the former having had the higher standard of living before instituting socialism and the latter a much higher standard of living afterwards. Other countries—India, Germany, China, New Zealand, South Korea, Sri Lanka—have experienced sharp upturns in their economies when they freed those economies from many government controls and relied more on prices to allocate resources. As of 1960, India and South Korea were at comparable economic levels but, by the late 1980s, South Korea's per capita income was ten times that in India.

India remained committed to a government-controlled economy for many years after achieving independence in 1947. However, in the 1990s, India "jettisoned four decades of economic isolation and planning, and freed the country's entrepreneurs for the first time since independence," in the words of the London magazine *The Economist*. There followed a new growth rate of 6 percent a year, making it "one of the world's fastest-growing big economies."

In China, government controls were relaxed in particular economic sectors and in particular geographic regions during the reforms of the 1980s, leading to stunning economic contrasts within the same country, as well as rapid economic growth overall. Back in 1978, less than 10 percent of China's agricultural output was sold in open markets but, by 1990, 80 percent was. The net result was more food and a greater variety of food available to city dwellers in China and a rise in farmers' income by more than 50 percent within a few years. In contrast to China's severe economic problems when there was heavy-handed government control under Mao, who died in 1976, the subsequent freeing up of prices in the marketplace led to an astonishing economic growth rate of 9 percent per year between 1978 and 1995.

While history can tell us that such things happened, economics helps explain *why* they happened—what there is about prices that allows them to accomplish what political control of an economy can seldom match. There is more to economics than prices, but understanding how prices function is the foundation for understanding much of the rest of economics.

In a society of millions of consumers, no given individual or set of government decision-makers sitting around a table can possibly know just how much these millions of consumers prefer one product to another, much less thousands of products to thousands of other products—quite aside from the problem of knowing how much of each of thousands of resources should be used to produce which products. In an economy coordinated by prices, no one has to know. Each producer is simply guided by what price that producer's product can sell for and by how much must be paid for the ingredients that go into making that product.

Knowledge is one of the most scarce of all resources and a pricing system economizes on its use by forcing those with the most knowledge of their own particular situation to make bids for goods and resources based on that knowledge, rather than on their ability to influence other people. However much articulation may be valued by intellectuals, it is not nearly as efficient a way of conveying accurate information as confronting people with a need to "put your money where your mouth is."

Human beings are going to make mistakes in any kind of economic system. In a price-coordinated economy, any producer who uses ingredients that are more valuable elsewhere is likely to discover that the costs of those ingredients cannot be repaid from what the consumers are willing to pay for the product. After all, he has had to bid these resources away from alternative users, paying more than these resources are worth to some of those alternative users. If it turns out that these resources are not more valuable in the uses to which he puts them, then he is going to lose money. There will be no choice but to discontinue making that product with those ingredients. For those producers who are too blind or too stubborn to change, continuing losses will force their businesses into bankruptcy, so that the waste of society's resources will be stopped that way.

In a price-coordinated economy, employees and creditors insist on being paid, regardless of whether the managers and owners have made mistakes. This means that capitalist businesses can make only so many mistakes for so long before they have to either stop or get stopped—whether by an inability to get the labor and supplies they need or by bankruptcy. In a feudal economy or a socialist economy, leaders can continue to make the same mistakes indefinitely. The consequences are paid by others in the form of a standard of living lower than it would be if there were greater efficiency in the use of scarce resources.

As already noted, there were many products which remained unsold in stores or in warehouses in the Soviet Union, while there were desperate shortages of other things. But, in a price-coordinated economy, the labor, management, and physical resources that went into producing unwanted products would have had to go into producing something that could pay its own way from sales. That means producing something that the consumers wanted more than they wanted what was actually produced. In the absence of compelling price signals and the threat of financial losses to the producers that they convey, inefficiency and waste in the Soviet Union could continue until such time as each waste reached proportions big enough and blatant enough to attract the attention of central planners in Moscow, who were preoccupied with thousands of other decisions.

Ironically, the problems caused by trying to run an economy by fiat or by arbitrarily-imposed prices created by government dictates were foreseen by Karl Marx and Friedrich Engels, whose ideas the Soviet Union claimed to be following. Engels pointed out that price fluctuations have "forcibly brought home to the commodity producers what things and what quantity of them society requires or does not require." Without such a mechanism, he demanded to know "what guarantee we have that necessary quantity and not more of each product will be produced, that we shall not go hungry in regard to corn and meat while we are choked in beet sugar and drowned in potato spirit, that we shall not lack trousers to cover our nakedness while trouser buttons flood us in millions." Marx and Engels apparently understood economics much better than their latter-day followers. Or perhaps Marx and Engels were more concerned with economic efficiency than with maintaining political control from the top.

PRICES IN ACTION

There is perhaps no more basic or more obvious principle of economics than the fact that people tend to buy more at a lower price and less at a higher price. By the same token, people who produce goods or supply services tend to supply more at a higher price and less at a lower price. Yet the implications of these two principles, singly or in combination, cover a remarkable range of economic activities and issues—and contradict an equally remarkable range of misconceptions and fallacies.

When people try to quantify a country's "need" for this or that product or service, they are ignoring the fact that there is no fixed or objective "need."

The fact that people demand more at a lower price and less at a higher price may be easy to understand, but it is also easy to forget. Seldom, if ever, is there a fixed quantity demanded. For example, communal living in an Israeli kibbutz was based on its members' collectively producing and supplying their members' needs without resort to money or prices. However, supplying electricity and food without charging prices led to a situation where people often did not bother to turn off electric lights during the day and members would bring friends from outside the kibbutz to join them for meals. But, after the kibbutz began to charge prices for electricity and food, there was a sharp drop in the consumption of both. In short, there was no fixed quantity of "need" or demand.

Likewise, there is no fixed supply. Statistics on the amount of petroleum, iron ore, or other natural resources seem to indicate that this is just a simple matter of how much physical stuff there is in the ground. In reality, most natural resources are available at varying costs of discovery, extraction, and processing. There is some oil that can be produced for $10 a barrel and other oil that cannot pay for all its costs at $20 a barrel, but which can at $30 a barrel. *The quantity supplied varies directly with the price*, just as the quantity demanded varies inversely with the price.

When the price of oil falls, certain low-yield oil wells are shut down because the cost of extracting and processing the oil from these wells would exceed the price it would sell for in the market. If the price later rises—or if the cost of extraction or processing is lowered by some new technology—then such oil wells will be put back in operation again. There is no fixed supply of oil—or of most other things.

When people project that there will be a shortage of engineers or teachers or housing in the years ahead, they usually either ignore prices or implicitly assume that there will be a shortage at today's prices. But shortages are precisely what cause prices to rise. At higher prices, it may be no harder to fill vacancies for engineers or teachers than today and no harder to find housing, as rising rents cause more homes and apartment buildings to be built. Price fluctuations are a way of letting a little knowledge go a long way. Price changes guide people's decisions through trial and error adjustments to what other people can and will pay as consumers, as well as what they can and will supply as producers.

The producer whose product turns out to have the combination of features that are closest to what the consumers really want may be no wiser than his competitors. Yet he can grow rich while his competitors who guessed wrong

go bankrupt. But the larger result is that society as a whole gets more benefits from its limited resources by having them directed toward where those
resources produce the kind of output that millions of people want, instead of
producing things that they don't want.

Rationing by Prices

There are all kinds of prices. The prices of consumer goods are the most obvious examples but labor also has prices called wages or salaries, and borrowed money has a price called interest. In addition to prices for tangible
things, there are prices for services ranging from haircuts to brain surgery
and from astrology to advice on speculating in gold or soybeans. Prices provide incentives to conserve. That is why the Israeli kibbutz used less electricity and less food after it began to charge its members for these things, and
why American enterprises used less input for a given output than their Soviet counterparts that did not have to worry about prices or profits.

In so far as prices—whether of soybeans or surgery—result from supply
and demand in a free market, they effectively allocate scarce resources which
have alternative uses. So long as people are free to spend their money for
what they see fit, price changes in response to supply and demand direct resources to where they are most in demand and direct people to where their
desires can be satisfied most fully by the existing supply.

Simple as all this may seem, it contradicts many widely held ideas. For example, high prices are often blamed on "greed" and people often speak of
something being sold for more than its "real" value, or of workers being paid
less than they are "really" worth.

To treat prices as resulting from greed implies that sellers can set prices
where they wish, that prices are not determined by supply and demand. It
may well be true that some—or all—sellers prefer to get the highest price
that they can. But it is equally true that buyers usually wish to pay the lowest
price they can for goods of a given quality. More important, the competition
of numerous buyers and numerous sellers results in prices that leave each individual buyer and seller with very little leeway. Any deal depends on both
parties agreeing to the same terms. Anyone who doesn't offer as good a deal
as a competitor is likely to find nobody willing to make a deal at all.

The fact that prices fluctuate over time, and occasionally have a sharp rise
or a steep drop, misleads some people into concluding that prices are deviat-
ing from their "real" values. But their usual level under usual conditions is no

more real or valid than their much higher or much lower levels under different conditions.

When a large employer goes bankrupt in a small community, or simply moves away to another state or country, many of the business' former employees may decide to move away themselves—and when their numerous homes go on sale in the same small area at the same time, the prices of those houses are likely to be driven down by competition. But this does not mean that they are selling their homes for less than their "real" value. The value of living in this particular community has simply declined with the decline of job opportunities, and housing prices reflect that underlying fact. The new and lower prices reflect the new reality as well as the previous prices reflected the previous reality. A survey of home prices in a number of upstate New York cities that were losing population in the 1990s found that home prices were falling in those particular communities, while home prices were rising elsewhere in the state and around the country. This is exactly what one should expect on the basis of basic economic principles.

Conversely, when some natural disaster such as a hurricane or flood suddenly destroys many homes in a given area, the price of hotel rooms in that area may suddenly rise, as many people compete for a limited number of rooms, in order to avoid sleeping outdoors or having to double up with relatives and friends, or having to relocate out of the community. People who charge higher prices for hotel rooms, or for other things in short supply in the wake of some disaster, are especially likely to be condemned for "greed," but in fact the relationship between supply and demand has changed. Prices are simply performing one of their most important functions—rationing scarce resources. When some disaster suddenly makes those resources even more scarce than usual, it is important that prices reflect that underlying reality, so as to reduce the demands that each individual makes on the reduced supply.

Regardless of what hotel owners charge, a sudden and widespread destruction of housing in a given area means that there may be not nearly enough hotel rooms for all the displaced people to get the kinds of accommodations they would like. If prices had remained at their previous levels after the hurricane, a family of four might well rent two rooms—one for the parents and one for the children. But when hotel prices shoot up well beyond their usual level, all four family members may crowd into one room, in order to save money, leaving the other room for other people who have likewise lost their homes and are equally in need of shelter. The more stringent scarcity of housing in the wake of a widespread destruction of homes is inherent, even if temporary, and prices merely reflect that underlying reality. If the government were to impose price controls under these conditions, then those who happened to get to the hotels first would take up more space and leave more latecomers without a place to sleep indoors in that community.

Similarly, if local electric power lines were put out of commission for a few days, the demand for flashlights in that community might suddenly increase, causing prices to rise before new shipments of flashlights could arrive. Had prices remained at their previous level, a family might buy several flashlights, so that each member could have one. But, at the suddenly higher prices, they would more likely buy only one or two, leaving more flashlights for others with a similarly urgent need. In short, prices force people to share, whether or not they are aware of sharing. Prices perform this function both in normal times and in emergency times. While sharply higher prices may be resented during emergencies, their functions are even more urgently needed at such times.

Prices and Supplies

Prices not only ration existing supplies, they also act as powerful incentives to cause supplies to rise or fall in response to changing demand. When a crop failure in a given region creates a sudden increase in demand for imports of food into that region, food suppliers elsewhere rush to be the first to get there, in order to capitalize on the high prices that will prevail until more supplies arrive and drive food prices back down again. What this means, from the standpoint of the hungry people in that region, is that food is being rushed to them at maximum speed by "greedy" suppliers, probably much faster than if the same food were being transported to them by salaried government employees sent on a humanitarian mission.

Those spurred on by greed may well drive throughout the night or take short cuts over rough terrain, while those operating "in the public interest" are more likely to proceed at a less hectic pace and by safer or more comfortable routes. In short, people tend to do more for their own benefit than for the benefit of others. Freely fluctuating prices can make that turn out to be beneficial to others. In the case of food supplies, earlier arrival can be the difference between temporary hunger and death by starvation. Where there are local famines in Third World countries, it is not at all uncommon for food supplied by international agencies to the national government to sit spoiling on the docks while people are dying of hunger inland.[2] Much as we may deplore private greed, it is likely to move food much faster, saving far more lives.

In other situations, the consumers may not want more, but less. Prices also convey this. When automobiles began to displace horses and buggies in the early twentieth century, the demand for saddles, horseshoes, carriages and other such paraphernalia declined. As the manufacturers of such products faced losses instead of profits, many began to abandon their businesses or were shut down by bankruptcy. In a sense, it is unfair when some people are unable to earn as much as others with similar skills, diligence, and other virtues. Yet this unfairness to particular individuals is what makes the economy as a whole operate more efficiently for the benefit of vastly larger numbers of others.

---

[2]The same thing can happen when the food arrives by land. See "Death by Bureaucracy," on page 40 of the December 8, 2001 issue of *The Economist*, for examples of Afghan refugees dying of starvation while waiting for paperwork to be completed by aid workers.

Chapter 3

Price Controls

Facts are stubborn things, and whatever may be our wishes, our inclinations, or the dictates of our passions, they cannot alter the state of facts and evidence.

—JOHN ADAMS

Just as nothing makes us appreciate the value of water like a drought, nothing shows more vividly the role of price fluctuations in a free market than the *absence* of such price fluctuations when the market is controlled. What happens when prices are not allowed to fluctuate freely according to supply and demand, but instead are set by law, as under various kinds of price-control laws? Price controls have existed, at one time or another, in countries around the world, over a period of centuries—in fact, for thousands of years—and have applied to everything from food to housing to medical services.

Typically, price controls are imposed in order to keep prices from rising to the levels that they would reach in response to supply and demand. The political rationales for such laws have varied from place to place and from time to time, but there is seldom a lack of rationales whenever it becomes politically expedient to hold down someone's prices in the interests of someone else whose political support seems more important. However, in addition to laws putting a "ceiling" on how high prices will be allowed to rise, there are also laws establishing "floor" prices, which limit how far prices will be allowed to fall.

Many countries have set limits to how low certain agricultural prices will be allowed to fall, sometimes with the government being legally obligated to buy up the farmer's output whenever free market prices go below the specified levels. Equally widespread are minimum wage laws, which set a limit to how low a worker's wage rate may be. Here the government seldom offers to buy up the surplus labor which the free market does not employ, though it usually offers unemployment compensation, covering some proportion of the wages that might otherwise have been earned.

To understand the effects of price control, it is necessary to understand how prices rise and fall in a free market. There is nothing esoteric about it, but it is important to be very clear about what happens. Prices rise because the amount demanded exceeds the amount supplied *at existing prices*. Prices fall because the amount supplied exceeds the amount demanded *at existing prices*. The first case is called a "shortage" and the second is called a "surplus"—but both depend on *existing prices*. Simple as this might seem, it is often misunderstood, sometimes with disastrous consequences.

A closer examination shows why shortages persist when the government sets a maximum price that is lower than what it would be in a free market and why a surplus persists when the government sets minimum prices that are higher than these prices would be in a free market.

PRICE CEILINGS AND SHORTAGES

When there is a "shortage" of a product, there is not necessarily any less of it, either absolutely or relative to the number of consumers. During and immediately after the Second World War, for example, there was a very serious housing shortage in the United States, even though the country's population and its housing supply had both increased about 10 percent from their prewar levels—and there was no shortage when the war began. In other words, even though the ratio between housing and people had not changed, nevertheless many Americans looking for an apartment during this period had to spend weeks or months in an often vain search for a place to live, or else resorted to bribes to get landlords to move them to the top of waiting lists. Meanwhile, they doubled up with relatives, slept in garages or used other makeshift living arrangements.

Although there was no less housing space per person than before the war, the shortage was very real *at existing prices*, which were kept artificially lower than they would have been because of rent control laws that had been passed during the war. At these artificially low prices, more people had a demand for more housing space than before rent control laws were enacted. This is a practical consequence of the simple economic principle already noted in Chapter 2, that the quantity demanded varies with how high or how low the price is. When some people used more housing than usual, other people found less housing available.

Demand Under Rent Control

Some people who would normally not be renting their own apartments, such as young adults still living with their parents or some single or widowed elderly people living with relatives, were enabled by the artificially low prices created by rent control to move out and into their own apartments. These artificially low prices also caused others to seek larger apartments than they would ordinarily be living in or to live alone when they would otherwise have to share an apartment with a room-mate, in order to be able to afford the rent. More tenants seeking both more apartments and larger apartments created a shortage, even though there was not any greater physical scarcity of housing relative to the population.[1] When rent control ended, the housing shortage quickly disappeared. As rents rose in a free market, some childless couples living in four-bedroom apartments decided that they could live in two-bedroom apartments. Some late teenagers decided that they could continue living with mom and dad a little longer, until their pay rose enough for them to afford their own apartments, now that apartments were no longer artificially cheap. The net result was that families looking for a place to stay found more places available, now that rent-control laws were no longer keeping such places occupied by people with less urgent requirements.

None of this was peculiar to the United States. Rent control had very much the same effects in Sweden. As of 1940, there were approximately 6,330,000 people living in Sweden and there were about 1,960,000 dwelling units to house them—about 31 housing units for every 100 people. Over the years, the number of housing units rose relative to the population—to 36 units per 100 people in 1965 and 43 units per 100 people by 1973—and yet the average waiting time for getting a place to live also rose.

---

[1]My own family, which occupied a two-bedroom apartment in 1939, occupied two apartments with a total of four bedrooms in 1944, and of course two kitchens and two bathrooms. Yet we were as baffled as everyone else as to why there was suddenly a housing shortage.

There was a 9-month wait in 1950, a 23-month wait in 1955 and a 40-month wait by 1958, for example. In short, the longer waits for housing was not due to any less housing in proportion to the population. *There was a lessening scarcity but a growing shortage.*

As incomes in Sweden rose much faster than rents were allowed to rise under rent control laws, more and more people could afford to occupy their own independent housing units, making it harder for others to find places to live, even with a massive, government-sponsored program to build more dwelling units. Before rent control, less than one-fourth of all unmarried adults in Sweden had their own separate housing units in 1940, but that proportion rose until just over half did by 1975.

Not only was the actual physical amount of housing no less than before, Sweden was in fact building more housing per person than any other country in the world during this period. Nevertheless, the housing shortage persisted and got worse. As of 1948, there were about 2,400 people on waiting lists for housing in Sweden but, a dozen years later, the waiting list had grown to ten times as many people, despite a frantic building of more housing. When eventually rent control laws were repealed in Sweden, a housing *surplus* suddenly developed, as rents rose and people curtailed their use of housing as a result. Again, this shows that "shortages" and "surpluses" are matters of *price*, not matters of physical scarcity, either absolutely or relative to the population. With rent control ended, private developers in Sweden now began building more housing as rents rose—and produced housing more in keeping with what the public wanted, as distinguished from the kind of housing produced by the government under political and bureaucratic incentives. Therefore it was the government-sponsored housing which became vacant—so much so as to become a drain on the public treasury.

Think of all the needless grief and wasted resources that could have been avoided if the Swedish voters had been familiar with basic economic principles and understood that the source of their housing problems were the very attempts to make housing more "affordable" by rent control. No doubt there were Swedish economists who understood this, but there are seldom enough economists in any country to have enough votes to sway decisions made by politicians. Nor are economists always clear or convincing enough to affect pubic opinion.

During the period when rent control laws were in effect in Australia, they had the same effect as they had in Sweden—many dwelling units with only a single occupant and long waits for others seeking housing. Similarly, a study of housing in New York City found 175,000 apartments where one person occupied 4 or more rooms—mostly elderly people in rent-controlled apartments. In San Francisco, a study in 2001 showed that 49 percent of that city's rent-controlled apartments had only a single occupant, while a severe housing shortage in the city had thousands of people living at considerable distances and making long commutes to their jobs in San Francisco.

In the normal course of events, people's demand for housing space changes over a lifetime. Their demand for space usually increases when they get married and have children. But, years later, after the children have grown up and moved away, the parents' demand for space tends to decline and it often declines yet again after a spouse dies and a widow or widower moves into smaller quarters or goes to live with relatives. In this way, a society's total stock of housing is shared and circulated among people according to their changing individual demands at different stages of their lives.

The individuals themselves do not do this out of a sense of cooperation, but because of the prices—rents in this case—which confront them. In a free market, these prices are based on the value that other tenants put on housing. Young couples with a growing family are often willing to bid more for housing, even if that means buying fewer consumer goods and services, in order to have enough money to pay for additional housing space. Parents may go out to restaurants or movies less often, or wait longer to buy new clothes or new cars, in order that each child may have his or her own bedroom. But, once the children are grown and gone, such sacrifices may no longer make sense, when additional other amenities can now be enjoyed by reducing the amount of housing space being rented.

Given the crucial role of prices in this process, suppression of the process by rent control laws leaves elderly people with little incentive to vacate apartments that they would normally vacate, if that would result in a significant reduction in rent, leaving them more money with which to improve their living standards in other respects. Moreover, the chronic housing shortages which accompany rent control greatly increase the time and effort required to search for a new and smaller apartment, while reducing the financial reward for finding one. In short, rent control reduces the rate of housing turnover.

New York City has had rent control longer and more stringently than any other major American city. One consequence has been that the annual rate of turnover of apartments in New York is less than half the national average and the proportion of tenants who have lived in the same apartment for 20 years or more is more than double the national average. As the *New York Times* summarized the situation:

New York used to be like other cities, a place where tenants moved frequently and landlords competed to rent empty apartments to newcomers, but today the motto may as well be: No Immigrants Need Apply. While immigrants are crowded into bunks in illegal boarding houses in the slums, upper-middle-class locals pay low rents to live in good neighborhoods, often in large apartments they no longer need after their children move out.

Supply Under Rent Control

Rent control has effects on supply as well as on demand. Nine years after the end of World War II, not a single new building had been built in Melbourne, Australia, because of rent control laws there which made buildings unprofitable. Declines in building construction have likewise followed in the wake of rent control laws elsewhere. After rent control was instituted in Santa Monica, California in 1979, building permits declined to less than one-tenth of what they were just five years earlier. A housing study in San Francisco in 2001 found that three quarters of its rent-controlled housing was more than half a century old and 44 percent of it was more than 70 years old.

Not only is the supply of new apartment construction less after rent control, even the supply of existing housing tends to decline, as fewer people are willing to rent to others after the rents are kept artificially low by law. During 8 years of rent control in Washington during the 1970s, that city's available rental housing stock declined absolutely, from just over 199,000 units on the market to just under 176,000 units. After rent control was introduced in Berkeley, California, the number of private housing units available to students at the university there declined by 31 percent in five years.

Sometimes the reduction in housing units on the market occurs because people who had been renting rooms or apartments in their own homes, or bungalows in their back yards, decide that it is no longer worth the bother, when rents are kept artificially low under rent control laws. In addition, there are often conversions of apartments to condominiums and an accelerated deterioration of the existing housing stock, as landlords provide less maintenance and repair under rent control, since the housing shortage makes it unnecessary for them to maintain the appearance of their premises in order to attract tenants. Studies of rent control in the United States, England, and France have found rent-controlled housing to be deteriorated far more often than non-rent-controlled housing.

Typically, the rental housing stock is relatively fixed in the short run, so that a shortage occurs first because more people want more housing at the artificially low price. Later, there may be a real increase in scarcity as well, as rental units deteriorate more rapidly with reduced maintenance, while not enough new units are being built to replace them as they wear out, because new privately built housing would be unprofitable under rent control. Under rent control in England and Wales, for example, privately-built rental housing fell from being 61 percent of all housing in 1947 to being 14 percent by 1977. A study of rent control in North America and in Britain, France, Germany, and the Netherlands concluded: "New investment in unsubsidized rented housing is essentially nonexistent in all the European countries surveyed, except for luxury housing."

In short, a policy intended to make housing affordable for the poor has had the net effect of shifting resources toward housing affordable only by the affluent or the rich, since luxury housing is often exempt from rent control. Among other things, this illustrates the crucial importance of making a distinction between intentions and consequences. Economic policies need to be analyzed in terms of the incentives they create, rather than the hopes that inspired them. In terms of incentives, it is easy to understand what happened in England when rent control was extended in 1975 to cover furnished rental units. According to *The Times* of London:

> Advertisements for furnished rental accommodations in the *London Evening Standard* plummeted dramatically in the first week after the Act came into force and are now running about 75 percent below last year's levels.

Since furnished rooms are particularly likely to be in people's homes, these represent housing units that are easily withdrawn from the market when the rents no longer compensate for the inconveniences of having renters living with you. The same principle applies where there are small apartment buildings like duplexes, where the owner is also one of the tenants. Within three years after rent control was imposed in Toronto in 1976, 23 percent of all rental units in owner-occupied dwellings were withdrawn from the housing market.

Even when rent control applies to apartment buildings where the landlord does not live, eventually the point may be reached where the whole building becomes sufficiently unprofitable that it is simply abandoned. In New York City, for example, many buildings have been abandoned after their owners found it impossible to collect enough rent to cover the costs of services that they are legally required to provide, such as heat and hot water. Such owners have simply disappeared, in order to escape the legal consequences of their abandonment, and such buildings often end up vacant and boarded up, though still physically sound enough to house people, if maintained.

The number of abandoned buildings taken over by the New York City government over the years runs into the thousands. It has been estimated that there are at least four times as many abandoned housing units in New York City as there are homeless people living on the streets there. Homelessness is not due to a physical scarcity of housing, but to a price-related shortage, which is painfully real nonetheless.

Such inefficiency in the allocation of resources means that people are sleeping outdoors on the pavement on cold winter nights—some dying of exposure—while the means of housing them already exist, but are not being used because of laws designed to make housing "affordable." Once again, this demonstrates that the efficient or inefficient allocation of scarce resources is not just some abstract economic notion, but has very real consequences, which can even include matters of life and death. It also illustrates that the goal of a law—"affordable housing," in this case—is far less important than its actual consequences.

Just as rent control reduces the housing stock, so the end of rent control often marks the beginning of private building, as it did in Sweden. In Massachusetts, a statewide ban on local rent control laws in 1994 led to the construction of new apartment buildings in formerly rent-controlled cities for the first time in 25 years. In short, with housing as with other things, less is supplied at a lower price than at a higher price—less both quantitatively and qualitatively. Polls of economists have found virtually unanimous agreement that declines in product quantity and quality are the usual effects of price controls in general. Of course, there are not enough economists in the entire country for their votes to matter very much to politicians.

The Politics of Rent Control

Politically, rent control is often a big success, however many serious economic and social problems it creates. Politicians know that there are always more tenants than landlords and more people who do not understand economics than people who do.

Often it is politically effective to represent rent control as a way to keep greedy rich landlords from "gouging" the poor with "unconscionable" rents. In reality, rates of return on investments in housing are seldom higher than on alternative investments and landlords are often people of very modest means. This is especially so for owners of small, low-end apartment buildings that are in constant need of repair. Many of the landlords with buildings like this are handymen who use their own skills and labor to maintain the premises, while trying to pay off the mortgage with the rents they collect. In short, the kind of housing likely to be rented by the poor often has owners who are by no means rich.

Where rent control applies to luxury housing, the tenants may be quite affluent. In Manhattan, for example, the chairman of the New York Stock Exchange paid less than $700 a month for a rent-controlled apartment on fashionable Central Park South. Another tenant on Central Park South paid just $400 a month for a six-room apartment. With rent-controlled prices so low, some people who did not even live in New York had apartments there for use when they were in town. Hollywood actress Shelley Winters, who owned a home in Beverly Hills, also rented a two-bedroom apartment in Manhattan for a rent-controlled price of less than $900 a month. New York Mayor Ed Koch paid less than half of that for his rent-controlled apartment in Washington Square, which he kept during the entire 12 years when he lived in Gracie Mansion, the official residence of the mayor.

Meanwhile, city welfare agencies have paid much higher rents than these when they housed poverty-stricken families in cramped and roach-infested apartments in run-down hotels. The idea that rent control protects poor tenants from rich landlords may be politically effective, but often it bears little resemblance to the reality.

San Francisco's rent control laws are not as old as those in New York City but they are similarly severe—and have produced very similar results. A study published in 2001 showed that more than one-fourth of the occupants of rent-controlled apartments in San Francisco had household incomes of more than $100,000 a year. It should also be noted that this was the first empirical study of rent control commissioned by the city of San Francisco. Since rent control began there in 1979, this means that for more than two decades these laws were enforced and extended with no serious attempt to gauge their actual economic and social consequences, as distinguished from their political popularity.

Where rent control laws apply on a blanket basis to all housing in existence as of the time the law goes into effect, luxurious housing becomes low-rent housing. Then, after the passage of time makes clear that no new housing is likely to be built unless it is exempted from rent control, such exemptions or relaxations of rent control for new housing mean that even new apartments that are very modest in size and quality may rent for far more than older, more spacious and more luxurious apartments that are still under rent control. This non-comparability of rents has been common in European cities under rent control, as well as in New York and other American cities. Similar incentives produce similar results in many different settings.

Ironically, cities with strong rent control laws, such as New York and San Francisco, tend to end up with higher average rents than cities without rent control. Where such laws apply only to rents below some specified level, presumably to protect the poor, builders then have incentives to build only apartments luxurious enough to be above the rent-control level. Rich and poor alike who move into the city after rent control has created a housing shortage typically cannot find a rent-controlled apartment, and so have available only housing that costs more than it would in a free market, because of the housing shortage. Not surprisingly, homelessness tends to be greater in cities with rent control—New York and San Francisco again being classic examples.

Scarcity Versus Shortage

In order to demonstrate in a different way the crucial distinction between an increased scarcity—where fewer goods are available relative to the population—and a "shortage" as a *price* phenomenon, we can consider a situation where the actual amount of housing suddenly declined in a given area without any price control. This happened in the wake of the great San Francisco earthquake and fire of 1906. More than half the city's housing supply was destroyed during that catastrophe in just three days and not a single major hotel remained standing. Yet there was no housing shortage. When the *San Francisco Chronicle* resumed publication a month after the earthquake, its first issue contained 64 advertisements of apartments or homes for rent, compared to only 5 ads from people seeking apartments to live in.

Of the 200,000 people suddenly made homeless by the earthquake, temporary shelters housed 30,000 and an estimated 75,000 left the city. Still, that left nearly 100,000 people to be absorbed into the local housing market. Yet the newspapers of that time mention no housing shortage. Rising prices not only allocated the existing housing, they provided incentives for rebuilding. In short, just as there can be a shortage without any greater physical scarcity, so there can be a greater physical scarcity without any shortage. People made homeless by the San Francisco earthquake found housing more readily than people made homeless by New York's rent control laws that took thousands of building off the market.

Similar economic principles apply in other markets. During the American gasoline "crisis" of 1972 and 1973, when oil prices were kept artificially low by the federal government, there were long lines of automobiles waiting at filling stations in cities across the United States, but there was in fact 95 percent as much gasoline sold in 1972 as there was in the previous year, when there were no gasoline lines at the filling stations, no shortage and no crisis atmosphere. Similarly, during the gasoline crisis of 1979, the amount of gasoline sold was only 3.5 percent less than in the record-breaking year of gasoline sales in 1978. In fact, the amount of gasoline sold in 1979 was greater than the gasoline consumption in any other previous year in the history of the country except 1978. In short, there was a minor increase in scarcity but a major shortage, with long lines of motorists waiting at filling stations, sometimes for hours, before reaching the pump.

The usual function of prices in directing goods and resources to where they are most in demand no longer operates under price controls, so that gasoline remained in short supply in many cities, even though it was more available in various communities to which people were driving less, such as rural or recreational areas. With prices being frozen in both places, there was little or no incentive to move the gasoline from one area to another, as would normally happen with free market prices responding to supply and demand. Commenting on the unusual 1979 gasoline shortages in the United States, two Soviet economists pointed out an analogy with what happened regularly in the government-controlled economy of the Soviet Union:

> In an economy with rigidly planned proportions, such situations are not the exception but the rule—an everyday reality, a governing law. The absolute majority of goods is either in short supply or in surplus. Quite often the same product is in both categories—there is a shortage in one region and a surplus in another.

In a free market, supply and demand would cause prices to rise where goods are in short supply and fall where they are abundant, providing incentives to move things from regions where there is a surplus to regions where there is a shortage. But where prices are fixed by law, no such price movements occur and there is no incentive to move goods between the two regions. Theoretically, a government planning commission could either issue orders to move these goods or change the prices to provide incentives for others to move them. In reality, Soviet planning commissions were overwhelmed by having to set more than 20 million prices and could hardly respond as quickly as a market where prices fluctuate freely by supply and demand. The U.S. government, with much less experience trying to manage an economy, was even less able to micro-manage the gasoline market.

Just as price controls on apartments cause a cutback inpainting, maintenance, and other auxiliary services that go with apartments, so price controls on gasoline led to a cutback on the hours that filling stations remained open for their customers' convenience. Because of the long lines of automobiles waiting to buy gasoline during the shortage, filling stations could sell gas continuously for a relatively few hours and then shut down for the day, instead of having to stay open around the clock to dispense the same amount of gasoline at a normal pace, with cars stopping in at whatever times were convenient to the motorists. In New York City, for example, the average filling station was open 110 hours a week in September 1978, before the shortage, but only 27 hours a week in June 1979, during the shortage. Yet the total amount of gasoline pumped differed by only a few percentage points between these two periods.

In short, the problem was not a substantially greater physical scarcity, but a shortage at artificially low prices. Shortages mean that the seller no longer has to please the buyer. That is why landlords can let maintenance and other services deteriorate under rent control. In this case, the filling station owners could save on the time during which they had to pay for electricity and other costs of remaining open long hours. No doubt many or most of the motorists whose daily lives and work were disrupted by having to spend hours waiting in line behind other cars at filling stations would gladly have paid a few cents more per gallon of gasoline, in order to avoid such problems and stresses. But price control prevents buyers and sellers from making mutually advantageous transactions on terms different from those specified in the law.

Black Markets

Bolder and less scrupulous buyers and sellers make mutually advantageous transactions outside the law. Price controls almost invariably produce black markets, where prices are not only higher than the legally permitted prices, but also higher than they would be in a free market, since the legal risks must also be compensated. While small-scale black markets may function in secrecy, large-scale black markets usually require bribes to officials to look the other way. In Russia, for example, a local embargo on the shipment of price-controlled food beyond regional boundaries was dubbed the "150-ruble decree," since this was the cost of bribing police to let the shipments pass through checkpoints.

Statistics on black market activity are by nature elusive, since no one wants to let the whole world know that they are violating the law. However, sometimes there are indirect indications. Under American wartime price controls that remained in effect immediately after World War II, employment in meat-packing plants declined as meat was diverted from legitimate packing houses into black markets. This often translated into empty meat counters in butcher shops and grocery stores.[2]

A 1946 government survey of retail outlets reported: "Approximately 85 percent of the stores had no veal, more than four-fifths were without pork loins, ham or bacon and almost seven out of ten had no beef or lamb." As in other cases, however, this was not due to an actual physical scarcity of meat but to its diversion into black markets. Within one month after price controls were ended, employment in meat-packing plants rose from 93,000 to 163,000 and then rose again to 180,000 over the next two months. This nearly doubling of employment in meat-packing plants in just three months indicated that meat was clearly no longer being diverted from the packing houses after price controls were ended.

PRICE FLOORS AND SURPLUSES

Just as a price set below the level that would prevail by supply and demand in a free market tends to cause more to be demanded and less to be supplied, creating a shortage at the imposed price, so a price set *above* the free market level tends to cause more to be supplied than demanded, creating a surplus. Simple as this principle seems, it is often lost sight of in the swirl of more complex events and more politically popular beliefs.

One of the classic examples of a lower limit to prices imposed by government have been agricultural price-support programs. As often happens, a real but transient problem led to the establishment of enduring government programs, which long outlived the conditions that initially caused them to be created.

Among the many tragedies of the Great Depression of the 1930s was the fact that many farmers simply could not make enough money from the sale of their crops to pay their bills. The prices of farm products fell much more drastically than the prices of the things that farmers had to buy. As many

---

[2]In many cases, goods in short supply were kept in the back of the store for sale to those people who were willing to offer more than the legal price. Black markets were not always separate operations, but were also a sideline of some otherwise legitimate businesses.

farmers lost their farms because they could no longer pay the mortgages, and as other farm families suffered privations as they struggled to hang on to their farms and their traditional way of life, the federal government sought to restore "parity" between agriculture and other sectors of the economy by intervening to keep farm prices from falling so sharply.

This intervention took various forms. One approach was to reduce by law the amount of various crops that could be grown and sold, so as to prevent the supply from driving the price below the level that the federal government had decided upon. Thus, supplies of peanuts and cotton were restricted by law. Supplies of citrus fruit, nuts and various other farm products were regulated by local cartels of farmers, backed up by the authority of the Secretary of Agriculture to issue "marketing orders" and prosecute those who violated these orders by producing and selling more than they were authorized to produce and sell. Such arrangements continued for decades after the poverty of the Great Depression was replaced by the prosperity of the boom following World War II.

These indirect methods of keeping prices artificially high were only part of the story. The key factor in keeping farm prices artificially higher than they would have been under free market supply and demand was the government's willingness to buy up the surpluses created by its control of prices. This they did for such farm products as corn, rice, tobacco, and wheat, among others.

Price control in the form of a "floor" under prices, preventing them from falling further, produced surpluses as dramatic as the shortages produced by price control in the form of a "ceiling" preventing them from rising higher. In some years, the federal government bought more than one-fourth of all the wheat grown in the country and took it off the market, in order to maintain prices at a pre-determined level.

During the Great Depression of the 1930s, agricultural price support programs led to vast amounts of food being deliberately destroyed at a time when malnutrition was a serious problem in the United States and hunger marches were taking place in cities across the country. For example, the federal government bought 6 million hogs in 1933 alone and destroyed them. Huge amounts of farm produce were plowed under, in order to keep it off the market and maintain prices at the fixed level, and vast amounts of milk were poured down the sewers for the same reason. Meanwhile, many American children were suffering from diseases caused by malnutrition.

Still, there was a food surplus. A surplus, like a shortage, is a *price* phenomenon. A surplus does not mean that there is some excess relative to the people.

There was not "too much" food relative to the population during the Great Depression. The people simply did not have enough money to buy everything that was produced at the artificially high prices set by the government. A very similar situation existed in poverty-stricken India at the beginning of the twenty-first century, where there was a surplus of wheat and rice under government price supports. The *Far Eastern Economic Review* reported:

> India's public stock of food grains is at an all-time high, and next spring, it will grow still further to a whopping 80 million tonnes, or four times the amount necessary in case of national emergency. Yet while that wheat and rice sits idle—in some cases for years, to the point of rotting—millions of Indians don't have enough to eat.

A report from India in the *New York Times* told a very similar story under the headline, "Poor in India Starve as Surplus wheat Rots":

> Surplus from this year's wheat harvest, bought by the government from farmers, sits moldering in muddy fields here in Punjab State. Some of the previous year's wheat surplus sits untouched, too, and the year's before that, and the year's before that.
>
> To the south, in the neighboring state of Rajasthan, villagers ate boiled leaves or discs of bread made from grass seeds in late summer and autumn because they could not afford to buy wheat. One by one, children and adults—as many as 47 in all—wilted away from hunger-related causes, often clutching pained stomachs.

A surplus or "glut" of food in India, where malnutrition is still a serious problem, may seem like a contradiction in terms. But food surpluses under "floor" prices are as real as the housing shortages under "ceiling" prices. In the United States, the vast amount of storage space required to keep surplus crops off the market once led to such desperate expedients as storing these farm products in unused warships, when all the storage facilities on land had been filled to capacity. Otherwise, American wheat would have had to be left outside to rot, as in India. A series of bumper crops in the United States could lead to the federal government's having more wheat in storage than was grown by American farmers all year. In India, it was reported in 2002 that the Indian government was spending more on storage of its surplus produce than on agriculture, rural development, irrigation and flood control combined.

None of this is peculiar to the United States and India. The countries of the European Union spent $39 billion in direct subsidies in 2002, and their consumers spent twice as much in the inflated food prices created by these agricultural programs. Meanwhile, the surplus food was sold below cost on the world market, driving down the prices that Third World farmers could get for their produce. In all these countries, not only the government but also the consumers are paying for agricultural price-support programs—the government directly in payments to farmers and storage companies, the consumers in inflated food prices. As of 2001, American consumers were paying $1.9 billion a year in artificially higher prices for products containing sugar and the government was paying $1.4 million per *month* just to store the surplus sugar. Meanwhile, the *New York Times* reported that sugar producers were "big donors to both Republicans and Democrats" and that the costly sugar price support program had "bipartisan support."

In 2002, the U.S. Congress passed a farm subsidy bill that was estimated to cost the average American family more than $4,000 over the next decade in taxes and inflated food prices. Nor was this a new development. During the mid–1980s, when the price of sugar on the world market was four cents a pound, the wholesale price within the United States was 20 cents a pound. The government was subsidizing the production of something that Americans could have gotten cheaper by not producing it at all and buying it in the world market. This has been true of sugar for decades. Moreover, sugar is not unique in this respect, nor is the United States. In the nations of the European Union, the prices of lamb, butter, and sugar are all more than twice as high as their world market prices. As a writer for the *Wall Street Journal* put it, every cow in the European Union gets more subsidies per day than most Africans have to live on.

Although the original rationale for the American price-support programs was to save family farms, in practice more of the money went to big agricultural corporations, some of which received millions of dollars each, while the average farm received only a few hundred dollars. Most of the money from the 2002 bipartisan farm bill will likewise go to the wealthiest 10 percent of farmers—including David Rockefeller, Ted Turner, and a dozen companies on the *Fortune* 500 list. In Mexico as well, 85 percent of agricultural subsides go to the largest 15 percent of farmers.

What is crucial from the standpoint of understanding the role of prices in the economy is that persistent surpluses are as much a result of keeping prices artificially high as persistent shortages are of keeping prices artificially low. Nor were the losses simply the sums of money extracted from the taxpayers or the consumers for the benefit of agricultural corporations and farmers. These are internal transfers within a nation, which do not directly reduce the total wealth of the country. The real losses to the country as a whole come from the misallocation of scarce resources which have alternative uses.

Scarce resources such as land, labor, fertilizer, and machinery are needlessly used to produce more food than the consumers are willing to consume at the artificially high prices decreed by the government. All the vast resources used to produce sugar in the United States are wasted when sugar can be imported from countries in the tropics, where it is produced much more cheaply. Poor people, who spend an especially high percentage of their income on food, are forced to pay far more than necessary to get the amount of food they receive, leaving them with less money for other things. Those on food stamps are able to buy less food with those stamps when food prices are artificially inflated. From a purely economic standpoint, it is working at cross purposes to subsidize farmers by forcing food prices up and then subsidize some consumers by bringing down their particular costs of food with subsidies—as is done in both India and the United States. However, from a political standpoint, it makes perfect sense to gain the support of two different sets of voters, especially since most of them do not understand the full economic implications of the policies.

Even when agricultural subsidies and price controls originated during hard times as a humanitarian measure, they have persisted long past those times because they developed an organized constituency which threatened to create political trouble if these subsidies and controls were removed or even reduced. Farmers have blocked the streets of Paris with their farm machinery when the French government showed signs of scaling back its agricultural programs or allowing more foreign farm produce to be imported. In Canada, farmers protesting low wheat prices blocked highways and formed a motorcade of tractors to the capital city of Ottawa.

It has not been uncommon for governments in the European Community to spend more than half of their annual budgets on agricultural subsidies.

While roughly one-fifth of farming income in the United States comes from government subsidies, more than 40 percent of farming income in countries of the European Union comes from such subsidies, as does an absolute majority of the farming income in Japan.

QUALITY DETERIORATION

One of the reasons for the political success of price controls is that part of their costs are concealed. Even the visible shortages do not tell the whole story. *Quality* deterioration, such as already noted in the case of housing, has been common with many other products and services whose prices have been kept artificially low by government fiat.

One of the fundamental problems of price control is defining just what it is whose price is being controlled. Even something as simple as an apple is not easy to define because apples differ in size, freshness, and appearance, quite aside from the different varieties of apples. Produce stores and super-markets spend time (and hence money) sorting out different kinds and qual-ities of apples, throwing away those that fall below a certain quality that their respective customers expect. Under price control, however, the amount of ap-ples demanded at an artificially low price exceeds the amount supplied, so there is no need to spend so much time and money sorting out apples, as they will all be sold anyway. Some apples that would ordinarily be thrown away under free market conditions may, under price control, be kept for sale to those people who arrive after all the good apples have been sold.

As with apartments under rent control, there is less incentive to maintain high quality when everything will sell anyway during a shortage.

Some of the most painful examples of quality deterioration have occurred in countries where there are price controls on medical care. At artificially low prices, more people go to doctors' offices with minor ailments that they might otherwise ignore, or treat with over-the-counter medications, perhaps with a pharmacist's advice. Alternatively, they might make a quick phone call to their doctor for advice, instead of coming to his office for a visit that would take up more of their time and his. But all this changes when price controls reduce the cost of visits to the doctor's office, and especially when these visits are paid for by the government and are therefore free to the patient.

In short, more people make more claims on doctors' time under price con-trol, leaving less time for other people with more serious, or even urgent, medical problems. Thus, under Britain's government-controlled medical sys-tem, a twelve-year-old girl was given a breast implant while 10,000 people waited 15 months or more for surgery, including a woman with cancer who had her operation postponed so many times that the malignancy eventually became inoperable. The priorities which prices automatically cause individu-als to consider are among the first casualties of price controls.

In countries around the world, the amount of time that physicians spend per patient visit has been shorter under government-controlled medical care, compared to the time spent by physicians where prices are not controlled. Such other common features of price controls as waiting lines and black markets have also been found in medical care. In China and Japan, black markets have taken the form of bribes to doctors to get expedited treatment.

In short, whether the product or service has been housing, apples, or medical care, quality deterioration under price control has been common in the most disparate settings.

THE POLITICS OF PRICE CONTROLS

Simple as basic economic principles may be, their ramifications can be quite complex, as we have seen with the various effects of rent control laws and agricultural price support laws. However, even this basic level of economics is seldom understood by the public, which often demands political "solutions" that turn out to make matters worse. Nor is this a new phenomenon of modern times in democratic countries. In 1628, a local harvest shortfall in Italy led to reduced supplies of food in that area, which in turn led to a public reaction similar to what has been seen in many other times and places:

> People implored the magistrates to take measures, measures which the crowd considers simple, just and certain to bring out the hidden, walled-up, buried grain, and to bring back plenty. The magistrates did do something: fixed the maximum price for various foodstuffs, threatened to punish those who refused to sell, and other edicts of the sort. Since such measures, however vigorous, do not have the virtue of diminishing the need for food, growing crops out of season, or attracting supplies from areas of surplus, the evil lasted, and grew. The crowd attributed that effect to the incompleteness and weakness of the remedies, and shouted for more generous and decisive ones.

Since this was a local food shortage, the ordinary effect of supply and demand would have been to cause local prices to rise, attracting more food into the area. Price controls prevented that. Nor was this perverse reaction peculiar to Italy.

When a Spanish blockade in the sixteenth century tried to starve Spain's rebellious subjects in Antwerp into surrender, the resulting high prices of food within Antwerp caused others to smuggle food into the city, even through the blockade, enabling the inhabitants to continue to hold out. However, the authorities within Antwerp decided to solve the problem of high food prices by laws fixing the maximum price to be allowed to be charged for given food items and providing severe penalties for anyone violating those laws. There followed the classic consequences of price control—a larger consumption of the artificially lower priced goods and a reduction in the supply of such goods, since people were less willing to run the risk of sending food through the blockade without the additional incentive of higher prices. Therefore, the net effect of the price controls were that "the city lived in high spirits until all at once provisions gave out" and Antwerp had to surrender to the Spaniards.

Halfway around the world, in eighteenth-century India, a local famine in Bengal brought a government crackdown on food dealers and speculators, imposing price controls on rice. Here the resulting shortages lead to widespread deaths by starvation. However, when another famine struck India in the nineteenth century, under the colonial rule of British officials and during the heyday of classical economics, opposite policies were followed, with opposite results:

> In the earlier famine one could hardly engage in the grain trade without becoming amenable to the law. In 1866 respectable men in vast numbers went into the trade; for the Government, by publishing weekly returns of the rates in every district, rendered the traffic both easy and safe. Everyone knew where to buy grain cheapest and where to sell it dearest and food was accordingly brought from the districts which could best spare it and carried to those which most urgently needed it.

As elementary as all this may seem, in terms of economic principles, it was made possible politically only because the British colonial government was not accountable to local public opinion. In an era of democratic politics, the same actions would require either a public familiar with basic economics or political leaders willing to risk their careers to do what needed to be done. It is hard to know which is less likely.

Chapter 4

An Overview

... we need education in the obvious more than investigation of the obscure.

—Justice Oliver Wendell Holmes

Understanding any subject requires that it first be defined, so that you are clear in your own mind as to what you are talking about—and what you are not talking about. It is not merely the subject matter which defines economics, but also its methods and its purposes. Just as a poetic discussion of the weather is not meteorology, so an issuance of moral pronouncements or political creeds about the economy is not economics. Economics is a study of *cause-and-effect* relationships in an economy. Its purpose is to discern the consequences of various ways of allocating scarce resources which have alternative uses. It has nothing to say about social philosophy or moral values, any more than it has anything to say about music, literature, or medical science.

These other things are not necessarily any less important, they are simply not what economics is about. No one expects mathematics to explain love and no one should expect economics to be something other than what it is or to do something other than what it can. But both mathematics and economics can be very important where they apply. Careful and complex mathematical calculations can be the difference between having an astronaut who is returning to earth from orbit end up crashing in the Himalayas or landing safely in Florida. We have also seen similar social disasters from misunderstanding the basic principles of economics.

Even where no money is involved, economic principles may still apply. During the Second World War, Japanese fighter pilots were initially very formidable adversaries for American fighter pilots, who lacked aerial combat experience, such as the Japanese had already gotten while fighting in China and elsewhere. But, as the war went on, the two countries followed different policies with regard to their combat pilots. American pilots were systematically taken out of combat after flying a certain number of missions, and were then used as instructors who could spread some of their experience to new and inexperienced pilots being trained for combat. Meanwhile, Japan followed policies similar to those of its German ally, whose motto was "fly till you die"—a macho approach to war that ignored economic principles.

These military policies were also economic policies because aerial combat experience is a scarce and valuable resource which has alternative uses—either in continuing to fly combat missions or training others to fly them. Because of the element of chance in aerial combat, even the top aces can eventually get shot down if they fly long enough. As the war went on and many of the top Japanese fighter pilots were eventually shot down, they were replaced by inexperienced pilots who had to learn the hard way in aerial combat, where small mistakes can be fatal. Meanwhile, American fighter pilots who had been trained by veterans of aerial combat began to get the upper hand.

How much the relative skills of the opposing pilots had changed during the course of the war was demonstrated dramatically in an air battle near the end of that war, over the Marianas chain of islands in the Pacific. This became known as "the great Marianas turkey shoot" because American pilots shot down hundreds of Japanese planes while losing a relative handful of their own.

By this time, so many of the leading Japanese aces had already been killed that a Japanese fighter pilot who was now given a rare public commendation for his exploits no longer considered that an exalted honor because his potential competitors, the "great pilots of our Navy—Nishshizawa, Ota, Sasai, and others—were dead." In his postwar memoirs, this Japanese ace mentioned that the Americans "had virtually wiped out all our carrier-based planes in the Marianas." Japanese military leaders had not treated aerial combat experience as a scarce and valuable resource. Their failure to allocate this resource efficiently to its alternative uses was a mistake in economics, though there was no money involved—just dire military consequences.

CAUSE AND EFFECT

Analyzing economic actions in cause-and-effect terms means examining the logic of the incentives being created, rather than simply the goals being sought. It also means examining the empirical evidence of what actually happens under such incentives.

The causation at work in an economy is often *systemic interaction*, rather than the kind of simple one-way causation involved when one billiard ball hits another billiard ball and knocks it into a pocket. Systemic causation involves more complex reciprocal interactions, such as adding lye to hydrochloric acid and ending up with salty water,[1] because both chemicals are transformed by their effects on one another, going from being two deadly substances to becoming one harmless one.

In an economy as well, the plans of buyers and sellers are transformed as they discover each other's reactions to supply and demand conditions and the resulting price changes that force them to reassess their plans. For example, those who start out planning to buy a mansion at the beach may end up settling for a bungalow further inland, after they discover the high prices of mansions at the beach. Likewise, suppliers sometimes end up selling their goods for less than they paid to buy them or produce them, when the demand is inadequate to get any higher price from the consuming public and the alternative is to get nothing at all for an item that is unsalable at the price originally planned.

Systemic Causation

Because systemic causation involves reciprocal interactions, rather than one-way causation, that in turn reduces the role of individual intentions. As Friedrich Engels put it, "what each individual wills is obstructed by everyone else, and what emerges is something that no one willed." Economics is concerned with what emerges, not what anyone intended. Similar reasoning had appeared even earlier in the writings of Adam Smith, where the benefits of competitive capitalism were said to be "no part" of the capitalist's intention. (That is why Adam Smith had a high opinion of capitalism, despite his low

---

[1] Do *not* try this at home. Professional chemists can handle these dangerous chemicals, with appropriate safeguards, in a laboratory but either can be fatal in other hands.

opinion of capitalists.) If the stock market closes at 10,463 on a given day, that is the end result of a process of complex interactions among innumerable buyers and sellers of stocks, none of whom may have intended for the market to close at 10,463, even though it was their own actions in pursuit of other intentions which caused it to do so.

While causation can sometimes be explained by intentional actions and sometimes by systemic interactions, too often the results of systemic interactions are falsely explained by individual intentions. Just as primitive peoples tended to attribute such things as the swaying of trees in the wind to some intentional action by an invisible spirit, rather than to such systemic causes as variations in atmospheric pressure, so there is a tendency toward intentional explanations of systemic events in the economy, when people are unaware of basic economic principles. While rising prices are likely to reflect changes in supply and demand, people ignorant of economics may attribute the rises to "greed."

Such an intentional explanation raises more questions than it answers. For example, if greed is the explanation, why do prices vary so much from one time to another or from one place to another? Does greed vary that much and in the same pattern? In the Los Angeles basin, for example, homes near the ocean sell for much higher prices than similar homes located in the smoggy interior. Does this mean that fresh air promotes greed, while smog makes home sellers more reasonable? To say that prices are due to greed is to imply that sellers can set prices by an act of will. If so, no company would ever go bankrupt, since it could simply raise its prices to cover whatever its costs happened to be. But the systemic interactions of the marketplace through supply and demand force the high-cost company to keep its prices down to where their competitors' price are, thereby leading to losses and bankruptcy. Keeping their prices up would simply mean losses of sales and faster bankruptcy.

People shocked by the high prices charged in stores in low-income neighborhoods have often been quick to blame greed or exploitation on the part of the people who run such businesses. Similarly when they notice the much higher interest rates charged by pawnbrokers and small finance companies which operate in low-income neighborhoods, as compared to the interest rates charged by banks in middle-class communities. Yet studies show that profit rates are generally no higher in inner city businesses than elsewhere, and the fact that many businesses are leaving such neighborhoods—and others, such as supermarket chains, are staying away—reinforces that conclusion.

The painful fact that poor people end up paying more than affluent people for many goods and services has a very plain—and systemic—explanation. It often costs more to deliver goods and services in low-income neighborhoods. Higher insurance costs and higher costs for various security precautions, due to higher rates of crime and vandalism, are just some of systemic reasons that get ignored by those seeking an explanation in terms of personal intentions. For example, an inner city shopping center in one midwestern city had to spend 15 percent more on security guards and lighting than a comparable suburban shopping complex. All these costs get passed along to the local customers in higher prices.

In addition, the cost of doing business tends to be higher per dollar of business in low-income neighborhoods. Lending $100 each to fifty low-income borrowers at pawn shops or local finance companies takes more time and costs more money to process the applications than lending $5,000 at a bank to one middle-class customer, even though the same total sum of money is involved in both cases.[2]

An armored car delivering money in small denominations to a small check-cashing agency in a ghetto costs just as much as an armored car delivering a hundred times as much value of money, in larger bills, to a bank in a suburban shopping mall. With the cost of business being higher per dollar of business in the low-income community, it is hardly surprising that these higher costs get passed on in higher prices and higher interest rates. Higher prices for people who can least afford them is a tragic end-result, but its causes are systemic.

This is not merely a philosophical distinction. There are major practical consequences to the way causation is understood. Treating the causes of higher prices and higher interest rates in low-income neighborhoods as being personal greed or exploitation, and trying to remedy it by imposing price controls and interest rate ceilings only ensures that even less will be

---

[2]In many cases, the middle-class borrower who already has a checking account at the bank from which he wishes to borrow also has an automatic line of credit available with that checking account. When the need for a $5,000 loan arises, there may be no need even to file an application. The borrower simply writes $5,000 more in checks than there is money in the account, and the automatic line of credit covers it, with minimum time and trouble to both the borrower and the bank, since the potential borrower's credit rating was already established when the account was first opened and the size of the line of credit was established on the basis of that credit rating.

supplied in low-income neighborhoods thereafter. Just as rent control reduces the supply of housing, so price controls and interest rate controls can reduce the number of stores, pawn shops, and local finance companies willing to operate in neighborhoods with higher costs, when those costs cannot be covered by legally permissible prices and interest rates. The alternative, for many residents of low-income neighborhoods, may be to go outside the legal money-lending organizations and borrow from loan sharks, who charge even higher rates of interest and have their own methods of collecting.

When stores and financial institutions close down in low-income neighborhoods, more people in such neighborhoods are then forced to travel to other neighborhoods to shop for groceries or other goods, paying money for bus fare or taxi fare. Such business closings have already occurred for a variety of reasons, including riots and higher rates of shoplifting, with the result that many people in low-income neighborhoods already have to go elsewhere for shopping or banking.

An old adage says: "First, do no harm." Understanding the distinction between systemic causation and intentional causation is one way to do less harm with economic policies. It is especially important to do no harm to people who are already in painful economic circumstances.

It is also worth noting that most people are not criminals, even in high-crime neighborhoods. The fraction of dishonest people in such neighborhoods are the real source of many of the higher costs behind the higher prices charged by businesses operating in those neighborhoods. But it is both intellectually and emotionally easier to blame high prices on those who collect them, rather than on those who cause them. It is also more politically popular to blame outsiders, especially if those outsiders are of a different ethnic background.

Systemic causes, such as are often found in economics, provide no such emotional release for the public or moral melodrama for the media and politicians as such intentional causes as "greed," "exploitation," "gouging," "discrimination," and the like. Intentional explanations of cause and effect may also be more natural, in the sense that less sophisticated individuals and less sophisticated societies tend to turn first to such explanations. In some cases, it has taken centuries for intentional explanations embodied in superstitions about nature to give way to systemic explanations based on science. It is not yet clear whether it will take that long for the basic principles of economics to replace many people's natural tendency to try to explain systemic results by someone's intentions.

Complexity and Causation

Although the basic principles of economics are not very complicated, the very ease with which they can be learned also makes them easy to dismiss as "simplistic" by those who do not want to accept analyses which contradict their cherished beliefs. Evasions of the obvious are often far more complicated than the facts. Nor is it automatically true that complex effects must have complex causes. The ramifications of something very simple can become enormously complex. For example, the simple fact that the earth is tilted on its axis causes innumerable very complex reactions in plants, animals, and people, as well as in such non-living things as ocean currents, weather changes and changes in the length of night and day.

If the earth stood straight up on its axis,[3] night and day would be the same length all year around and in all parts of the world at the same time. Climate would still differ between the equator and the poles but, at any given place, the weather would be the same in winter as in summer. The fact that the earth is tilted on its axis means that sunlight is striking the same country at different angles at different points during the planet's annual orbit around the sun, leading to changing warmth and changing lengths of night and day. In turn, such changes trigger complex biological reactions in plant growth, animal hibernations and migrations, as well as psychological changes in human beings and many seasonal changes in their economies. Changing weather patterns affect ocean currents and the frequency of hurricanes, among many other phenomena. Yet all of these complications are due to the one simple fact that the earth is tilted on its axis, instead of being straight up.

In short, complex effects may be a result of either simple causes or complex causes. The specific facts can tell us which. *A priori* pronouncements about what is "simplistic" cannot.

Few things are more simple than the fact that people tend to buy more at lower prices and buy less at higher prices. But, putting that together with the fact that producers tend to supply more at higher prices and less at lower prices, that is enough to predict all sorts of complex reactions to price controls, whether in the housing market or in the market for food, electricity, or

---

[3]Purists may say that there is no up or down in space, but that simply requires rephrasing the same facts by saying that the axis on which the earth rotates is not perpendicular to the plane of the planet's orbit around the sun.

medical care. Moreover, these reactions have been found on all inhabited continents and over thousands of years of recorded history. Simple causes and complex effects have been common among wide varieties of peoples and cultures.

Individual Versus Systemic Rationality

The tendency to personalize causation leads not only to charges that "greed" causes high prices in market economies, but also to charges that "stupidity" among bureaucrats is responsible for many things that go wrong in government programs. In reality, many of the things that go wrong in these programs are due to perfectly rational actions, *given the incentives* faced by government officials who run such programs and given the constraints on the amount of knowledge available to any given decision-maker or set of decision-makers.

Where a policy or institution has been established by top political leaders, officials subject to their authority may well hesitate to contradict their beliefs, much less point out the counterproductive consequences that later follow from these policies and institutions. Messengers carrying bad news could be risking their careers or—under Stalin or Mao—their lives.

Officials carrying out particular policies may be quite rational, however negative the impact of these policies may prove to be for society at large. During the Stalin era in the Soviet Union, for example, there was at one time a severe shortage of mining equipment, but the manager of a factory producing such machines kept them in storage after they were built, rather than sending them out to the mines, where they were sorely needed. The reason was that the official orders called for these machines to be painted with red, oil-resistant paint and the manufacturer had on hand only green, oil-resistant paint and red varnish that was not oil-resistant. Disobeying official orders in any respect was a serious offense under Stalin and "I don't want to get eight years," the manager said.

When he explained the situation to a higher official and asked for permission to use the green, oil-resistant paint, this official's response was: "Well, I don't want to get eight years either." However, the higher official cabled to his ministry for their permission to give his permission. After a long delay, the ministry eventually granted his request and the mining machinery was finally shipped to the mines. None of these people was behaving stupidly or irrationally. They were responding quite rationally to the incentives and constraints of the system in which they worked. Under any economic or political system, people can make their choices only among the alternatives actually available—and different systems present different alternatives.

INCENTIVES VERSUS GOALS

Because economics is a study of cause and effect among human beings, it deals with incentives and their consequences. That often leads to radically different conclusions from those reached by people who think primarily or solely in terms of goals. As already noted in Chapter 3, the goal of providing "affordable housing" for the poor through rent control can lead to diverting resources toward the building of luxury housing or office buildings, when the latter are exempted from rent control and therefore offer a rate of return on investment that is higher that what is available by building housing for the poor. In short, the consequences are the exact opposite of the goal.

In addition to the incentives that rent control creates for builders, it also creates incentives for tenants, who seek to occupy more housing than they would if they had to pay the full value of that housing, as measured by what others would be willing to bid for it. For landlords, rent control not only constrains their profits—sometimes to zero or below—it creates incentives for them not to maintain the existing housing as well as they would in a free market, where they would have to compete for tenants, rather than in a rent-controlled market, where there are more applicants than apartments. Given these incentives and constraints, it is hardly surprising to discover empirically that rent control has been followed by housing shortages, a reduction in the building of new housing, and a faster deterioration of existing housing as it receives less maintenance.

It must be emphasized that these are *empirical* consequences, because some people seem to think that the role of prices in the economy is simply a theory by those with "faith in the market." However, it was a Swedish socialist—presumably lacking such "faith" in the capitalist market—who said that rent control "appears to be the most efficient technique known to destroy a city—except for bombing." He was an economist familiar with the empirical evidence.

Another comparison between bombing and rent control was made by an official of the Communist government of Vietnam, some years after the Vietnam war. "The Americans couldn't destroy Hanoi" by bombing it during the war, he said, "but we have destroyed our city by very low rents." As a Communist with no bias toward the free market, he had learned the hard way that artificially low rents encouraged demand while discouraging supply—a very simple principle, indeed, but one with major impacts on those who fail to heed it.

While bombing does more immediate damage to a city, wars end and many cities have been rapidly rebuilt in the postwar world. Rent control does more long-lasting damage because most people do not understand the basic economics of it and that allows it to continue reducing the housing supply for decades.

Economics was christened "the dismal science" precisely because its analysis frustrated so many hopes and desires. On the other hand, knowing what is not possible can spare us many disappointments and avoid many disasters. Because human beings can be as wrong in their pessimism as in their optimism, economics has also served to expose the fallacies of many doom-and-gloom prophets. This will become especially apparent in Chapter 12, which includes an analysis of the economic reasons why so many predictions of natural resource exhaustion have repeatedly turned out to be so wrong, by such huge margins, for so many years or even generations.

Incentives matter because most people will usually do more for their own benefit than for the benefit of others. Incentives link the two concerns together. A waitress brings food to your table, not because of your hunger, but because her salary and tips depend on it. In the absence of such incentives, service in restaurants in the Soviet Union was notoriously bad. Unsold goods piling up in warehouses were not the only consequences of a lack of a free market price system.

Prices not only help determine which particular things are produced, they are also one of the ways of rationing the inherent scarcity of all goods and service. However, prices do not create that scarcity, which will require some form of rationing under any other economic system.

Simple as all this may seem, it goes counter to many programs and policies designed to make various goods and services "affordable" or to keep them from becoming "prohibitively expensive." Being prohibitive is precisely how prices limit how much each person uses. If everything were made affordable by government decree, there would still not be any more to go around than when things were prohibitively expensive. There would simply have to be some alternative rationing method. Whether that method was through ration coupons, political influence, black markets, or just fighting over things when they go on sale, the rationing would still have to be done, since artificially making things affordable does not create any more total output. On the contrary, price "ceilings" tend to cause less to be produced.

While scarcity is inherent, shortages are not. Scarcity simply means that there is not enough to satisfy everyone's desires completely. Only in the Garden of Eden was there enough to do that. A shortage, however, means that there are people who are willing to pay the price of the product but are unable to find it. Price is an integral part of what a shortage is all about, even though many people mistakenly believe that there is a greater physical scarcity of goods during a shortage. However, as Sweden discovered, even the fastest rate of home-building in the world did not prevent an ever-worsening housing shortage, for the waiting list for housing grew faster, as rising incomes and the artificially low prices of housing under rent control caused many people to use more housing than they would have if they had had to pay the full value of the resources used in producing it.

Many apparently humanitarian policies have backfired throughout history because of a failure to understand the role of prices. Attempts to keep food prices down by imposing price controls have led to hunger and even starvation, whether in seventeenth-century Italy, eighteenth-century India, France after the French Revolution, Russia after the Bolshevik revolution, or in a number of African countries after they obtained independence during the 1960s. Some of these African countries, like some of the countries in Eastern Europe, once had such an abundance of food that they were exporters of food before the era of price control and government planning turned them into countries unable to feed themselves.

The motivation behind price controls on food may have been to make food affordable to the poor, but affordability did not mean any more food. In fact, it led to less food being available when the prices failed to repay the costs and labor required to grow crops or raise animals. Under the changed incentives created by price controls, farmers tended to produce less food and to keep much of what they produced for themselves and their families. Some farmers even gave up farming entirely as unprofitable, and moved to the city, simultaneously reducing the supply of food and adding to the number of urban consumers of food.

None of this is new or peculiar to a modern capitalist economy. Back in the days of the Roman Empire, the emperor Diocletian issued imperial decrees which set the prices of many goods. Then "people brought provisions no more to markets," as a contemporary put it. It would be much the same story nearly two thousand years later in America, when price controls during the Nixon administration led to declining supplies of the goods subject to those controls.

In Ghana, the country lost its long-standing position as the world's number one producer of cocoa when the government limited how much money would be paid to farmers growing cocoa—and Ghana regained that position after the disastrous decline in the cocoa crop that followed forced the government to change its policy. Similarly, after the government of India allowed wheat prices to rise, wheat production rose more than 5 percent per year from 1967 to 1977. This not only ended India's historic and catastrophic famines, it produced such a supply of wheat as to allow India to donate food to ease Ethiopia's famine in the 1980s.

Failure to supply goods, as a result of political restrictions on the economy, must be sharply distinguished from an inability to produce them. Food can be in short supply in a country with extraordinarily fertile soil, as in post-Communist Russia that had not yet achieved a free-market economy:

> Undulating gently through pastoral hills 150 miles south of Moscow, the Plava River Valley is a farmer's dream come true. This is the gateway to what Russians call "Chernozym"—"Black Earth Country"—which boasts some of the most fertile soil in Europe, within three hours' drive of a giant, hungry metropolis . . . Black Earth country has the natural wealth to feed an entire nation. But it can barely feed itself.

It is hard even to imagine, in a free market economy, a hungry city, dependent on imports of foreign food, when there is extraordinarily fertile farmland not far away. Yet the people on that very fertile farmland were as poor as the city dwellers were hungry. The workers harvesting that land earned the equivalent of about $10 a week, with even this small amount being paid in kind—sacks of potatoes or cucumbers—because of a lack of money. As the mayor of a town in this region said:

> We ought to be rich. We have wonderful soil. We have the scientific know-how. We have qualified people. But what does it add up to?

If nothing else, it adds up to a reason for understanding economics as a means of achieving an efficient allocation of scarce resources which have alternative uses. All that was lacking in Russia was a market to connect the hungry city with the products of the fertile land and a government that would allow such a market to function freely. In some places, local Russian officials forbad the movement of food across local boundary lines, in order to assure low food prices within their own jurisdictions, and therefore local political support for themselves. Again, it is necessary to emphasize that this was not a stupid policy, from the standpoint of officials trying to gain local popularity with consumers by maintaining low food prices. This protected their political careers, however disastrous such policies were for the country as a whole.

While systemic causation is in one sense impersonal, in the sense that its outcomes are not specifically predetermined by anyone, "the market" is ultimately a way by which people's individual personal desires are reconciled with one another. Too often a false contrast is made between the impersonal marketplace and the compassionate policies of various government programs. But both systems face the same scarcity of resources and both systems make choices within the constraints of that scarcity. The difference is that one system involves each individual making choices for himself or herself, while the other system involves a smaller number of people making choices for millions of others. The mechanisms of the market are impersonal but the choices made by individuals are as personal as choices made anywhere else.

It may be fashionable for journalists to refer to "the whim of the marketplace," as if that were something different from the desires of people, just as it was once fashionable to refer to "production for use, rather than profit"— as if profits could be made by producing things that people cannot use or do not want to use. The real contrast is between choices made by individuals for themselves and choices made for them by others who presume to define what these individuals "really" need.

SCARCITY AND COMPETITION

Scarcity means that everyone's desires cannot be satisfied completely, regardless of which particular economic system or economic policy we choose—and regardless of whether an individual or a society is poor or affluent. Therefore competition among people for these resources is inherent. It is not a question whether we like or dislike competition. Scarcity means that we do not have the option to *choose* whether or not to have an economy in which people compete. That is the only kind of economy that is possible—and our only choice is among the particular methods that can be used for this competition.

Economic Institutions

One way in which competition for scarce resources might take place would be for those who hold political power to decide how resources should be allocated to different uses and shared among different people. This has happened in ancient despotisms and under modern communism. Conceivably, the people themselves might decide voluntarily how to share things, as in some tribal societies or in an Israeli kibbutz, though it is hard to imagine how that could happen in societies consisting of millions of people.

Yet another method of sharing resources among competing uses and competing individuals is by having them bid for these resources and the products resulting from them. In this system—a price-coordinated economy—those who want to use wood to produce furniture must bid against those who want to use it to produce paper, houses, or baseball bats. Those who want to use milk to produce cheese must bid against those who want to use it to produce yogurt or ice cream. Most people may be unaware that they are competing and simply see themselves as deciding how much of various things to buy at whatever prices they find, but scarcity ensures that they are competing with others, even if they are conscious only of weighing their own purchasing decisions against the amount of money they have available.

One of the incidental benefits of competing and sharing through prices is that different people are not as likely to think of themselves as rivals, nor to develop the kinds of hostility that rivalry can breed. For example, much the same labor and construction material needed to build a Protestant church could be used to build a Catholic church. But, if a Protestant congregation is raising money to build a church for themselves, they are likely to be preoccupied with how much money they can raise and how much is needed for the kind of church they want. Construction prices may cause them to scale back some of their more elaborate plans, in order to fit within the limits of what they can afford. But they are unlikely to blame Catholics, even though the competition of Catholics for the same construction materials makes their prices higher than otherwise.

If, instead, the government were in the business of building churches and presenting them to different religious groups, Protestants and Catholics would be explicit rivals for this largess and neither would have any financial incentive to cut back on their building plans to accommodate the other. Instead, each would have an incentive to make the case, as strongly as possible, for the full extent of their desires and to resent any suggestion that they scale back their plans. The inherent scarcity of materials and labor would still limit what could be built, but that limit would now be imposed politically and would be seen by each as due to the rivalry of the other. The Constitution of the United States of course prevents the American government from building churches for religious groups, no doubt in order to prevent just such political rivalries and the bitterness, and sometimes bloodshed, to which such rivalries have led in other countries.

The same economic principle, however, applies to groups that are not based on religion but on ethnicity, geographical regions, or age brackets. All are inherently competing for the same resources, simply because these resources are scarce. However, competing indirectly by having to keep your demands within the limits of your own pocketbook is very different from seeing your desires for government benefits thwarted by the rival claims of some other group. Market rationing limits the amount of your claims on the output of others to what your own productivity has created, while political rationing limits your claims by the competing claims and clout of others.

Incremental Substitution

Because economic resources are not only scarce but have alternative uses, the efficient use of these resources requires both consumers and producers to make trade-offs and substitutions. Prices provide the incentives for doing so. When the price of oranges goes up, some consumers switch to tangerines. When bacon becomes more expensive, some consumers switch to ham. When the cost of a vacation at the beach rises, some people decide to go on a cruise instead. Note that what is happening here is not just substitution—it is *incremental* substitution. Not everybody stops eating oranges when they become more pricey. Some people continue to eat the same number of oranges they always ate, some cut back a little, some cut back a lot, and others forget about oranges completely and go on to some other fruit.

When the price of oranges rises, it is very likely because the number of oranges demanded at the existing price exceeds the number of oranges actually available. Something has to give. Incremental substitution, because of price increases, causes the loss to be minimized by being borne more by those who are relatively indifferent as between oranges and other substitutes, rather than by those who are so devoted to oranges that they will simply pay the higher prices and continue to eat the same number of oranges as before, cutting back somewhere else in their budget to offset the additional money spent on oranges.

Incremental substitutions take place in production as well as consumption. Petroleum, for example, can be used to make heating oil or gasoline, among many other things. More petroleum is turned into heating oil during the winter, when the demand for heating oil is greatest, and more into gasoline during the summer, when many people are doing more driving to recreational areas. This is not a total substitution, since some petroleum is turned into both products (and many others) throughout the year. It is *incremental* substitution—somewhat more of *A* at the cost of somewhat less of *B*. Prices facilitate this kind of substitution, as they reflect incrementally changing demands, leading to incremental changes in the amount supplied.

Trade-offs and substitution can take place either intentionally or systemically. An intentional trade-off has been made by LTV, a steel manufacturer in Cleveland, whose equipment has been set up to shift automatically from oil to natural gas when the price of oil rises above a given level. Automobiles have also been adjusted intentionally by becoming more fuel-efficient. Thus, the average American car drove 2,000 miles more in 1998 than in 1973, but used about 200 gallons less gasoline than a quarter of a century earlier. This was because of high-tech equipment added to engines, obviously at a cost, but with the cost of this technology substituting incrementally for the cost of gasoline.

A systemic trade-off occurs when the economy as a whole uses less oil because the composition of its output changes. As a higher proportion of the output of the American economy has over the years come to consist of services, rather than material goods, less fuel is needed in their production. It takes less fuel to create more advanced software than to manufacture steel or automobiles. Over all, the amount of fuel used per dollar of national output in the American economy has declined steadily since the early 1970s, when oil prices were raised dramatically by the international petroleum cartel.

As important as it is to understand the role of substitutions, it is also important to keep in mind that the efficient allocation of resources requires that these substitutions be *incremental*, not total. For example, one may believe that health is more important than amusements but, however reasonable that may sound as a general principle, no one really believes that having a twenty-year's supply of Band-Aids in the closet is more important than having to give up all music in order to pay for it. A price-coordinated economy facilitates incremental substitution, but political decision-making tends toward categorical *priorities*—that is, declaring one thing absolutely more important than another and creating laws and policies accordingly.

When a political figure says that we need to "set national priorities" about one thing or another, what that amounts to is making *A* categorically more important than *B*. That is the opposite of incremental substitution, in which the value of each depends on how much of each we already have at the moment, and therefore on the changing amount of *A* that we are willing to give up in order to get more *B*.

Incremental substitution means that the relative values of each varies with how much of each we already have available. This variation can be so great as to convert something that is beneficial into something that is detrimental, and vice versa. For example, human beings cannot live without salt, fat, and cholesterol, but most Americans get so much of all three that their lifespan is reduced. Conversely, despite the many problems caused by alcohol, from fatal automobile accidents to deaths from cirrhosis of the liver, studies show that very modest amounts of alcohol have health benefits that can be life-saving.[4] It is not categorically good or bad.

Whenever there are two things that each have some value, one cannot be categorically more valuable than another: Enough pennies will be worth more than any diamond. That is why incremental trade-offs tend to produce better results than categorical priorities.

Subsidies and Taxes

Ideally, prices allow alternative users to compete for scarce resources in the marketplace. However, this competition is distorted to the extent that special taxes are put on some products or resources but not on others, or when some products or resources are subsidized by the government but others are not. Prices charged to the consumers of such specially taxed or specially subsidized goods and services do not convey the real costs of producing them and therefore do not produce the same trade-offs as if they did. Yet there is always a political temptation to subsidize "good" things and tax "bad" things.

---

[4]Men who drank either nothing alcoholic or just one drink per week had a reduction in cardiovascular disease when they increased their alcohol intake by from one to six drinks per week. However, among men who already averaged seven or more alcoholic drinks per week, an increase in their drinking led to more cardiovascular disease, according to the *Journal of the American Medical Association*, September 25, 2000 issue. The medical publication *The Lancet* reported that "light-to-moderate alcohol consumption is associated with a reduced risk of dementia in individuals 55 years or older" in its January 26, 2002 issue.

However, when neither good things nor bad things are good or bad categorically, this prevents our finding out just how good or how bad any of these things is by letting people choose freely, uninfluenced by politically changed prices.

One of the factors in California's periodic water crises, for example, is that California farmers' use of water is subsidized so heavily that its price to farmers is less than one percent of what the same amount of water costs people living in Los Angeles or San Francisco. The net result is that agriculture, which accounts for about 3 percent of the state's output, consumes more than four-fifths of its water. Another consequence of subsidized water is that farmers grow crops requiring great amounts of water, such as rice and cotton, in California's semi-desert climate, where such crops would never be grown if farmers had to pay the real costs of the water they use. Inspiring as it may be to some that California's arid lands have been enabled to produce vast amounts of fruits and vegetables with the aid of subsidized water, those same fruits and vegetables could be produced more cheaply elsewhere with water supplied free of charge from the clouds.

The way to tell whether the California produce is worth what it costs to grow is to allow all those costs to be paid by California farmers who compete with farmers in other states that have higher rainfall levels. There is no need for government officials to decide arbitrarily—and categorically— whether it is a good thing or a bad thing for particular crops to be grown in California with water artificially supplied from federal irrigation projects. Such questions can be decided incrementally through price competition in a free market.

California is, unfortunately, not unique in this respect. In fact, this is not a peculiarly American problem. Halfway around the world, the government of India provides "almost free electricity and water" to farmers, according to *The Economist*, encouraging farmers to plant too much "water-guzzling rice," with the result that water tables in the Punjab "are dropping fast." Making anything artificially cheap usually means that it will be wasted, whatever that thing might be and wherever it might be located.

From standpoint of the allocation of resources, government should either not tax resources, goods, and services or else tax them all equally, so as to minimize the distortions of choices made by consumers and producers. For similar reasons, particular resources, goods, and services should not be subsidized, even if particular people are subsidized out of humanitarian concern over their being the victims of natural disasters, birth defects, or other misfortunes beyond their control.

From a political standpoint, however, politicians win votes by doing special favors for special interests or putting special taxes on whoever or whatever might be unpopular at the moment.

The Meaning of "Costs"

In light of the role of trade-offs and substitutions, it is easier to understand the real meaning of costs as the foregone opportunities to use the same resources elsewhere. Because an economy deals with scarce resources which have alternative uses, every benefit has a cost in the alternative uses that could have been made of the same resources that created a particular benefit. We do not simply "put" a price on things. Things have inherent costs and our political choice is only between trying to suppress the conveying of those costs to the users in prices or allowing these inherent costs to be expressed in the marketplace.

Free-market prices are not mere arbitrary obstacles to getting what people want. Prices are symptoms of an underlying reality that is not nearly as susceptible to political manipulation as the prices are. Prices are like thermometer readings—and a patient with a fever is not going to be helped by plunging the thermometer into ice water to lower the reading. On the contrary, if we were to take the new readings seriously and imagine that the patient's fever was over, the dangers would be even greater, now that the underlying reality was being ignored.

Despite how obvious all this might seem, there are never-ending streams of political schemes designed to escape the realities being conveyed by prices—whether through direct price controls or by making this or that "affordable" with subsidies or by having the government itself supply various goods and services free, as a "right." There are probably more ill-conceived economic policies based on treating prices as just nuisances to get around than on any other single fallacy. What all these schemes have in common is that they exempt some things from the process of weighing costs and benefits against one another.

Sometimes the rationale for removing particular things from the process of weighing costs against benefits is expressed in some such question as: "How can you put a price on art?"—or education, health, music, etc. The fundamental fallacy underlying this question is the belief that prices are simply "put" on things. So long as art, education, health, music, and thousands of other things all require time, effort, and material resources, the costs of these inputs are the prices that are inherent. These costs do not go away because a law prevents them from being conveyed through prices in the marketplace. Ultimately, to society as a whole, costs are the other things that could have been produced with the same resources. Money flows and price movements are symptoms of that fact—and suppressing these symptoms will not change the underlying fact.

PART II: INDUSTRY AND COMMERCE

Chapter 5

The Rise and Fall of Businesses

*Failure is part of the natural cycle of business. Companies
are born, companies die, capitalism moves forward.*

-FORTUNE MAGAZINE

Ordinarily, we tend to think of businesses as simply money-making enterprises, but that can be very misleading, in at least two ways. First of
all, most businesses go out of business within a very few years after getting
started, so it is likely that at least as many businesses are losing money as are
making money. More important, from the standpoint of economics, is not
what money the business owner hopes to make or whether he succeeds, but
how all this affects the use of scarce resources which have alternative uses—
and therefore how it affects the economic well-being of millions of other
people in the society at large.

ADJUSTING TO CHANGES

The businesses we hear about, in the media and elsewhere, are usually those
which have succeeded, and especially those which have succeeded on a grand
scale—Microsoft, Sony, General Motors, Lloyd's of London, Credit Suisse.
In an earlier era, Americans would have heard about the A & P grocery
chain, once the largest retail chain in any field, anywhere in the world. Its
15,000 stores in 1929 were more than any other retailer ever had in America,

before or since. The fact that A & P has shrunk to a minute fraction of its former size, and is now virtually unknown, suggests that industry and commerce are not static things, but dynamic processes, in which individual companies and whole industries rise and fall, as a result of relentless competition under changing conditions.

Half the companies on the "*Fortune* 500" list of the largest American businesses in 1980 were no longer on that list a decade later. In just one year—between 2001 and 2002—38 businesses dropped off the list, including Enron, which had been the fifth largest company in America the previous year. Nor are such falls from the financial peaks confined to the United States. At one time, the largest bank in the world, Japan's Mizuho, had a $20 billion loss in its fiscal year ending in 2003 and the value of its stock fell by 93 percent. The amount by which its total stock value fell was greater than the Gross Domestic Product of New Zealand.

At the heart of all of this is the role of profit—and of *losses*. Each is equally important from the standpoint of forcing companies and industries to use scarce resources efficiently. Industry and commerce are not just a matter of routine management, with profits rolling in more or less automatically. Masses of ever-changing details, within an ever-changing surrounding economic and social environment, mean that the threat of losses hangs over even the biggest and most successful businesses. There is a reason why business executives usually work far longer hours than their employees, and why so many businesses fail within a few years after getting started. Only from the outside does it look easy.

Just as companies rise and fall over time, so do profit rates—even more quickly. When compact discs began rapidly replacing long-playing records in the late 1980s, Japanese manufacturers of CD players "thrived" according to the *Far Eastern Economic Review*. But "within a few years, CD-players only offered manufacturers razor-thin margins." This has been a common experience with many products in many industries. The companies which first introduce a product that consumers like may make large profits, but those very profits attract more investments into existing companies and encourage new companies to form, both of which add to output, driving down prices and profit margins through supply and demand. Sometimes profits then turn to losses, forcing some firms into bankruptcy until the industry's supply and demand balance at levels that are sustainable.

Even the largest corporations can see profit turn to losses and vice versa. Sony lost $354 million in a six-month period and then, about a year later, had profits that topped one billion dollars. General Motors lost $30 billion during a three-year period in the early 1990s but rebounded under new management to earn nearly $4 billion in profits in 2002.

Companies superbly adapted to a given set of conditions can be left behind when those conditions change suddenly and their competitors are quicker to respond. During the 1920s, for example, the A & P grocery chain in the United States was making a phenomenal rate of profit on its investment—never less than 20 percent per year, about double the national average—and it continued to prosper on through the decades of the 1930s and 1940s. But all this began to change drastically in the 1950s, when A & P lost more than $50 million in one 52-week period. A few years later, it lost $175 million over the same span of time. Its decline had begun.

A & P's fate, both when it prospered and when it lost out to rival grocery chains, illustrates the dynamic nature of a price-coordinated economy and the role of profits and losses. When A & P was prospering up through the 1940s, it did so by charging *lower* prices than competing grocery stores. It could do this because its efficiency kept its costs lower than those of competing grocery stores and chains, and the resulting lower prices attracted vast numbers of customers. When A & P began to lose customers to other grocery chains, this was because these other chains could now sell for lower prices than A & P. Changing conditions in the surrounding society brought this about—together with differences in the speed with which different companies spotted these changes and realized their implications.

What were these changes? In the years following the end of World War II, suburbanization and the American public's rising prosperity gave huge supermarkets in shopping malls with vast parking lots decisive advantages over neighborhood stores located along the streets in the central cities. As the ownership of automobiles, refrigerators and freezers became far more widespread, this completely changed the economics of the grocery industry.

The automobile, which made suburbanization possible, also made possible greater economies of scale for both customers and supermarkets. Shoppers could now buy far more groceries at one time than they could have carried home in their arms from an urban neighborhood store before the war. That was the crucial role of the automobile. Moreover, refrigerators and freezers now made it possible to stock up on perishable items like meat and dairy products. This led to fewer trips to the grocery store, with larger purchases each time.

What this meant to the supermarket itself was a larger volume of sales at a given location, which could now draw customers with automobiles from miles around, whereas a neighborhood store in the central city was unlikely to draw customers on foot from ten blocks away. High volume meant savings in delivery costs from the wholesale warehouses to the supermarket, as compared to delivering the same total amount of groceries in smaller individual lots to many neighborhood stores, whose total sales would add up to what one supermarket sold.

This also meant savings in the cost of selling within the supermarket itself, because it did not take as long to check out one customer buying $50 worth of groceries at a supermarket as it did to check out ten customers buying $5 worth of groceries each at a neighborhood store. Because of these and other differences in the costs of doing business, supermarkets could be very profitable while charging prices lower than those in neighborhood stores that were struggling to survive.

All this not only lowered the costs of delivering groceries to the consumer, it changed the relative economic advantages and disadvantages of different locations for stores. Some supermarket chains, such as Safeway, responded to these radically new conditions faster and better than A & P did. The A & P stores lingered in the central cities longer and also did not follow the shifts of population to California and other sunbelt regions.

A & P was also reluctant to sign long leases or pay high prices for new locations where the customers and their money were now moving. As a result, after years of being the lowest-price major grocery chain, A & P suddenly found itself being undersold by rivals with even lower costs of doing business.

Lower costs reflected in lower prices is what made A & P the world's leading retail chain in the first half of the twentieth century. Similarly, lower costs reflected in lower prices is what enabled other supermarket chains to take A & P's customers away in the second half of the twentieth century. While A & P succeeded in one era and failed in another, what is far more important is that the economy as a whole succeeded in both eras in getting its groceries at the lowest prices possible at the time—from whichever company happened to have the lowest prices. By the early twenty-first century, general merchandiser Wal-Mart had moved to the top of the grocery industry, with nearly double the number of stores selling groceries as Safeway.

Many other corporations that once dominated their fields have likewise fallen behind in the face of changes or have even gone bankrupt. For decades, the Graflex Corporation produced most of the cameras used by press photographers. Movies and newsreels of the 1930s and 1940s almost invariably showed news photographers using a big, bulky camera with a bellows called a Speed Graphic, produced by Graflex. Then, in the early 1950s, outstanding photographs of the Korean war were made with a 35mm Leica camera, using lenses produced by a Japanese manufacturer that also made a new camera called the Nikon.

Advances in lens design and films now made it possible for newspaper and magazine photographers to take pictures with smaller cameras that had enough sharpness and detail for their pictures to compete with pictures taken by much bulkier cameras. Within a decade, smaller cameras rapidly replaced Speed Graphics and other large cameras made by the Graflex Corporation. The last Speed Graphic was produced in 1973 and the Graflex Corporation itself became extinct, after decades of dominating its field.

Similar stories could be told in industry after industry. Pan American Airlines, which pioneered in commercial flights across the Atlantic and the Pacific, went out of business in the wake of the deregulation of the American airline industry in the 1970s. Famous newspapers like the *New York Herald-Tribune*, with a pedigree going back more than a century, stopped publishing in a new environment, after television became a major source of news and newspaper unions made publishing more costly. Between 1949 and 1989, the number of newspapers sold daily in New York City fell from more than 6 million to less than 3 million. The *Herald-Tribune* was one of many local newspapers across the country to go out of business with the rise of television. The *New York Daily Mirror*, with a daily circulation of more than a million readers in 1949, went out of business in 1963.

By 2003, three of the four American newspapers with daily circulations of a million or more were newspapers sold nationwide—*USA Today*, *The Wall Street Journal* and the *New York Times*. In fourth place, the *Los Angeles* sold just over a million copies. Back in 1949, two local newspapers in New York each sold more than a million copies daily—the *Daily Mirror* at 1,020,879 and the *Daily News* at 2,254,644. The role of television was apparent in the fact that it was the afternoon newspapers that suffered the greatest declines in circulation. Before, people caught up on events of the day by reading afternoon papers on their way home from work. Now they waited until they got home and turned on television.

Smith-Corona dominated the typewriter industry for decades, but then laptop computers appeared on the scene and displaced portable typewriters, while desktop computers began displacing other typewriters. Like A & P before it, Smith-Corona began losing millions of dollars under changed conditions. It went five years in a row without making a profit during the 1980s. Only by beginning to produce word processors, a sort of half-way house between typewriters and computers, was Smith-Corona able to survive and begin making money again. Yet the relentless spread of personal computers continued to shrink the market for these alternatives. Although Smith-Corona manufactured over half the typewriters and word processors sold in North America as late as 1989, six years later it filed for bankruptcy.

Other great industrial and commercial firms that have declined or become extinct are likewise a monument to the unrelenting pressures of competition. So is the rising prosperity of the consuming public. The fate of particular companies or industries is not what is most important. Consumers are the principal beneficiaries of lower prices made possible by the more efficient allocation of scarce resources which have alternative uses.

The key roles in all of this are played not only by prices and profits, but also by losses. These losses force businesses to change with changing conditions or find themselves losing out to competitors who spot the new trends earlier or who understand their implications better. Knowledge is one of the scarcest of all resources in any economy, and the insight distilled from knowledge is scarcer still. An economy based on prices, profits, and losses gives decisive advantages to those with greater knowledge and insight.

Put differently, knowledge and insight can guide the allocation of resources, even if most people, including the country's political leaders, do not share that knowledge or do not have the insight to understand what is happening. Clearly this is not true in the kind of economic system where political leaders control economic decisions, for then the limited knowledge and insights of those leaders become decisive barriers to the progress of the whole economy. Even when leaders have more knowledge and insight than the average member of the society, they are unlikely to have nearly as much knowledge and insight as exists scattered among the millions of people subject to their governance.

Knowledge and insight need not be technological or scientific for it to be economically valuable and decisive for the material well-being of the society as a whole. Something as mundane as retailing changed radically during the course of the twentieth century, revolutionizing both department stores and grocery stores—and raising the standard of living of millions of Americans by lowering the costs of delivering goods to them.

Names like Sears and Ward's came to mean department store chains to most Americans in the twentieth century. However, neither of these enterprises began as department store chains. Montgomery Ward—the original name of Ward's department stores—began as a mail-order house in the nineteenth century. Under the conditions of that time, before automobiles or trucks and with most Americans living in small rural communities, the high costs of delivering consumer goods to widely-scattered local stores was re-flected in the high prices that were charged. These high prices, in turn, meant that ordinary people could seldom afford many of the things that we today regard as basic.

Montgomery Ward cut delivery costs by operating as a mail-order house, selling directly to consumers all over the country from its huge warehouse in Chicago. Its high volume of sales also reduced its cost per sale and allowed it to cut its prices below those charged by local stores in small communities. Under these conditions, Montgomery Ward became the world's largest re-tailer in the late nineteenth century. Sears then arose as a competing mail-order house and eventually surpassed Montgomery Ward in sales. One indication of the size of these two retail giants was that each had railroad tracks running through its Chicago warehouse.

More important than the fates of these two businesses was the fact that millions of people were able to afford a higher standard of living than if they had to be supplied with goods through costlier channels. Meanwhile, there were changes in American society, with more and more people beginning to live in urban communities. This was not a secret, but not everyone noticed such gradual changes and even fewer had the insight to understand their im-plications for retail selling. It was 1920 before the census showed that, for the first time in the country's history, there were more Americans living in urban areas than in rural areas.

One man who liked to pore over such statistics was Robert Wood, an ex-ecutive at Montgomery Ward. Now, he realized, selling merchandise through a chain of urban department stores would be more efficient and more profitable than selling exclusively by mail order. Not only were his in-sights not shared by the head of Montgomery Ward, Wood was fired for his suggestion.

Meanwhile, a man named James Cash Penney had the same insight and was already setting up his own chain of department stores. From very mod-est beginnings, the J. C. Penney chain grew to almost 300 stores by 1920 and more than a thousand by the end of the decade. Their greater efficiency in delivering goods to urban consumers was a boon to consumers—and a big economic problem for the mail order giants Sears and Montgomery Ward, both of which began losing money. The fired Robert Wood went to work for Sears and was more successful there in convincing their top management to begin building department stores of their own. After they did, Montgomery Ward had no choice but to do the same belatedly, though it was never able to catch up to Sears again.

Rather than get lost in the details of the histories of particular businesses, we need to look at this from the standpoint of the economy as a whole and the standard of living of the people as a whole. One of the biggest advantages of an economy coordinated by prices and operating under the incentives created by profit and loss is that it can tap scarce knowledge and insights, even when most of the people—or even their political and intellectual elites—do not have such knowledge or insights. The competitive advantages of those who are right can overwhelm the numerical, or even financial, advantages of those who are wrong.

James Cash Penney began as just a one-third partner in a store in a little town in Wyoming, at a time when Sears and Montgomery Ward were unchallenged giants of nationwide retailing. Yet his insights into the changing conditions of retailing eventually forced these giants into doing things his way, on pain of extinction. While Robert Wood failed to convince Montgomery Ward to change, competition and red ink on the bottom line finally convinced them. In a later era, a clerk in a J.C. Penney store named Sam Walton would learn retailing from the ground up and later put his knowledge and insights to work in his own store, which would eventually expand to become the Wal-Mart chain, with sales larger than those of Sears and J. C. Penney combined.

One of the great handicaps of government-run economies, whether under medieval mercantilism or modern communism, is that insights which arise among the masses have no such powerful leverage as to force those in authority to change the way they do things. Under any form of economic or political system, those at the top tend to become complacent, if not arrogant. Convincing them of anything is not easy, especially when it is some new way of doing things that is very different from what they are used to. The big advantage of a free market is that you don't have to convince anybody of anything. You simply compete with them in the marketplace and let that be the test of what works best.

Imagine a system in which J. C. Penney had to verbally convince the heads of Sears and Montgomery Ward to expand beyond mail-order retailing and build a nationwide chain of stores. Their response might well have been: "Who is this guy Penney—a part-owner of some little store in a hick town nobody ever heard of—to tell us how to run the largest retail companies in the world?"

In a market economy, Penney did not have to convince anybody of anything. All he had to do was deliver the merchandise to the consumers at a lower price. His success and the millions of dollars in losses suffered by Sears and Montgomery Ward left these giants no choice but to imitate this up-start, in order to become profitable again and regain their leadership of the retail merchandise industry. J. C. Penney grew up in worse poverty than most people who are on welfare today. Yet his ideas and insights prevailed against some of the richest men of his time, who finally realized that they would be ruined financially if they did not follow his lead by setting up their own department stores. They would not have remained rich for long if Penney and others had kept taking away their customers, leaving their companies with millions of dollars in losses each year.

Mere words could not have persuaded Sears or Montgomery Ward to become department store chains. The firing of Robert Wood at Montgomery Ward was all too typical of what can happen to those who tell people things they do not want to hear. Years later, during the post-World War II era, a similar fate awaited those executives at Montgomery Ward who tried to tell its chief executive officer, Sewell Avery, that the company needed to establish stores in suburban shopping malls. Avery got rid of these executives—but then the market eventually got rid of him, amid great dissatisfaction among stockholders, as his ideas failed the test of competition.

Many things that we take for granted as features of a modern economy today were resisted when first proposed and had to fight uphill to establish themselves by the power of the marketplace. Even something as widely used today as credit cards were initially resisted. When Mastercard and Bankamericard first appeared in the 1960s, leading New York department stores such as Macy's and Bloomingdale's said that they had no intention of accepting credit cards as payments for purchases in their stores, even though there were already millions of people with such cards in the New York metropolitan area.

Only after the success of credit cards in smaller stores did the big department stores finally relent and begin accepting credit cards—and eventually issuing their own. By 2003, *Fortune* magazine reported that a number of companies made more money from their own credit card business, with its interest charges, than from selling goods and services. Sears made more than half its profits from its credit cards and Circuit City made all of its profits from its credit cards, while losing $17 million on its sales of electronic merchandise.

What is important is not the success or failure of particular individuals or companies, but the success of particular knowledge and insights in prevailing despite the blindness or resistance of particular business owners and managers. Given the scarcity of such mental resources, an economy in which knowledge and insights have such decisive advantages is an economy which itself has great advantages in creating a higher standard of living for the population at large. A society in which only members of a hereditary aristocracy, a military junta, or a ruling political party can make major decisions is a society that has thrown away much of the knowledge, insights, and talents of most of its people.

A society in which such decisions can only be made by males has thrown away half of its knowledge, talents, and insights.

Contrast societies with such restricted sources of ability with a society in which a farm boy who walked eight miles to Detroit to look for a job could end up creating the Ford Motor Company and changing the face of America with mass-produced automobiles—or a society in which a couple of young bicycle mechanics could create the airplane and change the whole world. Neither a lack of pedigree nor a lack of academic degrees nor even a lack of money could stop ideas that worked, for investment money is always looking for a winner to back and cash in on. A society which can tap all kinds of talents from all kinds of sources has obvious advantages over societies in which only the talents of a preselected few are allowed to determine its destiny.

No economic system can depend on the continuing wisdom of its current leaders. A price-coordinated economy with competition in the marketplace does not have to, because those leaders can be forced to change course—or be replaced—whether because of red ink, irate stockholders, outside investors ready to take over, or because of bankruptcy. Given such economic pressures, it is hardly surprising that economies under the thumbs of kings or commissars have seldom matched the track record of capitalist economies.

THE COORDINATION OF KNOWLEDGE

In medieval times, when craftsmen produced everything from swords to plowshares on a direct order from the customer, there was no problem of knowing what was wanted by whom. But a modern economy—whether capitalist or socialist—faces an entirely different situation. Today's supermarket or department store stocks an incredible variety of goods without knowing who will buy how much of what. Automobile dealers, bookstores, florists, and other businesses likewise keep a stock on hand to sell, without really knowing what the consumers will turn out to want. In a capitalist economy, wrong guesses can lead to anything from clearance sales to bankruptcy.

Under both capitalism and socialism, the scarcity of knowledge is the same, but the way these different economies deal with it can be quite different. The problem is not simply with the over-all scarcity of knowledge, but also with the fact that this knowledge is often fragmented into tiny bits and pieces, the totality of which is not known to anybody.

Imagine the difficulties of an oil company headquartered in Texas trying to decide how much gasoline—and what kinds—will be needed in a filling station at the corner of Market and Castro Streets in San Francisco during the various seasons of the year, as well as in thousands of other locations across the country. The people who actually own and operate the filling stations at all these locations have far better knowledge of what their particular customers are likely to buy at different times of the year than anybody in a corporate headquarters in Texas can hope to have.

Variations can be great, even within a single city at a single time. If people who live in the vicinity of Market and Castro Streets in San Francisco own more sports cars than people who live near the filling station at 19th Avenue and Irving Street, then the filling station owner at Market and Castro is likely to order more premium gasoline than the filling station owner who sells to people with cheaper cars that use cheaper gasoline or to truckers who want diesel fuel. No single person at any given location—whether at a filling station or in corporate headquarters—can possibly have all this information for the whole country at his fingertips, much less keep updating it for thousands of filling stations from coast to coast as the seasons and the neighborhoods change. But that is wholly unnecessary in an economy where each kind of fuel simply goes wherever the money directs it to go.

The amount of such highly localized information, known to thousands of individual filling station owners scattered across the United States, is too enormous to be transmitted to some central point and then be digested in time to lead to government allocations of fuel with the same efficiency as a price-coordinated market can achieve. No oil company knows or cares about all this detailed information. All they know is that orders are pouring in for diesel fuel in North Dakota this month, while Massachusetts is buying lots of premium gasoline and Ohio is buying mostly regular unleaded. Next month it may be a totally different pattern and the oil company may not have any more clue about the reasons for the new pattern than about the reasons for the old. But all that the oil company has to do is to supply the demand, wherever it is and for whatever reason. Their job is infinitely easier than the task facing central planners under socialism.

The significance of free market prices in the allocation of resources can be seen most clearly by looking at situations where prices are not allowed to function. Two Soviet economists described a situation in which their government raised the price it would pay for moleskins, leading hunters to get and sell more of them:

> State purchases increased, and now all the distribution centers are filled with these pelts. Industry is unable to use them all, and they often rot in warehouses before they can be processed. The Ministry of Light Industry has already requested Goskomsten twice to lower the prices, but "the question has not been decided" yet. This is not surprising. Its members are too busy to decide. They have no time: besides setting prices on these pelts, they have to keep track of another 24 million prices.

However overwhelming it might be for a government agency to try to keep track of millions of prices, a country with hundreds of millions of people can far more easily keep track of those prices individually, because no given individual or business enterprise has to keep track of more than the relatively few prices relevant to their own decision-making. The situation as regards pelts was common for other goods during the days of the Soviet Union's centrally planned economy, where a recurrent problem was a piling up of unsold goods in warehouses at the very time when there were painful shortages of other things that could have been produced with the same resources.

Like oil company executives in the United States, the executives who ran Soviet enterprises had no way to keep track of all the thousands of local conditions and millions of individual desires in a country that stretched all the way across the Eurasian land mass from Eastern Europe to the Pacific Ocean. Unlike American executives, however, their Soviet counterparts did not have the same guidance from fluctuating prices or the same incentives from profits and losses. The net result was that many Soviet enterprises kept producing things in quantities beyond what anybody wanted, unless and until the problems became so huge and so blatant as to attract the attention of central planners in Moscow, who would then change the orders they sent out to manufacturers. But this could be years later and enormous amounts of resources would be wasted in the meantime.

The wastefulness of a centrally planned economic system translated into a painfully low standard of living for millions of Soviet citizens, living in a country with some of the richest natural resources anywhere in the world.

Their standard of living was low, not only by comparison with that in the United States, but also compared to the standard of living in countries with far fewer natural resources, such as Japan and Switzerland. Efficiency is more than just an abstract concept of economists and accountants. It directly translates into the well-being of hundreds of millions of human beings.

The problems faced by the Soviet economy were not due to deficiencies peculiar to Russians or the other peoples of the Soviet Union. Americans faced very similar problems when the U. S. government was controlling the price of gasoline and its allocation during the 1970s. Under these conditions, both individuals and businesses had to drastically curtail their use of gasoline in some locations, such as New York and Washington, while in some other places—mostly rural areas—there was a surplus of unsold gasoline.

This was not due to stupidity on the part of government allocators, but to the fact that a process that is relatively simple, when prices direct resources and products where millions of individuals want them to go, is enormously complex when a set of central planners seeks to substitute their necessarily very limited knowledge for the knowledge scattered among all those vast numbers of people in highly varying circumstances. The federal government issued 3,000 pages of regulations, supplemented by various official "clarifications," but none of this allocated gasoline as smoothly as the ordinary operations of a free market price system.

To know how much gasoline should be sent where and when requires an enormous amount of knowledge of when and where it is most in demand at any given moment—and that changes throughout the year, as well as varying from place to place. People drive more to particular vacation spots during the summer and more diesel-powered trucks carry produce to and from other places at harvest time, in addition to other changing uses of motor vehicles for all sorts of other reasons. Nobody in any kind of economic or political system can possibly know the specifics of all these things. The advantage of a price-coordinated economy is that nobody has to. The efficiency of such an economy comes from the fact that vast amounts of knowledge do not ever have to be brought together, but are coordinated automatically by prices that convey in summary and compelling form what innumerable people want.

The difference between the limited knowledge of a business executive and the similarly limited knowledge of a government official is that the business executive is *receiving* instructions from others via the marketplace on what to do—whom to supply, and when, with what kinds of fuel, in this case—while the government official is *giving* instructions to others and compelling them to obey. In short, economic decisions are ultimately being directed or con-

trolled by those who have specific knowledge in a price-coordinated economy, while those decisions move in the opposite direction—from those with
less knowledge, who are giving orders to those with more knowledge—in a
centrally planned economy. The difference is fundamental and profound in
its implications for the material well-being of the population at large.

During the episodic gasoline shortages of the 1970s, Americans experienced in one industry for a limited period of time the severe economic problems that were common across the board in the Soviet Union for more than
half a century. Because such an experience was so rare and shocking to
Americans, they were receptive to all sorts of false political explanations and
conspiracy theories for such an extraordinary situation, when in fact such situations were common in other countries using government allocation. What
was uncommon was for such methods to be used in the United States.

The rationale at the time was that reduced oil supplies from the Middle
East required government intervention to prevent chaos in American oil
markets. Needless to say, politicians were not about to admit that it was precisely their intervention which brought chaos, since the reduction in the total
amount of gasoline in the country was just a few percentage points—the
kind of reduction in the amount supplied that is routinely handled in all sorts
of industries by a small price increase in a free market.

Indeed, a previous Arab oil embargo in 1967 had caused no such disloca-
tions because it was not accompanied by the kinds of price controls instituted by the Nixon administration and continued by the Ford and Carter
administrations. Nor were there long lines of cars waiting for hours at filling
stations in other Western industrial nations or Japan, even though most of
these other nations produced a far smaller percentage of their own petroleum
than the United States did. These other countries did not have price controls
on gasoline, so they did not have the shortages that go with price controls.

When government control of gasoline prices was ended in 1981—amid
widespread warnings that this would lead to drastically higher prices—what
followed was virtually a lesson in elementary economics. Higher prices led to
a greater quantity of gasoline being supplied and a smaller amount demanded. Oil exploration shot up and existing wells whose costs could not
have been covered at the controlled prices began pumping oil again. Within
months, gasoline prices fell below what they had been under complex government controls. This fall continued over the years until gasoline prices
reached an all-time low in real terms. Additional taxes were then piled onto
the prices at the pump, but the gas itself was cheaper than ever—and there
were no waiting lines.

Often the knowledge that is economically crucial is highly specific to a particular location or a particular group of people—and is therefore unlikely to be known widely. One of the reasons for the success of the A & P grocery chain in the first half of the twentieth century and of the McDonald's chain in the second half was the great amount of time and attention they devoted to acquiring detailed knowledge of specific locations being considered for their respective outlets, so as to have their outlets be accessible to the maximum number of customers. Real estate agents often say that the three most important factors in the value of real estate are "location, location, and location." The same is also true of many businesses serving the public. There is a reason why filling stations are usually located on corners and McDonald's are usually located in the middle of the block.

Highly specific knowledge of particular groups of people can prove to be as economically decisive as knowledge of particular places. At the beginning of the twentieth century, an Italian immigrant in San Francisco, well aware that other Italian immigrants regularly saved money, even out of small incomes, and were reliable in repaying loans, established a bank that he called the Bank of Italy, so as to attract depositors and borrowers whom the other banks overlooked. His bank began in a little office with three wooden desks, some chairs, an adding machine, a safe, and one teller's window. But, capitalizing on its owner's understanding of the particular community it served, and his general business astuteness, the bank became so successful that it grew and eventually spread its branches across the state. Once firmly established, it began attracting so many depositors beyond the Italian American community that it became at one time the largest bank in the world under its new name, the Bank of America.

Chapter 6

The Role of Profits—
And Losses

Competition is the keen cutting edge of business,
always shaving away at costs.

—Henry Ford

To those who run businesses, profits are obviously desirable and losses deplorable. But economics is not business administration. From the standpoint of the economy as a whole, and from the standpoint of the central concern of economics—the allocation of scarce resources which have alternative uses—profits and losses play equally important roles in maintaining and advancing the standards of living of the population as a whole.

While part of the efficiency of a price-coordinated economy comes from the fact that goods can simply "follow the money," without the producers really knowing just why people are buying one thing here and something else there and yet another thing during a different season. However, it is necessary for them to keep track not only of the money coming in from the customers, it is equally necessary to keep track of how much money is going out to those who supply raw materials, labor, parts, and other inputs. Keeping careful track of these numerous flows of money in and out can make the difference between profit and loss. Therefore electricity, machines or cement cannot be used in the same careless way that caused far more of such things to be used per unit of output in the Soviet economy than in the American economy. From the standpoint of the economy as a whole, and of the consuming public, the threat of losses is just as important as the prospect of profits.

When one business enterprise in a market economy finds ways to lower its costs, competing enterprises have no choice but to scramble to try to do the same. After the general merchandising chain Wal-Mart began selling groceries in 1988, it moved up to become the nation's largest grocery seller by the early twenty-first century. Its lower costs benefitted not only its own customers, but those of other grocers as well. As the *Wall Street Journal* reported:

> When two Wal-Mart Supercenters and a rival regional grocery open near a Kroger Co. supermarket in Houston last year, the Kroger's sales dropped 10%. Store manager Ben Bustos moved quickly to slash some prices and cut labor costs, for example, by buying ready-made cakes instead of baking them in-house, and ordering precut salad-bar items from suppliers. His employees used to stack displays by hand. Now, fruit and vegetables arrive stacked and gleaming for display.
>
> Such moves have helped Mr. Bustos cut worker-hours by 30% to 40% from when the store opened four years ago, and lower the prices of staples such as cereal, bread, milk, eggs and disposable diapers. Earlier this year, sales at the Kroger facility finally edged up over the year before.

In short, the economy operated more efficiently, to the benefit of the consumers, not only because of Wal-Mart's ability to cut costs and lower prices, but also because this forced Kroger's to do the same. This is a microcosm of what happens throughout a free market economy. It is no accident that people in such economies tend to have higher standards of living.

PROFITS

Profits are perhaps the most misconceived subject in economics. Socialists have long regarded profits as simply "overcharge," as Fabian socialist George Bernard Shaw called it, or a "surplus value" as Karl Marx, called it. "Never talk to me about profit," India's first prime minister, Jawaharal Nehru, warned his country's leading industrialist. "It's a dirty word."

From all these men's perspectives, profits were simply unnecessary charges added on to the inherent costs of producing goods and services, driving up the cost to the customer. One of the great appeals of socialism, especially back when it was just an idealistic theory without any concrete examples in the real world, was that it sought to eliminate these supposedly unnecessary charges, making things generally more affordable, especially for people with lower incomes. Only after socialism went from being a theory to being an actual economic system in various countries around the world did the fact become painfully apparent that people in socialist countries had a harder time trying to afford things that most people in capitalist countries could afford with ease and took for granted.

With profits eliminated, prices should have been lower in socialist countries, according to theory, and the standard of living of the masses correspondingly higher. Why then was it not that way in practice?

Profits as Incentives

Let us go back to square one. The hope for profits and the threat of losses is what forces a business owner in a capitalist economy to produce at the lowest cost and sell what the customers are most willing to pay for. In the absence of these pressures, those who manage enterprises under socialism have far less incentive to be as efficient as possible under given conditions, much less to keep up with changing conditions and respond to them quickly, as capitalist enterprises must do if they expect to survive.

It was a Soviet premier who said that his country's enterprise managers shied away from innovation "as the devil shies away from incense." But, given the incentives of a socialist economy, why should these managers have stuck their necks out by trying new methods or new products, when they stood to gain little or nothing if they succeeded and might have lost their jobs (or worse) if they failed? Under Stalin, failure was often equated with sabotage, and was punished accordingly. Even under the milder conditions of democratic socialism, as in India for decades after its independence, innovation was by no means necessary for protected enterprises, such as automobile manufacturing.

Until the freeing up of markets that began in India in 1991, the country's most popular car was the Hindustan Ambassador—an unabashed copy of the British Morris Oxford. Moreover, even in the 1990s, *The Economist* reported that "the Ambassador is a 1954 Morris Oxford and unashamedly so." The magazine observed: "The Research and Development department of Hindustan Motor Corporation, Calcutta, employs no fewer than 250 people. Quite what they have been doing over the past 25 years is anyone's guess." A London newspaper, *The Independent*, reported: "Ambassadors have for years been notorious in India for their poor finish, heavy handling and proneness to alarming accidents." Nevertheless, there was a waiting list for the Ambassador—with waits lasting for months and sometimes years—as foreign cars were not allowed to be imported to compete with them.

Under capitalism, the incentives work in the opposite direction. Even the most profitable business can lose its market if it doesn't keep innovating, in order to avoid being overtaken by its competitors. For example, in the 1970s IBM computers measuring 3,000 cubic feet became obsolete when Intel created a chip smaller than a fingernail that could do the same things. Yet Intel itself was then constantly forced to improve that chip at an exponential rate, as rivals like Advanced Micro Devices (AMD), Cyrix, and others began catching up with them technologically. More than once, Intel poured such huge sums of money into the development of improved chips as to risk the financial survival of the company itself. But the alternative was to allow itself to be overtaken by rivals, which would have been an even bigger risk to Intel's survival.

Later, Advanced Micro Devices made equally strenuous attempts to overtake Intel with a more advanced chip—and in the process had losses of more than a billion dollars in 2002, while AMD stock lost four-fifths of its value. Even among corporate giants, competition can become desperate in a free market. Nor was AMD unique. In 2002, 120 of the *Fortune* 500 companies reported losses totaling in the aggregate more than $295 billion. Such losses play a vital role in the economy, forcing corporate giants to change what they are doing, under penalty of extinction, since no one can sustain losses of this magnitude indefinitely. Inertia may be a common tendency among human beings around the world, but businesses operating in a free market are forced by red ink on the bottom line to realize that they cannot keep drifting along like the Hindustan Motor Corporation, protected from competition by the Indian government. Even in India, the freeing of markets toward the end of the twentieth century created competition in cars, forcing Hindustan Motors to invest in improvements, producing new Ambassadors that were "much more reliable than their predecessors," according to *The Independent*.

While capitalism has a visible cost—profit—that does not exist under socialism, socialism has an invisible cost—inefficiency—that gets weeded out by losses and bankruptcy under capitalism. The fact that most goods are more widely affordable in a capitalist economy implies that profit is less costly than inefficiency. Put differently, profit is a price paid for efficiency. Clearly the greater efficiency must outweigh the profit or else socialism would in fact have had the more affordable prices and greater prosperity that its theorists expected, but which failed to materialize in the real world.

While capitalists have been conceived of as people who make profits, what a business owner really gets is legal ownership of whatever residual is left over after the costs have been paid out of the money received from customers. That residual can turn out to be positive, negative or zero. Workers must be paid and creditors must be paid—or else they can take legal action to seize the company's assets. The only person whose payment is contingent on how well the business is doing is the owner of that business. This is what puts unrelenting pressure on the owner to monitor everything that is happening in the business and everything that is happening in the market for the business' products.

In contrast to the layers of authorities monitoring the actions of those under them in a government-run enterprise, the business owner is essentially an *unmonitored monitor* as far as the economic efficiency of the business is concerned. Self-interest takes the place of external monitors, and forces far closer attention to details and far more expenditure of time and energy at work than any set of rules or authorities is likely to be able to do. That simple fact gives capitalism an enormous advantage. More important, it gives the people living in price-coordinated market economies visibly higher standards of living.

It is not just ignorant people, but also highly educated and highly intellectual people like George Bernard Shaw, Karl Marx, and Pandit Nehru, who have misconceived profits as arbitrary charges added on to the costs of producing goods and services. To many people, even today, high profits are often attributed to high prices charged by those motivated by "greed." In reality, most of the great fortunes in American history have resulted from someone's figuring out how to reduce costs, so as to be able to charge *lower* prices and therefore gain a mass market for the product. Henry Ford did this with automobiles, Rockefeller with oil, Carnegie with steel, and Sears, Penney, Walton and other department store founders with a variety of products.

A supermarket chain in a capitalist economy can be very successful charging prices that allow about a penny of clear profit on each dollar of sales. Because several cash registers are usually bringing in money simultaneously all day long in a big supermarket, those pennies can add up to a very substantial annual rate of return on the supermarket chain's investment, while adding very little to what the customer pays. If the entire contents of a store get sold out in about two weeks, then that penny on a dollar becomes more like a quarter on the dollar (26 cents, to be exact) over the course of a year, when that same dollar comes back to be re-used 25 more times a year.

Under socialism, that penny would be eliminated, but so too would be all the economic pressures on the management to keep costs down. Consumers in a socialist country, paying two hours' wages for what consumers under capitalism would get for one hours' wages, could have the satisfaction of knowing that none of the money they paid went for profits, but that might be small comfort for people with a lower standard of living.

When most people are asked how high they think the average rate of profit is, they usually suggest some number much higher than the actual rate of profit. From 1978 through 1998, American corporate profit rates on investment fluctuated between a low of just above 6 percent to a high of about 13 percent. As a percentage of national income, corporate profits after taxes never exceeded 9 percent and was often below 6 percent over a thirty-year period ending in 1998. However, it is not just the numerical rate of profit that most people misconceive. Many misconceive its whole role in a price-coordinated economy, which is to serve as incentives—and it plays that role wherever its fluctuations take it. Moreover, some people have no idea that there are vast differences between profits on sales and profits on investments.

Profit Rates

Profits on sales are very different from profits on investment. If a store buys widgets for $10 each and sells them for $15 each, some might say that it makes $5 in profits on each widget. But, of course, the store has to pay the people who work there, the utility company which supplies the electricity for the lights, cash registers and other electrical devices in the store, as well as other suppliers of other goods and services needed to keep the store running. What is left over after all these people have been paid is the net profit, usually a lot less than the gross profit. But that is still not the same as profit on investment. It is simply net profits on sales, which still ignores the cost of the investments which created the store in the first place.

When someone invests $10,000, what that person wants to know is what annual rate of return it will bring, whether it is invested in stores, real estate, or stocks and bonds. Profits on particular sales are not what matter most. It is the profit on the total capital that has been invested in the business that matters. That profit matters not just to those who receive it, but to the economy as a whole, for differences in profit rates in different sectors of the economy are what cause investments to flow into and out of these sectors, until profit rates are equalized, like water seeking its own level.

Things can be sold at prices that are much higher than what the seller paid for them and yet, if those items sit in the store for months before being sold, they may be less profitable than other items that have less of a mark-up in price but which sell out within a week. A store that sells pianos undoubtedly makes a higher percentage profit on each sale than a supermarket makes selling bread. But a piano sits in the store for a much longer time waiting to be sold than a loaf of bread does. Bread would go stale and moldy waiting for as long as a piano to be sold. When a supermarket chain buys $10,000 worth of bread, it gets its money back much faster than when a piano dealer buys $10,000 worth of pianos. Therefore the piano dealer must charge a higher percentage mark-up on the sale of each piano than a supermarket charges on each loaf of bread, if the piano dealer is to make the same annual percentage rate of return on a $10,000 investment. Profit rates tend to equalize, even when that requires different mark-ups to compensate for different turnover rates among the different products.

When the supermarket gets its money back in a shorter period of time, it can turn right around and re-invest it, buying more bread or other grocery items. In the course of a year, the same money turns over many times in a supermarket, earning a profit each time, so that a penny of profit on the dollar can produce a total profit for the year on the initial investment equal to what a piano dealer makes charging a much higher percentage markup on an investment that turns over much more slowly. Companies that made the *Fortune* magazine list of the 500 largest companies in America averaged "a return on revenue of a penny on the dollar" in 2002, compared to "6 cents in 2000, the peak profit year."

Profits on sales and profits on investment are not merely different concepts. They can move in opposite directions. One of the keys to the rise to dominance of the A & P grocery chain in the 1920s was a conscious decision by the head of the company to cut profit margins on sales, in order to increase the profit rate on investment. With the new and lower prices made possible by selling with lower profits per item, A & P was able to attract greatly increased numbers of customers, making far more total profit because of the increased volume of sales. Making a profit of only a few cents on the dollar on sales, but with the inventory turning over nearly 30 times a year, A & P's profit rate on investment soared. This low price and high volume strategy set a pattern that spread to other grocery chains and to other kinds of enterprises as well. In a later era, huge supermarkets were able to shave the profit margin on sales still thinner, because of even higher volumes, enabling them to displace A & P from industry leadership by charging still lower prices.

COSTS OF PRODUCTION

Since profits are the difference between what consumers pay and what the products cost to produce and distribute, it is important to be very clear about those costs. Unfortunately, costs are misconceived almost as much as profits.

Economies of Scale

First of all, there is no such thing as "the" cost of producing a given product or service. Henry Ford proved long ago that the cost of producing an automobile was very different when you produced 100 cars a year than when you produced 100,000. With a mass market for automobiles, it paid to invest in expensive mass production machinery, whose cost per car would turn out to be modest when spread out over a huge number of automobiles. But, if you sold only half as many cars as you expected, then the cost of that machinery per car would be twice as much.

It has been estimated that the minimum amount of automobile production required to achieve efficient production levels today runs into the hundreds of thousands. Back in 1896, the largest automobile manufacturer in the United States produced just six cars a year. At that level of output, with an average of two months of work required for producing each car, only the truly rich could afford to buy an automobile. It was Henry Ford whose mass production methods brought the cost of producing cars down within the price range of ordinary Americans.

Similar principles apply in other industries. It does not cost as much to deliver a hundred cartons of milk to one supermarket as it does to deliver ten cartons of milk to each of ten different neighborhood stores scattered around town. Economies in beer production include advertising. Although Annheuser-Busch spends millions of dollars a year advertising Budweiser and its other beers, its huge volume of sales means that its advertising costs per barrel of beer are about two dollars less than that of its competitors Coors and Miller.

Advertising has sometimes been depicted as simply another cost added on to the cost of producing goods and services. However, in so far as advertising causes more of the advertised product to be sold, economies of scale can reduce production costs, so that the same product may cost less when it is advertised. Advertising itself of course has costs, both in the financial sense and in the sense of using resources. But it is an empirical question, rather than a foregone conclusion, whether the costs of advertising are greater or less than the reductions of production costs made possible by the economies of scale which it promotes. [This can obviously vary from one industry to another.]

Economies of scale are only half the story. If economies of scale were the whole story, the question would then have to be asked: Why not produce cars in even more gigantic enterprises? If General Motors, Daimler-Chrysler, and Ford all merged together, would they not be able to produce cars even more cheaply and thereby make more profit than when they produce separately?

Probably not. There comes a point, in every industry, beyond which the cost of producing a unit of output no longer declines as the amount of production increases. In fact, costs per unit actually rise after an enterprise becomes so huge that it is difficult to monitor and control, when the right hand doesn't know what the left hand is doing. General Motors is the largest manufacturer of automobiles in the world, but its cost of production per car is estimated to be hundreds of dollars more than the costs of Ford, DaimlerChrysler, or leading Japanese manufacturers. A small airline in the United States, JetBlue, has more than 30 percent lower cost per seat per mile than giants like United Airlines or American Airlines. Problems associated with size can affect quality as well as price. When frequent flyers and travel professionals were asked by *BusinessWeek* magazine to rank the quality of airlines, the five top-rated in quality were all smaller airlines.

In short, while there are economies of scale, there are also what economists call "diseconomies of scale." Economies and diseconomies exist simultaneously at many different levels of output. That is, there may be things that a given business enterprise could do better if it were larger and other things that it could do better if it were smaller. As an entrepreneur in India put it, "What small companies give up in terms of financial clout, technological resources, and staying power, they gain in flexibility, lack of bureaucracy, and speed of decision-making." With increasing size, eventually the diseconomies begin to outweigh the economies, so it does not pay a firm to expand beyond that point. That is why industries usually consist of many firms, instead of one giant, super-efficient monopoly.

Diseconomies of Scale

In the Soviet Union, where there was a fascination with economies of scale and a disregard of diseconomies of scale, both the industrial and agricultural enterprises of the U.S.S.R. were the largest in the world. The average Soviet farm, for example, was ten times the size of the average American farm and employed more than ten times as many workers. But Soviet farms were notoriously inefficient. Among the reasons for this inefficiency cited by Soviet economists was "deficient coordination." One example may illustrate a general problem:

> In the vast common fields, fleets of tractors fanned out to begin the plowing. Plan fulfillment was calculated on the basis of hectares worked, and so it was to the driver's advantage to cover as much territory as quickly as possible. The drivers started by cutting deep furrows around the edge of the field. As they moved deeper into the fields, however, they began to lift the blade of the plow and race the tractor, and the furrows became progressively shallowed. The first furrow were nine to ten inches deep. A little farther from the road, they were five to six inches deep, and in the center of the field, where the tractor drivers were certain that no one would check on them, the furrows were as little as two inches deep. Usually, no one discovered that the furrows were so shallow in the middle of the field until it became obvious that some thing was wrong from the stunted nature of the crop.

Once again, counterproductive behavior from the standpoint of the economy was not irrational behavior from the standpoint of the person engaging in it. Clearly, the tractor drivers understood that their work could be more easily monitored at the edge of a field than in the center, and adjusted the kind and quality of work they did accordingly, so as to maximize their own pay, based on how much land they plowed. By not plowing as deeply into the ground where they could not be easily monitored by farm officials, they were able to cover more ground in a given amount of time, even if they covered it less effectively. No such behavior would be likely by a farmer plowing his own land because his actions would be controlled by the incentive of profit, rather than by external monitors.

The point at which the disadvantages of size begin to outweigh the advantages differs from one industry to another. That is why restaurants are smaller than steel mills. A well-run restaurant usually requires the presence of an owner with sufficient incentives to continuously monitor all the things necessary for successful operation, in a field where failures are all too common. Not only must the food be prepared to suit the tastes of the restaurant's clientele, the waiters and waitresses must do their jobs in a way that encourages people to come back for another pleasant experience, and the furnishings of the restaurant must also be such as to meet the desires of the particular clientele that it serves.

Moreover, these are not problems that can be solved once and for all. Food suppliers must be continuously monitored to see that they are still sending the kind and quality of produce, fish, meats, and other ingredients needed to satisfy the customers. Cooks and chefs must also be monitored to see that they are continuing to meet existing standards—as well as adding to their repertoires, as new foods and drinks become popular and old ones are ordered less often by the customers. The normal turnover of employees also requires the owner to be able to select, train, and monitor new people on an on-going basis. Moreover, changes outside the restaurant—in the kind of neighborhood around it, for example—can make or break its business. All these factors, and more, must be kept in mind and weighed by the owner, and continuously adjusted to, if the business is to survive, much less be profitable.

Such a spectrum of details, requiring direct personal knowledge and control by someone on the scene and with incentives going beyond a fixed salary, limits the size of restaurants, as compared to the size of steel companies, airplane manufacturers, or mining companies. Even where there are nationwide restaurant chains, often these are run by separate owners operating franchises from some national organization that supplies such things as advertising and general guidance and standards, leaving the numerous on-site monitoring tasks to local owners. Howard Johnson pioneered in restaurant franchising in the 1930s, supplying half the capital, with the local manager supplying the other half. This gave the local franchisee a vested interest in the restaurant's profitability, rather than simply a fixed salary.

Costs and Capacity

Costs vary not only with the volume of output, and to varying degrees from one industry to another, they also vary according to the extent to which existing capacity is being used. When an airplane with 200 seats is about to take off with 180 passengers on board, the cost of letting 20 "standby" passengers get on the flight is negligible. That is one reason for radically different prices being charged to people flying on the same plane. Some passengers bought guaranteed reservations and others essentially bought a chance of getting on board as standbys. Different levels of probability have different costs in airline tickets, as elsewhere. The passengers themselves also differ in how important it is for them to be at a particular place at a particular time. Those on urgent business may want a guaranteed reservation, even at a higher price, while others may be in a position where saving money is more important than being on one particular flight rather than another.

Unutilized capacity can cause price anomalies in many sectors of the economy. In Cancun, Mexico, the cheapest room available at the modest Best Western hotel was $180 a night in mid–2001, while the fancy Ritz-Carlton nearby was renting rooms for $169 a night. The Best Western happened to be filled up and the Ritz-Carlton happened to have vacancies. Nor was this peculiar to Mexico. A four-star hotel in Manhattan was renting rooms for less than a two-star hotel nearby and the posh Phoenician in Phoenix was renting rooms for less than the Holiday Inn in the same city. Why were normally very expensive hotels renting rooms for less than hotels that were usually much lower in price? Again, the key was the utilization of capacity.

Apparently tourists going to popular resorts on a limited budget had made reservations at the low-cost hotels well in advance, in order to be sure of finding something affordable. This meant that fluctuations in the number of tourists would be absorbed by the higher-priced hotels. A general decline in tourism in 2001 thus led to vacancies at the luxury hotels, which had no choice but to cut prices in order to attract more people to fill the rooms. Thus the luxurious Boca Raton Club & Spa in Florida gave guests their third night free and tourists were able to get last-minute bargains on beachfront villas at Hilton Head, South Carolina, where reservations usually must be made six months in advance. Conversely, a rise in tourism would also be absorbed by the luxury hotels, which could raise their prices even more than usual.

In many industries and enterprises, capacity must be built to handle the peak volume—which means that there is excess capacity at other times. The cost of accommodating more users of the product or service during the times when there is excess capacity is much less than the cost of handling those who are served at peak times. A cruise ship, for example, must receive enough money from its passengers to cover not only such current costs as paying the crew, buying food, and using fuel, it must also be able to pay such overhead costs as the purchase price of the ship and the expenses at the headquarters of the cruise line. To handle twice as many passengers on a given cruise at the peak season may mean buying another ship, as well as hiring another crew and buying twice as much food and fuel.

However, if the number of passengers in the off season is only one-third of what it is at the peak, then a doubling of the number of off-season passengers will not require buying another ship. Existing ships can simply sail with fewer empty cabins. Therefore, it pays the cruise line to try to attract economy-minded passengers by offering much reduced fares during the off season. Groups of retired people, for example, can usually schedule their cruises at any time of the year, not being tied down to the vacation schedules of their jobs or the schedule of their children's schools. It is common for seniors to get large discounts in off-season travel, both on land and at sea. Businesses in general can afford to do this because their costs are lower—and each particular business is forced to do it because their competition will take customers away from them if they don't.

Where the government itself provides a good or service and charges for it, there are few incentives for the officials in charge to match the prices with the costs—and sometimes they charge more to those who create the least cost. When a bridge, for example, is built or its capacity expanded, the costs created are essentially the cost of building the capacity to handle rush-hour traffic. The cars that drive across the bridge during off-peak hours cost almost nothing because the bridge has idle capacity during those hours. Yet, when tolls are charged, often there are books of tickets or electronic passes available at lower prices per trip than the prices charged to those who drive across the bridge only occasionally.

Although it is the regular rush-hour users who create the huge cost of building or expanding the bridge's capacity, they pay less because it is they who are more numerous voters and whose greater stake in toll policies makes them more likely to react politically to toll charges. What may seem like economic folly can be political prudence on the part of politically appointed officials operating the bridges.

SPECIALIZATION AND DISTRIBUTION

A business firm is limited, not only in its over-all size, but also in the range of functions that it can perform efficiently. General Motors makes millions of automobiles, but not a single tire. Instead, it buys its tires from Goodyear, Michelin and other tire manufacturers, who can produce this part of the car more efficiently than General Motors can. Nor do automobile manufacturers own their own automobile dealerships across the country. Typically, automobile producers sell cars to local people who in turn sell to the public.

There is no way that General Motors can keep track of all the local conditions across the length and breadth of the United States, which determine how much it will cost to buy or lease land on which to locate an automobile dealership, or which locations are best in a given community, much less evaluate the condition of local customers' used cars that are being traded in on new ones.

No one can sit in Detroit and decide how much trade-in value to allow on a particular Chevrolet in Seattle with some dents and scratches or a given Honda in mint condition in Miami. And if the kind of salesmanship that works in Los Angeles does not work in Boston, those on the scene are likely to know that better than anyone in Detroit can. In short, the automobile manufacturer specializes in manufacturing automobiles, leaving other functions to people who develop different knowledge and different skills needed to specialize in those particular functions.

Middle Men

The perennial desire to "eliminate the middleman" is perennially thwarted by economic reality. The range of human knowledge and expertise is limited for any given person or for any manageably-sized collection of people. Only a certain number of links in the great chain of production and distribution can be mastered and operated efficiently by the same set of people. Beyond some point, there are other people who can perform the next step in the sequence more cheaply or more effectively—and, therefore, at that point it pays a firm to sell its output to some other businesses that can carry on the next part of the operation more efficiently. Newspapers seldom, if ever, own and operate their own news stands, nor do furniture manufacturers typically own or operate furniture stores. Most authors do not do their own publishing, much less own their own bookstores.

Prices play a crucial role in all of this, as in other aspects of a market economy. Any economy must not only allocate scarce resources which have alternative uses, it must determine how long the resulting products remain in whose hands before being passed along to others who can handle the next stage more efficiently. Profit-seeking businesses are guided by their own bottom line, but this bottom line is itself determined by what others can do and at what cost. When an oil company discovers that it can make more money by selling gasoline to local filling stations than by owning and operating its own filling stations, then the gasoline passes out of its hands and is then dispensed to the public by others. In other words, the economy as a whole operates more efficiently when the oil company turns the gasoline over to others at this point, though the oil company itself does so only out of self-interest. What connects the self-interest of a company with the efficiency of the economy as a whole are prices. When a product becomes more valuable in the hands of somebody else, that somebody else will bid more for the product than it is worth to its current owner. The owner then sells, not for the sake of the economy, but for his own sake. However, the end result is a more efficient economy, where goods move to those who value them most.

Despite superficially appealing phrases about "eliminating the middle-man," middlemen continue to exist because they can do their phase of the operation more efficiently than others can. It should hardly be surprising that people who specialize in one phase can do that phase better than others.

Third World countries have tended to have more middle men than more industrialized nations, a fact much lamented by observers who have not considered the economics of the situation. Farm produce tends to pass through more hands between the African farmer who grows peanuts, for example, to the company that processes it into peanut butter than would be the case in the United States. Conversely, boxes of matches may pass through more hands between the manufacturer of matches to the African consumer who buys them. A British economist in mid-twentieth century West Africa described and explained such situations there:

> West African agricultural exports are produced by tens of thousands of Africans operating on a very small scale and often widely dispersed. They almost entirely lack storage facilities, and they have no, or only very small, cash reserves. The large number and the long line of intermediaries in the purchase of export produce essentially derive from the economies to be obtained from bulking very large numbers of small parcels . . . In produce marketing the first link in the chain may be the purchase, hundreds of miles from Kano, of a few pounds of groundnuts, which after several stages of bulking arrive there as part of a wagon or lorry load of several tons.

Instead of ten farmers in a given area all taking time off from their farming to drive their individually small amounts of produce to a distant town for sale, one middleman can collect the produce of the ten farmers and drive it all to a produce buyer at one time, allowing ten farmers to apply their scarce resource—time and labor—to its alternative uses in growing more produce. Society as a whole thus saves on the amount of resources required to move produce from the farm to the next buyer, as well as on the number of individual negotiations required at the points of sale. The saving of time is particularly important during the harvest season, when some of the crop may become over-ripe before it is picked or spoil afterwards if it is not picked promptly and gotten into a storage or processing facility.

In a wealthier country, each farm would have more produce, and motorized transport on modern highways would reduce the time required to get it to the next point of sale, so that the time lost per ton of crop would be less and fewer middlemen would be required to move it. Moreover, modern farmers in prosperous countries would be more likely to have their own storage facilities, harvesting machinery, and other aids. What is and is not efficient—either from the standpoint of the individual farmer or of society as a whole—depends on the circumstances. Since these circumstances can differ radically between rich and poor countries, very different methods may be efficient in each country and no given method need be right for both.

For similar reasons, there are often more intermediaries between the industrial manufacturer and the ultimate consumer in poor countries. However, the profits earned by each of these intermediaries is not just so much waste, as often assumed by third-party observers, especially observers from a different society. Here the limiting factor is the poverty of the consumer, which restricts how much can be bought at one time. Again, West Africa in the mid twentieth century provided especially clear examples:

> Imported merchandise arrives in very large consignments and needs to be distributed over large areas to the final consumer who, in West Africa, has to buy in extremely small quantities because of his poverty . . . The organization of retail selling in Ibadan (and elsewhere) exemplifies the services rendered by petty traders both to suppliers and to consumers. Here there is no convenient central market, and it is usual to see petty traders sitting with their wares at the entrances to the stores of the European merchant firms. The petty traders sell largely the same commodities as the stores, but in much smaller quantities.

This might seem to be the ideal situation in which to "eliminate the middleman," since the petty traders were camped right outside stores selling the same merchandise, and the consumers could simply walk right past them to buy the same goods inside at lower prices per unit. But these traders would sell in such tiny quantities as ten matches or half a cigarette, while it would be wasteful for the stores behind them to spend their time breaking down their packaged goods that much, in view of the better alternative uses of their labor and capital. The alternatives available to the African petty traders were seldom as remunerative, so it made sense for these traders to do what it

would not make sense for the European merchant to do. Moreover, it made
sense for the very poor African consumer to buy from the local traders, even
if the latter's additional profit raised the price of the commodity, because the
consumer often could not afford to buy the commodity in the quantities sold
by the European merchants.

Obvious as all this may seem, it has been misunderstood by renowned
writers[1] and—worse yet—by both colonial and post-colonial governments
hostile to middlemen.

Socialist Economies

As in other cases, one of the best ways of understanding the role of prices,
profits, and losses is to see what happens in their absence. Socialist
economies not only lack the kinds of incentives which force individual enterprises toward efficiency and innovation, they also lack the kinds of financial
incentives that lead each given producer in a capitalist economy to limit its
work to those stages of production at which it has lower production costs
than alternative enterprises. Capitalist enterprises buy components from
others who have lower costs in producing those particular components, and
sell their own output to whatever middlemen can most efficiently carry out
its distribution. But a socialist economy may forego these advantages of specialization.

In the Soviet Union, for example, many enterprises produced their own
components, even though specialized producers of such components could
manufacture them at lower cost. Two Soviet economists estimated that the
costs of components needed for a machine-building enterprise in the
U.S.S.R. were two to three times as great as the costs of producing those
same components in specialized enterprises. But what does cost matter in a
system where profits and losses are not decisive?

This was not peculiar to machine-building enterprises. According to these
same Soviet economists, "the idea of self-sufficiency in supply penetrates all
the tiers of the economic and administrative pyramid, from top to bottom."
Just over half the bricks in the U.S.S.R. were produced by enterprises that

---

[1]Gunnar Myrdal, for example, in his *Asian Drama* referred to a "proliferation of retail outlets and petty traders" in Third World countries in South Asia as being "clearly underutiliza-
tion of labor." But he provided neither evidence nor analysis to show that the middlemen had
alternative uses of their time that were more remunerative to them or more valuable to society.

were *not* set up for that purpose, but which made their own bricks in order to build whatever needed building to house their main economic activity. That was because these Soviet enterprises could not rely on deliveries from the Ministry of Construction Materials, which had no financial incentives to be reliable in delivering bricks on time or of the quality required.

For similar reasons, far more Soviet enterprises were producing machine tools than were specifically set up to do so. Meanwhile, specialized plants set up for this purpose worked below their capacity—which is to say, at higher production costs than if their overhead had been spread out over more output—because so many other enterprises were producing these things for themselves. Capitalist producers of bricks or machine tools have no choice but to produce what is wanted by the customer, and to be reliable in delivering it, if they intend to keep those customers in competition with other producers of bricks or machine tools. That, however, is not the case when there is one nationwide monopoly under government control, as was the situation in the Soviet Union.

In China's government-planned economy as well, enterprises generally supplied their own transportation for the goods they produced, unlike most companies in the United States that hire trucking firms or rail or air freight carriers to transport their products. As the *Far Eastern Economic Review* put it: "Through decades of state-planned development, nearly all big Chinese firms transported their own goods, however inefficiently."

Although theoretically firms specializing in transportation might operate more efficiently, the absence of financial incentives to satisfy their customers made specialized transport firms too unreliable, both as to times of delivery and as to the care—or lack of care—when handling goods in transit. A company manufacturing television sets in China might not be as efficient in transporting those sets as a specialized transport company would be, but at least they were less likely to damage their own TV sets by handling them roughly in transit.

One of the other side effects of unreliable deliveries has been that Chinese firms have had to keep more goods in inventory, foregoing the advantages of "just in time" delivery practices in Japan, which reduces the Japanese firms' costs of maintaining inventories. Dell Computers in the United States likewise operates with very small inventories, relative to their sales, but this is possible only because there are shipping firms like Federal Express or UPS that Dell can rely on to get components to them and computers to their customers quickly and safely. The net result is that China spends about twice as high a share of its national income on transportation as the United States does, even though the U.S. has a larger territory, including two states separated by more than a thousand miles from the other states.

Contrasts in the size—and therefore costs—of inventories can be extreme from one country to another. Japan carries the smallest inventories, while the Soviet Union carried the largest, with the United States in between. As two Soviet economists pointed out:

> Spare parts are used right "off the truck": in Japan producers commonly deliver supplies to their ordering companies three or four times a day. At Toyota the volume of warehoused inventories is calculated for only an hour of work, while at Ford the inventories are for up to three weeks.

In the Soviet Union, "we have in inventories almost as much as we create in a year." In other words, most of the people who work in Soviet industry "could take a year's paid vacation" and the economy could live on its inventories. This is not an advantage but a handicap because inventories cost money—and don't earn any. From the standpoint of the economy as a whole, the production of inventory uses up resources without adding anything to either the standard of living of the public or the current output of industry. As the Soviet economists put it, "our economy is always burdened by the heavy weight of inventories, much heavier than those that weigh on a capitalist economy during the most destructive recessions." Yet the decisions to maintain huge inventories were not irrational decisions, given the circumstances of the Soviet economy and the incentives and constraints inherent in those circumstances. Soviet enterprises had no real choice but to maintain these costly inventories. The less reliable the suppliers, the more inventory it pays to keep, so as not to run out of vital components.[2] Nevertheless, inventories add to the costs of production, which add to the price, which in turn reduces the public's purchasing power and therefore its standard of living.

American businesses have inventory practices closer to those of the Japanese than to those that existed in the Soviet Union. The Chrysler division of DaimlerChrysler unloads about 8,000 truckloads of materials at its

---

[2] Far from being excessive under the circumstances, inventories in the Soviet Union sometimes proved to be inadequate, as manufacturing enterprises still ran out of components. According to Soviet economists, "a third of all cars come off the assembly line with parts missing."

various plants each day. Closely following the pattern in Japan, Daimler-Chrysler keeps only two hours' supply of materials on hand. It can do this only because it can rely on the deliveries needed to keep their production lines operating.

American manufacturers whose deliveries to other companies are not on time or not up to specifications can either lose customers or find their customers deducting money when they pay the manufacturer's bill. As the *New York Times* reported:

> Increasingly, stores want products packaged in ways that cut the amount of time required to set them up on shelves or racks. And they will deduct a certain amount for each aspect of product delivery, which can quickly add up to thousands of dollars.

The computer game manufacturer Sega ended up in a lawsuit when K-Mart deducted millions of dollars from its bill because of disputed delivery problems. A socialist monopoly faces no such pressures to deliver what is wanted, when it is wanted, and how it is wanted.

The reason General Motors can produce automobiles, without producing any tires to go on them, is because it can rely on Goodyear, Michelin, and whoever else supplies their tires to have those tires waiting to go on the cars when they come off the production lines. If these suppliers failed to deliver, it would of course be a disaster for General Motors. But it would be even more catastrophic for the tire companies themselves. To leave General Motors high and dry, with no tires to go on its Cadillacs or Chevrolets, would be financially suicidal to a tire company, since it would lose a customer for millions of tires each year, quite aside from the billions of dollars in damages from lawsuits over breach of contract. Under these circumstances, it is hardly surprising that General Motors does not have to produce all its own components, as many Soviet enterprises did.

Reliability is an inherent accompaniment of the physical product when keeping customers is a matter of economic life and death under capitalism, whether at the manufacturing level or the retail level. Back in the early 1930s, when refrigerators were just beginning to become widely used, there were many technological and production problems with the first mass-produced refrigerators sold by Sears. The company had no choice but to honor its money-back guarantee by taking back 30,000 refrigerators, at a time when Sears could ill afford to do so, in the depths of the Great Depression, when businesses were as short of money as their customers were. This situation put enormous financial pressure on Sears to either stop selling refrigerators (which is what some of its executives and many of its store managers wanted) or else greatly improve their reliability, which is what they eventually did, thereby becoming one of the leading sellers of refrigerators in the country.

None of this was painless. Nor is it likely that a socialist monopoly would have been forced to undergo such economic trauma to please its customers. There was a reason why Soviet enterprises could not rely on their suppliers and chose instead to make many things for themselves, and why large Chinese companies often transported their own products, even though neither the Soviet nor the Chinese enterprises were specialists in these auxiliary activities. The suppliers did not have to please their customers. All they had to do was follow general orders from the central planners, who were in no position to monitor the specific details for thousands of enterprises spread across a huge nation. But this was not an adequate substitute for the incentives of the marketplace, where customers monitored their own specific details. In both countries, the population at large paid the price in a standard of living much below what their country's resources and technology were capable of producing.

Chapter 7

Big Business and Government

Competitive free markets are not the only kinds of markets, nor are government-imposed price controls the only interferences with the operations of such markets. Monopolies, oligopolies, and cartels also produce economic results very different from those of a free market.

A monopoly means literally one seller. However, a small number of sellers—an oligopoly, as economists call it—may cooperate with one another, either explicitly or tacitly, in setting prices and so produce results similar to those of a monopoly. Where there is a formal organization in an industry to set prices and output—a cartel—its results can be like those of a monopoly, even though there may be numerous sellers in the cartel. Although these various kinds of non-competitive industries differ among themselves, their generally detrimental effects have led to laws and government policies designed to prevent or counter these effects. Sometimes this government intervention takes the form of direct regulation of the prices and policies of monopolistic industries. In other cases, government prohibits particular practices without attempting to micro-manage the companies involved. The first and most fundamental question, however, is: How are monopolistic firms detrimental to the economy?

MONOPOLIES AND CARTELS

Sometimes one company produces the total output of a given good or service in a region or a country. For many years, each local telephone company in the United States was a monopoly in its region of the country and that remains true in some other countries. For about half a century before World War II, the Aluminum Company of America (Alcoa) produced all the virgin ingot aluminum in the United States. Such situations are unusual, but they are important enough to deserve some serious attention.

Most big businesses are not monopolies and not all monopolies are big business. In the days before the automobile and the railroad, a general store in an isolated rural community could easily be the only store for miles around, and was as much of a monopoly as any corporation on the *Fortune* 500 list, even though the general store was usually an enterprise of very modest size. Conversely, today multi-billion-dollar nationwide grocery chains like Safeway or Giant have too many competitors to be able to price the goods they sell the way a monopolist would price them.

Just as we can understand the function of prices better after we have seen what happens when they are not allowed to function, so we can understand the role of competition in the economy better after we contrast what happens in competitive markets with what happens in markets that are not competitive.

In earlier chapters, we have considered prices as they emerge in a free market with many competing enterprises. Such markets tend to cause goods and services to be produced at the lowest costs possible under existing technology and with existing resources. Take something as simple as apple juice. How do consumers know that the price they are being charged for apple juice is not far above the cost of producing it? After all, most people do not grow apples, much less process them into juice and then bottle the juice, transport and store it, so they have no idea how much any or all of this costs.

Competition in the marketplace makes it unnecessary to know. Those few people who do know such things, and who are in the business of making investments, have every incentive to invest wherever there are higher rates of return and to reduce their investments where the rates of return are lower or negative. If the price of apple juice is higher than necessary to compensate for the costs incurred in producing it, then high rates of profit will be made—and will attract ever more investment into this industry until the competition of additional producers drives prices down to a level that just compensates the costs with the same average rate of return on similar investments available elsewhere in the economy. Only then will the in-flow of investments from other sectors of the economy stop, with the incentives for these in-flows now being gone.

If, however, there were a monopoly in producing apple juice, this whole process would not take place. Chances are that monopoly prices would remain at levels higher than necessary to compensate for the costs and efforts that go into producing apple juice, including paying a rate of return on capital sufficient to attract the capital required.

Many people object to the fact that a monopolist can charge higher prices than a competitive business could. But its ability to transfer money from other members of the society to itself is not the sole harm done by a monopoly. From the standpoint of the economy as a whole, these internal transfers do not change the total wealth of the society, even though this redistributes that wealth in a manner that may be considered objectionable. What adversely affects the total wealth in the economy as a whole is the effect of a monopoly on the allocation of scarce resources which have alternative uses.

When a monopoly charges a higher price than it could charge if it had competition, consumers tend to buy less of the product than they would at a lower competitive price. In short, a monopolist produces less output than a competitive industry would produce with the same available resources, technology and cost conditions. The monopolist stops short at a point where consumers are still willing to pay enough to cover the cost of production (including a normal profit) of more output because the monopolist is charging more than the usual cost of production and making more than the usual profit. In terms of the allocation of resources which have alternative uses, the net result is that some resources which could have been used to produce more apple juice instead go into producing other things elsewhere in the economy, even if those other things are not as valuable as the apple juice that could and would have been produced in a free competitive market. In short, the economy's resources are used inefficiently when there is monopoly, because these resources would be transferred from more valued uses to less valued uses.

Fortunately, monopolies are very hard to maintain without laws to protect the monopoly firms from competition. The ceaseless search of investors for the highest rates of return virtually ensures that such investments will flood into whatever segment of the economy is earning higher profits, until the rate of profit in that segment is driven down by the increased competition caused by that flood of investment. It is like water seeking its own level. But, just as dams can prevent water from finding its own level, so government intervention can prevent a monopoly's profit rate from being reduced by competition.

In centuries past, government permission was required to open businesses in many parts of the economy, especially in Europe and Asia, and monopoly rights were granted to various businessmen, who either paid the government directly for these rights or bribed officials who had the power to grant such rights, or both. However, by the end of the eighteenth century, the development of economics had reached the point where increasingly large numbers of people understood how this was detrimental to society as a whole and counter-pressures developed toward freeing the economy from monopolies and government control. Monopolies have therefore become much rarer, at least at the national level, though it remains common in many cities where restrictive licensing laws limit how many taxis are allowed to operate, causing fares to be artificially higher than necessary and cabs less available than they would be in a free market.

Again, the loss is not simply that of the individual consumers. The economy as a whole loses when people who are perfectly willing to drive taxis at fares that consumers are willing to pay are nevertheless prevented from doing so by artificial restrictions on the number of taxi licenses issued, and thus either do some other work of lesser value or remain unemployed. If the alternative work were of greater value, and were compensated accordingly, then such people would never have been potential taxi drivers in the first place.

From the standpoint of the economy as a whole, this means that consumers of the monopolist's product are foregoing the use of scarce resources which would have a higher value to them than in alternative uses. That is the inefficiency which causes the economy as a whole to have less wealth under monopoly than it would have under free competition. It is sometimes said that a monopolist "restricts output," but this is not the intent, nor is the monopolist the one who restricts output. The monopolist would love to have the consumers buy more at its inflated price, but the consumers stop short of the amount that they would buy at a lower price under free competition. It is the monopolist's higher price which causes the consumers to restrict their own purchases and therefore causes the monopolist to restrict production to what can be sold. But the monopolist may be advertising heavily to try to persuade consumers to buy more.

Similar principles apply to a cartel—that is, a group of businesses which agree among themselves to charge higher prices or otherwise avoid competing with one another. In theory, a cartel could operate collectively the same as a monopoly. In practice, however, individual members of cartels tend to cheat on one another secretly—lowering the cartel price to some customers, in order to take business away from other members of the cartel. When this becomes widespread, the cartel becomes irrelevant, whether or not it formally ceases to exist.

Because cartels were once known as "trusts," legislation designed to outlaw monopolies and cartels became known as "anti-trust laws." However, such laws are not the only way of fighting monopolies and cartels. Private businesses that are not part of the cartel have incentives to fight them in the marketplace. Moreover, private businesses can take action much faster than the years required for the government to bring a major anti-trust case to a successful conclusion.

In the nineteenth-century heyday of American trusts, Montgomery Ward was one of their biggest opponents. Whether the trust involved agricultural machinery, bicycles, sugar, nails or twine, Montgomery Ward would seek out manufacturers that were not part of the trust and buy from them below the cartel price, reselling to the general public below the retail price of the goods produced by members of the cartel. Since Montgomery Ward was the number one mail-order business in the country at that time, it was also big enough to set up its own factories and make the product itself if need be.

The later rise of other huge retailers like Sears and A & P likewise confronted the big producers with corporate giants able to either produce their own competing products to sell in their own stores or to buy enough from some small enterprise outside the cartel to enable that enterprise to grow into a big competitor. Sears did both. It produced stoves, shoes, guns, and wallpaper, among other things, in addition to subcontracting the production of other products. A & P imported and roasted its own coffee, canned its own salmon, and baked half a billion loaves of bread a year for sale in its own stores.

While giant firms like Sears, Montgomery Ward and A & P were unique in being able to compete against a number of cartels simultaneously, smaller companies could also take away sales from cartels in their respective industries. Their incentive was the same as that of the cartel—profit. Where a monopoly or cartel maintains prices that produce higher than normal profits, other businesses are attracted to the industry. This additional competition then tends to force prices and profits down. In order for a monopoly or cartel to succeed in maintaining profits above the competitive level, it must find ways to prevent others from entering the industry. That is easier said than done.

One way to keep out potential competitors is to have the government make it illegal for others to operate in particular industries. Kings granted or sold monopoly rights for centuries, and modern governments have restricted the issuance of licenses for various industries and occupations, ranging from airlines to taxicabs to trucking to the braiding of hair. Political rationales are never lacking for these restrictions, but their net economic effect is to protect existing enterprises from additional potential competitors and therefore to maintain prices at artificially high levels. For much of the late twentieth century, the government of India not only decided which companies it would license to produce which products, it imposed limits on how much each company could produce.

Thus an Indian manufacturer of scooters was hauled before a government commission because he had produced more scooters than he was allowed to and a producer of medicine for colds was fearful that the public had bought "too much" of his product during a flu epidemic in India. Lawyers for the cold medicine manufacturer spent months preparing a legal defense for having produced and sold more than they were allowed to, in case they were called before the same commission. All this costly legal work had to be paid for by someone and that someone was ultimately the consumer.

In the absence of government prohibition of entry, various clever schemes can be used privately to try to erect barriers to keep out competitors and protect monopoly profits. But other businesses have incentives to be just as clever at evading these barriers. Accordingly, the effectiveness of barriers to entry have varied from industry to industry and from one era to another in the same industry. The computer industry was once difficult to enter, back in the days when a computer was a huge machine taking up a major part of a room, and the costs of manufacturing such machines was likewise huge. But the development of microchips meant that smaller computers could do the same work and chips were now inexpensive enough to produce that they could be manufactured by smaller companies. These include companies located around the world, so that even a nationwide monopoly does not preclude competition in an industry. Although the United States pioneered in the creation of computers, the actual manufacturing of computers spread quickly to East Asia, which supplied much of the American market with computers.

In addition to private responses to monopoly and cartels which arise more or less spontaneously in the marketplace, there are government responses. In the late nineteenth century, the American government began to respond to monopolies and cartels by both directly regulating the prices which monopolist and cartels were allowed to charge and by taking legal punitive action against these monopolies and cartels under the Sherman Anti-Trust Act of 1890 and other later antitrust legislation. When railroads were first built in the nineteenth century, there were many places where only one rail line existed, leaving these railroads free to charge whatever prices would maximize their profits where they had a monopoly. Complaints about this situation led to the creation of the Interstate Commerce Commission in 1887, the first of many federal regulatory commissions to control the prices charged by monopolists. During the era when local telephone companies were monopolies in their respective regions and their parent company—A.T.&T.—had a monopoly of long-distance service, the Federal Communications Commission controlled the prices charged by A.T.&T., while state regulatory agencies controlled the price of local phone service.

Another approach has been to pass laws against the creation or maintenance of a monopoly or against various practices, such as price discrimination, growing out of monopolistic behavior. These anti-trust laws were intended to allow businesses to operate without the kinds of detailed government supervision which exist under regulatory commissions, but with a sort of general surveillance, like that of traffic police, with intervention occurring only when there are specific violations of laws.

REGULATORY COMMISSIONS

Although the functions of a regulatory commission are fairly straightforward in theory, in practice its task is far more complex and, in some respects, impossible. Moreover, the political climate in which regulatory commissions operate often lead to policies and results directly the opposite of what was expected by those who created such commissions.

Ideally, a regulatory commission would set prices where they would have been if there were a competitive marketplace. In practice, there is no way to know what those prices would be. Only the actual functioning of a market itself could reveal such prices, as the less efficient firms were eliminated by bankruptcy and only the most efficient survived, with their lower prices now being the market prices. No outside observers can know what the most efficient ways of operating a given firm or industry are. Indeed, many managements within an industry discover the hard way that what they thought was the most efficient way to do things was not efficient enough to meet the competition, and end up losing customers as a result. The most that a regulatory agency can do is accept what appear to be reasonable production costs and allow the monopoly to make what seems to be a reasonable profit over and above such costs.

Determining the cost of production is by no means always easy. As noted in Chapter 6, there may be no such thing as "the" cost of production. The cost of generating electricity, for example, can vary enormously, depending on when and where it is generated. When you wake up in the middle of the night and turn on a light, that electricity costs practically nothing to supply, because the electricity-generating system has much unused capacity in the middle of the night, when most people are asleep. But, when you turn on your air conditioner on a hot summer afternoon, when millions of other homes and offices already have their air conditioners on, that may help strain the system to its limit and necessitate turning on costly standby generators, in order to avoid blackouts. It has been estimated that the cost of supplying the electricity required to run a dishwasher, at a time of peak usage, can be 100 times larger than the cost of running that same dishwasher at a time when there is a low demand for electricity.

There are many reasons why additional electricity, beyond the usual capacity of the system, may be many times more costly per kilowatt hour than the usual costs when the system is functioning within its usual capacity. The main system that supplies vast numbers of consumers can make use of economies of scale to produce electricity at its lowest cost, while standby generators typically produce less electricity and therefore cannot take full advantage of economies of scales, but must produce at higher costs per kilowatt hour. Sometimes technological progress gives the main system lower costs, while obsolete equipment is kept as standby equipment, rather than being junked, and the costs of producing additional electricity with this obsolete equipment is of course higher. Where additional electricity has to be purchased from outside sources when the local generating capacity is at its limit, the additional cost of transmitting that electricity from greater distances raises the cost of the additional electricity to much higher levels than the cost of electricity generated closer to the consumers.

More variations in "the" cost of producing electricity come from fluctuations in the costs of the various fuels—oil, gas, coal, nuclear—used to run the generators. Since all these fuels are used for other things besides generating electricity, the demands for these fuels from other industries, or for use in homes or automobiles, makes their prices unpredictable. Hydroelectric dams likewise vary in how much electricity they can produce when rainfall varies, increasing or reducing the amount of water that passes through the generators. When the fixed costs of the dam are spread over differing amounts of electricity, the cost per kilowatt varies accordingly.

How is a regulatory commission to set the rates to be charged consumers of electricity, given that the cost of generating it can vary widely and unpredictably? If state regulatory commissions set electricity rates based on "average" costs of generating electricity, then when there is a higher demand or a shorter supply within the state, out-of-state suppliers may be unwilling to sell electricity at prices lower than their own costs of generating the additional electricity from standby units. This was part of the reason for the much-publicized blackouts in California in 2001. "Average" costs are irrelevant when the costs of generation are far above average at a particular time or far below average at other times.

Because the public is unlikely to be familiar with all the economic complications involved, they are likely to be outraged at having to pay electricity rates far higher than they are used to. In turn, this means that politicians are tempted to step in and impose price controls based on the old rates. And, as already noted in other contexts, price controls create shortages—in this case, blackouts. A larger quantity demanded and a smaller quantity supplied has been a very familiar response to price controls, going back in history long before electricity came into use. However, politicians' success does not depend on their learning the lessons of history or of economics. It depends far more on their going along with what is widely believed by the public and the media, which may include conspiracy theories or belief that higher prices are due to "gouging" or "greed."

Halfway around the world at the same time, attempts to raise electricity rates in India were being met by street demonstrations, as they were in California. In the state of Karnataka, controlled politically by the Congress Party at the time, efforts to change electricity rates were opposed in the streets by one of the opposition parties. However, in the neighboring state of Andhra Pradesh, where the Congress Party was in the opposition, it led similar street demonstrations against electricity rate increases. In short, what was involved in these demonstrations was neither ideology nor party, but an opportunistic playing to public misconceptions.

The economic complexities involved when regulatory agencies set prices are compounded by political complexities. Regulatory agencies are often set up after some political crusaders have successfully launched investigations or publicity campaigns that convince the authorities to establish a permanent commission to oversee and control a monopoly or some group of firms few enough in number to be a threat to behave in collusion as if they were one monopoly. However, after a commission has been set up and its powers established, crusaders and the media tend to lose interest over the years and turn their attention to other things. Meanwhile, the firms being regulated continue to take a keen interest in the activities of the commission and to lobby the government for favorable regulations and favorable appointments of individuals to these commissions.

The net result of these asymmetrical outside interests on these agencies is that commissions set up to keep a given firm or industry within bounds, for the benefit of the consumer, often metamorphose into agencies seeking to protect the existing regulated firms from threats arising from new firms with new technology or new organizational methods. Thus, in the United States, the Interstate Commerce Commission responded to the rise of the trucking industry, whose competition in carrying freight threatened the economic viability of the railroads, by extending its control over trucking.

The original rationale for regulating railroads was that these railroads were often monopolies in particular areas of the country. But now that trucking undermined that monopoly, the response of the I.C.C. was not to say that the need for regulating transportation was now less urgent or perhaps even unnecessary. Instead, it sought—and received from Congress—broader authority under the Motor Carrier Act of 1935, in order to restrict the activities of truckers. This allowed railroads to survive under new economic conditions, despite truck competition that was more efficient for various kinds of freight hauling. Trucks were now permitted to operate across state lines only if they had a certificate from the Interstate Commerce Commission declaring that the trucks' activities served "public necessity and convenience" as defined by the I.C.C.

In short, freight was no longer hauled in whatever way required the use of the least resources, as it would be under open competition, but only by whatever way met the arbitrary requirements of the Interstate Commerce Commission. The I.C.C. might, for example, authorize a particular trucking company to haul freight from New York to Washington, but not from Philadelphia to Baltimore, even though these cities are on the way. If the certificate did not authorize freight to be carried back from Washington to New York, then the trucks would have to return empty, while other trucks carried freight from D.C. to New York. From the standpoint of the economy as a whole, enormously greater costs were incurred than were necessary to get the work done. But what this arrangement accomplished politically was to allow far more companies—both truckers and railroads—to survive and make a profit than if there were an unrestricted competitive market, where the transportation companies would have no choice but to use the most efficient ways of hauling freight. The use of more resources than necessary entailed the survival of more companies than were necessary.

While open and unfettered competition would have been economically beneficial to the society as a whole, such competition would have been politically threatening to the regulatory commission. Firms facing economic extinction because of competition would be sure to resort to political agitation and intrigue against the survival in office of the commissioners and against the survival of the commission and its powers. Labor unions also had a vested interest in keeping the status quo safe from the competition of technologies and methods that might require fewer workers to get the job done.

After the I.C.C.'s powers to control the trucking industry were eventually reduced by Congress in 1980, freight charges declined substantially and shippers reported a rise in the quality of the service. This was made possible by greater efficiency in the industry, as there were now fewer trucks driving around empty and more truckers hired workers whose pay was determined by supply and demand, rather than by union contracts. Because truck deliveries were now more dependable in a competitive industry, businesses using their services were able to carry smaller inventories, saving in the aggregate tens of billions of dollars.

The inefficiencies created by regulation were indicated not only by such savings after federal deregulation, but also by the difference between the costs of interstate shipments and the costs of *intrastate* shipments, where strict state regulation continued after federal regulation was cut back. For example, shipping blue jeans within the state of Texas from El Paso to Dallas cost about 40 percent more than shipping the same jeans internationally from Taiwan to Dallas.

Gross inefficiencies under regulation were not peculiar to the Interstate Commerce Commission. The same was true of the Civil Aeronautics Board, which kept out potentially competitive airlines and kept the prices of airfares in the United States high enough to ensure the survival of existing airlines, rather than force them to face the competition of other airlines that could carry passengers cheaper or with better service. Once the CAB was abolished, airline fares came down, some airlines went bankrupt, but new airlines arose and in the end there were far more passengers being carried than at any time under the constraints of regulation. Savings to airline passengers ran into the billions of dollars. These were not just zero-sum changes, with airlines losing what passengers gained. The country as a whole benefitted from deregulation, for the industry became more efficient. Just as there were fewer trucks driving around empty after trucking deregulation, so airplanes began to fly with a higher percentage of their seats filled after airline deregulation and passengers usually had more choices of carriers on a given route than before.

In these and other industries, the original rationale for regulation was to keep prices from rising excessively but, over the years, this turned into regulatory restrictions against letting prices *fall* to a level that would threaten the survival of existing firms. Political crusades are based on plausible rationales but, even when those rationales are sincerely believed and honestly applied, their actual consequences may be completely different from their initial goals. When major mistakes are made in a competitive economy, those who were mistaken can be forced from the marketplace by the losses that follow. But, in politics, those who were mistaken can often continue to survive by doing things that were never contemplated when their positions and their powers were created.

ANTI-TRUST LAWS

With anti-trust laws, as with regulatory commissions, a sharp distinction must be made between their original rationales and what they actually do. The basic rationale for anti-trust laws is to prevent monopoly and other conditions which allow prices to rise above where they would be in a free and competitive marketplace. In practice, most of the great anti-trust cases in the United States have involved some business that charged *lower* prices than its competitors. Often it has been complaints from these competitors which caused the government to act.

The basis of many government prosecutions under the anti-trust laws is that some company's actions threatens competition. However, the most important thing about competition is that it is a *condition* in the marketplace. This condition cannot be measured by the number of competitors existing in a given industry at a given time, though politicians, lawyers and assorted others have confused the existence of competition with the number of surviving competitors. But competition as a condition is precisely what eliminates many competitors.

Obviously, if it eliminates all competitors, then the surviving firm would be a monopoly and could then charge far higher prices than in a competitive market. But that is extremely rare. However, the specter of monopoly is often used to justify government policies of intervention where there is no serious danger of a monopoly. For example, back when the A & P grocery chain was the largest retail chain in the world, it still sold less than one-fifth of the groceries in the United States. Yet the Justice Department brought an anti-trust action against it, using the company's low prices, and the methods by which it achieved those low prices, as evidence of unfair competition against rival grocers and grocery chains. Throughout the history of anti-trust prosecutions, there has been an unresolved confusion between what is detrimental to competition and what is detrimental to competitors. In the midst of this confusion, the question of what is beneficial to the consumer has often been lost sight of.

What has often also been lost sight of is the question of the efficiency of the economy as a whole, which is another way of looking at the benefits to the consuming public. Fewer scarce resources are used when products are bought and sold in carload lots, as large chain stores are often able to do, than when the shipments are sold and delivered in much smaller quantities to numerous smaller stores. Both delivery costs and selling costs are less per unit of product when the product is bought and sold in large enough amounts to fill a railroad boxcar. Production costs are also lower when the producer receives a large enough order to be able to schedule production far ahead, instead of finding it necessary to pay overtime to fill many small and unexpected orders that happen to arrive at the same time.

Unpredictable orders also increase the likelihood of slow periods when there is not enough work to keep all the workers employed. Workers who have to be laid off at such times may find other jobs and not return when the first employer has more orders to fill, thus making it necessary for the employer to hire new workers, which entails training costs and lower productivity until the new workers gain enough experience to reach peak efficiency. Moreover, employers unable to offer steady employment may find recruiting workers to be more difficult, unless they offer higher pay to offset the uncertainties of the job. In all these ways, production costs are higher when there are unpredictable orders than when a large purchaser, such as a major department store chain, can contract for a large amount of the supplier's output, enabling cost savings to be made in production, part of which go to the chain in lower prices as well as to the producer as lower production costs.

Despite such economies of scale, the government took action against the Morton Salt Company in the 1940s for giving discounts to buyers who bought carload lots of their product. Businesses that bought less than a carload lot of salt were charged $1.60 a case, those who bought carload lots were charged $1.50 a case, and those who bought 50,000 cases or more in a year's time were charged $1.35. Because there were relatively few companies that could afford to buy so much salt and many more that could not, "the competitive opportunities of certain merchants were injured," according to the Supreme Court, which upheld the Federal Trade Commission's actions against Morton Salt. The government likewise took action against the Standard Oil Company in the 1950s for allowing discounts to those dealers who bought oil by the tank car. The Borden company was similarly brought into court in the 1960s for having charged less for milk to big chain stores than to smaller grocers. In all these cases, the key point was that such price differences were considered "discriminatory" and "unfair" to those competing firms unable to make such large purchases.

While the sellers were allowed to defend themselves in court by referring to cost differences in selling to different classes of buyers, the apparently simple concept of "cost" is by no means simple when argued over by rival lawyers, accountants and economists. Where neither side could prove anything conclusively about the costs—which was common—the accused lost the case. In a fundamental departure from the centuries-old traditions of Anglo-American law, the government need only make a superficial or *prima facie* case, based on gross numbers, to shift the burden of proof to the accused. This same principle and procedure were to reappear, years later, in employment discrimination cases under the civil rights laws. As with anti-trust cases, these employment discrimination cases likewise produced many consent decrees and large out-of-court settlements by companies well aware of the virtual impossibility of proving their innocence, regardless of what the facts might be.

The rarity of genuine monopolies in the American economy has led to much legalistic creativity, in order to define various companies as monopolistic or as potential or "incipient" monopolies. How far this could go was illustrated when the Supreme Court in 1966 broke up a merger between two shoe companies that would have given the new combined company less than 7 percent of the shoe sales in the United States. It likewise that same year broke up a merger of two local supermarket chains which, put together, sold less than 8 percent of the groceries in the Los Angeles area. Similarly arbitrary categorizations of businesses as "monopolies" were imposed in India under the Monopolies and Restrictive Trade Practices Act of 1969, where any enterprise with assets in excess of a given amount (about $27 million dollars) were declared to be monopolies and restricted from expanding their business.

A standard practice in American courts and in the literature on anti-trust laws is to describe the percentage of sales made by a given company as the share of the market it "controls." By this standard, such now defunct companies as Graflex and Pan American "controlled" a substantial share of their respective markets, when in fact the passage of time showed that they controlled nothing, or else they would never have allowed themselves to be forced out of business. The severe shrinkage in size of such former giants as A & P and Smith-Corona likewise suggests that the rhetoric of "control" bears little relationship to reality. But such rhetoric remains effective in courts of law and in the court of public opinion.

Even in the rare case where a genuine monopoly exists on its own—that is, has not been created or sustained by government policy—the consequences in practice have tended to be much less dire than in theory. During the decades when the Aluminum Company of America (Alcoa) was the only producer of virgin ingot aluminum in the United States, its annual profit rate on its investment was about 10 percent after taxes. Moreover, the price of aluminum went down to a fraction of what it had been before Alcoa was formed. Yet Alcoa was prosecuted under the anti-trust laws and lost. Why were aluminum prices going down under a monopoly, when in theory they should have been going up? Despite its "control" of the market for aluminum, Alcoa was well aware that it could not jack up prices at will, without risking the substitution of other materials—steel, tin, wood, plastics—for aluminum by many users.

This raises a question that applies far beyond the aluminum industry. Percentages of the market "controlled" by this or that company ignore the role of substitutes that may be classified as products of other industries, but which can nevertheless be used as substitutes by many buyers, if the price of the monopolized product rises significantly. A technologically very different product may serve as a substitute, as laptop computers did when they replaced portable typewriters, or as television did when it replaced many newspapers as sources of information and entertainment. In Spain, when a high-speed train began to operate between Madrid and Seville, the division of passenger traffic between rail and air travel went from 33 percent rail and 67 percent air to 82 percent rail and 18 percent air.

Advertising is clearly a market that encompasses technologically very different media, ranging from billboards to brochures, sky-writing, the Internet, newspapers and magazine ads, and commercials on television and radio. Different businesses spend differing proportions of their respective advertising budgets in these various media and change those proportions over time. Any particular advertising firm's "control" of any given percentage of the advertising in its own particular medium—say, billboards—would mean little if jacking up its prices would lead advertisers to switch their advertising to newspaper ads, radio commercials, or some other medium.

Those bringing anti-trust lawsuits generally seek to define the relevant market narrowly, so as to produce high percentages of the market "controlled" by the targeted enterprise. In the famous anti-trust case against Microsoft at the turn of the century, for example, the market was defined as that for computer operating systems for stand-alone personal computers using microchips of the kind manufactured by Intel. This left out not only the operating systems running Apple computers but also other operating systems such as those produced by Sun Microsystems for multiple computers or the Linux system for stand-alone computers.

In this narrowly defined market, Microsoft clearly had a "dominant" share. The anti-trust lawsuit, however, did not accuse Microsoft of jacking up prices unconscionably, in the classic monopoly manner. Rather, Microsoft had added an Internet browser to its Windows operating system free of charge, undermining rival browser producer Netscape. The existence of all the various sources of potential competition from outside the narrowly defined market may well have had something to do with the fact that Microsoft did not raise prices, as it could have gotten away with in the short run—but at the cost of jeopardizing its long-run sales and profits, since other operating systems could have been adaptable as substitutes if their prices were right. In 2003, the city government of Munich in fact switched from using Microsoft Windows in 14,000 computers to using Linux—one of the systems excluded from the definition of the market that Microsoft "controlled."

The spread of international free trade means that even a genuine monopoly of a particular product in a particular country may mean little if that same product can be imported from other countries. If there is only one producer of widgets in Brazil, that producer is not a monopoly in any economically meaningful sense if there are a dozen widget manufacturers in neighboring Argentina and hundreds of widget makers in countries around the world. Only if the Brazilian government prevents widgets from being imported does the lone manufacturer in the country become a monopoly in a sense that would allow higher prices to be charged than would be charged in a competitive market. As of 1982, the number of American manufacturers of electric portable typewriters was down to one. But although Smith-Corona now "controlled" 100 percent of the market, that was not enough to keep them out of the red, much less enable them to make monopoly profits. Partly that was because the market for electric portable typewriters was itself declining and because there were now more imported electric portables sold in the United States than American-made electric portables.

If it seems silly to arbitrarily define a market and "control" of that market by a given firm's sales of domestically produced products, it was not too silly to form the basis of a landmark

U.S. Supreme Court decision in 1963, which defined the market for shoes in terms of "domestic production of nonrubber shoes." By eliminating sneakers, deck shoes, and imported shoes of all kinds, this definition increased the defined market share of the firms being charged with violating the anti-trust laws—who in this case were convicted. In a later anti-trust case, against Microsoft, the market was defined as operating systems for personal computers using Intel-type chips. This definition eliminated not only all Apple computers, but also all network computers and other computers using different technologies—all of which inflated Microsoft's defined share of sales of operating systems, which is to say, its "control" of the market, thereby facilitating its conviction under the anti-trust laws.

Thus far, whether discussing widgets, shoes, or computer operating systems, we have been considering markets defined by a given product performing a given function. But often the same function can be performed by technologically different products. For example, typewriters, word processors, and computers can all produce printed letters or manuscripts. In this situation, a complete monopoly of typewriter production by one company would mean virtually nothing, if the consumers were free to have their letters and manuscripts produced by word processors or computers. If the typewriter monopolist raised its prices in disregard of these alternatives, it could find typewriter sales plummeting. On the other hand, it would still be eligible to be convicted of anti-trust law violations, based on its complete "control" of the market for its technologically defined product.

Even products that have no functional similarity may nevertheless be substitutes in economic terms. If golf courses were to double their fees, many casual golfers might play the game less often or give it up entirely, and in either case seek recreation by taking cruises or by pursuing a hobby like photography or skiing, using money that might otherwise have been used for playing golf. The fact that these other activities are functionally very different from golf does not matter. In economic terms, when higher prices for *A* cause people to buy more of *B*, then *A* and *B* are substitutes, whether or not they look alike or operate alike. But laws and government policies seldom look at things this way, especially when defining how much of a given market a given firm "controls."

Domestically, as well as internationally, as the area that can be served by given producers expands, the degree of statistical dominance or "control" by local producers in any given area means less and less. For example, as the number of newspapers published in given American communities declined after the middle of the twentieth century with the rise of television, much concern was expressed over the growing share of local markets "controlled" by the surviving papers. In many communities, only one local newspaper survived, making it a monopoly as defined by the share of the market it "controlled." Yet the fact that newspapers published elsewhere became available over wider areas made such statistical "control" economically less and less significant.

For example, someone living in the small community of Palo Alto, California, 30 miles south of San Francisco, need not buy a Palo Alto newspaper to find out what movies are playing in town, since that information is readily available from the *San Francisco Chronicle*, which is widely sold in Palo Alto, with home delivery being easy to arrange. Still less does a Palo Alto resident have to rely on a local paper for national or international news. Technological advances have enabled *The New York Times* or *The Wall Street Journal* to be printed in California as readily as in New York, and at the same time, so that these became national newspapers, available in communities large and small across America. *USA Today* achieved the largest circulation in the country with no local origin at all. The net result was that many local "monopoly" newspapers had difficulties even surviving financially, much less making any extra profits associated with monopoly. Yet anti-trust policies based on market shares continued to impose restrictions on mergers of local newspapers, lest such mergers leave the surviving newspapers with too much "control" of their local market. But the market as defined by the location of the producer had become largely irrelevant economically.

An extreme example of how misleading market share statistics can be was the case of a local movie chain that showed 100 percent of all the first-run movies in Las Vegas. It was prosecuted as a monopoly but, by the time the case reached the 9th Circuit Court of Appeals, another movie chain was showing more first-run movies in Las Vegas than the "monopolist" that was being prosecuted. Fortunately, sanity prevailed in this instance. Judge Alex Kozinski of the 9th Circuit Court of Appeal pointed out that the key to monopoly is not market share—even when it is 100 percent—but the ability to keep others out. A company which cannot keep competitors out is not a monopoly, no matter what percentage of the market it may have at a given moment. That is why the *Palo Alto Weekly* is not a monopoly in any economically meaningful sense, even though it is the only newspaper published in town, because newspapers published in San Francisco or even New York are at least as widely available locally and more likely to be delivered to homes in Palo Alto.

Focusing on market shares at a given moment has also led to a pattern in which the U. S. government has prosecuted leading firms in an industry just when they were about to lose that leadership. In a world where it is common for particular companies to rise and fall over time, anti-trust lawyers can take years to build a case against a company that is at its peak—and about to head over the hill. For example, an anti-trust case against the A & P grocery chain ended in 1949, just three years before A & P lost $50 million and began a long and catastrophic economic decline.[1]

The "control," "power," and "dominance" of A & P, which the government lawyers depicted so convincingly in court proved to be of little consequence in the marketplace, when other supermarket chains were able to sell at lower prices. A major anti-trust case can take a decade or more to be brought to a final conclusion. Markets often react much more quickly than this against monopolies and cartels, as early twentieth century trusts found when giant retailers like Sears, Montgomery Ward and A & P outflanked them long before the government could make a legal case against them.

Perhaps the most clearly positive benefit of American anti-trust laws has been a blanket prohibition against collusion to fix prices. This is an automatic violation, subject to heavy penalties, regardless of any justification that might be attempted. Whether this outweighs the various negative effects of other anti-trust laws on competition in the marketplace is another question. The more stringent anti-monopoly laws in India produced many clearly counterproductive results before they were eventually repealed in 1991. Some of India's leading industrialists were prevented from expanding their highly successful enterprises, lest they exceed an arbitrary financial limit used to define a "monopoly"—regardless of how many competitors that "monopolist" might have. As a result, India entrepreneurs often applied their efforts and capital outside of India, providing goods, employment, and taxes in other countries where they were not so restricted. One such entrepreneur, for example, produced fiber in Thailand from pulp bought in Canada and sent this fiber to his factory in Indonesia to be exported to Belgium, where it would be made into carpets.

It is impossible to know how many other Indian businesses invested outside of India because of the restrictions against "monopoly." What is known is that the repeal of the Monopolies and Restrictive Trade Practices Act in

---

[1] Why did A & P not adjust to the new conditions as fast as Safeway? Partly, the answer may be that there are always differences among individuals in how fast they notice changes, realize their implications, and respond. Another factor in the case of A & P was that the company was owned and operated for nearly a century by the same family, and the death of the last brother to run it in 1951 brought to leadership a man who had served faithfully under the old system. Was such a man at such a time, in the wake of his leader's death, likely to turn the company upside down and throw away the managerial legacy he had received?

1991 was followed by an expansion of large-scale enterprises in India, both by Indian entrepreneurs and by foreign entrepreneurs who now found India a better place to establish or expand businesses. What also increased dramatically was the country's economic growth rate, reducing the number of people in poverty and increasing the Indian government's ability to help them, because tax revenues rose with the rising economic activity in the country.

Chapter 8

An Overview

In a society where most people are employees and consumers, it is easy to think of businesses as "them"—as impersonal organizations, whose internal operations are largely unknown and whose sums of money may sometimes be so huge as to be unfathomable. Perhaps the most overlooked fact about industry and commerce is that they are run by people who differ greatly from one another in insight, foresight, leadership, organizational ability, and dedication—just as people do in every other walk of life. According to *Forbes* business magazine, "other automakers can't come close to Toyota on how much it costs to build cars" and this shows up on the bottom line. "Toyota earned $1,800 for very vehicle sold, GM made $300 and Ford lost $240," *Forbes* reported.

If the economy is to achieve the most efficient use of its scarce resources, there must be some way of weeding out those business owners or managers who do not get the most from those resources. Losses accomplish that. Bankruptcy shuts down the entire enterprise that is failing to come up to the standards of its competitors or is producing a product that has been superseded by some other product. Before reaching that point, however, losses can force a firm to make internal reassessments of its policies and personnel. These include the chief executive, who can be replaced by irate stockholders who are not receiving the dividends they expected.

The whole management team of a corporation can be replaced when outside financial interests realize that the business would be worth more if managed by someone else, and who therefore take over the business, in order to run it better and more profitably with a different set of managers. Sometimes just a few shifts in key management personnel can turn a company around, as happened at General Motors which, in 1997, required about 10 more hours of labor per car than Toyota but narrowed the gap to less than 3 hours by 2001.

A poorly managed company is more valuable to outside investors, when they convinced that they can improve its performance, than it is to existing owners. These outside investors can therefore offer existing stockholders more for their stock than it is currently worth and still make a profit, if that stock's value later rises to the level expected when existing management is replaced by better managers. For example, if the stock is selling in the market for $50 a share under inefficient management, outside investors can start buying it up at $75 a share until they own a controlling interest in the corporation.

After using that control to fire existing managers and replace them with a more efficient management team, the value of the stock may then rise to $100 a share. While this profit is what motivates the investors, from the standpoint of the economy as a whole what matters is that such a rise in stock prices usually means that either the business is now serving more customers, or offering them better quality or lower prices, or is operating at lower cost—or some combination of these things.

Thus profits and losses work together in a market economy to replace personnel, products and whole companies and industries with better alternatives. The net effect of achieving higher levels of efficiency is a higher standard of living for the consuming public. Moreover, this process is never-ending because its problems can never be solved once and for all. Changes in technology, in the company's internal personnel and in the surrounding economy and society present ever-changing challenges to be dealt with, all under the constant threat of losses, as well as opportunities for profit.

CHANGING CONDITIONS

The Great Depression of the 1930s left many business leaders very cautious about expanding their operations, especially if this required borrowing money that might be hard to repay if the economy turned down. Even highly profitable businesses could decide to save their money for a rainy day, rather than risk it in new ventures. Against this background, it is not surprising that the dramatic changes in the American economy and society between the Great Depression of the 1930s and the booming prosperity that began after World War II were perceived very differently by different business leaders.

Fear that a new depression might be coming caused the managements of Montgomery Ward and A & P to be reluctant to pay high prices for suburban locations for new stores, while Sears and Safeway plunged ahead with expansion into such areas, to which much of the most affluent population was now moving. In this case, those who gambled won and those who played it safe lost. In other cases under other circumstances, those who expanded met disaster. The W. T. Grant variety store chain, once one of the biggest retailers in America during the first half of the twentieth century, became in the 1970s one of the biggest bankruptcies in the history of the country, after financing a costly expansion which did not work out.

Grocery stores and department stores were not the only businesses presented with a radically changed environment as a result of the rapid increase of automobile ownership during the post-World War II boom and suburbanization. Although urban newspapers suffered huge declines in circulation, and many leading big-city papers went out of business, suburban newspapers had dramatic increases in their circulation. Changes were equally dramatic in the fast-food industry.

McDonald's fast-food restaurants were entirely a postwar phenomenon, going from one hamburger stand in southern California operated by the McDonald brothers in 1955 to 4,000 nationwide just 20 years later and 8,000 a decade after that. By 2001, there were more than 29,000 McDonald's restaurants in 121 countries. When McDonald's first spread across America, many of its restaurants were built on highways or at other locations from which they could draw customers in automobiles from miles around. In previous decades—from the 1920s into the 1950s—White Castle was the dominant hamburger chain in the United States. People walked to White Castle hamburger restaurants, which meant that these restaurants had to be located in places with high population densities, so as to generate a large volume of pedestrian traffic coming in, enabling White Castle to sell to many people who came from a limited distance. Accordingly, White Castles were often located near factories or in crowded working class neighborhoods in central cities. And they stayed open around the clock.

Financing was also very different in that earlier era. Unlike later fast-food chains, White Castle did not have franchises. The parent company owned each restaurant and built new ones only when it had the money on hand to pay cash to do so. This enabled White Castle to ride out the Great Depression of the 1930s, when many other businesses, homes, and farms were lost because mortgages could not be paid at a time when money was so scarce.

Indeed, White Castle expanded during the Depression. It was almost ideally adapted to the world in which it existed. But it lost its unchallenged leadership of the industry and began a decline into obscurity when the economy and society changed around its restaurants in the middle of the twentieth century.

As middle-class and even working class people became more prosperous, acquired automobiles, and moved out of the central cities into the suburbs, reducing population densities in the cities, White Castle could no longer count on the heavy urban pedestrian traffic on which it had thrived. Its conservative financing policies meant that it could not expand as rapidly into the suburbs as other businesses which went into debt to do so, or raised capital by requiring their franchisees to put up part of the money needed. The rising crime and violence of the central cities in the 1960s were more of a problem for White Castle than for other hamburger chains located in suburban shopping malls. Staying open all night in low-income urban neighborhoods was no longer safe, financially or otherwise.

At the heart of the changed environment for fast-food chains was the automobile. Unlike White Castle, McDonald's did not have to adapt to the world of the automobile, because McDonald's began in that part of the country where automobile ownership was most widespread—southern California—and was geared to that environment from the beginning. As automobile ownership and suburbanization spread across the country, so did McDonald's. By 1988, half of McDonald's sales in America were made at drive-through windows, which were capable of handling a car every 25 seconds, or well over a hundred per hour.

As with the supermarkets, this high turnover represented extremely low costs of selling, enabling prices to be kept down to levels that were highly competitive. Drive-through restaurants in general require far less land per customer served than does a sit-down restaurant. This of course lowers the cost of doing business. Such economies enable prices to be kept down, while competition forces them to be kept down.

Just as neighborhood grocery stores, catering to pedestrian customers in central cities during the pre-World War II era, were eclipsed in the postwar world by suburban supermarkets serving customers coming from miles around in their cars, so local fast food restaurants serving customers walking in off the street were surpassed—and often forced out of business—by competition from drive-in fast food restaurants, serving people arriving in automobiles. Although at one time there were hundreds of White Castle hamburger restaurants and only one restaurant operated by the McDonald brothers, by 1996 White Castle's sales were just one percent of McDonald's.

In a society that is constantly evolving, the conditions surrounding a given company or industry are always changing, and not all business leaders are equally quick to spot the changes or grasp their implications. For example, the changing age-structure of the American population created a huge market for hamburgers as the baby boom generation reached adolescence and young adulthood. The number of Americans aged 18 to 24 years nearly doubled between 1960 and 1980, but then began to drop. Accordingly, the total number of hamburgers sold in the United States eventually dropped for the first time in 1989, as baby boomers began reaching the ages when many people start going to salad bars and upscale restaurants. Such demographic changes, combined with a growing emphasis on the calorie and fat content of foods, and what the *Washington Post* characterized as a "savage price war with competitor Burger King" all took an economic toll on McDonald's. In 2002, the chain had its first quarter operating at a loss—$390 million in the red—since McDonald's became a public corporation back in 1965. *The Economist* attributed this to the "top management" at McDonald's being "long-time insiders, shaped by the previous, out-of-date strategy." If so, it would not be the first time that a formula for success became a formula for failure when times changed. Only the future will tell. However, what is already clear is that even the most successful businesses cannot rest on their past achievements.

The economic pressures to keep abreast of changes in the industry, the economy and the society force business owners and managers to seek a wide range of knowledge, going beyond the internal management of their own enterprises. Among the responses to this imperative have been trade associations, which provide highly detailed data on what is happening in their respective industries. A trade association for hotels, for example, provides detailed statistics on such things as what percentages of what kinds of hotels provide king-size, queen-size, and twin beds, cable television, voice mail, video games in the rooms, ironing boards, written material in foreign languages, and even what percentage of what kinds of hotels provide liquid soap in their bathrooms.

An individual hotel needs this kind of information because it competes with other hotels, and cannot afford to fall behind in what it provides to the public. Small economy motels do not need to match everything provided by large luxury resorts, but a given small motel cannot afford to fall too far behind other small motels and still expect to survive.

LEADERSHIP

Given the importance of the human factor and the variability among people—or even with the same person at different ages—it can hardly be surprising that dramatic changes in the relative positions of businesses have been the norm. In the nineteenth century, Montgomery Ward was the biggest retailer in the country at a time when Richard Sears was just a young railroad agent who sold watches on the side. Yet the small company that Sears founded grew over the years to eventually become several times the size of Montgomery Ward—and it outlasted the demise of its rival in 2001, when the latter closed its doors for the last time under its more recent name, Ward's department stores. Differences in management had much to do with the different fates of these two companies, long after both Aaron Montgomery Ward and Richard Warren Sears were gone.

Some business leaders are very good at some aspects of management and very weak in other aspects. The success of the business then depends on which aspects happen to be crucial at the particular time. Sometimes two executives with very different skills and weaknesses combine to produce a very successful management team, whereas either one of them might have failed completely if operating alone. Ray Kroc, founder of the McDonald's chain, was a genius at operating details and may well have known more about hamburgers, milk shakes, and French fries than any other human being—and there is a lot to know—but he was out of his depth in complex financial operations. These matters were handled by Harry Sonneborn, who was an innovative genius whose financial improvisations rescued the company from the brink of bankruptcy more than once during its rocky early years. But Sonneborn didn't even eat hamburgers, much less have any interest in how they were made or marketed. However, as a team, Kroc and Sonneborn made McDonald's one of the leading corporations in the world.

Some executives are very successful during one era in the country's evolution, or during one period in their own lives, and very ineffective at a later time. Sewell Avery, for example, was for many years a highly successful and widely praised leader of U.S. Gypsum and then of Montgomery Ward. Yet his last years were marked by public criticism and controversy over the way he ran Montgomery Ward, and by a bitter fight for control of the company that he was regarded as mismanaging. When Avery resigned as chief executive officer, the value of Montgomery Ward's stock rose immediately. Under his leadership, Montgomery Ward had put aside so many millions of dollars as a cushion against an economic downturn that *Forbes* magazine called it "a bank with a store front." Meanwhile, rivals like Sears were using their money to expand into new markets.

When an industry or a sector of the economy is undergoing rapid change through new ways of doing business, sometimes the leaders of the past find it hardest to break the mold of their previous experience. For example, when the fast food revolution burst forth in the 1950s, existing leaders in restaurant franchises such as Howard Johnson were very unsuccessful in trying to compete with upstarts like McDonald's. Even when Howard Johnson set up imitations of the new fast food restaurants under the name Howard Johnson Jr., these imitations were unable to compete successfully, because they carried over into the fast food business approaches and practices that had been successful in conventional restaurants, but which slowed down operations too much to be successful in the new fast food sector, where rapid turnover with inexpensive food was the key to profits.

Selecting managers can be as chancy as any other aspects of a business. Only by trial and error did the new McDonald's franchise chain discover back in the 1950s what kinds of people were most successful at running their restaurants. The first few franchisees were people with business experience who did very poorly. The first two really successful McDonald's franchisees—who were *very* successful—were a working class married couple who drained their life savings in order to go into business for themselves. They were so financially strained at the beginning that they even had trouble coming up with the $100 needed to put into the cash register on their opening day, so as to be able to make change. But they ended up millionaires.

Other working class people who put everything they owned on the line to open a McDonald's restaurant also succeeded on a grand scale, even when they had no experience in running a restaurant or managing a business. When McDonald's set up its own company-owned restaurants, they did not succeed nearly as well as restaurants owned by people whose own life's savings were at stake. But there was no way to know this in advance.

Neither individuals nor companies are successful forever. Death alone guarantees turnover in management. An A & P executive during its declining years summarized its problems by saying: "The simple fact is that A & P had only one major management problem—the company was unable to replace Mr. John," the name long used inside the company for John Hartford, the last member of the founding family to run A & P. The decline of A & P began with his death. His successors could not simply continue his policies, for the whole retail grocery industry and the society around it were changing rapidly. "You cannot run a retail business from memory," John Hartford himself once remarked. What was needed after his death were not the particular policies and practices that were geared to his day. What was needed was the same kind of foresight, dedication, and imagination that had raised A & P to its pinnacle in the first place—and such talents are not readily available, certainly not continuously and indefinitely in one company.

Like so many other things, running a business looks easy from the outside. On the eve of the Bolshevik revolution, V. I. Lenin declared that "accounting and control" were the key factors in running an enterprise and that capitalism had already "reduced" the administration of businesses to "extraordinarily simple operations" that "any literate person can perform"—that is, "supervising and recording, knowledge of the four rules of arithmetic, and issuing appropriate receipts." Such "exceedingly simple operations of registration, filing and checking" could, according to Lenin, "easily be performed" by people receiving ordinary workmen's wages.

After just a few years in power, however, Lenin confronted a very different—and very bitter—reality. He himself wrote of a "fuel crisis" which "threatens to disrupt all Soviet work," of economic "ruin, starvation, and devastation" in the country and even admitted that peasant uprisings had become "a common occurrence" under Communist rule. In short, the economic functions which had seemed so easy and simple before having to perform them now loomed menacingly difficult.

Belatedly, Lenin saw a need for people "who are versed in the art of administration" and admitted that "there is nowhere we can turn to for such people except the old class"—that is, the capitalist businessmen. In his address to the 1920 Communist Party Congress, Lenin warned his comrades: "Opinions on corporate management are all too frequently imbued with a spirit of sheer ignorance, an anti-expert bias." The apparent simplicities of just three years earlier now required experts. Thus began Lenin's New Economic Policy, which allowed more market activity, and under which the economy began to revive.

KNOWLEDGE AND DECISIONS

Knowledge is one of the scarcest of all resources. Glib generalities abound, but specific hard facts about particular places and particular things at particular times that are relevant to economic decisions are something entirely different. In some respects, governments are able to assemble vast amounts of knowledge, but the kind of knowledge involved is often in the form of statistical generalities or verbal generalities known as "expertise," which are no substitute for the kind of knowledge that someone in the middle of a particular economic situation has.

Agriculture is especially difficult for a government agency to plan because of the amount of highly specific knowledge required. The qualities of the soil can vary significantly on a single acre, much less on a whole farm or on all the farms spread out across a nation. Someone sitting on a central planning board in a distant capital city cannot know where on a given farm it would be better to grow carrots and where wheat would better suit local conditions of weather, soil, and insects. Without having a minutely detailed map of the country—which would itself probably cover several square miles—they would have little chance of deciding which farms would have land best suited for which crops.

Moreover, the products of agriculture are more perishable than the products of industry. Central planners may be able to look at official documents that tell them how many tons of what kind of steel exist in which warehouses around the country, but strawberries would have spoiled before any such nationwide data could be collected. Specific knowledge is one of the scarcest of all resources, regardless of how many people there may be who can talk in glib generalities. The net result of all this is that even countries which have long been food exporters often begin to have difficulty feeding themselves after the government has taken control of agriculture. This has happened repeatedly over the centuries and in many countries, among people of every race, and under governments ranging from democracies to totalitarian dictatorships.

Even the centrally planned economies of the Soviet Union and the Soviet bloc in Eastern Europe ended up having to allow a larger role for individual farming decisions, made by farmers guided by prices and sales, than they would permit in industry. Nevertheless, they did not permit a fully free market in agriculture and so ended up repeatedly being forced to import large amounts of food to feed their populations. Ironically, many of these countries in the Soviet bloc, including Russia and the Ukraine, had been large exporters of food for centuries before the Communists took power and took control of agriculture. In the last peacetime year of the czarist regime, 1913, Russia exported more than 9 million tons of grain.

While central planning has an unimpressive record in industry as well, the fact that its agricultural failures are usually far worse, and more often catastrophic, suggests the crucial role of knowledge. Industrial products and industrial production processes have a far greater degree of uniformity than is

found in agriculture. Orders from Moscow on how to make steel in Vladivostok had more chances of achieving their goal than orders from Moscow
on how to grow carrots or strawberries in Vladivostok.

One of the most dangerous powers of any government, democratic or
despotic, is the power to foreclose knowledge from affecting decisions. Given
that most specific knowledge is widely scattered in fragments among vast
numbers of human beings, decisions made by any manageably small number
of government planners is likely to be based on far less knowledge than is
available in the society as a whole. Yet, once the government's decisions have
been turned into laws and policies, it no longer matters whether the beliefs
on which they were based are true or false. Power trumps truth. The economic history of the Soviet Union is a monument to counterproductive policies behind widespread poverty in one of the most richly endowed countries
on the face of the earth.

While many examples of the difficulties faced by government planning of
economic activity have come from the Soviet Union, similar results have
marked the history of similar efforts in other countries. One of the classic
disasters of government planning involved the British government's attempts
to grow peanuts in colonial Rhodesia after World War II. Yet ordinary farmers around the world had been deciding for generations where and how to
grow peanuts, each on his own particular land, whose individual characteris-
tics were known directly from personal experience. Even a single acre of land
usually has variations in its chemical composition and its slope, which determines how water runs off after a rainfall, and may vary as well in the degree
to which is it shaded by trees, hills, or other things. All this affects what will
grow best where.

No officials sitting in London could know land in Africa so intimately.
Even a trip to Rhodesia by "experts" could not find out the widely varying
qualities of the soil from place to place the way each farmer could on his own
plot of land, much less understand all the insects, birds, animals, and rainfall
patterns in various localities and what effect they might have on the peanut
crop. Yet even an illiterate farmer would almost automatically know such
things from experience on his own farm.

Theoretically, the experts could have asked each individual farmer in
Rhodesia about such things. But, aside from the improbability of experts
with university degrees deferring to farmers with much less formal schooling, the accurate transmission of knowledge would depend crucially on how
articulate and precise these farmers were in what they said. Since verbal precision is hardly universal, even among highly educated people, this would be

a very chancy way to gather information. A price-coordinated economy does not depend on anything so fragile. Each farmer decides individually whether or not to grow peanuts—and how many—at the prices that peanuts can be sold for in the marketplace. These prices are a much more accurate means of communication because each farmer and each buyer of peanuts knows that one mistake in weighing all the various factors can spell economic disaster. When it is no longer a question of talking to strangers, but of protecting your own economic future, there should be no surprise that markets generally work better than government planning.

In the Soviet Union as well, what was lacking was not expertise but highly specific knowledge. There were Soviet economists who were as much aware of general economic principles as Western economists were and highly trained experts on various aspects of agriculture. What the U.S.S.R. did not have were decision-making individuals with the same range of highly specific hard facts about each particular farm as an individual farm owner would have at his disposal. Power and knowledge were separated in their central planning system, as in all centrally planned economies.

Commercial and industrial enterprise managers knew what the specific equipment, personnel, and supplies at their disposal could and could not do, but central planners in Moscow did not—and it was the central planners who held the power to make the ultimate decisions. Nor could the central planners possibly be sufficiently knowledgeable about all the industries, technologies, and products under their command to be able to determine what would be best for each, independently of what the respective enterprise managers told them. Central planners could be skeptical of the self-serving statements and demands of the enterprise managers, but skepticism is not knowledge. Moreover, changing circumstances would almost inevitably be known first to the local managers on the scene and often much later, if at all, to the central planners, who had far too many industries and products to oversee to be able keep up with day-to-day changes for them all.

A price-coordinated economy may have no more total knowledge over all than a centrally-planned economy, but that knowledge is distributed very differently, as is decision-making power. When the owner of a gas station located on a highway in a capitalist country sees that the highways is being torn up for repairs, he knows to order less gasoline than usual from his supplier, because there will not be nearly as much traffic going past his station as before, at least until the repairs are completed.

This local gas station owner does not need the permission of anybody to change how much gasoline he orders or what hours he will stay open. The knowledge and the power are combined in the same person. Moreover, that person is operating under the incentives and constraints inherent in the prospect of profits and the threat of losses, rather than under orders from distant bureaucrats. Nor is this peculiar to gas stations. The same instant and local decision-making power by those with the facts before their eyes is common throughout a price-coordinated market economy. That is one of its advantages over a centrally-planned economy and one of the factors behind the enormous differences in results between the two kinds of economies.

Agents

As a scarce resource, knowledge can be bought and sold in various ways in a market economy. The hiring of agents is essentially the purchase of the agent's knowledge to guide one's own decisions. Real estate agents commonly charge 6 percent of the sale price of a home and literary agents typically charge 15 percent of a writer's royalties. Why would a writer surrender 15 percent of his royalties, unless 85 percent of what the agent can get for him is worth more than 100 percent of what he can get for himself? And why would a publisher be willing to pay more to an agent than to a writer for the same manuscript? Similarly, why would a home-owner accept 6 percent less for his house when sold through a real estate agent, unless the agent could either get a higher price or a quicker sale, both of which amount to the same thing, since delay and its accompanying stresses are both costs to the home-owner?

Let's go back to a basic principle of economics: The same physical object does not necessarily have the same value to different people. This applies to an author's manuscript as well as to a house, a painting or an autograph from a rock star. What a literary agent knows is where a particular manuscript is likely to have its greatest value. If it is a cookbook, the agent knows which publishers and which editors have the knowledge and the connections to promote such a book in places that are very interested in such things— gourmet magazines, cooking programs on television, and the like. This cookbook would be far more valuable to such editors and publishers than to others who specialize in technology, social issues, or other subjects, or to editors whose knowledge of food does not extend much beyond hamburgers and fried chicken. Even if an agent is not able to get any more money out of a given publisher than a writer could have gotten, the agent knows which publishers are most likely to pay top dollar for a given kind of book, because that particular publisher can probably sell more copies.

A real estate agent is similarly more knowledgeable than the average home-owner as to the channels through which a given home can be marketed most quickly and for the highest sale price. Often there are little defects in the home that need to be corrected, or cosmetic changes that need to be made, before the house goes on the market. An agent who keeps up with changing fashions in homes and their furnishings is not only more likely to know what these things are but also whether or to what extent money spent upgrading the house will be recouped in a higher sale price, or whether it is better to sell the house "as is" as a bargain "fixer-upper." The agent is also more likely to be knowledgeable as to which particular contractors are more reliable or more reasonable in price for doing whatever repairs or remodelling are called for, as well as which financial institutions are best to deal with for the buyer and seller of this particular house. Therefore, the same house is likely to bring in more money when sold through a real estate agent, just as a writer's manuscript is likely to sell for more through a literary agent.

Franchises

Knowledge is shared in both directions when hotels, restaurants and other businesses are franchised. The knowledge offered by the chain that does the franchising is based on its experience with similar businesses in various locations around the country. It is also likely to be more knowledgeable about where and how to advertise and how to deal with suppliers. However, the local franchisee is likely to be more knowledgeable about things that only someone on the scene can know—the local labor market, changes in the surrounding community and of course all the details that have to be monitored on the premises day to day.

Chains and franchises are not synonymous. The first great hamburger chain—the chain that put the hamburger on the map in the 1920s—was the White Castle chain, which owned all of its hundreds of restaurants. Its top management, however, had much local experience before going regional and then national—and they made many visits to their local outlets to keep in touch. The era of the franchised restaurant chain began with Howard Johnson in the 1930s and the heyday of franchised hamburger stands began with McDonald's in the 1950s. By and large, franchises have been more successful in these fields. By 1990, more than one-third of all revenues from retail sales of goods and services in the United States went to franchise outlets. Nearly three-quarters of all revenues from hotels and motels were earned by those affiliated with chains.

MARKET VERSUS NON-MARKET ECONOMIES

The fact that profits are contingent on efficiency in producing what consumers want, at a price that consumers are willing to pay—and that losses are an ever-present threat if a business fails to provide that—explains much of the economic prosperity found in economies that operate under free market competition. Profits as a realized end-result are crucial to the individual business, but it is the *prospect* of profits—and the threat of losses—that is crucial to the functioning of the economy as a whole. For the economy as a whole, profits are a minor item, about 10 percent of what the American economy produces, for example. But it is a major item as an incentive to efficiency in producing the other 90 percent.

There are many other possible ways of allocating resources, and many of these alternatives are particularly attractive to those with political power. However, none of these alternative ways of organizing an economy has matched the track record of economies where prices direct what resources go where and in what quantities.

Anyone who saw East Berlin and West Berlin, during the years when communism prevailed in the eastern part of the city and a market economy in the rest of it, could not help noticing the drastic contrast between the prosperity of West Berlin and the poverty in East Berlin. Indeed, it was hard to avoid being shocked by it, especially since people of the same race, language, culture and history lived in both parts of the same city.

Monopoly is the enemy of efficiency, whether under capitalism or socialism. The difference between the two systems is that monopoly is the norm under socialism. Even in a mixed economy, with some economic activities being carried out by government and others being carried out by private industry, the government's activities are typically monopolies, while those in the private marketplace are typically activities carried out by rival enterprises.

Thus, when a hurricane, flood, or other natural disaster strikes some part of the United States, emergency aid usually comes both from the Federal Emergency Management Agency (FEMA) and from private insurance companies whose customers' homes and property have been damaged or destroyed. FEMA has been notoriously slower and less efficient than the private insurance companies. Allstate Insurance cannot afford to be slower in getting money into the hands of its policy-holders than State Farm Insurance is in getting money to the people who hold its policies. Not only would existing customers in the disaster area be likely to switch insurance companies if one dragged its feet in getting money to them, while their neighbors received substantial advances to tide them over from a different insurance company, word of any such difference would spread like wildfire across the country, causing millions of people elsewhere to switch billions of dollars worth of insurance business from the less efficient company to the more efficient one. A government agency, however, faces no such pressure. No matter how much FEMA may be criticized or ridiculed for its failure to get aid to disaster victims in a timely fashion, there is no rival government agency that these people can turn to for the same service. Moreover, the people who run these agencies are paid according to fixed salary schedules, not by how quickly or how well they serve people hit by disaster.

Inertia is common to people under both capitalism and socialism. In the early twentieth century, both Sears and Montgomery Ward were reluctant to begin operating out of stores, after decades of great success selling exclusively from their mail order catalogs. It was only when the 1920s brought competition from chain stores that cut into their profits and caused red ink to start appearing on the bottom line that they had no choice but to become chain stores themselves. (In 1920, Montgomery Ward lost nearly $10 million and Sears was $44 million in debt.) Under socialism, they could have remained mail order retailers and there would have been little incentive for the government to pay to set up rival chain stores to complicate everyone's life.

Henry Ford likewise wanted to keep on doing what he had always done—producing the same standard model car, year after year, painted just one color (black). But, when a new company named General Motors started changing the styling of their cars and painting them different colors, the Ford Motor company started losing customers and GM replaced Ford as the number one auto maker in the industry. Only then did Ford automobiles begin to change their styling and become available in whatever colors the customers wanted.

Socialist and capitalist economies differ not only in the quantity of output they produce but also in the quality. Everything from cars and cameras to restaurant service and airline service were of notoriously low quality in the Soviet Union. Nor was this a happenstance. The incentives are radically different when the producer has to satisfy the consumer, in order to survive financially, than when the test of survivability is carrying out production quotas set by central planners. The consumer is going to look not only at quantity but quality. But a central planning commission is too overwhelmed with the millions of products they oversee to be able to monitor much more than gross output.

That this low quality is a result of incentives, rather than being due to traits peculiar to Russians or other Eastern Europeans, is shown by the quality deterioration that has taken place in the United States or Western Europe when free market prices are replaced by rent control or other forms of price controls and government allocation. Both excellent service and terrible service can occur in the same country, when there are different incentives, as a salesman in India found:

> Every time I ate in a roadside cafe or dhaba, my rice plate would arrive in three minutes flat. If I wanted an extra roti, it would arrive in thirty seconds. In a saree shop, the shopkeeper showed me a hundred sarees even if I did not buy a single one. After I left, he would go through the laborious and thankless job of folding back each saree, one at a time, and placing it back on the shelf. In contrast, when I went to buy a railway ticket, pay my telephone bill, or withdraw money from my nationalized bank, I was treated or regarded as a nuisance, and made to wait in a long queue. The bazaar offered outstanding service because the shopkeeper knew that his existence depended on his customer. If he was courteous and offered quality products at a competitive price, his customer rewarded him. If not, his customers deserted him for the shop next door. There was no competition in the railways, telephones, or banks, and their employees could never place the customer in the center.

London's *The Economist* magazine likewise pointed out that in India one can "watch the tellers in a state-owned bank chat amongst themselves while the line of customers stretches out on to the street." Comparisons of government-run institutions with privately-run institutions often overlook the fact that ownership and control are not the only differences between them. Government-run institutions are almost always monopolies, while privately-run institutions usually have competitors. Competing government institutions performing the same function are referred to negatively as "duplication" or "needless duplication." Whether the frustrated customers waiting in line at a government-run bank would consider an alternative bank to be needless duplication is another question.

While some businesses can and do give poor service or cut corners on quality in a free market, they do so at the risk of their survival. The great financial success stories in American industry have often involved companies almost fanatical about maintaining the reputation of their products, even when these products have been quite inexpensive.

McDonald's built its reputation on a standardized hamburger and maintained quality by having its own inspectors make unannounced visits to its meat suppliers in the middle of the night, to see what was being put into the meat it was buying. Colonel Sanders was notorious for showing up unexpectedly at Kentucky Fried Chicken restaurants. If he didn't like the way the chickens were being cooked, he would dump them all into a garbage can, put on an apron, and proceed to cook some chickens himself, to demonstrate how he wanted it done. His protégé Dave Thomas later followed similar practices when he created his own chain of Wendy's hamburger stands. Although Colonel Sanders and Dave Thomas could not be everywhere in a nationwide chain, no local franchise owner could take a chance on seeing his profits being thrown into a garbage can by the head honcho of the chain.

When the processed food industry first began in nineteenth century America, it was common for producers to adulterate food items with less expensive fillers. Horseradish, for example, was often sold in colored bottles, to conceal the adulteration. But when Henry J. Heinz began selling unadulterated horseradish in clear bottles, this gave him a decisive advantage over his competitors, who fell by the wayside while the Heinz company went on to become one of the enduring giants of American industry, still in business in the twenty-first century. Similarly with the British food processing company Crosse & Blackwell, which sold quality foods not only in Britain but in the United States as well. It too remained one of the giants of the industry through the twentieth century and into the twenty first.

Quality control is of course even more important to financial success with more expensive products and services. The producers of Linhof cameras— made in Germany and costing thousands of dollars each—not only buy their lenses from the world's leading optical companies, they also subject each individual lens put on one of their cameras to their own tests and standards, even though these lenses have already passed tests performed by the manufacturers. Linhof's standards are sufficiently more stringent that an identical make and model of lens on a Linhof camera sells for a higher price, both new and used, than the same lens sells for when bought independently. Even if the lens is being bought to be put on another camera, the fact that it came off a Linhof brings a higher price than the identical model of lens by the identical manufacturer that did not come from a Linhof.

Behind all of this is the basic fact that a business is selling not only a physical product, but also the reputation which surrounds that product. Motorists traveling in an unfamiliar part of the country are more likely to turn into a hamburger stand that has a McDonald's or Wendy's sign on it than one that does not. That reputation translates into dollars and cents—or, in this case, millions and billions of dollars. People with that kind of money at stake are unlikely to be very tolerant of anyone who would compromise their reputation. Ray Kroc, the founder of the McDonald's chain, would explode in anger if he found a McDonald's parking lot littered. His franchisees were expected to keep not only their own premises free of litter, but also to see that there was no McDonald's litter on the streets within a radius of two blocks of their restaurants.[1]

When speaking of quality in this context, what matters is the kind of quality that is relevant to the particular clientele being served. Hamburgers and fried chicken may not be regarded by others as either gourmet food or health food, nor can a nationwide chain mass-producing such meals reach quality levels achievable by more distinctive, fancier, and pricier restaurants. What the chain can do is assure quality within the limits expected by their particular customers.

While a market economy is essentially an impersonal mechanism for allocating resources, some of the most successful businesses have prospered by their attention to the personal element. One of the reasons for the success of the F. W. Woolworth retail chain was Woolworth's insistence on the importance of courtesy to the customers. This came from his own painful memories of store clerks treating him like dirt when he was a poverty-stricken farm boy who went into stores to buy or look. Ray Kroc's zealous insistence on maintaining McDonald's reputation for cleanliness paid off at a crucial juncture when he desperately needed a loan to stay in business, for the financier who toured McDonald's restaurants said later: "If the parking lots had been dirty, if the help had grease stains on their aprons, and if the food wasn't good, McDonald's never would have gotten the loan." Similarly, Kroc's good relations with his suppliers—people who sold cups, milk, napkins, etc., to

---

[1] A history of McDonald's noted: "On his frequent visits to restaurants, Kroc commonly picked up waste paper on the lot before going inside to see the franchisee." In later years he hired a staff of inspectors and evaluators who went around to the restaurants. One of these inspectors, named Gus Karos, "initiated a practice of taking photographs" when there were dirty units. "When he noticed McDonald's litter strewn about the yards in the neighborhood of a store in New Jersey, it was obvious that the operator had ignored the system's requirement for policing the area within a two-block radius of the store. Karos picked up all the litter he could carry, marched into the franchisee's office, and dumped the trash on his desk." John F. Love, *McDonald's: Behind the Arches*, revised edition, p. 147.

McDonald's—had saved him before when these suppliers agreed to lend him money to bail him out of an earlier financial crisis.

What is called "capitalism" might more accurately be called consumerism. It is the consumers who call the tune, and those capitalists who want to remain capitalists have to learn to dance to it. The twentieth century began with high hopes for replacing the competition of the marketplace by a more efficient and more humane economy, planned and controlled by government in the interests of the people. However, by the end of the century, all such efforts were so thoroughly discredited by their actual results in countries around the world that even Communist nations abandoned central planning, while socialist governments in democratic countries began selling off government-run enterprises, whose losses were a heavy burden to the taxpayers.

Privatization was embraced as a principle by such conservative governments as those of Prime Minister Margaret Thatcher in Britain and President Ronald Reagan in the United States. But the most decisive evidence for the efficiency of the marketplace was that even those who were philosophically opposed to capitalism turned back towards it after seeing what happens when industry and commerce operate without the guidance of prices, profits and losses.

WINNERS AND LOSERS

Many people who appreciate the prosperity created by market economies may nevertheless lament the fact that particular individuals, groups, industries, or regions of the country do not share fully in the general economic advances, and some may even be worse off than before. Political leaders or candidates are especially likely to deplore the inequity of it all and to propose various government actions to "correct" the situation.

Whatever the merits or demerits of various political proposals, what must be kept in mind when evaluating them is that the good fortunes and misfortunes of different sectors of the economy may be closely related as cause and effect—and that preventing bad effects may prevent good effects. It was not accidental that Smith Corona was losing millions of dollars on its typewriters while Dell was making millions on its computers. It was not accidental that Safeway surged to the top of the grocery business while A & P fell from its peak to virtual oblivion. It was not accidental that coal-mining regions suffered economic declines with the rise of alternative fuel sources or that the number of pay telephones declined as more people acquired their own cellular phones.

The efficient allocation of scarce resources which have alternative uses means that some must lose their ability to use those resources, in order that others can gain the ability to use them. Smith-Corona had to be *prevented* from using scarce resources, including both materials and labor, to make typewriters, when those resources could be used to produce computers that the public wanted more. Nor was this a matter of anyone's fault. No matter how fine the typewriters made by Smith-Corona were or how skilled and conscientious its employees, typewriters were no longer what the public wanted after they had the option to achieve the same end result—and more—with computers.

Scarcity implies that resources must be taken from some places, in order to go to other places. Few individuals or businesses are going to want to give up what they have been used to doing, especially if they have been successful at it, for the greater good of society as a whole. But, in one way or another, under any economic or political system, they are going to have to be forced to relinquish resources and change what they themselves are doing, if rising standards of living are to be achieved and sustained.

The financial pressures of the free market are just one of the ways in which this can be done. Kings or commissars could instead simply order individuals and enterprises to change from doing A to doing B. No doubt other ways of pursuing the same goals are possible, with varying degrees of effectiveness and efficiency. What is crucial, however, is that it must be done. Put differently, the fact that some people, regions, or industries are being "left behind" or are not getting their "fair share" of the general prosperity is not necessarily a problem with a political solution, as abundant as such proposed solutions may be, especially in election years.

However more pleasant and uncomplicated it might be if all sectors of the economy grew simultaneously at the same lockstep pace, that has never been the reality in any dynamic economy. As an entrepreneur in India put it:

> The history of how country after country went from poverty to prosperity over the past two hundred years teaches us that the transformation was generally powered by one sector, which became the engine of its economic growth. In Britain, it was textiles; in the United States, the industrial revolution was led by the railways. Timber and timber products were responsible for Sweden's take-off; milk and dairy products did the same for Denmark.

PART III:
WORK AND PAY

Chapter 9

Productivity and Pay

Genius begins great works; labor alone finishes them.

-Joseph Joubert

In discussing the allocation of resources, we have so far been concerned largely with inanimate resources. But people are part of the economy too, and not just as consumers. People are a key part of the inputs which produce output. Most people are not volunteers, so they must be either forced to work or paid to work, since the work has to be done in any case, if we are to live at all, much less enjoy the various amenities that go into our modern standard of living. In a free society, people are paid to work.

How much they are paid depends on many things. Stories about the astronomical pay of professional athletes, movie stars, or chief executives of corporations often cause journalists and others to question how much this or that person is "really" worth.

Fortunately, since we know from Chapter 2 that there is no such thing as "real" worth, we can save all the time and energy that others put into such unanswerable questions. Instead, we can ask a more down-to-earth question: What determines how much people get paid for their work? To this question there is a very down-to-earth answer: Supply and Demand. However, that is just the beginning. Why does supply and demand cause one individual to earn more than another?

Workers would obviously like to get the highest pay possible and employers would like to pay the least possible. Only where there is overlap between what is offered and what is acceptable can anyone be hired. But why does that overlap take place at a pay rate that is several times as high for an engineer as for a messenger?

Messengers would of course like to be paid what engineers are paid, but there is too large a supply of people capable of being messengers to force the employer to raise his offer to that level. Because it takes a long time to train an engineer and not everyone is capable of mastering such training, there is no such abundance of engineers relative to the demand. That is the supply side of the story. But what determines the demand for labor? What determines the limit of what an employer is willing to pay?

It is not merely the fact that engineers are scarce that makes them valuable. It is what an engineer can add to a company's earnings that makes an employer willing to bid for his services—and sets the limit to how high the bids can go. An engineer who added $100,000 to a company's earnings and asked for a $200,000 salary would not be hired. On the other hand, if the engineer added a quarter of a million dollars to a company's earnings, it would obviously pay to hire him at $200,000—provided there were no other engineers who would do the same thing for a lower salary.

The term "productivity" is sometimes used loosely to describe an employee's contribution to a company's earnings. The problem is that this word is also defined in other ways and sometimes the implication is left that each worker has a certain productivity that is inherent in that worker, rather than being dependent on surrounding circumstances as well. A worker using the latest modern equipment can produce more output than the very same worker employed in another firm whose equipment is not quite as up-to-date or whose management does not have things organized as well. For example, Japanese-owned cotton mills in China during the 1930s paid higher wages than Chinese-owned cotton mills there, but the Japanese-run mills had lower labor costs per unit of output because they had higher output per worker. This was not due to different equipment—they both used the same machines—but to more efficient management brought over from Japan.

Similarly, in the early twenty-first century, an international consulting firm found that American-owned manufacturing enterprises in Britain had far higher productivity than British-owned manufacturing enterprises. The British magazine *The Economist* said that "British industrial companies have underperformed their American counterparts badly," that when it comes to "economy in the use of time and materials," fewer than 40 percent of British manufacturers "have paid any attention to this" and that "Britain's top engineering graduates prefer to work for foreign-owned companies." In short, lower productivity in British-owned companies reflects management practices, even when productivity is measured in terms of labor. In general, the productivity of any input in the production process depends on the quantity and quality of other inputs, as well as its own.

The same principle applies outside what we normally think of as economic activities. In baseball, a slugger gets more chances to hit home runs if he is batting ahead of another slugger. But, if the batter hitting after him is not much of a home run threat, pitchers are more likely to walk the slugger in a tight situation, so that he will get fewer opportunities to hit home runs over the course of a season.

During Ted Williams's career, for example, he had one of the highest percentages of home runs—in proportion to his times at bat—in the history of baseball. Yet he had only one season in which he hit as many as 40 homers, because he was walked as often as 162 times a season—averaging more than one walk per game during the era of the 154-game season. By contrast, when Roger Maris hit 61 home runs in 1961, breaking the record at that time, he was walked less than a hundred times because Mickey Mantle was batting right after him, and Mantle hit 54 home runs that season. There was no percentage in walking Maris to pitch to Mantle with one more man on base. Maris' productivity as a home-run hitter was greater because he batted with Mickey Mantle in the on-deck circle.

In virtually all jobs, the quality of the equipment, management and other workers goes into determining a given worker's productivity. Movie stars like to have good supporting actors, good make-up artists and good directors, all of whom enhance the star's performance. Scholars depend heavily on their research assistants, and generals rely on their staffs, as well as their troops, to win battles.

Whatever the source of a given individual's productivity, that productivity determines the upper limit of how far an employer will go in bidding for that person's services. That is the demand side of the equation.

Employers seldom bid as much as they would if they had to, because there are other individuals willing and able to supply the same services for less. By the same token, consumers would pay a lot more for their food than they do, if there were no competing sellers and their only choice was to pay what a monopolist charged or starve. In short, it is the *combination* of supply and demand which determines pay, as it determines the prices of goods and services in general.

PAY DIFFERENCES

Wages and salaries serve the same economic purposes as other prices—that is, they guide the utilization of scarce resources which have alternative uses. Yet because these scarce resources are human beings, we tend to look on wages and salaries differently. Often we ask questions that are quite emotionally powerful, even if they are logically meaningless. For example: Are the wages "fair"? Are the workers "exploited"? Is this "a living wage"?

Such questions seldom get asked about the prices of inanimate things, such as a can of peas or a share of stock in General Motors. But people are believed to be entitled to pay that is "fair," even if no one can define what that means. "Exploitation" and "a living wage" are likewise emotionally powerful expressions without concrete meanings. If a worker is living, how can he be receiving less than "a living wage"[1]—unless he is, as some have said thoughtlessly, "living below subsistence"?

No one likes to see fellow human beings living in poverty and squalor, and many are prepared to do something about it, as shown by the vast billions of dollars that donated to a wide range of charities every year, on top of the additional billions spent by governments in an attempt to better the condition of less fortunate people. These socially important activities occur alongside an economy coordinated by prices, but the two things serve different purposes. Attempts to make prices, including the prices of people's labor and talents, be something other than signals to guide resources to their most valued uses, make those prices less effective for their basic purpose, on which the prosperity of the whole society depends. Ultimately, it is economic prosperity that makes it possible for billions of dollars to be devoted to helping the less fortunate.

Income "Distribution"

Nothing is more straightforward and easy to understand than the fact that some people earn more than others, for a variety of reasons. Some people are simply older than others, for example, and their additional years have given them opportunities to acquire more experience, skills, formal education and

---

[1] Sometimes a "living wage" is defined as a wage that will support a family of four— which is to say that one person is to make a decision (to have a family) and another is to pay the price of that decision by paying whatever it takes to support that family.

on-the-job-training—all of which allows them to do a given job more efficiently or to take on more complicated jobs that would be overwhelming for
a beginner or for someone with limited experience or training. With the
passing years, older individuals may also become more knowledgeable about
job opportunities, while increasing numbers of other people become more
aware of them and their individual abilities, leading to offers of new jobs or
promotions. These and other commonsense reasons for income differences
among individuals are often lost sight of in abstract discussions of the am-
biguous term "income distribution."

Although people in the top income brackets and the bottom income
brackets—"the rich" and "the poor," as they are often called—may be discussed as if they were different classes of people, often they are the very same
people at different stages of their lives. An absolute majority of those Americans who were in the bottom 20 percent in income in 1975 were also in the
top 20 percent at some point over the next 16 years. This is not surprising.
After 16 years, people usually have had 16 years more experience, perhaps
including on-the-job training or formal education. Those in business or the
professions have had 16 years in which to build up a clientele. It would be
surprising if they were not able to earn more money as a result. It is not uncommon for most of the people in the top 5 percent of income-earners to be
45 years old and up.

None of this is unique to the United States. A study of eleven European
countries found similar patterns. One-half of the people in Greece and two-
thirds of the people in Holland who were below the poverty line in a given
year had risen above that line within two years. A study in Britain found
similar patterns when following thousands of individuals over a six-year period. At the end of six years, nearly two-thirds of the individuals who were
initially in the bottom 20 percent in income had risen out of that bracket.
Thirty-nine percent moved up and out of it in just one year and only 5 percent remained in the bottom 20 percent in income for the whole six years.
Studies in New Zealand likewise showed significant rises of individuals out
of the bottom 20 percent of income earners in just one year and of course
larger numbers rising out of this bracket over a period of several years. There
are similar patterns in Canada.

When some people are born, live, and die in poverty, while others are
born, live, and die in luxury, that is a very different situation from one in
which young people have not yet reached the income level of older people,
such as their parents. But the kind of statistics often cited in the media, and
even in academia, typically do not distinguish these very different situations.

Moreover, those who publicize such statistics usually proceed as if they are talking about differences between classes rather than differences between age brackets. Because of the movement of people from one income bracket to another over the years, the degree of income inequality over a lifetime is not the same as the degree of income inequality in any given year. A study in New Zealand found that the degree of income inequality over a working lifetime was less than the degree of inequality in *any* given year during those lifetimes.

Much discussion of "the rich" and "the poor"—or of the top or bottom 10 or 20 percent—fail to say just what kinds of incomes qualify to be in these categories. As of 2001, a household income of $84,000 was enough to put those who earned it in the top 20 percent of Americans. Even to make the top 5 percent required a household income of just over $150,000—that is, about $75,000 apiece for a working couple. That is a nice income, but rising to that level after working for decades is hardly a sign of being rich. Even among the truly rich, there is turnover. When *Forbes* magazine ran its first list of the 400 richest Americans in 1982, that list included 14 Rockefellers, 23 du Ponts and 11 Hunts. Twenty years later, the list included 3 Rockefellers, one Hunt and no du Ponts. Incidentally, the nation's 400 richest people lost a total of $80 billion in net worth in one year, which may be one reason for such turnover, in addition to new people like Bill Gates coming along.

Describing people in certain income brackets as "rich" is false for a more fundamental reason: Income and wealth are different things. No matter how much income passes through your hands in a given year, your wealth depends on how much you have accumulated over the years. If you receive a million dollars in a year and spend a million and a half, you are not getting rich. But many frugal people on modest incomes have been found, after their deaths, to have left surprisingly large amounts of wealth to their heirs.

Although there is much talk about "income distribution," most income is of course *not* distributed at all, in the sense in which newspapers or Social Security checks are distributed from some central place. Most income is distributed only in the figurative statistical sense in which there is a distribution of heights in a population—some people being 5 foot 4 inches tall, others 6 foot 2 inches, etc.—but none of these heights was sent out from some central location. Yet it is all too common to read journalists and others discussing how "society" *distributes* its income, rather than saying in plain English that some people make more money than others.

More is involved than a misleading metaphor. Often the very units in which income differences are discussed are as misleading as the metaphor.

Family income or household income are not like individual income. An individual always means the same thing—one person—but the sizes of families and households differ substantially from one time period to another, from one racial or ethnic group to another, and from one income bracket to another. For example, a detailed analysis of U.S. Census data showed that there were 39 million people in the bottom 20 percent of households but 64 million people in the top 20 percent of households. Although the unwary might assume that these quintiles represent dividing the country into "five equal layers," as two well-known economists have misstated it in a popular book, there is nothing equal about those layers. They represent grossly different numbers of people.

Not only do the numbers of people differ considerably between low-income households and high-income households, the proportions of people who work also differ by very substantial amounts between these households. In the year 2000, the top 20 percent of households contained 19 million heads of households who worked, compared to fewer than 8 million heads of households who worked in the bottom 20 percent of households. When it comes to working full-time the year around, even the top 5 percent of households contained more heads of household who worked full-time for 50 or more weeks than did the bottom 20 percent. That is, there were more heads of household *in absolute numbers*—3.9 million versus 3.3 million—working full-time and year-around in the top 5 percent of households compared to the bottom 20 percent. At one time, back in the 1890s, people in the top 10 percent in income worked fewer hours than people in the bottom 10 percent, but that situation has long since reversed.

The sizes of families and households have differed not only from one income bracket to another at a given time, but also have differed over time. These differences are not incidental. They radically change the implications of "income distribution" statistics. For example, real income per American household rose only 6 percent over the entire period from 1969 to 1996, but real per capita income rose 51 percent over the same period. The discrepancy is due to the fact that the average size of families and households was declining during these years, so that smaller households were now earning about the same as larger households had earned a generation earlier.

Rising prosperity was one reason for more people to be able to go set up their own individual households, instead of continuing to live with parents or as roomers elsewhere, or by sharing an apartment with a roommate. Yet these consequences of prosperity generate household statistics that are widely used to suggest that there has been no real economic progress. A

Washington Post writer, for example, declared that "the incomes of most American households have remained stubbornly flat over the past three decades." It might be more accurate to say that some writers have remained stubbornly blind to economic facts. When two people in one household today earn the same total amount of money that three people were earning in one household in the past, that is a 50 percent increase in income per person—even when household income remains the same.

Despite some confused or misleading discussions of "the rich" and "the poor," based on people's transient positions in the income streams, genuinely rich and genuinely poor people exist—people who are going to be living in luxury or in poverty all their lives—but they are much rarer than gross income statistics would suggest. Just as most American "poor" do not stay poor, so most rich Americans were not born rich. Four-fifths of American millionaires earned their fortunes within their own lifetimes, having inherited nothing. Moreover, the genuinely rich are rare, like the genuinely poor. Even if we take a million dollars in net worth as our criterion for being rich, only about 3.5 percent of American households are at that level. This is in fact a fairly modest level, given that net worth counts everything from household goods and clothing to the total amount of money in an individual's pension fund. If we count as genuinely poor that 3 percent of the population which remains in the bottom 20 percent over a period of years, then the genuinely rich and the genuinely poor—put together—add up to a small fraction of the American population. Nevertheless, some political rhetoric might suggest that most people are either "haves" or "have nots."

It is a common but misleading practice to try to determine whether inequality is increasing or decreasing by comparing the incomes of those in the top 20 percent with the incomes of those in the bottom 20 percent. If our concern is the well-being of flesh-and-blood human beings, rather than with statistical categories, then we need to consider not only those who are in given income brackets in a given year but also those who are constantly moving in and out of those brackets from year to year. When an absolute majority of those in the bottom 20 percent in income in 1975 were also in the top 20 percent at some point by 1991, you cannot determine the degree of income inequality between *people* by looking at inequality between income brackets at a given time.

If our concern is with the economic well-being of flesh-and-blood people, as distinguished from statistical comparisons between brackets, then we need to look at real income per capita, because people do not live on percentage shares. They live on real income. Among those individuals who were in the bottom 20 percent in 1975, 98 percent had higher real incomes by 1991 and two-thirds had higher real incomes in 1991 than the average American had back in 1975. Moreover, even when narrowly focusing on income brackets, that fact that the share of the bottom 20 percent of households declined from 4 percent of all income in 1985 to 3.6 percent in 2001 did not prevent the real income of the households in these brackets from rising by thousands of dollars in absolute terms—quite aside from the movement of actual people out of the bottom 20 percent between the two years.

While, in some senses, those who are called "the poor" are not as badly off as instantaneous statistics might suggest, in other respects they are worse off. Those who are poor on a long-term basis and live in poverty-stricken neighborhoods must often pay higher prices for inferior goods and services, because of the higher costs of delivering those goods and services to such neighborhoods. As already noted in Chapters 4 and 6, a suburban supermarket has lower costs of delivering groceries to its customers than does a typical neighborhood store in the inner city, and that translates into higher prices charged to low-income customers than to high-income customers. Being poor is expensive. Fortunately, most people in most modern Western countries do not remain poor very long.

Differences in Skills

Among the many reasons for differences in productivity and pay is that some people have more skills than others. No one is surprised that engineers earn more than messengers or that experienced shipping clerks tend to earn higher pay than inexperienced shipping clerks—and experienced pilots tend to earn more than either. Although workers may be thought of as people who supply labor, what most people supply is not just their ability to engage in physical exertions, but their ability to apply mental proficiency to their tasks. The time when "a strong back and a weak mind" were sufficient for many jobs is long past in most modern economies. Obvious as this may seem, its implications are not equally obvious nor always widely understood.

In those times and places where physical strength and stamina have been the principal work requirements, productivity and pay have tended to reach their peak in the youthful prime of life, with middle-aged laborers receiving less pay or less frequent employment, or both. A premium on physical strength likewise favored male workers over female workers. In some desperately poor countries living close to the edge of subsistence, such as China in times past, the sex differential in performing physical labor was such that it was not uncommon for the poorest people to kill female infants. While a mother was necessary for the family, an additional woman's productivity in arduous farm labor on small plots of land with only primitive tools might not produce enough food to keep her alive, and her drain on the food produced by others would thus threaten the survival of the whole family, at a time when malnutrition and death by starvation were ever-present dangers. One of the many benefits of economic development has been making such desperate and brutal choices unnecessary.

The rising importance of skills and experience relative to physical strength has changed the relative productivities of youth compared to age and of women compared to men. This has been especially so in more recent times, as the power of machines has replaced human strength in industrial societies and as skills have become crucial in high-tech economies. Even within a relatively short span of time, the age at which most people receive their peak earnings has shifted upward.

In 1951, most Americans reached their peak earnings between 35 and 44 years of age, and people in those age brackets earned about half again as much as workers in their early twenties. By 1973, people in the 35 to 44-year-old brackets earned more than double the income of the younger workers. Twenty years later, the peak earnings bracket had moved up to 45 to 54 years of age, and people in those brackets earned more than three times what workers in their early twenties earned.

Meanwhile, the dwindling importance of physical strength also reduced or eliminated the premium for male workers in an ever-widening range of occupations. This did not require all employers to have enlightened self-interest. Those who persisted in paying more for male workers who were not correspondingly more productive were at a competitive disadvantage compared to rival firms that got their work done at lower costs by eliminating the male premium, equalizing the pay of women and men to match their productivities. The most unenlightened or prejudiced employers had higher labor costs, which risked the elimination of their businesses by the ruthlessness of market competition. Thus the pay of women began to equal that of men of similar qualifications even before there were laws mandating equal pay.

While the growing importance of skills tended to reduce economic inequalities between the sexes, it tended to increase the inequality between those with and without skills. Moreover, the rising earnings in general, growing out of a more productive economy with more skilled people, tended to increase the inequality between those who worked regularly and those who did not. As already noted, there are striking differences between the number and proportions of people who work and those who don't as between the top income brackets and the bottom income brackets.

Job Discrimination

While pay differences often reflect differences in skills, experience, or willingness to do hard or dangerous work, they may also reflect discrimination against particular segments of society, such as ethnic minorities, women, lower castes, or other groups. However, in order to determine whether there is discrimination or how severe it is, we need to define what we mean.

Sometimes discrimination is defined as judging individuals from different groups by different standards when hiring, paying or promoting. In its severest form, this can mean refusal to hire at all. "No Irish Need Apply" was a stock phrase in advertisements for many desirable jobs in nineteenth- and early twentieth-century America. Before World War II, many hospitals in the United States would not hire black doctors or Jewish doctors, and some prestigious law firms would not hire anyone who was not a white Protestant male from the upper classes. In other cases, people might be hired from a number of groups, but individuals from different groups were channeled into different jobs.

None of this has been peculiar to the United States or to the modern era. On the contrary, members of different groups have been treated differently in laws and practices all around the world and for thousands of years of recorded history. It is the idea of treating individuals the same, regardless of what group they come from, that is relatively recent as history is measured.

Overlapping with discrimination, and often confused with it, are employment differences based on very substantial differences in skills, experience, and work habits from one group to another. Mohawk Indians, for example, have long been sought after to work on the construction of skyscrapers, for they walk around high up on the steel frameworks with no apparent fear or distraction from their work. Chinese laborers on rubber plantations in colonial Malaya were found to collect twice as much sap from rubber trees in a given amount of time as Malay workers did. During the industrialization of the Soviet Union in the 1920s and 1930s, large numbers of German, American, and other foreign workers, technicians, and engineers were imported at attractive salaries. More than 10,000 Americans alone went to work in the U.S.S.R. during a one-year period beginning in September 1920.

While preferences for some groups and reluctance or unwillingness to hire others have often been described as due to "bias," "stereotypes" or "perceptions," third-party observers cannot so easily dismiss the first-hand knowledge of those who are backing their beliefs with their own money. Even in the absence of different beliefs about different groups, application of the same employment criteria to different groups can result in very different proportions of these groups being hired, fired, or promoted. Distinguishing discrimination from differences in qualifications and performances is not easy in practice, though the distinction is fundamental in principle. Seldom do statistical data contain sufficiently detailed information on skills, experience, performance, or absenteeism, much less work habits and attitudes, to make possible comparisons between truly comparable individuals from different groups.

Women, for example, have long had lower incomes than men, but most women give birth to children at some point in their lives and many stay out of the labor force until their children reach an age where they can be put into some form of day care while their mothers go to work. These interruptions of their careers cost women workplace experience and seniority, which in turn inhibit the rise of their incomes over the years relative to that of men who have been working continuously in the meantime. However, as far back as 1971, women who worked continuously from high school through their thirties earned slightly *more* than men of the same description, even though women as a group earned substantially less than men as a group.

This suggests that employers were willing to pay women of the same experience the same as men, and that women with the same experience may even outperform men and earn more, but that differences in domestic responsibilities prevent the sexes from having identical workplace experience or identical incomes based on that experience. In 1991, women without children earned 95 percent of what men earned, while women with children earned just 75 percent of what men earned. Moreover, the very possibility of having children makes different occupations have different attractions to women, even before they become mothers. Occupations like librarians or teachers, which one can resume after a few years off to take care of small children, are more attractive to women who anticipate becoming mothers than occupations such as computer engineers, where just a few years off from work can leave you far behind in this rapidly changing field. In short, women and men make different occupational choices and prepare for many of these occupations by specializing in a very different mix of subjects while being educated.

The question as to whether or how much discrimination women encounter in the labor market is a question about whether there are substantial differences in pay between women and men in the same fields with the same qualifications. The question as to whether there is or is not income parity between the sexes is very different, since differences in occupational choices, educational choices, and continuous employment all affect incomes. Men also tend to work in more hazardous occupations, which tend to pay more than similar occupations that are safer. As one study noted, "although 54 percent of the workplace is male, men account for 92 percent of all job-related deaths."

Similar problems in trying to compare comparable individuals make it difficult to determine the presence and magnitude of discrimination between groups that differ by race or ethnicity. It is not uncommon, both in the United States and in other countries, for one racial or ethnic group to differ in age from another by a decade or more—and we have already seen how age makes a big difference in income. While gross statistics show large income differences between American racial and ethnic groups, finer breakdowns usually show much smaller differences. For example, black, white, and Hispanic males of the same age (29) and IQ (100) have all had average annual incomes within a thousand dollars of one another. In New Zealand, while there are substantial income differences between the Maori population and the white population, these differences likewise shrink drastically when comparing Maoris with other New Zealanders of the same age and with the same skills and literacy levels.

Whatever the amount and magnitude of discrimination, it is important to be aware of what economic factors tend to cause it to be larger or smaller. While it is obvious that discrimination imposes a cost on those being discriminated against, in the form of lost opportunities for higher incomes, it is also true that discrimination can impose costs on those who do the discriminating, where they too lose opportunities for higher incomes. For example, when a landlord refuses to rent an apartment to people from the "wrong" group, that can mean leaving the apartment vacant longer.

Clearly, that represents a loss of rent—if this is a free market. However, if there is rent control, with a surplus of applicants, then such discrimination costs the landlord nothing.

Similar principles apply in job markets. An employer who refuses to hire qualified individuals from the "wrong" groups risks leaving his jobs unfilled longer in a free market. This means that he must either leave some work undone and some orders unfilled or else pay overtime to existing employees to get it done, losing money either way. However, in a market where wages are set artificially above the level that would exist through supply and demand, the resulting surplus of applicants can mean that discrimination costs the employer nothing. Whether these artificially higher wages are set by a labor union or by a minimum wage law does not change the principle. Empirical evidence strongly indicates that racial discrimination tends to be greater when the costs are lower and lower when the costs are greater.

Even in South Africa during the era of apartheid, where racial discrimination was required by law, white employers in competitive industries hired more blacks and in higher occupations than they were permitted to do by the government, and were often fined when caught doing so. This was because it was in the employers' economic self-interest to hire blacks. Similarly, whites who wanted homes built in Johannesburg typically hired illegal black construction crews, often with a token white nominally in charge to meet the requirements of the apartheid laws, rather than pay the higher price of hiring a white construction crew as the government wanted them to do. Landlords likewise often rented to blacks in areas where only whites were legally allowed to live.

The cost of discrimination to the discriminators is crucial for understanding such behavior. Employers who are spending other people's money—government agencies or non-profit organizations, for example—are much less affected by the cost of discrimination. In countries around the world, discrimination by government has been greater than discrimination by businesses operating in private, competitive markets. Understanding the basic economics of discrimination makes it easier to understand why blacks were starring on Broadway in the 1920s, at a time when they were not permitted to enlist in the U. S. Navy and were kept out of many civilian government jobs as well. Broadway producers were not about to lose big money that they could make by hiring black entertainers who could attract big audiences, but the costs of government discrimination were paid by the taxpayers, whether they realized it or not.

Just as minimum wage laws reduce the cost of discrimination to the employer, maximum wage laws increase the employer's cost of discrimination. One of the few examples of maximum wage laws in recent centuries were the wage and price controls imposed in the United States during World War II. Because wages were not allowed to rise to the level that they would reach under supply and demand, there was a shortage of workers, just as there is a shortage of housing under rent control. Many employers who had not hired blacks or women, or who had not hired them for desirable jobs, before the war now began to do so. The "Rosy the Riveter" image that came out of World War II was in part a result of wage and price controls.

CAPITAL, LABOR, AND EFFICIENCY

While everything requires some labor for its production, practically nothing can be produced by labor alone. Farmers need land, taxi drivers need cars, artists need something to draw on and something to draw with. Even a stand-up comedian needs an inventory of jokes, which is his capital, as much as hydroelectric dams are the capital of companies that produce electricity.

Capital complements labor in the production process, but it also competes with labor for employment. In other words, many goods and services can be produced either with much labor and little capital or much capital and little labor. When transit workers' unions force bus drivers' pay rates much above what they would be in a competitive labor market, transit companies tend to add more capital, in order to save on the use of the more expensive labor. Busses grow longer, sometimes becoming essentially two busses with a flexible connection between them, so that one driver is using twice as much capital as before and is capable of moving twice as many passengers.

Some may think that this is more "efficient" but efficiency is not so easily defined. If we arbitrarily define efficiency as output per unit of labor, as the U.S. Department of Labor sometimes does, then it is merely circular reasoning to say that having one bus driver moving more passengers is more efficient. It may in fact cost more money per passenger to move them, as a result of the additional capital needed for the expanded busses and the more expensive labor of the drivers.

If bus drivers were not unionized and were paid no more than was necessary to attract qualified people, then undoubtedly their wage rates would be lower and it would then be profitable for the transit companies to hire more of them and use shorter busses. This would in turn mean that passengers would have less time to wait at bus stops because of the shorter and more numerous busses. This is not a small concern to people waiting on street corners on cold winter days or in high-crime neighborhoods at night.

"Efficiency" cannot be meaningfully defined without regard to human desires and preferences. Even the efficiency of an automobile engine is not simply a matter of physics. All the energy generated by the engine will be used in some way—either in moving the car forward, overcoming friction among the moving parts, or shaking the automobile body in various ways. It is only when we define our goal—moving the car forward—that we can regard the percentage of the engine's power that is used for that task as indicating its efficiency and the other power dissipated in various other ways as being "wasted."

Europeans long regarded American agriculture as "inefficient" because output per acre was much lower in the United States than in much of Europe. On the other hand, output per agricultural worker was much higher in the United States than in Europe. The reason was that land was far more plentiful in the U.S. and labor was more scarce. An American farmer would spread himself thinner over far more land and would have correspondingly less time to devote to each acre. In Europe, where land was more scarce, and therefore more expensive because of supply and demand, the European farmer concentrated on the more intensive cultivation of what land he could get, spending more time clearing away weeds and rocks, or otherwise devoting more attention to ensuring the maximum output per acre.

Similarly, Third World countries often get more use out of given capital equipment than do wealthier and more industrialized countries. Such tools as hammers and screw-drivers may be plentiful enough for each worker in an American factory or shop to have his own, but that is much less likely to be the case in a much poorer country, where such tools are more likely to be shared, or shared more widely, than among Americans making the same products. Looked at from another angle, each hammer in a poor country is likely to drive more nails per year, since it is shared among more people and has less idle time. That does not make the poorer country more "efficient." It is just that the relative scarcities are different. Capital tends to be scarcer and more expensive in poorer countries, while labor is more abundant and cheaper. Such countries tend to economize on the more expensive factor, just as richer countries economize on a different factor that is more expensive and scarce there, namely labor. It is just that, in richer countries, capital is more plentiful and cheaper, while labor is more scarce and more expensive.

When a freight train comes into a railroad yard or onto a siding, workers are needed to unload it. When a freight train arrives in the middle of the night, it can either be unloaded then and there, so that the train can proceed on its way, or the boxcars can be left on a siding until the workers come to work the next morning. In a country where such capital as railroad box cars are very scarce and labor is plentiful, it makes sense to have the workers available around the clock, so that they can immediately unload box cars and this very scarce resource does not remain idle. But, in a country that is rich in capital, it may often be better to let box cars sit idle on a siding, waiting to be unloaded, rather than to have expensive workers sitting around idle waiting for the next train to arrive.

It is not just a question about these particular workers' paychecks or this particular railroad company's monetary expenses. From the standpoint of the economy as a whole, the more fundamental question is: What are the alternative uses of these workers' time and the alternative uses of the railroad boxcars? In other words, it is not just a question of money. The money only reflects underlying realities that would be the same in a socialist, feudal or other non-market economy. Whether it makes sense to leave the boxcars idle waiting for the workers to arrive or to leave the workers idle waiting for trains to arrive depends on the relative scarcities of labor and capital and their relative productivity in alternative uses.

During the era of the Soviet Union and Cold War competition, the Soviets used to boast of the fact that an average Soviet box car moved more freight per year than an average American box car. But, far from indicating that their economy was more efficient, this showed that Soviet railroads lacked the abundant capital of the American railroad industry, and that Soviet labor had less valuable alternative uses of its time than did American labor. Similarly, a study of West African economies in the mid-twentieth century noted that trucks there "are in service twenty-four hours a day for seven days a week and are generally tightly packed with passengers and freight."

For similar reasons, automobiles tend to have longer lives in poor countries than in richer countries. Remember that economics is the study of scarce resources which have alternative uses. The alternative uses of American labor are too valuable for it to be used keeping ten-year-old cars repaired—except for those Americans wealthy enough to be able to indulge a hobby of collecting vintage automobiles or those poor enough that the alternative uses of their time are not very remunerative and they are unable to afford a new car.

By and large, it pays Americans to junk their cars, refrigerators, and other capital equipment in a shorter time than it would pay people in poorer countries to do so. Nor is this a matter of being able to afford "waste." It would be a waste to keep repairing this equipment, when the same efforts elsewhere in the American economy would produce more than enough wealth to buy replacements. But it would not make sense for poorer countries, whose alternative uses of time are not as productive, to junk their equipment at the same times when American junk theirs. Accordingly, many older American cars, planes, and sewing machines may be bought second-hand and then used for years longer in Third World countries after they have been junked in the United States. This can be an efficient way of handling the situation for both kinds of countries.

A book by two Soviet economists pointed out that in the U.S.S.R. "equipment is endlessly repaired and patched up," so that the "average life of capital stock in the U.S.S.R. is forty-seven years, as against seventeen in the United States." They were not bragging. They were complaining.

Chapter 10

Controlled Labor Markets

Just as inanimate resources and their resulting products can have their prices set either by free competition or by monopolies, so people's pay and employment conditions may or may not be a result of free market competition. Pay or working conditions may be controlled by law, custom, or organizations of employers or employees, as well as by the government. Among the major factors behind such controls have been desires for job security and for collectively-set limits on how high or how low pay scales will be allowed to go in particular occupations or industries.

Here as elsewhere, we are concerned not so much with the goals or rationales of such policies, but with the incentives created by these arrangements and the consequences to which such incentives lead. These consequences extend beyond the workers themselves to the economy as a whole, where labor is one of the scarce resources which have alternative uses.

JOB SECURITY

Virtually every modern industrial nation has faced issues of job security, whether they have faced these issues realistically or unrealistically, successfully or unsuccessfully. At the most simplistic level, some people advocate that every worker be guaranteed a job, with the government if necessary. In some countries, laws make it difficult and costly for a private employer to fire anyone. Labor unions try to do this in many industries and in many countries around the world. Teachers' unions in the United States are so successful at this that it can easily cost a school district tens of thousands of dollars—or more than a hundred thousand in some places—to fire just one teacher, even if that teacher is grossly incompetent.

Job security laws and policies restrict an employer's ability to lay off workers for economic reasons or to fire them for unsatisfactory work. The obvious purpose of such laws is to reduce unemployment but that is very different from saying that this is their actual effect. Countries with such laws typically do not have lower unemployment rates, but instead have higher unemployment rates, than countries without widespread job protection laws. In Germany, which has some of the world's strongest job security laws, double-digit unemployment rates are not uncommon, while in the United States, where there are no such national laws mandating job security in the private sector, Americans become alarmed when the unemployment rate rises to 6 percent.

Although the United States has no national job security laws imposed by government on private employers, the government itself has laws protecting the job security of its own civilian employees who have acquired permanent status and federal judges have lifetime tenure.

The very thing that makes a modern industrial society so efficient and so effective in raising living standards—the constant quest for newer and better ways of getting work done and more goods produced—makes it impossible to keep on having the workers doing the same jobs in the same way. For example, back at the beginning of the twentieth century, the United States had about 10 million farmers and farm laborers to feed a population of 76 million people. By the end of the twentieth century, there were less than one-fifth this many farmers and farm laborers, feeding a population more than three times as large. Yet, far from having less food, Americans' biggest problems now included obesity and trying to find export markets for their surplus crops. All this was made possible because farming became a radically different enterprise, using machinery, chemicals and methods unheard of when the century began—and requiring far fewer people.

Farming is of course not the only sector of the economy to be revolutionized during the twentieth century. Whole new industries have sprung up, such as aviation and computers, and even old industries like retailing have seen radical changes in which companies and which methods have survived. In little over a decade, between 1985 and 1996, Sears lost 131,000 jobs while Wal-Mart gained 624,000 jobs. Altogether, more than 17 million workers throughout the American economy lost their jobs between 1990 and 1995. But there were never 17 million Americans unemployed during this period, nor anything close to that. In fact, the unemployment rate in the United States fell to its lowest point in years during the 1990s. Americans were moving from one job to another, rather than relying on "job security" in one place. The average American has nine jobs between the ages of 18 and 34.

In Europe, where job security laws and practices are much stronger than in the United States, jobs have in fact been harder to come by. During the decade of the 1990s, the United States created jobs at triple the rate of industrial nations in Europe. In the private sector, Europe actually lost jobs, and only its increased government employment led to any net gain at all. This should not be surprising. Job security laws make it more expensive to hire workers. Like anything else that is made more expensive, labor is less in demand at a higher price than at a lower price. The one exception is government employment, where the employers are spending other people's money—the taxpayers' money.

Job security policies save the jobs of existing workers, but at the cost of reducing the flexibility and efficiency of the economy as a whole, thereby inhibiting the creation of wealth needed for the creation of new jobs for other workers. Because job security laws make it risky for private enterprises to hire new workers during periods of rising demand for their products, existing employees may be worked overtime instead or capital may be substituted for labor, such as using huge busses instead of hiring more drivers for regular-sized busses. However it is done, increased substitution of capital for labor leaves other workers unemployed. For the working population as a whole, this is no net increase in job security. It is a concentration of the insecurity on those who happen to be on the outside looking in. Meanwhile, the total number of jobs can decrease, or be less than it would have been otherwise, as a result of job security laws and policies which increase the costs of employing workers.

It is much the same story in the American academic world, where associate professors and full professors usually have lifetime tenure, while assistant professors, lecturers and instructors work on short-term contracts. The job insecurity of the latter faculty members can be far greater than in other sectors of the economy where there is no tenure, and therefore where there are more new jobs opening up. But, in academia, tenured professors have unchallenged possession of jobs that would otherwise be available. Again, those on the inside looking out benefit at the expense of those on the outside looking in, while the higher expenses entailed by tenure make the whole system more expensive to those who pay tuition and taxes to support it.

Even military personnel in the NATO countries have job security. One consequence is that the average age of soldiers in Belgium's armed forces is 40, compared to 28 in the American military. Soldiers are unionized in

Europe and, through job security and other policies, absorb a much higher percentage of NATO's military spending, leaving less for spending on equipment and weapons. Thus, while the United States spends about 36 percent of its military budget on personnel, Belgium spends 68 percent and Portugal 81 percent. The result is obsolete NATO military equipment that can cost lives in the event of combat. Meanwhile, NATO troops get generous vacations and work light enough schedules to allow many of them to pursue part-time civilian careers. In one Belgian military hospital, "doctors now work four-hour days for full-time pay, allowing some of them to set up private practices," according to a news item in the *Wall Street Journal*. What all this will mean if NATO armies have to fight, using over-age soldiers and obsolete equipment, is a question that can get ignored by those politicians who do not think beyond the next election, where their generosity with the taxpayers' money can be expected to pay off in votes from those who have benefitted.

Even in the absence of formal laws and policies on job security, there are many efforts to preserve jobs threatened by technological change, foreign imports or other sources of cheaper or better products. Virtually all these efforts likewise ignore the danger that greater security for some given set of workers can come at the expense of lessened job opportunities for other workers, as well as needlessly high prices for consumers.

One of the emotionally powerful arguments heard in politics and the media during the "down-sizing" of many large American corporations during the 1990s was that workers were being laid off in industries where sales and profits were going up and the top executives were getting large and rising pay. For example, the workforce at General Motors was cut by 50,000 in just 5 years, while sales were rising and the price of General Motors stock increased 50 percent. From an economic standpoint, this meant that it was possible to do more business with fewer workers, creating better prospects for profit, which in turn led to rising stock prices.

Should General Motors have kept these workers on, as a humanitarian good deed? The argument for doing this might have been stronger if the workers had nowhere to go and no other means of supporting themselves and their families. But the unusually low rates of unemployment in the American economy as a whole during this period of widespread corporate down-sizing suggests that these workers had plenty of places to go. They were classic examples of scarce resources which have alternative uses. If unneeded workers had been retained at General Motors as disguised welfare cases, they would not have added to the output of other parts of the economy where there was much genuine work for them to do. Moreover, consumers would have had to pay needlessly higher price for automobiles to subsidize featherbedding, as well as losing the benefits of all the other goods and services that the displaced automobile workers produced in other sectors of the economy to which they were forced to move.

It has sometimes seemed especially galling that corporate executives who got rid of thousands of workers were rewarded by pay increases for themselves. However, it is worth considering the consequences of the situation in government, where executives are likely to be rewarded according to how many people they supervise and how large a budget they administer. These different situations create opposite incentives—to get as much work done with as few people and resources as possible in private industry and with as many people and resources as available in government. This is one reason why it often costs much less for private companies to perform the same tasks as a government agency performs. The public pays the costs of the government's inefficiencies, whether as consumers or as taxpayers.

MINIMUM WAGE LAWS

Just as we can better understand the economic role of prices in general when we see what happens when prices are not allowed to function, so we can better understand the economic role of workers' pay by seeing what happens when that pay is not allowed to vary with supply and demand. Historically, authorities set maximum wage levels centuries before they set minimum wage levels. Today, however, only the latter are widespread.

Minimum wage laws make it illegal to pay less than the government-specified price for labor. By the simplest and most basic economics, a price artificially raised tends to cause more to be supplied and less to be demanded than when prices are left to be determined by supply and demand in a free market. The result is a surplus, whether the price that is set artificially high is that of farm produce or labor. Minimum wage laws are almost always discussed politically in terms of the benefits they supposedly confer on workers receiving those wages. Unfortunately, the real minimum wage is always zero, regardless of the laws, and that is the wage that many workers receive in the wake of the creation or escalation of a government-mandated minimum wage, because they lose their jobs. Making it illegal to pay less than a given amount does not make a worker's productivity worth that amount—and, if it is not, that worker is unlikely to be employed.

Unemployment

Because the government does not hire surplus labor the way it buys surplus agricultural output, a labor surplus takes the form of unemployment, which tends to be higher under minimum wage laws than in a free market. Because people differ in many ways, those who are unemployed are not likely to be a random sample of the labor force. In country after country around the world, those whose employment prospects are reduced most by minimum wage laws are those who are younger, less experienced, and less skilled. This pattern has been found in New Zealand, France, Canada, the Netherlands, and the United States, for example.

As in other cases, a "surplus" is a price phenomenon, just as "shortages" are. Unemployed workers are not surplus in the sense of being useless or in the sense that there is no work around that needs doing. Most of these workers are perfectly capable of producing goods and services, even if not to the same extent as more skilled workers. The unemployed are made idle by wage rates artificially set above the level of their productivity. Those who are idled in their youth are of course prevented from acquiring the job skills and experience which could make them more productive—and therefore higher earners—later on.

Although most modern industrial societies have minimum wage laws, not all do. Switzerland and Hong Kong have been among the exceptions—and both have had very low unemployment rates. In 2003, *The Economist* magazine reported: "Switzerland's unemployment neared a five-year high of 3.9% in February." Back in 1991, when Hong Kong was still a British colony, its "unemployment rate fell to a seasonally adjusted 1.4% in the three months ended Nov. 30—the lowest level in 10 months, easing from 1.3 a year earlier and dropping sharply from 1.8% in the preceding three months," according to the *Wall Street Journal*. Although Hong Kong still did not have a minimum wage law at the end of the twentieth century, in 1997 new amendments to its labor law under China's rule mandated many new benefits for workers. This imposed increase in labor costs was followed, predictably, by a higher unemployment rate that reached 7.3 percent in 2002—not high by European standards but a multiple of what it had been for years.

Minimum wage rates in Europe tend generally to be set higher than in the United States, and European countries tend to have correspondingly higher unemployment rates than the United States—and job growth rates only a fraction of the American rate. A belated recognition of the connection between minimum wage laws and unemployment has caused some countries to allow their real minimum wage levels to be eroded by inflation, avoiding the political risks of trying to repeal these laws explicitly.

Among 11 million Americans earning at or near the minimum wage in 2001, just over half were from 16 to 24 years of age. Just over half worked part time. Yet political campaigns to increase the minimum wage often talk in terms of providing "a living wage" sufficient to support a family of four— such families as most minimum wage workers do not have and would be ill-advised to have before they reach the point where they can feed and clothe their children.

The huge financial, political, emotional, and ideological investment of various groups in issues revolving around minimum wage laws means that dispassionate analysis is not always the norm. Moreover, the statistical complexities of separating out the effects of minimum wages on employment from all the other ever-changing variables that also effect employment mean that honest differences of opinion are possible. However, when all is said and done, most empirical studies indicate that minimum wage laws reduce employment in general, and especially the employment of younger, less skilled and minority workers. A majority of professional economists surveyed in Britain, Germany, Canada, Switzerland, and the United States agreed that minimum wage laws increase unemployment among low-skilled workers. Economists in France and Austria did not. However, the majority among Canadian economists was 85 percent and among American economists 90 percent.

Those officially responsible for administering minimum wages laws, such as the U. S. Department of Labor and various local agencies, prefer to claim that these laws do not create unemployment. So do labor unions, for whom minimum wage laws serve as tariff barriers against potential competitors for their members' jobs. Even though most studies show that unemployment tends to increase as minimum wages are imposed or increased, those few studies that seem to indicate otherwise are hailed as having "refuted" this "myth," while the devastating criticisms of the defects of such studies by economists are ignored.

One common problem with research on the employment effects of minimum wage laws is that surveys of employers before and after a minimum wage increase can survey only those businesses which survived in both periods. Given the high rates of business failures in many fields, the results for the survivors may becompletely different from the results for the industry as a whole.[1] Using such research methods, you can interview people who have played Russian roulette and "prove" from their experience that it is a harmless activity, since those for whom it was not harmless are unlikely to be around to be interviewed. Thus you would have "refuted" the "myth" that Russian roulette is dangerous.

It would be comforting to believe that the government can simply decree higher pay for low-wage workers, without having to worry about unfortunate repercussions, but the validity of that belief is open to doubts that cannot be dispelled by the kind of research that would lead to the conclusion that Russian roulette is harmless. The preponderance of evidence indicates that labor is not exempt from the basic economic principle that artificially high prices cause surpluses. In the case of surplus human beings, that can be a special tragedy when they are already from low-income, unskilled, or minority backgrounds and urgently need to get on the job ladder if they are ever to move up the ladder by acquiring skills and experience.

Informal Minimum Wages

Sometimes a minimum wage is imposed not by law, but by custom, informal government pressures, labor unions or—especially in the case of Third World countries—by international public opinion pressuring multinational companies to pay Third World workers the kinds of wages usually found in more industrially developed countries. Although organized public pressures for higher pay for Third World Workers in Southeast Asia and Latin America have made news in the United States in recent years, such pressures are not new nor confined to Americans. Similar pressures were put on companies operating in colonial West Africa in the middle of the twentieth century.

---

[1] Imagine that an industry consists of 7 firms, each hiring 1,000 workers before a minimum wage increase, for an industry total of 7,000 employees. If two of these firms go out of business between the first and the second surveys, and only one new firm enters the industry, then only the five firms that were in existence both "before" and "after" can be surveyed and their results reported. Both they and the new firm may now have 1,100 employees each, but the industry as a whole will have 6,600 employees— 400 fewer than before the minimum wage increase. Yet this study can show a 10 percent increase in employment in the five firms surveyed, rather than the 6 percent decrease for the industry as a whole. Since minimum wages can cause unemployment by (1) reducing employment among all the firms, (2) by pushing marginal firms into bankruptcy, or (3) discouraging the entry of replacement firms, false reports based on surveying only survivors are a clear danger.

Informal minimum wages imposed in these ways have had effects very similar to those of explicit minimum wage laws. An economist studying colonial West Africa in the mid-twentieth century found signs telling job applicants that there were "no vacancies" almost everywhere. Nor was this peculiar to West Africa. The same economist—Professor P. T. Bauer of the London School of Economics—noted that it was "a striking feature of many under-developed countries that money wages are maintained at high levels" while "large numbers are seeking but unable to find work." These were of course not high levels compared to what was earned by workers in more industrialized economies, but high relative to Third World workers' productivity and high relative to their alternative earning opportunities in sectors of the economy not subject to external pressures to maintain an artificially inflated level of earnings, such as agriculture, domestic service, or self-employment as street vendors and the like.

The magnitude of the unemployment created by artificially high wages that multinational companies felt pressured to pay in West Africa was indicated by Professor Bauer's first-hand investigations:

> I asked the manager of the tobacco factory of the Nigerian Tobacco Company (a subsidiary of the British-American Tobacco Company) in Ibadan whether he could expand his labour force without raising wages if he wished to do so. He replied that his only problem would be to control the mob of applicants. Very much the same opinion was expressed by the Kano district agent of the firm of John Hold and Company in respect of their tannery. In December 1949 a firm of produce buyers in Kano dismissed two clerks and within two days received between fifty and sixty applications for the posts without having publicized the vacancies. The same firm proposed to erect a groundnut crushing plant. By June 1950 machinery had not yet been installed; but without having advertised a vacancy it had already received about seven hundred letters asking for employment . . . I learnt that the European-owned brewery and the recently established manufacturers of stationery constantly receive shoals of applications for employment.

The misfortunes of eager but frustrated African job applicants were only part of the story. The output that they could have produced, if employed, would have made a particularly important contribution to the economic well-being of the consuming public in a very poor region, lacking many things that others take for granted in more prosperous societies. It is not at all clear that workers as a class are benefitted by artificially high wage rates in the Third World. Employed workers—those on the inside looking out—obviously benefit, while those on the outside looking in lose. The only category of clear beneficiaries are people living in richer countries who enjoy the feeling that they are helping people in poorer countries.

Just as a price set below the free market level tends to cause quality deterioration in the product that is being sold, because a shortage means that buyers will be forced to accept things of lower quality than they would have otherwise, so a price set above the free market level tends to cause a rise in average quality, as the surplus allows the buyers to cherry-pick and purchase only the better quality items being sold. What that means in the labor market is that job qualification requirements are likely to rise and that some workers who would ordinarily be hired in a free market may become "unemployable" when there are minimum wage laws. Unemployability, like shortages and surpluses, is not independent of price. In a free market, low-productivity workers are just as employable at a low wage rate as high-productivity workers are at a high wage rate.

Differential Impact

Some countries in Europe have lower minimum wages for teenagers than for adults and New Zealand simply exempted teenagers from the coverage of its minimum wage law until 1994. This was tacit recognition of the fact that those workers less in demand were likely to be hardest hit by unemployment created by minimum wage laws.

Another group disproportionately affected by minimum wage laws are members of unpopular racial or ethnic minority groups. Indeed, minimum wage laws were once advocated explicitly because of the likelihood that they would reduce or eliminate the competition of particular minorities, whether they were Japanese in Canada during the 1920s or blacks in the United States and South Africa at about the same time. Such expressions of overt racial discrimination were both legal and socially accepted in all three countries at that time.

Again, it is necessary to note how price is a factor even in racial discrimination. That is, surplus labor resulting from minimum wage laws makes it cheaper to discriminate against minority workers than it would be in a free market, where there is no chronic excess supply of labor. Passing up qualified minority workers in a free market means having to hire more other workers to take the jobs they were denied, and that in turn usually means either having to raise the pay to attract the additional workers or lowering the job qualifications at the existing pay level—both of which amount to the same thing economically, higher labor costs for getting a given amount of work done.

The history of black workers in the United States illustrates the point. The American federal minimum wage law—the Fair Labor Standards Act—was passed in 1938. However, wartime inflation had the effect of repealing this law for all practical economic purposes during the 1940s, since the wages set in the marketplace for even unskilled labor rose well above what the law specified. The real impact of the law began to be felt after 1950, when the first major revision of the Act began a series of escalations of the federal minimum wage.

From the late nineteenth-century on past the middle of the twentieth century, the labor force participation rate of American blacks was slightly higher than that of American whites. In other words, during this long period before the escalation of minimum wage rates, blacks were just as employable at the wages they received as whites were at their very different wages. The minimum wage law changed that and those particularly hard hit by the resulting unemployment have been black teenage males.

Even though 1949—the year before the series of minimum wage escalations began—was a recession year, black male teenage unemployment that year was lower than it was to be at any time during the later boom years of the 1960s. The usual explanations of high unemployment among black teenagers—inexperience, lack of skills, racism—cannot explain their rising unemployment, since all these things were worse during the earlier period when black teenage unemployment was much lower.

Taking the more normal year of 1948 as a basis for comparison, black male teenage unemployment then was less than half of what it would be at any time during the decade of the 1960s and less than one-third of what it would be in the 1970s. Moreover, unemployment among 16 and 17-year-old black males was no higher than among white males of the same age in 1948. It was only after a series of minimum wage escalations began that black male teenage unemployment not only skyrocketed itself but became more than double the unemployment rates among white male teenagers. In the early twenty-first century, the unemployment rate for black teenagers exceeded 30 percent.

COLLECTIVE BARGAINING

So far we have been considering labor markets in which both workers and employers are numerous and compete individually and independently. However, these are not the only kinds of markets for labor. Some labor markets are controlled by laws or by collective bargaining agreements, or both. Some workers are members of labor unions which negotiate pay and working conditions with employers, whether employers are acting individually or in concert as members of an employers' association.

Employer Organizations

In earlier centuries, it was the employers who were more likely to be organized and setting pay and working conditions as a group. In medieval guilds, the master craftsmen collectively made the rules determining the conditions under which apprentices and journeymen would be hired and how much customers would be charged for the products. Today, major league baseball owners collectively make the rules as to what is the maximum total salaries any given ball club can pay to its players.

Clearly, pay and working conditions tend to be different when determined collectively than in a labor market where employers compete against one another individually for workers and workers compete against one another individually for jobs. It would obviously not be worth the trouble of organizing employers if they were not able to keep the salaries they pay lower than they would be in a free market.

Much has been said about the fairness or unfairness of the actions of medieval guilds, modern labor unions or other forms of collective bargaining. Here we are studying their economic consequences—and especially their effects on the allocation of scarce resources which have alternative uses.

Almost by definition, all these organizations exist to keep the price of labor from being what it would be otherwise in free and open competition in the market. Just as the tendency of market competition is to base rates of pay on the productivity of the worker, thereby bidding labor away from where it is less productive to where it is more productive, so organized efforts to make wages artificially low or artificially high defeat this process and thereby make the allocation of resources less efficient in the economy as a whole.

For example, if an employers' association keeps wages in the widget industry below the level that workers of similar skills receive elsewhere, fewer of these workers are likely to apply for jobs producing widgets than if the pay rate were higher. If widget manufacturers are paying $10 an hour for labor that would get $15 an hour if employers had to compete with each other for workers in a free market, then some workers will go to other industries that pay $12 an hour. From the standpoint of the economy as a whole, this means that people capable of producing $15 an hours' worth of output are instead producing only $12 an hours' worth of output. This is a clear loss to the consumers—that is, to society as a whole.

The fact that it is a more immediate and more visible loss to the workers in the widget industry does not make that the most important fact from an economic standpoint. Losses and gains between employers and employees are social or moral issues, but they do not change the key *economic* issue, which is how the allocation of resources affects the total wealth available to society as a whole. What makes the total wealth produced by the economy less than it would be in a free market is that wages set below the market level cause workers to work where they are not as productive, but where they are paid more because of a competitive labor market.

The same principle applies where wages are set above the market level. If a labor union is successful in raising the wage rate for the same workers in the widget industry to $20 an hour, then employers will employ fewer workers at this higher rate than they would at either the $10 an hour they set under employer collusion or the $15 an hour that would have prevailed in free market competition. In fact, the only workers it will pay the employers to hire are workers whose productivity is $20 an hour or more. This higher productivity can be reached in a number of ways, whether by retaining only the most skilled and experienced employees, by adding more capital to enable the labor to turn out more products per hour, or by other means—none of them free.

Those workers displaced from the widget industry must go to their second-best alternative. Those worth $15 an hour producing widgets may end up working in another industry at $12 an hour. Again, this is not simply a loss to those particular workers but a loss to the economy as a whole, because scarce resources are not being allocated where their productivity is highest.

Where unions set wages above the level that would prevail under supply and demand in a free market, widget manufacturers are not only paying more money for labor, they are also paying for additional capital or other complementary resources to raise the productivity of labor above the $20 an hour level. Higher productivity may seem on the surface to be greater "efficiency," but producing fewer widgets at higher cost per widget does not benefit the economy, even though less labor is being used. Other industries receiving more labor than they normally would, because of the workers displaced from the widget industry, can expand their output. But that expanding output is not the most productive use of the additional labor. It is only the artificially-imposed union wage rate which causes the shift from a more productive use to a less productive use.

Note that either artificially low wage rates caused by an employer association or artificially high wage rates caused by a labor union reduces employment in the widget industry. Another way of saying the same thing is that the maximum employment in any industry is achieved under free and open market competition, without organized collusion among either employers or employees. Looked at more generally, the only individual bargains that can be made anywhere in a free market are those whose terms are acceptable to both sides—that is, buyers and sellers of labor, computers, shoes or whatever. Any other terms, whether set higher or lower, and whether set by collective actions of employers or unions or imposed by government decree, favors one side or the other and therefore causes the disfavored side to make fewer transactions.

From the standpoint of the economy as a whole, the real loss is that things that both sides wanted to do now cannot be done because the range of mutually acceptable terms has been artificially narrowed. One side or the other must now go to their second-best alternative—which is also second-best from the standpoint of the economy as a whole, because scarce resources have not been allocated to their most valued uses.

The parties engaged in collective bargaining are of course preoccupied with their own interests, but those judging the process as a whole need to focus on how such a process affects the economic interests of the entire society, rather than the internal division of economic benefits among contending members of the society.

Labor Unions

Labor unions often boast of the pay rate and other benefits they have gotten for their members and of course that is what enables unions to continue to attract members. The wage rate per hour is typically a key indicator of a union's success, but the further ramifications of that wage rate seldom receive as much attention. Legendary labor leader John L. Lewis, head of the United Mine Workers from 1925 to 1960, was enormously successful in winning higher pay for his union's members. However, an economist also called him "the world's greatest oil salesman," because the resulting higher price of coal and the disruptions in its production due to numerous strikes caused many users of coal to switch to using oil instead. This of course reduced employment in the coal industry.

By the 1960s, declining employment in the coal industry left many mining communities economically stricken and some virtual ghost towns. Media stories of their plight seldom connected their current woes with the former glory days of John L. Lewis. In fairness to Lewis, he made a conscious decision that it was better to have fewer miners doing dangerous work underground and more heavy machinery down there, since machinery could not be killed by cave-ins, explosions and the other hazards of mining.

To the public at large, however, these and other trade-offs were largely unknown. Many simply cheered at what Lewis had done to improve the wages of miners and, years later, were compassionate toward the decline of mining communities—but made little or no connection between the two things. Yet what was involved was one of the simplest and most basic principles of economics, that less is demanded at a higher price than at a lower price. That principle applies whether considering the price of coal, of the labor of mine workers, or anything else.

Very similar trends emerged in the automobile industry, where the danger factor was not what it was in mining. Here the United Automobile Workers' union was also very successful in getting higher pay, more job security and more favorable work rules for its members. In the long run, however, all these additional costs raised the price of automobiles and made American cars less competitive with Japanese and other imports, not only in the United States but around the world.

As of 1950, the United States produced three-quarters of all the cars in the world and Japan produced less than one percent of what Americans produced. Twenty years later, Japan was producing almost as many automobiles as the United States and, five years after that, more automobiles. By 1990, one-third of the cars sold in the United States were made in Japan. In 1996, the Honda Accord and the Toyota Camry each sold more cars in the United States than any car sold by General Motors. All this of course had its effect on employment. During the 1980s, the number of jobs in the American automobile industry declined by more than 100,000. By 1990, the number of jobs in the American automobile industry was 200,000 less than it had been in 1979.

Political pressures on Japan to "voluntarily" limit its export of cars to the U.S. led to the creation of Japanese automobile manufacturing plants in the United States, hiring American workers. By 1990, these transplanted Japanese factories were producing nearly as many cars as were being exported to the United States from Japan. Many of these transplanted Japanese car companies had workforces that were non-union—and which rejected unionization when votes were taken among the employees.

This was part of a more general trend among industrial workers in the United States. The United Steelworkers of America was another large and highly successful union in getting high pay and other benefits for its members. But here too the number of jobs in the industry declined by more than 200,000 in a decade, while the steel companies invested $65 million in machinery that replaced these workers, and while the towns where steel production was concentrated were economically devastated.

The once common belief that unions were a blessing and a necessity for workers was now increasingly mixed with skepticism about the unions' role in the economic declines and reduced employment in many industries. Faced with the prospect of seeing some employers going out of business or having to drastically reduce employment, some unions were forced into "givebacks"—that is, relinquishing various wages and benefits they had obtained for their members in previous years. Painful as this was, many unions concluded that it was the only way to save members' jobs.

The proportion of the American labor force that was unionized began to decline as skepticism about their economic effects spread among workers who increasingly voted against being represented by unions. Unionized workers were 32 percent of all workers in the middle of the twentieth century, but only 14 percent by the end of the century. Moreover, there was a major change in the composition of unionized workers.

In the first half of the century, the great unions were in mining, automobiles, steel, and trucking. But, by the end of the century, the largest and most rapidly growing unions were those of government employees. The largest union in the country by far was the union of teachers—the National Education Association. The economic pressures of the marketplace, which had created such problems for unionized workers in industry and commerce, did not apply to government workers. Government employees could continue to get pay raises, benefits, and job security without worrying that they would suffer the fate of miners, automobile workers, and other unionized industrial workers. Those who hired government workers were not spending their own money but the taxpayers' money, and so had little reason to resist union demands. Moreover, they faced no competitive forces in the market that could force them to lose business to imports or substitute products.

In private industry, many companies remained non-union by a policy of paying their workers at least as much as unionized workers received. Such a policy implies that the cost to an employer of having a union exceeds the wages and benefits paid to workers. The hidden costs of union rules on seniority and many other details of operations are for some companies worth being rid of for the sake of greater efficiency, even if that means paying their employees more than they would have to pay to unionized workers. The unionized big three American automobile makers, for example, required from 26 hours to 31 hours of labor per car, while the largely non-unionized Japanese auto makers required from 17 to 22 hours.

Chapter 11

An Overview

A lthough the basic economic principles underlying the allocation of labor are not fundamentally different from the principles underlying the allocation of inanimate resources, it is not equally easy to look at labor and its pay rates in the same way one looks at the prices of iron ore or bushels of wheat. Even aside from the human factor, the sheer magnitude of payments for work dwarfs payments for all other resources. Employee earnings are the largest category of income in the American economy, constituting about 80 percent of national income for decades on end. This is not uncommon in modern industrial economies.

Because wages and salaries are so important in the lives of most individuals, there is a tendency to look at income solely from the standpoint of the individuals receiving it. However, this overlooks the important role of the price of labor in allocating resources in ways which determine the standard of living in the society as a whole. Looking at income solely from the standpoint of individual recipients also tends to portray the economy as a zero-sum game, in which what is gained by some is lost by others. But there would obviously never have been the great rises in the general standard of living which have occurred over the years and generations if that were true.

THE MYSTIQUE OF "LABOR"

In various forms, the idea has persisted for centuries that labor is what "really" creates the output that we all live on and enjoy. In this view, it is the farmers who feed us and the factory workers who clothe us and provide us with furniture and television sets, while a variety of other workers build the homes we live in and produce the clothes we wear. Karl Marx took this vision to its logical conclusion by depicting capitalists, landlords and investors as people who, in one way or another, were enabled by the institutions of capitalism to take away much of what labor had created—that is, to "exploit" labor. Echoes of this vision can still be found today, not only among a relative handful of Marxists but also among non-Marxists or even anti-Marxists, who use such terms as "unearned income" to describe profits, interest, rent and dividends.

This view that there is something special about labor as a source of output, and of the value of individual commodities, existed before Marx was born— and not only among radicals, but even among such orthodox economists as Adam Smith, the father of laissez-faire economics. The first sentence of Smith's classic *The Wealth of Nations* says: "The annual labour of every nation is the fund which originally supplies it with all the necessaries and conveniences of life which it annually consumes, and which consist always either in the immediate produce of that labour, or in what is purchased with that produce from other nations."

By the late nineteenth century, however, economists had given up the notion that it is primarily labor which determines the value of goods, since capital, management and natural resources all contribute to output and must be paid for from the price of that output, if these inputs into production are to continue to be supplied. More fundamentally, labor, like all other sources of production costs, was no longer seen as a source of value. On the contrary, it was the value of the goods to the consumers which made it worthwhile to produce those goods—provided that the consumer was willing to pay enough to cover their production costs.

This new understanding marked a revolution in the development of economics. It is also a sobering reminder of how long it can take for even highly intelligent people to get rid of a misconception whose fallacy then seems obvious in retrospect. It is not costs which create value; it is value which causes purchasers to be willing to repay the costs incurred in the production of what they want. Where costs have been incurred in excess of what the consumers are willing to pay, the business simply loses money, because those costs do not create value, whether they are labor costs or other costs.

In one sense, everything we consume is produced by human labor, especially if we broaden the term to include the work of those who plan, manage and coordinate the activities of those who directly lay their hands on the things that are being manufactured or built. Usually, however, the term "labor" or "worker" is reserved for those who are employed by others. Thus, someone who works 35 or 40 hours a week in a factory or office is called a worker, while someone who works 50 or 60 hours a week managing the enterprise is not. Clearly, the amount of work you do is not what makes you a worker or not, as that term is popularly used.

If labor were in fact the crucial source of output and prosperity, then we should expect to see countries where great masses of people toil long hours richer than countries where most people work shorter hours, in a more leisurely fashion, and under more pleasant conditions, often including air-conditioning, for example. In reality, we find just the opposite. Third World farmers may toil away under a hot sun and in difficult working conditions that were once common in Western nations that have long since gotten soft and prosperous under modern capitalism. If those who are not laborers derive their wealth from exploiting labor, then we should expect to see countries with many wealthy people having ordinary working people who are especially poor. The United States, for example, not only leads the world in the number of billionaires, but has nearly as many billionaires as the rest of the world combined, so ordinary Americans should be especially poor, if the exploitation theory is correct. But in fact ordinary Americans have long had the highest standard of living in the world.

The growth and development of such non-labor inputs as science, engineering and sophisticated investment and management policies, as well as the institutional benefits of a price-coordinated economy, have made the difference and given hundreds of millions of people higher standards of living. Again, this is not something that is difficult to grasp—once the misconceptions have been gotten rid of. However, those misconceptions tend to linger on wherever they can find refuge, even after they have been formally banished by logic and evidence. Official government statistics are still cast in such terms as "unearned income," and "productivity" is often defined as output divided by the labor that went into it. International trade is still discussed as if high-wage countries cannot compete successfully with low-wage countries, as if labor were the only cost of production. In reality, high-wage countries have been competing successfully with low-wage countries for centuries, precisely because of advantages in capital, technology and organization, which enable high-wage workers to produce so much more that the labor cost per unit of output is often lower than in low-wage countries.

For years, India banned imports of automobiles from the United States and Japan, in order to protect its own domestically produced cars, made by workers who were paid much less than American or Japanese workers. Consumers in India were for years forced to pay far higher prices for automobiles—and to get on waiting lists to buy them—because the products of their low-wage workers could not compete in price or quality with automobiles shipped thousands of miles from high-wage countries.

Misconceptions have practical consequences, sometimes needlessly holding down the standard of living of poor people. Antipathy toward "unearned incomes" has led to attempts to control or suppress profits in various countries at various periods of history, with the result of discouraging the investment of capital that those countries have desperately needed, in order to raise the standard of living of their people. In some cases, the more prosperous classes in these poor countries have invested their capital abroad, in richer industrial nations that do not tax or restrict capital so much—leading to international transfers of wealth from where it is most scarce to where it is most abundant, as a result of the domestic politics of envy and resentment, compounded by economic confusion.

What can be seen physically is always more vivid than what cannot be. Those who watch a factory in operation can see the workers creating a product before their eyes. They cannot see the investment that made that factory possible in the first place, much less the thinking that went into assessing whether the market for the product was sufficient to justify the expense, or the analysis and trial-and-error experience that made possible the technology with which the workers are working or the vast amounts of knowledge and insights required to deal with ever-changing markets in an ever-changing economy and society.

Ignoring or disregarding such things makes it possible to believe that only those currently handling tangible objects before our eyes are creating wealth and that any of that wealth which goes to others represents "exploitation" of its real producers. Crude as such a conception may be, it has held a powerful sway over numerous political leaders and their followers, in countries around the world.

Tanzania's legendary and charismatic leader Julius Nyerere, surveying with painful honesty his country's economic disasters under his socialist government, declared that at least he had prevented foreign capitalists from carrying away Tanzania's wealth for their own profit. Implicit in the fear of foreign "exploitation" is a vision of a zero-sum process, where one can gain only if others lose. Insupportable as such a vision would be if one paused to examine it, either logically or empirically, implicit assumptions survive precisely because they are not examined.

The kinds of ideas about exploitation which Julius Nyerere exemplified in Africa also long prevailed in Latin America. Under the influence of "depen-

dency theory," many Latin American nations restricted their economic transactions with wealthier industrial nations of North America and Western Europe, lest these capitalists exploit them. Only after many years of painful
economic failures in trying to produce internally the goods which could have
been bought more cheaply in the world market did Latin America's governments eventually abandon dependency theory and the self-destructive economic policies based on it. Perhaps even more remarkable, this theory
eventually lost ground even among Latin American intellectuals. Yet what a
price was paid in the meantime by those Latin American peoples whose standards of living were needlessly kept lower than they could have been with the
available resources and technology. Misconceptions are more than mere intellectual problems. They can have large and painful human consequences.

As is so often the case, the economic realities are not very complicated, but
there is nevertheless a great difficulty in extricating ourselves from tangled
myths and misconceptions. This is especially so when it comes to labor, for
people's work has been sufficiently central to their lives to help define who
they are, as reflected in the great number of family names which are based on
occupations—Smith, Shepherd, Weaver, Carpenter, Mason, Wright, Miller,
Brewer, Cook, Butler, and Steward, for example. But, however emotionally
powerful the role of labor may be, it is still part of the general economic pattern of the allocation of scarce resources which have alternative uses.

ALLOCATION AND INEQUALITIES

In an economy that never changed, it would be possible to establish some
permanent allocation of labor to its various uses and to establish some payment system—whether based on equal pay or some other principle—that
would also be permanent. But no such permanent arrangements are possible
in an economy that is growing in size and developing technologically. Unpredictable advances in organization and technology occur in different parts
of the economy at different times, requiring shifts in labor and other resources from one industry or sector to another, if the new potentialities are to
lead to greater output and the higher standards of living which depend on
greater output.

The allocation of human resources—with the inequalities this often entails—is inextricably bound up with the economic development on which
the prosperity of all depends. Unless workers are to be ordered to move from
one industry, region, or occupation to another, as under totalitarianism, eco-

nomic incentives and constraints must accomplish these transfers in a market economy. Higher pay may attract workers to the newer and more productive sectors or unemployment may force them out of sectors whose products or technologies are becoming obsolete.

Simple and obvious as this may seem, it is often misunderstood by those who are shocked to see some sectors of the economy prospering at the same time when others are being "left behind" or are even suffering losses of business and jobs. Too often there is no sense that these are all part of the same process, rather than separate happenstances that are good for some and bad for others.

There were, for example, many laments in nineteenth century England for the plight of the handloom weavers, increasingly displaced by power looms that produced cloth more cheaply and thereby made clothing more affordable to millions. Today, in an affluent age, when physically adequate clothing is so widely available that only issues of style and brand name concern most people in modern industrial societies, it is difficult to imagine the hardships endured by many people in centuries past who were unable to afford enough clothing to provide adequate protection against the elements[1]—or what a blessing it was to them to have the prices of clothes brought down to a level where they could finally afford them, because of advances in the mechanization of production. Their good fortune and the misfortunes of the handloom weavers were inseparably part of the same process.

In the late twentieth century, China's robust economic growth rate in the wake of opening up more of the economy to free markets after the death of Mao in 1978 led to rising real incomes in those regions of the country where free markets were first allowed. Nationally, this meant a growing income inequality, since the state-run industries and sectors remained inefficient and poor. Here was the situation before the reforms took effect, as described by *The Economist* magazine:

> When the economic reform era began in the late 1970s, urban residents enjoyed guaranteed jobs for life, free housing and health care. Unemployment was virtually non-existent and rural residents were banned from moving into urban areas. There was no private enterprise. Most people's lives were spartan.

---

[1] At one time, centuries ago, hospitals in parts of Europe had to take precautions to see that clothing was not stolen from the bodies of people who had died, when there were so many people desperate for adequate clothing.

This government-guaranteed subsidence for all at a poverty level was referred to as "the iron rice bowl" and it was egalitarian. When the new leader, Deng Xiaoping, announced a new policy of seeking to raise the economic level of the country as a whole, he said: "Let some people get rich first" by allowing the kinds of incentives that exist in prosperous capitalist countries. This policy led to rapid growth rates for China's economy, with spectacular results for particular regions, sectors and individuals. The reasons for growing inequalities, were not just that those left out of these experimental reforms did not experience the same prosperity, but also that to some extent enterprises in the state-owned and state-run sector suffered from competition with more efficient private enterprises.

While about 9 percent of the people in China's cities lived below the official poverty level of 1,800 yuan in annual income—$217 in American money—the percentage was much higher in particular cities. For example, the poverty rate was 30 percent in the city of Xian, with 2.7 million people and was even more widespread "in some northeastern cities that are home to many of the worst-performing state-owned industries," according to *The Economist*. Here 60 percent of the 1.8 million people in the city of Shuangyashan lived below the official poverty level. In short, the rising prosperity of China was accompanied by growing internal inequalities, as has happened in other countries at various times in history.

It would be a mistake to regard a given level of inequality at a particular time in this on-going process as a permanent inequality. That is not necessarily so for a nation any more than it is for individuals or families. As market reforms spread through China, more regions, sectors, and populations in China began to share in the resulting prosperity by becoming more productive in response to changing incentives. In India, differing levels of economic development in different regions likewise led to differences in income in general and different levels of poverty in particular. At the end of the twentieth century, the percentage of the population of India that lived below that country's official poverty level was 47 percent in the state of Orissa but only 6 percent in the Punjab.

The alternative to uneven economic development, and the income inequalities this entails, can be egalitarian stagnation in poverty. In an ever-changing economy with new and more productive technologies emerging unpredictably and more efficient methods of organization being devised, to keep workers employed where they are already working is to force society to forego the economic benefits of such new developments.

Even within a given occupation, technology affects people of different abilities differently. Local entertainers of modest abilities could earn a modest living more easily before motion pictures, television, and compact disks enabled the most talented entertainers in the world to become available to audiences around the world. People thousands of miles away could hear Pavarotti sing or watch Andre Agassi play tennis or Tiger Woods play golf. Just as the televising of major league baseball made minor league baseball less attractive, so the availability of superstars in many fields led to what one economist called "a 'winner-take-all' effect, where only the best do well, and those lucky few command enormous incomes."

Focusing on such growing internal inequalities in a given occupation overlooks the vastly larger numbers of other people who benefit from hearing Pavarotti or seeing a wider array of highly talented people in a variety of fields. Moreover, it is by no means clear that most people are as preoccupied with income differences as intellectuals in academia and the media seem to be. One classic study, *Equality* by R. H. Tawney, lamented that the public seemed less resentful of the rich than fascinated by their goings-on.

Occupational Pay Differentials

Pay differentials are typically reflections of productivity differences and are part of the process of allocating scarce labor resources which have alternative uses. Again, a fairly obvious economic fact can become very confused when intertwined with very different moral questions about whether one group of people merit so much more than others. Productivity and merit are wholly different things. Someone born and raised in highly favorable circumstances may find it easier to become a brain surgeon than someone born and raised in highly unfavorable circumstances may find it to become a carpenter. But that is very different from saying that brain surgeons are paid "too much" or carpenters "too little."

In policy terms, making it easier for people born in less fortunate circumstances to acquire the knowledge and skills to become brain surgeons is very different from simply decreeing that pay differentials between brain surgeons and carpenters be reduced or eliminated. The latter policy affects the allocation of resources, affecting not only how hard existing brain surgeons will work or how early they will retire, but also how many replacements they will have, as young people decide whether or not it is worth all the years and effort it takes to become a brain surgeon.

Those who have the biggest stake in all this are people suffering from medical conditions that require brain surgery. Despite a tendency in some quarters to see economic choices as a zero-sum activity involving a trade-off between the interests of two competing groups, very often the third parties who are ignored are affected most of all. Moreover, seeing economic issues as simply issues about how to divide up money ignores the larger role of financial incentives in allocating resources. From the standpoint of society as a whole, money is just an artifact used to get real things done. How well those real things are done is what determines the material well-being of the people in that society.

Unmerited misfortunes and windfall gains leave many people uneasy, especially when these undeserved happenstances have large effects on someone's whole way of life. The desire to help the less fortunate may be especially strong, but whether a particular policy will in fact have that effect is not an easy question to answer—except for those who simply want to "do something" to express their sympathy or solidarity, without regard to the actual consequences.

Income Distribution

So-called "income distribution" issues often include concern about the rich and the disproportionate share of the national income that they receive. Where the term "rich" simply refers to the top 10 percent or 20 percent of income earners as of a given time, then these are more likely to be people who have simply reached their peak earnings years—usually in their forties or fifties—rather than people who are genuinely rich in the sense of having enough wealth to live on without continuing to work. However, even considering the genuinely rich, how much do they cost the rest of society? Their total wealth is not subtracted from the total output of the country, but only what they actually consume, which is typically a tiny fraction of what they own, as well as a fraction of the wealth that they have created for others in the process of earning their fortunes.

Often there is a sense of amazement, or even resentment in some quarters, when the rich spend huge sums of money on such things as rare stamps or antique furniture. But often these are items of little or no use or interest to most people, even though their prices may be bid up to astronomical levels by a few rich people bidding against one another. The loss to the society is typically trivial. For example, a rare camera used by the Japanese navy in World War II was put on sale for $40,000, but better photographs can be taken with cameras on sale today for less than one percent of that. In such cases, the rich are paying for the distinction of having something rare, while others suffer no real loss in their standard of living.

It is not only in buying expensive things from the past that the rich may seek the distinction of ownership. They can also acquire distinction by buying new products that are too expensive for most other people to buy. When the first television sets were sold around 1940, they were so expensive that only truly wealthy people could afford them. Sales to the rich is what enabled television manufacturers to survive and to have the time to continually improve their product over the years, meanwhile improving their production methods as well, so that by 1980 even poor people could afford television sets far superior to what the rich had paid much higher prices for in earlier years.

Nor was television unique. Many products taken for granted today were able to develop to the point of being within the budgets of millions of people only because their high initial costs were paid by the wealthy. An American popular song of the 1920s had lyrics that said: "We won't have it known, dear, that we own a telephone, dear."[2] Two generations later, such lyrics would make no sense, because virtually every American had a telephone.

Those who look only at a static picture of events as they appear at a given moment often want to heavily tax things that are "luxuries of the rich," without considering that it may be only a matter of time when those very same things will be part of the standard of living of ordinary people. As late as the middle of the twentieth century, college was largely a luxury of the affluent and the wealthy. Had it been heavily taxed, instead of being heavily subsidized, it might well have continued to be a luxury confined to the rich.

By 1994, most American households *living below the official poverty line* had a microwave oven and a videocassette recorder, things that less than one percent of all American households had in 1971. For the population at large, homes were much bigger, automobiles were much better, and more Americans were connected to the Internet at the end of the twentieth century than were connected to a water supply at the beginning of that century. This was clearly not a zero-sum activity, in which what was gained by some was lost by others. Other countries have shown similar patterns. In New Zealand, for example, most people whose incomes were in the lowest quarter owned a videocassette recorder, a freezer, a washing machine, and a vehicle.

---

[2] The song was "Tea for Two."

Media and even academic preoccupation with instant snapshot statistics create major distortions of economic reality. "The rich" and "the poor" have become staples of income discussions, even though most people in the top and bottom income categories may be the same people at different stages of their lives, at least in Western countries, rather than fixed classes of people who remain at the top and bottom throughout their lives. Even among American millionaires, studies show that four-fifths of them did not inherit their fortune but earned it during their own lifetimes. The great historic American fortunes—Carnegie, Ford, Vanderbilt, etc.—were often created by people who began in modest or even humble circumstances. Richard Warren Sears, Aaron Montgomery Ward, and James Cash Penney all began working to support themselves in lowly jobs as teenagers, too young to be allowed to work under today's child labor laws, though each eventually rose to become fabulously wealthy as creators of the retail store chains that bore their respective names.

Similar stories could be told of teenage Henry Ford, who became fed up with farm work and walked eight miles to Detroit to look for a job. David Sarnoff, who went on in later life to create the NBC broadcasting network, likewise began working to support himself as a teenager by selling newspapers on the streets. Another teenager who supported himself was an immigrant lumberyard worker named Frederick Weyerhauser, who went on to establish a wood products empire. The list goes on and on.

While such stories have long been part of what has been called the American Dream, dramatic social mobility has not been confined to the United States. Despite India's reputation as a rigid, caste-ridden society, it has likewise had its rags-to-riches stories, especially as more free markets emerged toward the end of the twentieth century. Dhiruhai Ambani, for example, was born in poverty and was able to go as far as high school only because he was admitted as a "free student"—and he was too poor to continue on to college. His first job was pumping gas at a filling station, his second job was as a shipping clerk. But from there on he rose, step by step, eventually establishing his own business, making synthetic yarn. From there he branched out into petrochemicals and eventually created India's largest company and the world's largest multifeed refinery. By 1995, his company had 2.4 million stockholders and their annual meetings had to be held in a football stadium.

Such stories have often been seen as just examples of individual good fortune for exceptional people. But the more fundamental point is the great advantage for any society that can tap the talents of people from all across the social spectrum to develop its economy and thereby raise the living standards of its population as a whole. That is what Carnegie, Ford, Sears, and Penney did in America and what people from modest or even poverty backgrounds have begun to do in India after it moved in the direction of freer markets at the end of the twentieth century.

Infosys was started by six Indian computer engineers with a total capital of $600 among them, and it grew until the company was worth $15 billion. Its Chief Executive Officer received his education at one of the local engineering colleges because, although he had been admitted to the more prestigious Indian Institute of Technology, his father could not afford to pay the $20 a month required for a place for him to live away from home.

Another Indian entrepreneur who rose from poverty was Sam Pitroda, born in a village where there was no electricity, no telephones, and no running water. His early education was in a one-room school where most of the children had neither books nor shoes. He somehow made his way to the United States, where he rose to become a millionaire in telecommunications. Then he returned to India and proceeded to revolutionize their antiquated and bureaucratically dominated telephone system. From a country with only 12,000 telephones for 700 million people, India had by 1990 become a country with 5 million telephones. Before the end of the decade India had nearly 20 million phones and the years-long waiting lists of the past had virtually disappeared. That Pitroda became wealthy during this process is a footnote to history. It is what he did for millions of people in India that was historic.

Neither poverty nor caste has died out in India. While most of India's managers and professionals come from upper-caste backgrounds, the modern sectors of the Indian economy have fewer caste barriers. With vast sums of money being able to be made by supplying what people want through a freer marketplace, the cost of discrimination by caste becomes enormous when there are educated and talented individuals who can make a company hugely profitable. The bottleneck has been producing such individuals in an educational system where, as a leading Indian entrepreneur put it, "our schools and colleges were only creating an army of unemployables." Yet the new Indian entrepreneurs also set about creating private education in practical skills in the computer industry. In short, the more market-oriented economy of late twentieth-century India opened new avenues of social mobility for those at the bottom, in contrast to the previous decades of socialist emphasis on helping "the poor" while they remained poor.

Individuals and groups have often been accused of reducing the wealth of nations, when in fact they have contributed to its increase. Many highly productive immigrant groups in many parts of the world—the overseas Chinese in Southeast Asia, the Lebanese in West Africa, and the Indians in Fiji, among others—have been accused of draining away the wealth of the countries in which they settled because they have sent money back to members of their families still living in the countries from which they came. But these earnings are almost invariably due to providing goods and services which their customers and clients obviously valued more than the money they paid.

On net balance, these productive groups have drained nothing but have added to the wealth of both the countries in which they settled and the countries from which they came. It has not been a zero-sum process. As in many other cases, the economic facts are fairly straightforward and uncomplicated. It is the myths and misconceptions which become complicated, especially those revolving around "income distribution."

Fights over which individuals and groups get how big a slice of the pie create the kind of emotions and controversy on which the media, politicians, and intellectuals thrive. But the economic reality is that the main reason most Americans have prospered is that the pie itself has gotten much bigger, not because this group or that group changed a few percentage points in its share. For example, American families in the bottom quintile in income earned 4 percent of the income of all U.S. families in 1967 and this fell to 3.6 percent by the year 2000. Over that same span, however, the median real income of families in the bottom quintile rose by more than $4,000. That is not even counting the fact that most American families in the bottom quintile do not stay there permanently—and, indeed, most are also in the top quintile at some point over the years.

The changing allocation of scarce resources which makes continuing prosperity possible may change these percentages back and forth over time, as changing pay and employment prospects direct individuals to where their productivity would be higher and away from where it is lower. But it is changes in productivity and allocation which are crucial to the economic well-being of the population as a whole, not the few percentage point changes in relative shares which attract so much media, political, and other attention.

PART IV:
TIME AND RISK

Chapter 12

Investment and Speculation

A tourist in New York's Greenwich Village decided to have his portrait sketched by a sidewalk artist. He received a very fine sketch, for which he was charged $100.

"That's expensive," he said to the artist, "but I'll pay it, because it is a great sketch. But, really, it took you only five minutes."

"Twenty years and five minutes," the artist said.

Artistic ability is only one of many things which are accumulated over time for use later on. If the earlier sacrifices and risks are ignored, then the reward for what was done within the present time period may often seen exorbitant. Oil wells can repay their costs many times over—but they must also cover the costs of all the dry holes that were drilled in the ground while searching in vain for petroleum deposits before finally striking oil.

Add to this the cost of keeping people alive while waiting for their artistic talent to develop, their oil exploration to pay off, or their academic credits to finally add up to enough to earn their degree, and there may be a considerable investment to be repaid. The repaying of the investment is not a matter of morality, but of economics. If the return on the investment is not enough to make it worthwhile, fewer people will make that particular investment in the future, and consumers will therefore be denied the use of the goods and services that would otherwise have been produced. No one is under any obligation to make all investments pay off, but how many need to pay off, and to what extent, is determined by how many consumers value the benefits of other people's investments.

Where the consumers do not value what is being produced, the investment should *not* pay off. When people insist on specializing in a field for which there is little demand, their investment has been a waste of scarce resources that could have produced something else that others wanted. The low pay and sparse employment opportunities in that field are a compelling signal to them—and to others coming after them—to stop making such investments.

The principles of investment are involved in activities that do not pass through the marketplace, and are not normally thought of as economic. Putting things away after you use them is an investment of time in the present to reduce the time required to find them in the future. Explaining yourself to others can be a time-consuming, and even unpleasant, activity but it is engaged in as an investment to prevent greater unhappiness in the future from misunderstandings.

Investments take many forms, whether the investment is in human beings, steel mills, or transmission lines for electricity. Risk is an inseparable part of these investments and others. Among the ways of dealing with risk are speculation, insurance and the issuance of stocks and bonds. Among the kinds of investments to be considered here are investments in human beings, as well as investments in machinery, farm crops and hydroelectric dams.

While human capital can take many forms, there is a tendency of some to equate it with formal education. However, not only may many other valuable forms of human capital be overlooked this way, the value of formal schooling may be exaggerated and its counterproductive consequences in some cases not understood.

The industrial revolution was not created by highly educated people but by people with practical industrial experience. The airplane was invented by a couple of bicycle mechanics who had never gone to college. Electricity and many inventions run by electricity became central parts of the modern world because of a man with only three months of formal schooling, Thomas Edison.

Education has of course also made major contributions to economic development. But this is not to say that all kinds of education have. From an economic standpoint, some education has great value, some has no value and some can even have a negative value. While it is easy to understand the great value of specific skills in medical science or engineering, for example, or the more general foundation for a number of professions provided by mathematics or a command of the English language, other subjects such as literature make no pretense of producing marketable skills but are available for whatever they may contribute in other ways. In a country where education or higher levels of education are new, those who have obtained diplomas or degrees may feel that many kinds of work are now beneath them. In such societies, even engineers may prefer the desk to standing in the mud in hip boots at a construction site. Depending on what they have studied, the newly educated may have higher levels of expectations than they have higher levels of ability to create the wealth from which their expectations can be redeemed. In the Third World especially, those who are the first members of their respective families to reach higher education typically do not study difficult and demanding subjects like science, medicine, or engineering, but instead tend toward easier and fuzzier subjects which provide them with little in the way of marketable skills, which is to say, skills that can create prosperity for themselves or their country.

Large numbers of young people with schooling, but without economically meaningful skills, have produced much unemployment in Third World nations. Since the marketplace has little to offer such people that would be commensurate with their expectations, governments have created swollen bureaucracies to hire them, in order to neutralize their potential for political disaffection, civil unrest or insurrection. In turn, these bureaucracies and the voluminous and time-consuming red tape they generate can become obstacles to others who do have the skills and entrepreneurship needed to contribute to the country's economic advancement. In India, for example, two of its leading entrepreneurial families, the Tatas and the Birlas, were repeatedly frustrated in their efforts to obtain the necessary government permission to expand their enterprises:

> The Tatas made 119 proposals between 1960 and 1989 to start new businesses or expand old ones, and all of them ended up in the wastebaskets of bureaucrats. Aditya Birla, the young and dynamic inheritor of the Birla empire, who had trained at MIT, was so disillusioned with Indian policy that he decided to expand Birla enterprises outside India, and eventually set up dynamic companies in Thailand, Malaysia, Indonesia, and the Philippines, away from the hostile atmosphere of his home.

The vast array of government rules micro-managing businesses "ensured that every businessman would break some law or other every month," according to an India executive. Large businesses in India set up their own bureaucracies in Delhi, parallel to those of the government, in order to try to

keep track of the progress of their applications for the innumerable government permissions required to do things that businesses did on their own in
free market economies, and to pay bribes as necessary to secure these permissions. The consequences of suffocating bureaucratic controls in India have
been shown not only by such experiences while they were in full force but
also by the country's dramatic economic improvements after many of these
controls were relaxed or eliminated. The economy's growth rate increased
dramatically after reforms in 1991 freed many of its entrepreneurs from some
of the worst controls, and foreign investment in India rose from $150 million
to $3 billion.

Hostility to entrepreneurial minorities like the Chinese in Southeast Asia
or the Lebanese in West Africa has been especially fierce among the newly
educated indigenous people, who see their own diplomas and degrees bringing them much less economic reward than the earnings of minority business
owners who may have less formal schooling than themselves.

In short, more schooling is not automatically more human capital. It can
in some cases reduce a country's ability to use the human capital that it already possesses.

SPECULATION

Most market transactions involve buying things that exist, based on whatever value they have to the buyer and whatever price is charged by the seller.
Some transactions, however, involve buying things that do not yet exist or
whose value has yet to be determined—or both. For example, the price of
stock in the Internet company Amazon.com rose for years before the company made its first dollar of profits. People were obviously speculating that
the company would eventually make profits or that others would keep bidding the price up, so that the initial stockholder could sell the stock for a
profit, whether or not Amazon.com itself ever made a profit. After years of
operating at a loss, Amazon.com finally made its first profit in 2001.

Exploring for oil is a costly speculation, since millions of dollars may be
spent before discovering whether there is in fact any oil at all where the exploration is taking place, much less whether it is enough oil to repay the
money spent. Many other things are bought in hopes of future earnings
which may or may not materialize—scripts for movies that may never be
made, pictures painted by artists who may or may not become famous some
day, and foreign currencies that may go up in value over time, but which

could just as easily go down. Speculation as an economic activity may be engaged in by people in all walks of life but there are also professional speculators for whom this is their career. One of the professional speculator's main roles is in relieving other people from having to speculate as part of their regular economic activity.

When an American wheat farmer in Idaho or Nebraska is getting ready to plant his crop, he has no way of knowing what the price of wheat will be when the crop is harvested. That depends on innumerable other wheat farmers, not only in the United States but as far away as Russia or Argentina. If the wheat crop fails in Russia or Argentina, the world price of wheat will shoot up, causing American wheat farmers to get very high prices for their crop. But if there are bumper crops of wheat in Russia or Argentina, there may be more wheat on the world market than anybody can use, with the excess having to go into expensive storage facilities. That will cause the world price of wheat to plummet, so that the American farmer may have nothing to show for all his work and may be lucky to avoid taking a loss on the year. Meanwhile, he and his family will have to live on their savings or borrow from whatever sources will lend to them. In order to avoid having to speculate like this, the farmer may in effect pay a professional speculator to carry the risk, while the farmers sticks to farming.

The speculator signs contracts to buy or sell at prices fixed today for goods to be delivered at some future date. This shifts the risk of the activity from the person engaging in it—such as the wheat farmer, in this case—to someone who is, in effect, betting that he can guess the future prices better than the other person and has the financial resources to ride out the inevitable wrong bets, in order to make a profit on the bets that turn out better.

Speculation is often misunderstood as being the same as gambling, when in fact it is the opposite of gambling. What gambling involves, whether in games of chance or in actions like playing Russian roulette, is creating a risk that would otherwise not exist, in order either to profit or to exhibit one's skill or lack of fear. What economic speculation involves is coping with an *inherent* risk in such a way as to minimize it and to leave it to be borne by whoever is best equipped to bear it.

When a commodity speculator offers to buy wheat that has not yet been planted, that makes it easier for a farmer to plant wheat, without having to wonder what the market price will be like later, at harvest time. A futures contract guarantees the seller a specified price in advance, regardless of what the market price may turn out to be at the time of delivery. This separates farming from economic speculation, allowing each to be done by different people, in each case by the person best able to do it. The speculator uses his knowledge of the market, and of economic and statistical analysis, to try to arrive at a better guess than the farmer may be able to make, and thus is able to offer a price that the farmer will consider an attractive alternative to waiting to sell at whatever price happens to prevail in the market at harvest time.

Although speculators seldom make a profit on every transaction, they must come out ahead in the long run, in order to stay in business. Their profit depends on paying the farmer a price that is lower on average than the price which actually emerges at harvest time. The farmer also knows this, of course. In effect, the farmer is paying the speculator for carrying the risk. As with other goods and services, the question may be raised as to whether the service rendered is worth the price charged. At the individual level, each farmer can decide for himself whether the deal is worth it. Each speculator must of course bid against other speculators, as each farmer must compete with other farmers, whether in making futures contracts or in selling at harvest time. From the standpoint of the economy as a whole, competition determines what the price will be and therefore what the speculator's profit will be. If that profit exceeds what it takes to entice investors to risk their money in this volatile field, more investments will flow into this segment of the market until competition drives profits down to a level that just compensates the expenses, efforts, and risks.

Competition is visibly frantic among speculators who shout their offers and bids in commodity exchanges. Prices fluctuate from moment to moment and a five-minute delay in making a deal can mean the difference between profits and losses. Even a modest-sized firm engaging in commodity speculation can gain or lose hundreds of thousands of dollars in a day, and huge corporations can gain or lose millions in a few hours.

One of the most dramatic examples of what can happen with commodity speculation involved the rise and fall of silver prices in 1980. Silver was selling at $6.00 an ounce in early 1979 but skyrocketed to a high of $50.05 an ounce by early 1980. However, this price began a decline that reached $21.62 on March 26th. Then, in just one day, that price was cut in half to $10.80. In the process, the billionaire Hunt brothers, who were speculating heavily in silver, lost more than a billion dollars *within a few weeks*. Speculation is one of the financially riskiest activities for the individual speculator, though it reduces risks for the economy as a whole.

Speculation may be engaged in by people who are not normally thought of as speculators. As far back as the 1870s, a food-processing company headed by Henry Heinz signed contracts to buy cucumbers from farmers at prearranged prices, regardless of what the market prices might be when the cucumbers were harvested. Then as now, those farmers who did *not* sign futures contracts with anyone were necessarily engaging in speculation about prices at harvest time, whether or not they thought of themselves as speculators. Incidentally, the deal proved to be disastrous for Heinz when there was a bumper crop of cucumbers, well beyond what he expected or could afford to buy, forcing him into bankruptcy. Years later, he started over again, founding the H. J. Heinz company that continues to exist today.

Because risk is the whole reason for speculation in the first place, being wrong is a common experience, though being wrong too often means facing financial extinction. Predictions, even by very knowledgeable people, can be wrong by vast amounts. The distinguished British magazine *The Economist* predicted in March 1999 that the price of a barrel of oil "may be heading for $5," but in fact the price of oil *rose* to $25 a barrel by December. Anyone speculating in oil on the basis of *The Economist*'s statement could have been ruined financially. Had they signed a contract in March to sell oil at $10 a barrel in December, they might have expected a profit of $5 a barrel, but they would have ended up with losses of $15 a barrel, which can get very expensive for anyone selling an oil tanker's cargo.

Futures contracts are made for delivery of gold, oil, soybeans, foreign currencies and many other things at some price fixed in advance for delivery on a future date. Commodity speculation is only one kind of speculation. People also speculate in real estate, corporate stocks, or other things. For example, the stock of the Internet bookseller Amazon.com rose sharply for years before the company made a cent of profit. Why were buyers bidding up the price of this stock, which had yet to pay a dividend, from a company which as yet had no profits from which dividends might be paid if they wanted to? One reason was the belief that Amazon.com would eventually become profitable. Another reason was that the price of the stock was expected to continue to rise, so that the initial buyers could make a profit by selling to subsequent buyers, regardless of whether Amazon.com made a profit or not. This second reason was pure speculation.

The full cost of risk is not only the amount of money involved, it is also the worry that hangs over the individual while waiting to see what happens. A farmer may expect to get $100 a ton for his crop but also knows that it could turn out to be $50 a ton or $150. If a speculator offers to guarantee to buy his crop at $90 a ton, that price may look good if it spares the farmer months of sleepless nights wondering how he is going to support his family if the harvest price leaves him nothing to cover his costs. Not only may the speculator be better equipped financially to deal with being wrong, he may be better equipped psychologically, since the kind of people who worry a lot do not usually go into commodity speculation. A commodity speculator I know had one year when his business was operating at a loss going into December, but things changed so much in December that he still ended up with a profit for the year—to his surprise, as much as anyone else's. This is not an occupation for the faint of heart.

Economic speculation is another way of allocating scarce resources—in this case, knowledge. Neither the speculator nor the farmer knows what the prices will be when the crop is harvested. But the speculator happens to have more knowledge of markets and of economic and statistical analysis than the farmer, just as the farmer has more knowledge of how to grow the crop. My commodity speculator friend admitted that he had never actually seen a soybean and had no idea what they looked like, even though he had probably bought and sold millions of dollars worth of them over the years. He simply transferred ownership of his soybeans on paper to soybean buyers at harvest time, without ever taking physical possession of them from the farmer. He was not really in the soybean business, he was in the risk management business.

Speculation means that complementary knowledge is thus coordinated, creating greater efficiency in the production of products which have inherent risks associated with their production. These risks can never be eliminated, but they can be minimized by having them borne by those best able to bear them, both from the standpoint of specialized knowledge and skills and from the standpoint of having sufficient financial accumulations to ride out losing speculations while waiting for them to be offset by winning speculations in the long run.

INVENTORIES

Inherent risks must be dealt with by the economy not only through economic speculation but also by maintaining inventories.

Put differently, *inventory is a substitute for knowledge.* No food would ever be thrown out after a meal, if the cook knew beforehand exactly how much each person would eat and could therefore cook just that amount. Since inventory costs money, a business enterprise must try to limit how much inventory it has on hand, while covering the possibility that its best guess as to how much it will need may be inadequate. Having either too large or too small an inventory means losing money. One of the factors in the success of Dell computers has been its ability to operate with only enough inventory to last for five days, while its competitors' inventories are some multiple of that.

Clearly, those businesses which come closest to the optimal size of inventory will have their profit prospects enhanced. More important, the total resources of the economy will be allocated more efficiently, not only because each enterprise has an incentive to be efficient, but also because those firms which turn out to be right more often are more likely to survive and continue making such decisions, while those who repeatedly carry far too large an inventory, or far too small, are likely to disappear from the market through bankruptcy. Too large an inventory means excess costs of doing business, compared to the costs of their competitors, who are therefore in a position to sell at lower prices and take away customers. Too small an inventory means running out of what the customers want, not only missing out on immediate sales but also risking having those customers look elsewhere for more dependable suppliers in the future.

Some of the same economic principles involving risk apply to activities far removed from the marketplace. A soldier going into battle does not take just the number of bullets he will fire or just the amount of first aid supplies he will need if wounded in a particular way, because neither he nor anyone else has the kind of foresight required to do that. The soldier carries an inventory of both ammunition and medical supplies to cover various contingencies. At the same time, he cannot go into battle loaded down with huge amounts of everything that he might possibly need in every conceivable circumstance. That would slow him down and reduce his maneuverability, making him an easier target for the enemy. In other words, beyond some point, attempts to increase his safety can make his situation more dangerous.

RETURN ON INVESTMENT

Delayed rewards for costs incurred earlier are a return on investment, whether these rewards take the form of dividends paid on corporate stock or increases in incomes resulting from having gone to college or medical school. One of the largest investments in many people's lives consists of the time and energy expended over a period of years in raising their children. At one time, the return on that investment included having the children take care of the parents in old age, but today the return on this investment often consists only of the parents' satisfaction in seeing their children's well-being and progress. From the standpoint of society as a whole, each generation that makes this investment in its offspring is repaying the investment that was made by the previous generation in raising those who are parents today.

There are also investments made outside the family that transfer wealth back and forth across the generations. As noted in Chapter 9, income varies greatly with age. People in their forties and fifties tend to have much higher incomes than people in their twenties. People in the older generation often put their money into banks and other financial institutions, which in turn lend it to young people buying homes or getting an education. What this means is that the amount of income that older and higher-income people are entitled to spend is not in fact all spent by them. A significant amount of their money is spent by younger people who borrow through banks, for example, and use their elders' money to pay for mortgages, tuition, and the like. Later, when people in the older generation retire, they begin to consume more than they are currently producing by using money now being repaid to banks and other financial institutions, which share with them the interest and principal they are receiving back from the younger generation, whose incomes have usually been rising over the years.

Looking beyond money to the actual goods and services exchanged over the years, the younger generation acquires more cars, houses, education and furniture than they can afford at the moment and the older generation is repaid later in medical care, retirement homes, cruises, and golf carts.

Although making investments and receiving the delayed return on those investments takes many forms and has been going on all over the world throughout the history of the human race, misunderstandings of this process have also been long standing and widespread. Sometimes these delayed benefits are called "unearned" income, simply because they do not represent rewards for contributions made during the current time period. Investments that build a factory may not be repaid until years later, after workers and managers have been hired and products manufactured and sold. During the particular year when dividends finally begin to be paid, investors may not have contributed anything, but this does not mean that the reward they receive is "unearned," simply because it was not earned during that particular year.

As noted in Chapter 11, the activities taking place in a factory before our eyes are not the only source of the business' success. Risks are invisible, even when they are present risks, and the past risks surrounding the initial creation of the business are readily forgotten by observers who see only a successful enterprise after the fact. Also easily overlooked are the many management decisions that had to be made in determining where to locate, what kind of equipment to acquire, and what policies to follow in dealing with suppliers, consumers, and employees—any one of which decisions could spell the difference between success and failure. And of course what also cannot be seen are all the similar businesses that went out of business because they did not do all the things done by the surviving business before our eyes, or did not do them equally well.

Because what is immediately visible to the naked eye makes a more lasting impression than past or present factors invisible inside other people's heads, it is easy to regard the visible factors as the sole or most important factors, even when other businesses with those same visible factors went bankrupt, while an expertly managed enterprise in the same industry flourished and grew. Nor are such misunderstandings inconsequential. Elaborate ideologies and mass movements have been based on the notion that only the workers really create wealth, while others merely skim off profits, without having contributed anything to producing the wealth in which they unjustly share.

Similar misconceptions have had fateful consequences for money-lenders around the world. For many centuries, money-lenders have been widely condemned in many cultures for receiving back more money than they lent—that is, for getting an "unearned" income for waiting and taking risks. Often the social stigma attached to money lending has been so great that only minorities who lived outside the existing social system anyway have been willing to take on such stigmatized activities. Thus, for centuries, Jews predominated in such occupations in Europe, as the Chinese did in Southeast Asia, the Chettiars and Marwaris in India, and other minority groups in other parts of the world. At various times and places, the hostility to such groups has reached the point where these minorities have been expelled by governments or have been forced to flee from mob violence. Although often depicted as useless parasites, the contribution of money-lending minorities has been demonstrated after their departure by shortages of credit and general economic declines in the countries that forced them out.

Just as prices in general affect the allocation of resources from one place to another at a given time, so returns on investment affect the allocation of resources from one time period to another. A high rate of return provides incentives for people to save and invest more than they would at a lower rate of return. To say the same thing differently, a higher rate of return encourages people to consume less in the present, in order to consume more in the future. It allocates resources over time. The individual saver need not invest directly. Money saved in a bank, for example, may be lent out to someone else and invested in establishing or enlarging a business.

Investment plays another very important role in the economy. When teenage Henry Ford walked from the farm where he worked all the way into Detroit, in order to look for a job, he clearly did not have the kind of money needed to manufacture millions of automobiles. Where did he get that money, then? Obviously, someone else thought enough of his ideas and abilities to risk some money backing him to get started. As he proved himself at one step after another, more and more people were willing to put their money behind him, in order to cash in on the product and the mass-production industry that he was creating. Investment is a way of transferring resources to where they have alternative uses that are more valuable than where they are.

Nor was Henry Ford unique. The Hewlett Packard hi-tech corporate empire began in a garage rented with borrowed money. Numerous other entrepreneurs, starting with little more than an idea and determination, have found investors willing to take a chance on them, just as investors take chances on oil wells or soybean futures. Although willing to take risks, these investors cannot be reckless or they will end up with nothing to invest. In this way, entrepreneurial talent gets a chance to prove itself in the marketplace, even if that talent originates in someone with no money of his own and utterly unknown to the general public or to the political powers that be. It is yet another way in which a free market system taps knowledge and abilities that have no avenues to emerge in more restrictive societies. This is often looked at in terms of a benefit to a fortunate few who are allowed to rise in the economic system but its more consequential impact is in allowing whole populations to rise in prosperity by tapping the talents and insights of people scattered across a vast social spectrum.

PRESENT VALUE

Although many goods and services are bought for immediate use, many other benefits come in a stream over time, whether as a season's ticket to baseball games or an annuity that will make monthly pension payments to you after you retire. That whole stream of benefits may be purchased at a given moment for what economists call its "present value." However, more is involved than simply determining the price to be paid, important as that is. The implications of present value affect economic decisions and their consequences, even in areas that are not normally thought of as economic, such as determining the amount of natural resources available for future generations.

Prices and Present Values

Whether a home, business, or farm is maintained, repaired or improved today determines how long it will last and how well it will operate in the future. However, the owner who has put in these improvements does not have to wait to see the future effects on the property's value. These future benefits are immediately reflected in the property's *present value*. The "present value" of an asset is in fact nothing more than its anticipated future benefits, added up and discounted for the fact that they are delayed. Your home, business, or farm may be functioning no better than your neighbor's today, but if the prospective toll of wear and tear on your property over time is reduced by installing heavier pipes, stronger woods, or other more durable building materials, then your property's market value will *immediately* be worth more than that of your neighbor, even if there is no visible difference in the way they are functioning today.

Conversely, if the city announces that it is going to begin building a sewage treatment plant next year, on a piece of land next to your home, the value of your home will decline *immediately*, before the adjoining land has been touched. The present value of an asset reflects its future benefits or detriments, so that anything which is expected to enhance or reduce those benefits or detriments will immediately affect the price at which the asset can be sold today.

Present value links the future to the present. It makes sense for a ninety-year-old man to begin planting fruit trees that will take 20 years before they reach their maturity because his land will *immediately* be worth more as a result of those trees. He can sell the land a month later and go live in the Bahamas if he wishes, because he will be receiving additional value from the fruit that is expected to grow on those trees, years after he is no longer alive. Part of the value of his wealth today consists of the value of food that has not yet been grown—and which will be eaten by children who have not yet been born.

One of the big differences between economics and politics is that politicians are not forced to pay attention to future consequences that lie beyond the next election. An elected official whose policies keep the public happy up through election day stands a good chance of being voted another term in office, even if those policies will have ruinous consequences in later years.

There is no "present value" to make political decision-makers today take future consequences into account, when those consequences will come after election day.

Although the general public may not have sufficient knowledge or training to realize the long-run implications of today's policies, financial specialists who deal in government bonds do. Thus the Standard & Poor's bond-rating service downgraded California's state bonds in the midst of that state's electricity crisis in 2001, even though there had been no defaults on those bonds, nor any lesser payments made to those who had bought California bonds, and there were billions of dollars of surplus in the state's treasury. What Standard & Poor understood was that the heavy financial responsibilities taken on by the California government to meet the electricity crisis meant that heavy taxes or heavy debt were waiting over the horizon. That increased the risk of future defaults or delay in payments to bondholders—thereby reducing the present value of those bonds.

Any series of future payments can be reduced to a present value that can be paid immediately in a lump sum. Winners of lotteries who are paid in installments over a period of years can sell those payments to a financial institution that will give them a fixed sum immediately. So can accident victims who have been awarded installment payments from insurance companies. Because the present value of a series of payments due over a period of decades may be considerably less than the sum total of all those payments, due to discounting for delays, the lump sums paid may be less than half of those totals, causing some people who sold to relieve immediate financial problems to later resent the deal they made. Others, however, are pleased and return to make similar deals in the future.

Conversely, some individuals wish to convert a fixed sum of money into a stream of future payments. Elderly people who are retiring with what seems like an adequate amount to live on must be concerned with whether they will live longer than expected—"outlive their money" as the expression goes—and end up in poverty. In order to avoid this, they may use a portion of their money to purchase an annuity from an insurance company. For example, as of the year 2001, by purchasing an annuity for $100,000, a seventy year old man would receive $772 a month for life—whether that life was three more years or thirty more years. In other words, the risk would be shifted to the insurance company, for a price. As in other cases, the risk is not only shifted but reduced, since the insurance company can more accurately predict the lifespan of millions of people to whom it has sold annuities than any given individual can predict his own lifespan. Incidentally, a woman aged 70 would get somewhat smaller monthly payments—$725—for the same price, given that women usually live longer than men.

The key point is that the reduced risk comes from the greater predictability of large numbers. A news story some years ago told of a speculator who made a deal with an elderly woman who needed money. In exchange for her making him the heir to her house, he agreed to pay her a fixed sum every month as long as she lived. However, this one-to-one deal did not work out as planned because she lived far longer than anyone expected and the speculator died before she did. An insurance company not only has the advantage of large numbers, it has the further advantage that its existence is not limited to the human lifespan.

Natural Resources

Present value profoundly affects the discovery and use of natural resources. There may be enough oil underground to last for centuries, but its present value determines how much oil will repay what it costs anyone to discover it at any given time—and that may be no more than enough oil to last for a dozen or so years. A failure to understand this basic economic reality has led to numerous and widely publicized false predictions that we were "running out" of petroleum, coal, or some other natural resource.

In 1960, for example, a best-selling book said that the United States had only a 13-year supply of domestic petroleum at the existing rate of usage. At that time, the known petroleum reserves of the United States were not quite 32 billion barrels. At the end of the 13 years, the known petroleum reserves of the United States were more than 36 billion barrels. Yet the original statistics and the arithmetic based on them were accurate. Why then did the United States not run out of oil by 1973? Was it just dumb luck that more oil was discovered—or were there more fundamental economic reasons?

Just as shortages and surpluses are not simply a matter of how much physical stuff there is, either absolutely or relative to the population, so known reserves of natural resources are not simply a matter of how much physical stuff there is underground. For natural resources as well, prices are crucial. So are present values.

How much of any given natural resource is known to exist depends on how much it costs to know. Oil exploration, for example, is very costly. This includes not only the costs of geological exploration but also the costs of drilling expensive dry holes before finally striking oil. As these costs mount up while more and more oil is being discovered, the growing abundance of known supplies of oil reduces its price through supply and demand. Eventually the point is reached where the cost per barrel of finding more oil in a given place exceeds the present value per barrel of the oil you are likely to find there. At that point, it no longer pays to keep exploring. Depending on a number of circumstances, the total amount of oil discovered at that point may well be no more than the 13 years' supply which led to dire predictions that we were running out. Only as the existing supplies of oil are being used up will rising prices lead to more huge investments in oil exploration.

As one example of the kinds of costs that can be involved, a major oil exploration venture in the Gulf of Mexico spent $80 million on the initial exploration and leases, and another $120 million for exploratory drilling, just to see if it looked like there was enough oil to justify continuing further. Then there were $530 million spent for building drilling platforms, pipelines and other infrastructure, and—finally—$370 million for drilling for oil where there were proven reserves. This adds up to a total of $1.1 billion.

Imagine if the interest rate had been twice as high on this much money borrowed from banks or investors, making the total cost of exploration even higher. Or imagine that the oil companies had this much money of their own and could put it in a bank to earn twice the usual interest in safety. Would they have sunk as much money as they did into the more risky investment of looking for oil? Would you? Probably not. A higher interest rate would probably have meant less oil exploration and therefore smaller amounts of known reserves of petroleum. But that would not mean that we were any closer to running out of oil than if the interest rate were lower and the known reserves were correspondingly higher.

As more and more of the known reserves of oil get used up, the present value of the remaining oil begins to rise and once more exploration for additional oil becomes profitable. But, as of any given time, it never pays to discover all the oil that exists in the ground or under the sea. In fact, it does not pay to discover more than a minute fraction of that oil. What does pay is for people to write hysterical predictions that we are running out of natural resources. It pays not only in book sales and television ratings, but also in political power and in personal notoriety.

Even the huge usages of energy resources in the twentieth century have not reduced the known reserves of many of these resources. Given the enormous drain on energy resources created by such things as the spread of railroad networks, factory machinery, and the electrification of cities, it has been estimated that more energy was consumed in the first two decades of the twentieth century than in all the previously recorded history of the human race. Moreover, energy usage has continued to escalate since then. Yet known petroleum reserves have risen. At the end of the twentieth century, the known reserves of petroleum were more than ten times as large as they were in the middle of the twentieth century.

The economic considerations which apply to petroleum apply to other natural resources as well. No matter how much iron ore there is in the ground, it will never pay to discover more of it when its present value per ton is less than the cost of exploration and processing per ton. Yet, despite the fact that the twentieth century saw vast expansions in the use of iron and steel, the proven reserves of iron ore have grown several fold. So have the known reserves of copper, aluminum, and lead, among other natural resources. As of 1945, the known reserves of copper were 100 million metric tons. After a quarter of century of unprecedented use of copper, the known reserves of copper were *three times* what they were at the outset and, by 1999, copper reserves had doubled again.

The difference between the economic approach and the hysterical approach to natural resource usage was shown by a bet between the late economist Julian Simon and environmentalist Paul Ehrlich. Professor Simon offered to bet anyone that any set of five natural resources they chose would not have risen in real cost over any time period they chose. A group led by Professor Ehrlich took the bet and chose five natural resources. They also chose ten years as the time period for measuring how the real costs of these natural resources had changed. At the end of the decade, not only had the real cost of that set of five resources declined, so had the cost of every single resource which they had expected to rise in cost! Obviously, if we had been anywhere close to running out of those resources, their costs would have risen because the present value of these potentially more scarce resources would have risen.

In some ultimate sense, the total quantity of resources must of course be declining. However, a resource that is going to run out centuries after it becomes obsolete, or a thousand years after the sun grows cold, is not a serious practical problem. If it is going to run out within some time period that is a matter of practical relevance, then the rising present value of the resource whose exhaustion looms ahead will automatically force conservation, without either public hysteria or political exhortation.

Just as prices cause us to share scarce resources and their products with others at a given time, present value causes us to share those resources over time with future generations—without even being aware that we are sharing. It is of course also possible to share politically, by having the government assume control of natural resources, as it can assume control of other assets, or in fact of the whole economy.

The efficiency of political control versus impersonal control by prices in the marketplace depends in part on which method conveys the underlying realities more accurately. As already noted in earlier chapters, price controls and direct allocation of resources by political institutions requires far more explicit knowledge by a relatively small number of planners than is required for a market economy to be coordinated by prices to which millions of people respond according to their own first-hand knowledge of their own individual circumstances and preferences—and the relative handful of prices that each individual has to deal with. Planners can easily make false projections, either from ignorance or from various political motives, such as seeking more power, re-election, or other goals. For example, during the 1970s, a government scientist was asked to estimate the size of the American reserves of natural gas and how long it would last at the current rate of usage. His estimate was that the United States had enough natural gas to last for 4,000 years! While some might consider this good news, politically it was bad news at a time when the President of the United States was trying to arouse public support for more government programs to deal with the energy "crisis." This estimate was repudiated by the Carter administration and a new study begun, which reached more politically acceptable results.

Sometimes the known reserves of a natural resource seem especially small because the amount available at currently feasible costs is in fact nearing exhaustion in a few years. There may be vast amounts available at a slightly higher cost of extraction and processing, but these additional amounts will of course not be touched until the amount available at a lower cost is exhausted. For example, back when there were large coal deposits available on top of the ground, no one was going to the expense of digging even a few feet into the earth to get more, because the higher-cost coal underground could not compete in the marketplace with the cheaper coal found on the surface. During the interim, someone could sound an alarm that we are "running out" of coal that is "economically feasible" to use, coal that can be gotten without "prohibitive costs." But again, the whole purpose of prices is to be prohibitive. In this case, that prohibition prevented more costly resources from being used needlessly, so long as there were less costly sources of the same resource available.

If technology never improved, then all resources would become more costly over time, as the most easily obtained deposits were used up first and the less accessible, or less rich, or more difficult to process deposits were then resorted to. However, with improving technology, it can actually cost less to acquire future resources when their time comes, as happened with the resources that Julian Simon and Paul Ehrlich bet on. For example, the average cost of finding a barrel of oil fell from $15 in 1977 to $5 by 1998. It is hardly surprising that there were larger known oil reserves after the cost of knowing fell.

Although the reserves of natural resources in a nation are often discussed in terms of physical quantities, economic concepts of cost, prices, and present values must be considered if practical conclusions are to be reached. In addition to needless alarms about natural resources running out, there have also been, conversely, unjustifiably optimistic statements that some poor country has so many billions of dollars' worth of "natural wealth" in the form of iron ore or bauxite deposits or some other natural resource. Such statements mean very little without considering how much it would cost to extract and process those resources. A country with $10 billion worth of some natural resource might as well not have it if the costs of exploration, extraction and processing add up to $11 billion. Only if the demand for that resource rises enough in the future to raise its price above the costs of using it, or if future technological improvements lower the costs of producing it, would this resource become economically relevant.

Statistics on the physical totals of a natural resource may sometimes understate how much wealth that represents, if the costs of extraction and processing are especially low. It has been estimated that, in some parts of Russia, petroleum can be extracted at a cost of less than two dollars a barrel—less than one-tenth its selling price in the world market. In purely physical terms, Russia has larger petroleum reserves than any country outside the Middle East. But it is even better off in economic terms.

Chapter 13

Risks and Insurance

Risks inherent in economic activities can be dealt with in a wide variety of ways. In addition to the commodity speculation and inventory management discussed in the previous chapter, other ways of dealing with risk include stocks, bonds, and insurance. There are also other economic activities analogous to stocks, bonds, and insurance which deal with risks in ways that are legally different, though similar economically. Conversely, there are sources of income which seem similar to ordinary wages, salaries and profits but which are in fact quite different. These include capital gains. There are also systems that call themselves "social insurance" which are not insurance at all. Here, as in so many other places, we cannot go by words but must examine the underlying reality.

Whenever a home, a business, or any other asset increases in value over time, that increase is called a "capital gain." While it is another form of income, it differs from wages and salaries in not being paid right after it is earned, but usually only after an interval of some years. A thirty-year bond, for example, can be cashed in only after thirty years.

If you never sell your home, then whatever increase in value it has will be called an "unrealized capital gain." The same is true for someone who opens a grocery store that grows more valuable as its location becomes known throughout the neighborhood, and as it develops a set of customers who get into the habit of shopping at that particular store. Perhaps after the owner dies, his widow or children may decide to sell the store—and only then will the capital gain be realized.

Sometimes a capital gain comes from a purely financial transaction, where you simply pay someone a certain amount of money today in order to get back a somewhat larger amount of money later on. This happens when you put money into a savings account that pays interest, or when a pawnbroker lends money, or when you buy a $10,000 U. S. Treasury bond for somewhat less than $10,000.

However it is done, this is a trade-off of money today for money in the future. The fact that interest is paid implies that money today is worth more than the same amount of money in the future. How much more depends on many things, and varies from time to time, as well as from country to country at the same time.

BONDS

In the heyday of 19th-century British industrialization, railroad companies could raise the huge sums of money required to build miles of tracks and buy trains, by selling bonds that paid about 3 percent per year. This was possible only because the public had great confidence in both the railroads and the stability of the money. If inflation had been 4 percent a year, those who bought the bonds would have lost real value instead of gaining it. But the value of the British pound sterling was very stable and reliable during that era.

Since those times, inflation has become more common, so the interest rate would now have to cover whatever level of inflation was expected and still leave a prospect of a real gain in terms of an increase in purchasing power. The risk of inflation varies from country to country and from one era to another so the rate of return on investments must include an allowance for the risk of inflation, which also varies. At the beginning of the twenty-first century, Mexico's government bonds paid a quarter of a point higher interest than those of the United States, while those of Brazil paid half a point higher than those of Mexico. Brazil's interest rate then shot up another percentage point after the emergence of a left-wing candidate for president of the country. Varying risks are reflected in varying risk premiums added to interest rates. As of April 2003, short-term interest rates ranged from less than 2 percent in Hong Kong to 19 percent in Russia and 39 percent in Turkey.

Leaving inflation aside, however, how much would a $10,000 bond that matures a year from now be worth to you today? That is, how much would you pay today for a bond that can be cashed in for $10,000 next year? Clearly it would not be worth $10,000, because future money is not as valuable as the same amount of present money. Even if you felt certain that you would still be alive a year from now, and even if there were no inflation expected, you would still prefer to have the same amount of money right now rather than later. If nothing else, money that you have today can be put in a bank and earn a year's interest on it. For the same reason, if you had a choice between buying a bond that matures a year from now and another bond of the same face value that matures ten years from now, you would not be willing to bid as much for the one that matures a decade later. What this says is that the same nominal amount of money has different values, depending on how long you must wait to get a return on it.

At a sufficiently high interest rate, you might be willing to wait a long time to get your money back. People buy 30-year bonds regularly, though usually at a higher rate of return than what is paid on financial securities that mature in a year or a decade. On the other hand, at a sufficiently low interest rate, you would not be willing to wait any time at all to get your money back. Somewhere in between is an interest rate at which you would be indifferent between lending money or keeping it. At that interest rate, the present value of a given amount of future money is equal to some smaller amount of present money. For example if you are indifferent at 4 percent, then a hundred dollars today is worth $104 a year from now to you. Any business or government agency that wants to borrow $100 from you today with a promise to pay you back a year from now will have to make that repayment at least $104. If everyone else has the same preferences that you do, then the interest rate in the economy as a whole will be 4 percent.

What if everyone does not have the same preferences that you do? Suppose that others will lend only when they get back 5 percent more at the end of the year? In that case, the interest rate in the economy as a whole will be 5 percent, simply because businesses and government cannot borrow the money they want for any less and they do not have to offer any more. Faced with a national interest rate of 5 percent, you would have no reason to accept less, even though you would take 4 percent if you had to.

In this situation, let us return to the question of how much you would be willing to bid for a $10,000 bond that matures a year from now. With an interest rate of 5 percent being available in the economy as a whole, it would not pay you to bid more than $9,523.81 for a $10,000 bond that matures a year from now. By investing that same amount of money somewhere else today at 5 percent, you could get back $10,000 in a year. Therefore, there is no reason for you to bid more than $9,523.81 for the $10,000 bond. What if the interest rate in the economy as a whole had been 12 percent, rather than 5 percent? Then it would not pay you to bid more than $8,928.57 for a $10,000 bond that matures a year from now. In short, what people will bid for bonds depends on how much they could get for the same money by putting it somewhere else. That is why bond prices go down when the interest rate goes up, and vice-versa.

What this also says is that, when the interest rate is 5 percent, $9,523.81 in the year 2000 is the same as $10,000 in the year 2001. This raises questions about the taxation of capital gains. If someone buys a bond for the former price and sells it a year later for the latter price, the government will of course want to tax the $476.19 difference. But is that really the same as an increase in value, if the two sums of money are just equivalent to one another? What if there has been a one percent inflation, so that the $10,000 received back would not have been enough to compensate for waiting, if the investor had expected inflation to reduce the real value of the bond?

What if there had been a 5 percent inflation, so that the amount received back was worth no more than the amount originally lent, with no reward at all for waiting? Clearly, the investor would be worse off than if he or she had never bought the bond. How then can this "capital gain" really be said to be a gain?

These are just some of the considerations that make the taxation of capital gains more complicated than the taxation of such other forms of income as wages and salaries. Some governments in some countries do not tax capital gains at all, while the rate at which such gains are taxed in the United States remains a matter of political controversy.

VARIABLE RETURNS VERSUS FIXED RETURNS

There are many ways of confronting the fact that the real value of a given sum of money varies with when it is received and with the varying likelihood that it will be received at all. Stocks and bonds are just one way of dealing with differing risks. But people who have no interest in buying these financial securities must also confront the same principles in other ways, when choosing a career for themselves or when considering public policy issues for the country as a whole.

Stocks and Bonds

Bonds differ from stocks because bonds are legal commitments to pay fixed amounts of money on a fixed date. Stocks are simply shares of the business that issues them, and there is no guarantee that the business will make a profit in the first place, much less pay out dividends instead of re-investing these profits in the business. Bond-holders have a legal right to be paid what they were promised, whether the business is making money or losing money. In that respect, they are like the business' employees, to whom fixed commitments have been made as to how much they would be paid per hour or per week or month. They are legally entitled to those amounts, regardless of whether the business is profitable or unprofitable. The owners of a business—whether that is a single individual or millions of stockholders—are not legally entitled to anything, except whatever happens to be left over after a business has paid its employees, bond-holders and other creditors. Considering the fact that most new businesses fail within a few years, what is left over can just as easily be negative as positive. In other words, people who set up businesses may not only fail to make a profit but may even lose part or all of what they originally invested. In short, stocks and bonds have different amounts of risk. Moreover, the mixture of stocks and bonds sold by different kinds of businesses may reflect the inherent risks of those businesses themselves.

Imagine that someone is raising money to go into a business where (1) the chances are 50–50 that he will go bankrupt and (2) if the business does survive financially, the initial investment will increase ten-fold. Perhaps he is drilling for oil or speculating in foreign currencies. What if he wants you to contribute $5,000 to this venture? If you can afford the risk, would you be better off buying $5,000 worth of stock in this enterprise or $5,000 worth of this company's bonds?

If you buy bonds, your chances are only 50–50 of getting all your money back. And if this enterprise prospers, you are only entitled to whatever rate of return was specified in the bond at the outset, no matter how many millions of dollars the entrepreneur makes with your money. Buying bonds in such a venture does not seem like a good deal. Buying stocks, on the other hand, might make sense. If the business goes bankrupt, your stock could be worthless, while a bond would have some residual value, based on whatever assets might remain to be sold, even if that only pays the bondholders and other creditors pennies on the dollar. On the other hand, if the business succeeds and its assets increase ten-fold, then the value of your stock likewise increases ten-fold.

As a rule of thumb, it has been estimated that a venture capitalist needs at least a 50 percent rate of return on successful investments, in order to cover the losses on the many unsuccessful investments and come out ahead over all. In real life, rates of return on venture capital can vary greatly from year to year. For the 12 months ending September 30, 2001, venture capital funds lost 32.4 percent. That is, not only did these venture capitalists as a whole not make any net profit, they lost nearly one-third of the money they had invested. But, just a couple of years earlier, venture capitalists averaged a rate of return of 163 percent in 1999.

The question of whether this kind of activity is worthwhile from the standpoint of the venture capitalist can be left to the venture capitalist to worry about. From the standpoint of the economy as a whole, the question is whether this kind of financial activity represents an efficient allocation of scarce resources which have alternative uses. Although individual venture capitalists can go bankrupt, just like the companies they invest in, the venture capital industry as a whole usually does not lose money—that is, it does not waste the available resources of the economy. From the time when data began to be kept on venture capital in 1970, there was not a single year over the next 30 years in which venture capitalists as a whole lost money. However, the fact that they lost money in the 31st year means that nothing is a sure thing. It is in fact remarkable that something which looks as risky as venture capital usually works out from the standpoint of the economy as a whole, even if not from the standpoint of every venture capitalist.

Now look at stocks and bonds from the standpoint of the entrepreneur who is trying to raise money for a risky undertaking. Knowing that bonds would be unattractive to investors and that a bank would likewise be reluctant to lend to him because of the high risks, he would almost certainly try to raise money by selling stocks instead. At the other end of the risk spectrum, consider a public utility that supplies something the public always needs, such as water or electricity. There is usually very little risk involved in putting money into such an enterprise, so the utility can issue and sell bonds, without having to pay the higher amounts that investors would earn on stocks.[1]

In short, risks vary among businesses and their financial arrangements vary accordingly. At one extreme, a commodity speculator can go from profits to losses and back again, not only from year to year but even from hour to

---

[1] There are exceptions to virtually every rule. People who bought bonds in California's electric utility companies, as a safe investment for their retirement years, saw most of the value of those investments vanish into thin air during that state's electricity crisis of 2001. The state forced these utilities to sell electricity to their customers for less than they were paying their suppliers. As these utilities went billions of dollars into debt, their bonds were downgraded to the level of junk bonds.

hour on a given day. That is why there are television pictures of frantic shout-
ing and waving in commodity exchanges, where prices are changing so
rapidly that the difference between making a deal right now and making it
five minutes from now can be vast sums of money.

A more common pattern among those businesses that succeed is one of
low income or no income at the beginning, followed by higher earnings after
the enterprise becomes established. For example, a dentist first starting out
in his profession after graduating from dental school and buying the costly
equipment needed, may have little or no net income the first year, before becoming known widely enough in the community to attract a large clientele.
During that interim, the dentist's secretary may be making more money than
the dentist. Later on, of course, the situation will reverse and some observers
may then think if unfair that the dentist makes several times the income of
the secretary.

Even when variable sums of money add up to the same total as fixed sums
of money, they are unlikely to be equally attractive. Would you be equally as
likely to enter two occupations with the same average income—say, $50,000
a year—over the next decade if one occupation paid $50,000 every year while
the income in the other occupation might vary from $10,000 one year to
$90,000 the next year and back again, in an unpredictable pattern? Chances
are you would require a somewhat higher average income in the occupation
with variable pay, to make it equally attractive with the occupation with a re-
liably fixed income. Accordingly, stocks usually yield a higher average rate of
return than bonds, since stocks have a variable rate of return (including,
sometimes, no return at all), while bonds have a guaranteed fixed rate of return. It is not some moral principle that makes this happen. It happens because people will not take the risk of buying stocks unless they can expect a
higher average rate of return than they get from bonds.

The degree of risk varies not only with the kind of investment but also
with the period of time. For a period of one year, bonds are likely to be much
safer than stocks. But for a period of 20 or 30 years, the risk of inflation
threatens the value of bonds or other assets with fixed-dollar amounts, such
as bank accounts, while stock prices tend to rise with inflation like real estate,
factories, or other real assets. Being shares of real assets, stocks share in the
rising price of real assets during inflation. Moreover, even in the absence of
inflation, stock prices can generally be relied on to rise over a period of
decades, while bond prices and the prices of other fixed-dollar assets do not.
Therefore the relative safety of the two kinds of assets can be quite different
in the long run than in the short run.

Someone planning for retirement many years in the future may find a suitable mixture of stocks a much safer investment than someone who will need the money in a year or two. "Like money in the bank" is a popular phrase used to indicate something that is a very safe bet, but money in the bank is not particularly safe over a period of decades, when inflation can steal much of its value. The same is true of bonds. Eventually, after reaching an age when the remaining life expectancy is no longer measured in decades, it may be prudent to begin transferring money out of stocks and into bonds, bank accounts, and other assets with greater short-run safety.

Risk and Time

To take an extreme example of how risk can vary over time, while a dollar invested in bonds in 1801 would be worth nearly a thousand dollars by 1998, a dollar invested in stocks that same year would be worth more than half a million dollars. All this is in real terms, taking inflation into account. Meanwhile, a dollar invested in gold in 1801 would in 1998 be worth just 78 cents. The phrase "as good as gold" can be as misleading as the phrase "money in the bank," when talking about the long run. While there have been many short-run periods when bonds and gold held their values as stock prices plummeted, the relative safety of these different kinds of investments varies greatly with how long a time period you have in mind. Moreover, the pattern is not the same in all eras.

The real rate of return on American stocks was just 3.6 percent during the Depression decade from 1931 to 1940, while bonds paid 6.4 percent. However, bonds had a negative rate of return in real terms during the succeeding decades of the 1940s, 1950, 1960s and 1970s, while stocks had positive rates of return during that period. In other words, money invested in bonds during those inflationary decades would not buy as much when these bonds were cashed in as when the bonds were bought, even though larger sums of money were received in the end. With the restoration of price stability in the last two decades of the twentieth century, both stocks and bonds had positive rates of real returns.

Risk is always specific to the time at which a decision is made. "Hindsight is twenty-twenty," but risk always involves looking forward, not backward. During the early, financially shaky years of McDonald's, the company was so desperate for cash at one point that its founder, Ray Kroc, offered to sell half interest in McDonald's for $25,000—and no one accepted his offer. If anyone had, that person would have become a billionaire over the years. But, at the time, it was neither foolish for Ray Kroc to make that offer nor for others to turn it down.

The relative safety and profitability of various kinds of investments depends on your own knowledge. An experienced expert in financial transactions may grow rich speculating in gold, while people of more modest knowledge are losing big. However, with gold you are unlikely to be completely wiped out, since gold always has a value for jewelry and industrial uses, while any given stock can end up not worth the paper it is written on. Nor is it only novices who lose money in the stock market. Harvard's $13 billion endowment fell by 10 percent—more than a billion dollars—in less than three months. In the past, colleges and universities kept their endowments in safe investments like government bonds but, during the stock market boom of the 1990s, many went for higher rates of return in the private financial markets. As *The Wall Street Journal* put it, these academic institutions "are re-learning the lesson that high returns often are achieved by taking high risks."

Even top executives with inside knowledge can go wrong. The former Chief Executive Officer of Yahoo! Inc. sold $25 million worth of that company's stock that he owned in 2001—just before the stock's price shot up 65 percent. That same year, the 400 richest Americans lost a total of $80 billion.

Risk and Diversification

The various degrees and varieties of risk can be dealt with by having a variety of investments—a "portfolio," as they say—so that when one kind of investment is not doing well, other kinds may be flourishing, thereby reducing the over-all risk to your total assets. For example, as already noted, bonds may not be doing well during a period when stocks are very profitable, or vice versa. A portfolio that includes a combination of stocks and bonds may be much less risky than investing exclusively in either. Even adding an individually risky investment like gold, whose price is very volatile, to a portfolio can reduce the risk of the portfolio as a whole, since gold prices tend to move in the opposite direction from stock prices.

A portfolio consisting mostly—or even solely—of stocks can have its risks reduced by having a mixture of stocks from different companies. These may be a group of stocks selected by a professional investor who charges others for selecting and managing their money in what is called a "mutual fund." Where the selection of stocks bought by the mutual fund is simply a mixture based on whatever stocks make up the Dow Jones Industrial average or the

Standard & Poor's Index, then there is less management required and less may be charged for the service.

Theoretically, those mutual funds where the managers actively follow the various markets and then pick and choose which stocks to buy and sell should average a higher rate of return than those mutual funds which simply buy whatever stocks happen to make up the Dow Jones or Standard & Poor's index. Some actively managed mutual funds do in fact do better than index mutual funds, but in many years the index funds have had higher rates of return than most of the actively managed funds, much to the embarrassment of the latter.

On the other hand, the index funds offer little chance of a big killing, such as a highly successful actively managed fund might. A reporter for the *Wall Street Journal* who recommended index funds for people who don't have the time or the confidence to buy their own stocks individually said: "True, you might not laugh all the way to the bank. But you will probably smile smugly." However, index mutual funds lost 9 percent of their value in the year 2000, so there is no complete freedom from risk anywhere. For mutual funds as a whole—both managed funds and index funds—a $10,000 investment in early 1998 would by early 2003 be worth less than $9,000. Out of a thousand established mutual funds, just one made money every year of the decade ending in 2003.

While mutual funds made their first appearance in the last quarter of the twentieth century, the economic principles of risk-spreading have long been understood by those investing their own money. In centuries past, shipowners often found it more prudent to own 10 percent of ten different ships, rather than own one ship outright. The dangers of a ship sinking were much greater in the days of wooden ships and sails than in the modern era of metal, mechanically powered ships. Owning 10 percent shares in ten different ships increased the danger of a loss through sinking but greatly reduced how catastrophic that loss would be.

Investing in Human Capital

Investing in human capital is in some ways similar to investing in other kinds of capital and in some ways different. People who accept jobs with no pay, or with pay much less than they could have gotten elsewhere, are in effect investing their working time, rather than money, in hopes of a larger future return than they would get by accepting a job that pays a higher salary initially. But, where someone invests in another person's human capital, the return on this investment is not as readily recovered by the investor. Typically, those who use other people's money to pay for their education, for example, either receive that money as a gift—from parents or philanthropic individuals or organizations, for example—or else borrow the money.

While students can, in effect, issue bonds, they seldom issue stocks. That is, many students go into debt to pay for their education but rarely sell percentage shares of their future earnings. In the few cases where students have done that, they have often felt resentful in later years at having to continue contributing a share of their income after their payments have already covered all of the initial investment made in them. But dividends from corporations that issue stock likewise continue to be paid in disregard of whether the initial investment has been repaid. That is the difference between stocks and bonds.

It is misleading to look at this situation only after an investment in human capital has paid off. Stocks are issued precisely because of risks that the investment will not pay off. Given that a substantial number of college students will never graduate, and that even some of those who do may have meager incomes, the pooling of risks enables more private financing to be made available to college students in general. Ideally, if prospective students could and did issue both stocks and bonds in themselves, it would be unnecessary for parents or taxpayers to subsidize their education, and even poverty-stricken students could go to the most expensive colleges without financial aid. However, legal problems, institutional inertia, and social attitudes have kept such arrangements from becoming widespread in colleges and universities.

In some endeavors, however, it is feasible to have human beings in effect issue both stocks and bonds in themselves. Boxing managers have often owned percentage shares of their fighters' earnings. Thus many poor youngsters have received years of instruction in boxing that they would have been unable to pay for. Nor would simply going into debt to pay for this instruction be feasible because the risks are too high for lenders to lend in exchange for a fixed repayment. Some boxers never make it to the point where their earnings from fighting would enable them to repay the costs of their instruction and management. Nor are such boxers likely to have alternative occupations from which they could repay large loans to cover the costs of their failed boxing careers. Consider, for example, the fact that only one heavyweight champion ever had a college degree (Gene Tunney). More heavyweight champions than that have been on welfare or served time in prison.

Given the poor backgrounds from which most boxers have come and the high risk that they will never make any substantial amount of money, financing their early training in effect by stocks makes more sense than financing it by bonds. A fight manager can collect a dozen young men from tough neighborhoods as boxing prospects, knowing that most will never repay his investment of time and money, but calculating that a couple probably will, if he has made wise choices. Since there is no way to know in advance which ones these will be, the point is to have enough financial gains from shares in the winning fighters to offset the losses on the fighters who never make enough money to repay the investment.

For similar reasons, Hollywood agents have acquired percentage shares in the future earnings of young unknown actors and actresses who looked promising, thus making it worthwhile to invest time and money in the development and marketing of their talent. The alternative of having these would-be movie stars pay for this service by borrowing the money would be far less feasible, given the high risk that the majority who fail would never be able to repay the loans and might well disappear after it was clear that they were going nowhere in Hollywood.

At various times and places, it has been common for labor contractors to supply teams of immigrant laborers to work on farms, factories, or construction sites, in exchange for a percentage share of their earnings. In effect, the contractor owns stock in the workers, rather than bonds. Such workers have often been both very poor and unfamiliar with the language and customs of the country, so that their prospects of finding their own jobs individually have been very unpromising. In the nineteenth and early twentieth centuries, vast numbers of contract laborers from Italy went to countries in the Western Hemisphere and contract laborers from China went to countries in Southeast Asia, while contract laborers from India spread around the world to British Empire countries from Malaysia to Fiji to British Guiana.

In short, investment in human capital, as in other capital, has been made in the form of stocks as well as bonds. Although these terms have not been used legally, that is what they have amounted to economically.

These are just some of the ways in which risks can be spread, thereby reducing the total risk. Insurance is another example.

INSURANCE

Like commodity speculators, insurance companies deal with inherent and inescapable risks. Insurance both transfers and reduces those risks. In exchange for the premium paid by its policy-holder, the insurance company assumes the risk of compensating for losses caused by automobile accidents, houses catching fire, and numerous other misfortunes which befall human beings. There are more than 41,000 insurance carriers in the United States alone. That includes more than 11,000 life insurance companies, whose total assets exceed 3 trillion dollars.

In addition to transferring risks, an insurance company seeks to reduce them. For example, it charges lower prices to safe drivers and refuses to insure some homes until brush and other flammable materials near a house are removed. People working in hazardous occupations are charged higher premiums. In a variety of ways, it segments the population and charges different prices to people with different risks. That way it reduces its own over-all risks and, in the process, sends a signal to people working in dangerous jobs or living in dangerous neighborhoods, conveying to them the costs created by their chosen behavior or location.

The most common kind of insurance—life insurance—compensates for a misfortune that cannot be prevented. Everyone must die but the risk involved is in the time of death. If everyone were known in advance to die at age 70, there would be no point in life insurance, because there would be no risk involved. Each individual's financial affairs could be arranged in advance to take that predictable death into account. Paying premiums to an insurance company would make no sense, because the total amount to which those premiums grew over the years would have to add up to an amount no less than the compensation to be received by one's surviving beneficiaries. A life insurance company would, in effect, become an issuer of bonds redeemable on fixed dates. Buying life insurance at age 30 would be the same as buying a 40-year bond and buying life insurance at age 40 would be the same as buying a 30-year bond.

What makes life insurance different from a bond is that neither the individual insured nor the insurance company knows when that particular individual will die. The financial risks to others that accompany the death of a family breadwinner or business partner are transferred to the insurance company, for a price. Those risks are also reduced because the average death rate among millions of policy-holders is far more predictable than the death of any given individual. As with other forms of insurance, risks are not simply transferred from one party to another, but reduced in the process.

Where a given party has a large enough sample of risks, there may be no benefit from buying an insurance policy. The Hertz car rental agency, for example, owns so many automobiles that its risks are sufficiently spread that it need not pay an insurance company to assume those risks. It can use the same statistical methods used by insurance companies to determine the financial costs of its risk and incorporate that cost into what it charges people who rent cars. There is no point transferring a risk that is not reduced in the process, because the insurer must charge as much as the risk would cost the insured—plus enough more to pay the administrative costs of doing business and still leave a profit to the insurer. Self-insurance is therefore a viable option for those with a large enough sample of risks.

Insurance companies do not simply save the premiums they receive and later pay them out when the time comes. More than half of current premiums are paid out in current claims—61 percent for Allstate Insurance Company and 83 percent for State Farm Mutual Insurance, for example. Insurance companies can then invest what is left over after paying claims and other costs of doing business. Because of these investments, the insurance companies will have more money available than if they had let the money gather dust in a vault. About two-thirds of life insurance companies' income comes from the premiums paid by their policy-holders and about one-fourth from earnings on their investments. Obviously, the money invested has to be put into relatively safe investments—government securities and conservative real estate loans, for example, rather than commodity speculation.

Because insurance companies compete with one another for customers, the price of premiums is reduced by these investments, since the premiums paid in do not have to add up to the total amount that will be paid out to the policy-holders. The fact that the money taken in over the years grows because of the returns on the investments financed by insurance companies means that there can be more money at the end than was paid in by the policy-holders over the years.

While it might seem that an insurance company could just keep the profit from these investments for itself, in reality competition forces the price of insurance down, as it forces other prices down, to a level that will cover costs and provide a rate of return sufficient to compensate investors without attracting additional competing investment. In an economy where investors are always on the lookout for higher profits, an inflated rate of profit in the insurance industry would tend to cause new insurance companies to be created, in order to share in this bonanza. Sometimes this process can overshoot the mark, as periods of unusually high profits are followed by periods of unusually low profits, due to the additional competition that is attracted.

Insurance principles often conflict with political principles. For example, arguments are often made—and laws passed accordingly—that it is "unfair" that a safe young driver is charged a higher premium because other young drivers have higher accident rates,[2] or that young male drivers are charged more than female drivers the same age for similar reasons, or that people with similar driving records are charged different premiums according to where they live. A City Attorney in Oakland, California, called a press conference in which he asked: "Why should a young man in the Fruitvale pay 30 percent more for insurance" than someone living in another community. "How can this be fair?" he demanded.

Running through such political arguments is the notion that it is wrong for people to be penalized for things that are not their fault. But insurance is about risk—and risks are greater when you live where your car is more likely to be stolen, vandalized, or wrecked in a collision with local drag racers. These are all risks that differ from one place to another. Forcing insurance companies to charge the same premiums to groups of people with different risks means that premiums must rise over all, with safer groups subsidizing those who are either more dangerous in themselves or who live where they are vulnerable to more dangerous other people. In the case of automobile insurance, this means that more unsafe drivers can afford to be on the road, so that their victims pay the highest and most unnecessary price of all in injuries and deaths.

Government programs that deal with risk are often analogized to insurance, or may even be officially called "insurance" without in fact being insurance. For example, federal disaster relief in the United States helps victims of floods, hurricanes and other natural disasters to recover and rebuild. But, unlike insurance, it does not reduce the over-all risks. Often people rebuild homes and businesses in the well-known paths of hurricanes and floods, often to the applause of the media for their "courage." But the financial risks created are not paid by those who create them, as with insurance, but are instead paid by the taxpayers.

In short, there is now more risk than if there were no disaster relief available and more risk than if private insurance companies were charging these people premiums which cover the full cost of their risky behavior. Sometimes the government subsidizes insurance for earthquakes or other disasters for which private insurance would be "prohibitively expensive." What that

---

[2] Although fatality rates from motor vehicle deaths are highest for drivers age 16 to 19, the declining fatality rates with age end at around age 50 and then rise again, with drivers aged 80 to 84 having nearly as high a fatality rate from motor vehicle deaths as teenagers.

means is that the government makes it less expensive for people to live in risky places—and more costly to the society as a whole, when people distribute themselves in more risky patterns than they would do if they had to bear the costs themselves, either in higher insurance premiums or in financial losses and anxieties.

There is an almost politically irresistible inclination to help people struck by earthquakes, wildfires, tornadoes and other natural disasters. The tragic pictures on television over-ride any consideration of what the situation was when they decided to live where they did. But government-subsidized insurance is, in effect, disaster relief provided for them beforehand, and is therefore a factor in people's choices of where to live and what risks to take with other people's money.

Competition among insurance companies involves not only price but service. When flood, hurricanes or other disasters strike an area, insurance company *A* cannot afford to be slower than insurance company *B* in getting money to their policy-holders. Imagine a policy-holder whose home has been destroyed by a flood or hurricane, and who is still waiting for his insurance agent to show up, while his neighbor's insurance agent arrives on the scene within hours to advance a few thousand dollars immediately, so that the family can afford to go find shelter somewhere. Not only will the customer of the tardy insurance company be likely to change companies afterward, so will people all across the country, if word gets out as to who provides prompt service and who drags their feet. For the tardy insurance company, that can translate into losing billions of dollars worth of business. The lengths to which some insurance companies go to avoid being later than competing insurance companies was indicated by a *New York Times* story:

> Prepared for the worst, some insurers had cars equipped with global positioning systems to help navigate neighborhoods with downed street signs and missing landmarks, and many claims adjusters carried computer-produced maps identifying the precise location of every customer.

The kind of market competition which forces such extraordinary efforts is of course lacking in government emergency programs, which have no competitors. They may be analogized to insurance but do not have the same incentives or results. Political incentives can even delay getting aid to victims of natural disasters. When there were thousands of deaths in the wake of a huge cyclone that struck India in 1999, it was reported in that country's press that the government was unwilling to call on international agencies for help, for fear that this would be seen as admitting the inadequacies of India's own government. The net result was that many villages remained without either aid or information, two weeks after the disaster.

Insurance companies often sell annuities as well as insurance, using similar principles to pay off the living in installments, instead of paying survivors in a lump sum. Here too, government programs may be analogized to the activities of insurance companies, without in fact having either the same incentives or the same results. The most fundamental difference between private annuities and government pensions is that the former create real wealth by investing premiums, in order to be able to pay pensions later on, while the latter simply use current premiums from the working population to pay current pensions to the retired population.

What this means is that a private annuity invests the premiums that come in—creating homes, factories, or other tangible assets whose earnings will later enable the annuities to be paid to those whose money was used to create these assets. Government pension plans, such as Social Security in the United States, simply spend the premiums as they are received. Much of this money is used to pay pensions to current retirees, but the rest can be used to finance other government activities, ranging from fighting wars to paying for Congressional junkets. There is no wealth created to be used in the future to pay the pensions of those who are currently paying into the system.

The illusion of investment is maintained by giving the Social Security trust fund government bonds in exchange for the money that is taken from it and spent on current government programs. But these bonds represent no tangible assets. They are simply promises to pay money collected from future taxpayers. The country as a whole is not one dollar richer because these bonds were printed, so there is no analogy with private investments that create tangible wealth. If there were no such bonds, then future taxpayers would have to make up the difference when future premiums are insufficient to pay pensions to future retirees. That is exactly the same as what will have to happen when there are bonds. Accounting procedures may make it seem that there is an investment when the Social Security system holds government bonds but the economic reality is that neither the government nor anyone else can spend and save the same money.

What has enabled Social Security—and similar government pension plans in other countries—to postpone the day of reckoning is that a relatively small generation in the 1930s was followed by a much larger "baby boom" generation, earning much higher incomes and therefore paying large premiums, from which pensions could easily be paid to the retirees from the previous generation. Not only could the promises made to the 1930s generation be kept, additional benefits could be voted for them, with obvious political advantages to those awarding these additional benefits.

With the passage of time, however, a declining birthrate and an increasing life expectancy reduced the ratio of people paying into the system to people receiving money from the system. Unlike a private annuity, where each generation creates the wealth that will later pay its own pensions, government pensions pay the pensions of the retired generation from the premiums paid by the currently working generation. That is why private annuities are not jeopardized by changing demographics but government pension plans are.

Government pension plans enable current politicians to make promises which future governments will be expected to keep. These are virtually ideal political conditions for producing generous pension laws and future financial crises resulting from them. Nor are such incentives and results confined to the United States. Countries of the European Union likewise face huge financial liabilities as the size of their retired population continues to grow, not only absolutely but also relative to the size of the working populations whose taxes are paying their pensions. In Brazil, government pensions are already paying out more money than they are taking in, with the deficits being especially large in the pensions for unionized government workers. In other words, the looming financial crisis which American and European governments are dreading and trying to forestall has already struck in Brazil, whose government pensions have been described as "the most generous in the world." According to *The Economist*:

> Civil servants do not merely retire on full salary; they get, in effect, a pay rise because they stop paying contributions into the system. Most women retire at around 50 and men soon afterwards. A Soldier's widow inherits his pension, and bequeaths it to her daughters.

Given that Brazil's civil servants are an organized and unionized special interest group, such generosity is understandable politically. The question is whether the voting public in Brazil and elsewhere will understand the economic consequences well enough to be able to avoid the financial crises to which such unfunded generosity can lead—in the name of "social insurance." Such awareness is beginning to dawn on people in some countries. In New

Zealand, for example, a poll found that 70 percent of New Zealanders under the age of 40 believe that the pensions they have been promised will not be there for them when they retire.

In one way or another, the day of reckoning seems to be approaching in many countries for programs described as "social insurance" but which were in fact never insurance at all.

Chapter 14

An Overview

The purpose of capital markets is to direct scarce capital to its highest uses.

—ROBERT L. BARTLEY, WALL STREET JOURNAL

Time has sometimes been called the fourth dimension. It certainly adds a new dimension to economics, as it does to other aspects of life. Time produces both calculable risks and incalculable uncertainties. It is a calculable risk that playing Russian roulette will lead to death about one time out of six but there is simply uncertainty as to what the stock market will do next.

Various kinds of financial institutions have evolved to deal with various kinds of risk. In addition, financial markets transfer resources from one time period to another, as well as from one person to another and from one sector of the economy to another.

How much of a natural resource this generation will use, and how much it will leave for future generations, depends on the "present value" of that resource, which in turn depends on the interest rate, as well as estimates of the resource's future price, based on its future scarcity. If we were in fact likely to run out of some resource any time soon, its present value would skyrocket, with high prices forcing cutbacks in its use today—which is to say, forcing us to share it with future generations.

Not only the economy as a whole, but each individual as well, allocates his or her income over time by using financial institutions as intermediaries. As interest rates rise, people tend to consume less of their current incomes and save more, since the reward for saving is higher. In this way, the desire of businesses to invest more for the future is meshed with consumers' willingness to postpone some of their purchases, when these businesses are willing to pay more in higher interest, usually through an intermediary such as a bank that is charging interest to the businesses and paying interest to its depositors from the proceeds. From the standpoint of the economy as a whole, real resources—labor, electricity, raw materials—that would otherwise go into producing goods to be consumed today go instead into creating factories, power plants, or research laboratories to create goods to be consumed in the future.

Like other prices, interest rates also allocate resources as between competing contemporaries.

FINANCIAL INSTITUTIONS

Financial institutions allow individuals who do not know each other to use one another's incomes to redistribute their own incomes over time, in effect drawing on future income to pay for current purchases, or alternatively postponing purchases till a later time, when the interest received will enable larger purchases to be made. Everything depends on the current circumstances of each individual's life, with many—if not most—people being both debtors and creditors at different stages of their lives. People who are middle-aged, for example, tend to save more than young people, not only because their incomes are higher but also because of a need to prepare financially for retirement and for the higher medical expenses that old age can be expected to bring.

What makes such activities something more than matters of personal finance is that financial transactions are for the economy as a whole another way of allocating scarce resources which have alternative uses—allocating them over time, as well as among individuals and enterprises at a given time. Put differently, a society without well-functioning financial institutions has fewer opportunities to create wealth by joining the entrepreneurial talents of people who lack money to the savings of others, in order to finance new firms and industries. Since many, if not most, great American industries and individual fortunes began with entrepreneurs who had very limited financial resources at the outset—Henry Ford, Thomas Edison, Andrew Carnegie, etc.—the ability of poorer societies to follow similar paths are thwarted when they lack the financial institutions to allocate resources to those with great entrepreneurial ability but no money.

Such institutions took centuries to develop in the West. Nineteenth-century London was the greatest financial capital in the world, but there were earlier centuries when the British were so little versed in the complexities of finance that they were dependent on foreigners to run their financial institutions—notably the Jews and the Lombards. That is why there is a Lombard Street in London's financial district today. Not only Third World countries, but also some countries in the former Communist bloc of nations in Eastern Europe, have yet to develop the kinds of sophisticated financial institutions which promote economic development. They may now have capitalism, but they have not yet developed the financial institutions that would mobilize capital on a scale that Western countries can. It is not that the wealth is not there. Rather, this wealth cannot be collected from innumerable small sources, concentrated, and allocated without financial institutions equal to the task.

Financial institutions facilitate economic development by enabling strangers to transfer billions of dollars among themselves through an intermediary, when few would risk such transfers directly to people whom they have never met. The numerous small entrepreneurs often found in Third World countries have far fewer opportunities to garner the resources needed to expand into the kinds of large-scale businesses that are common in the West. Nor is this a problem that can be solved by simply transferring money to these countries, as numerous failed projects financed by foreign aid have demonstrated. In addition to a financial infrastructure, there needs to be a legal, cultural, and political infrastructure of intangibles, without which the tangible things will not work.

Unless the law protects contracts and property rights, huge sums of money are unlikely to be forthcoming for economic development, especially since huge sums of money are often a result of aggregating modest sums of money from millions of people, such as stockholders in giant corporations. Judges and politicians face a constant temptation to intervene in the economy, in order to do something "good" or at least popular, even when that infringes or violates contracts and property rights. At an extreme, property may be confiscated or, as it is phrased politically, "nationalized." Seldom does this lead to a more efficient operation of existing enterprises, quite aside from the deterrent effect against other enterprises which then avoid coming into a country where such actions are threatened, much less carried out.

The complexity of financial institutions means that relatively few people are likely to understand them, which makes them vulnerable politically. Where those who do have the expertise to operate such institutions are either foreigners or domestic minorities, they are especially vulnerable. Money-lenders have seldom been popular and terms like "Shylock" or even "speculator" are not terms of endearment. Many unthinking people in many countries and many periods of history have regarded financial activities as not "really" contributing anything to the economy and have regarded the people who engage in such financial activities as mere parasites.

This was especially so at a time when most people engaged in hard physical labor in agriculture or industry, and were both suspicious and resentful of people who simply sat around handling pieces of paper and money, while producing nothing that could be seen or felt. Centuries-old hostilities have arisen—and have been acted upon—against minority groups who played such roles, whether they were Jews in Europe, overseas Chinese minorities in Southeast Asia, or Chettiars in their native India or in Burma, East Africa, or Fiji. Often such groups have been expelled or harassed into leaving the country—sometimes by mob violence—because of popular beliefs that they were parasitic. Those with such misconceptions have then often been surprised to discover economic activity and the standard of living declining in the wake of their departure. An understanding of basic economics could have prevented many human tragedies, as well as many economic inefficiencies.

TIME AND MONEY

The old adage, "time is money" is not only true but has many serious implications. Among other things, it means that whoever has the ability to delay has the ability to impose costs on others—sometimes devastating costs.

People who are planning to build housing, for example, often borrow millions of dollars to finance the construction of homes or apartment buildings, and must pay the interest on these millions, whether or not their construction is proceeding on schedule or is being delayed by some legal challenge or by some political decision by officials who are in no hurry to decide. Huge interest payments can be added to the cost of the construction itself while claims of environmental damage are investigated or while local commissioners wrangle among themselves or with the builders over whether the builder should be required to add various amenities such as gardens, ponds, or bicycle paths, including amenities for the benefit of the general public, as well as those to whom homes will be sold or apartments rented. Weighing the costs of these amenities against the costs of delay, the builder may well decide to build things that neither he nor his customers want enough to pay for otherwise.

In general, wherever A pays a low cost to impose high costs on B through delay, then A can either extort money from B or thwart B's activities that A does not like, or some combination of the two.

Slow-moving government bureaucracies are a common complaint around the world, not only because bureaucrats usually receive the same pay whether they move slowly or quickly, but also because in some countries corrupt bureaucrats can add substantially to their incomes by accepting bribes to speed things up. The greater the scope of the government's power and the more red tape is required, the greater the costs that can be imposed by delay and the more lucrative the bribes that can be extorted.

In less corrupt countries, bribes may be taken in the form of things extorted indirectly for political purposes, such as forcing builders to build things that third parties want—or not build at all, where either local home owners or environmental movements prefer leaving the status quo undisturbed. The costs of demanding an environmental impact report may be quite low, compared to the costs of the delay which this will impose in the form of mounting interest charges on millions of dollars of borrowed money that is left idle while this process goes on. Even if the report ends up finding no environmental damage, it may nevertheless have imposed considerable economic damage, sometimes enough to force the builder to abandon plans to build in that community.

Similar principles apply when it comes to health regulations applied to imported fruits, vegetables, flowers, or other perishable things. While health regulations may have legitimate functions, just as environmental regulations may, it is also true that either or both can be used as ways of preventing people from doing what third parties object to, by the simple process of imposing high costs through delay.

Time is money in yet another way. Merely by changing the age of retirement, governments can help stave off the day of reckoning when the pensions they have promised exceed the money available to pay those pensions. Hundreds of billions of dollars may be saved by raising the retirement age by a few years. This violation of a contract amounts to a default on a financial obligation on which millions of people were depending. But, to those who do not stop to think that time is money, it may all be explained away politically in wholly different terms. Where the retirement age is not simply that of government employees but involves that of people employed by private businesses as well, the government not only violates its own commitments but violates prior agreements made between private employees and employers. In the United States, the government is explicitly forbidden by the Constitution from changing the terms of private contracts, but judges have over the years "interpreted" this Constitutional provision more or less out of existence.

Where the government has changed the terms of private employment agreements, the issue has often been phrased politically as putting an end to "mandatory retirement" for older workers. In reality, there has seldom, if ever, been any requirement for mandatory retirement. What did exist was simply an age beyond which a given business no longer employed those who worked for it. These people remained free to work wherever others wished to employ them, usually while continuing to receive their pensions. Thus a professor who retired from Harvard might go teach at one of the campuses of the University of California, military officers could go to work for companies producing military hardware, engineers or economists could work for consulting firms, while people in innumerable other occupations could market their skills to whoever wanted to hire them.

There was no mandatory retirement. Yet those skilled in political rhetoric were able to depict the government's partial default on its obligations to pay pensions at a given age as a virtuous rescue of older workers, rather than as a self-serving transfer of billions of dollars in financial liabilities from the government itself to private employers.[1]

Remembering that time is money is, among other things, a defense against rhetoric, as well as an important economic principle in itself.

---

[1] Elimination of the ability of private employers to cease employing people at a given age had further economic repercussions, the most obvious being that it now became harder for younger workers to move up the ladder, with older employees at the top blocking their rise by staying on. From the standpoint of the economy as a whole, there was a loss of efficiency. The elimination of a "mandatory retirement" age meant that, instead of automatically phasing out employees when they reached the age at which productivity usually begins to decline, employers now faced the prospect of having to prove that decline in each individual case to the satisfaction of third parties in government, in order to avoid an "age discrimination" lawsuit. The costs and risks of this meant that many older people would be kept employed when there were younger people who could perform their duties more efficiently. As for those older individuals whose productivity did not decline at the usual age, employers had always had a option to waive retirements on an individual basis. Neither for the employer nor the employee was there in fact a mandatory retirement age.

ECONOMIC ADJUSTMENTS

Time is important in another sense, in that most economic adjustments take time, which is to say, the consequences of decisions unfold over time—and markets adjust at different rates for different decisions. Even the most fervent believer in free market economics does not believe that you can throw yourself off a cliff and depend on someone to sell you a parachute on the way down. On the other hand, you can usually go spend a year in a city where you have never been before, and therefore have no idea where to get food, without any danger of starving, because the market will be sure to supply you. No doubt, if enough free market enthusiasts leaped off the same cliff regularly, someone would open a parachute store nearby, because the market does adjust, though not instantaneously.

The fact that economic consequences take time has enabled many people to have successful political careers by creating current benefits at future costs. Government-financed pension plans are perhaps a classic example, since great numbers of voters are pleased to be covered by pension plans, while only a few economists and actuaries point out that there is not enough wealth set aside to cover the promised benefits—and it will be decades before the economists and actuaries are proved right.

With time comes risk, given the limitations of human foresight. This *inherent* risk must be sharply distinguished from the kinds of risk that are created by such activities as gambling or playing Russian roulette. Economic activities for dealing with inescapable risks seek both to minimize these risks and shift them to those best able to carry them. Those who accept these risks typically have not only the financial resources to ride out short-run losses but also have lower risks from a given situation than the person who transferred the risk. A commodity speculator can reduce risks overall by engaging in a wider variety of risky activities than a farmer does, for example. While a wheat farmer can be wiped out if bumper crops of wheat around the world force the price far below what was expected when the crop was planted, a similar disaster would be unlikely to strike wheat, gold, cattle, and foreign currencies simultaneously, so that a professional speculator who speculated in all these things would be in less danger than someone who speculated in any one of them, as a wheat farmer does.

Whatever statistical or other expertise the speculator has further reduces the risks below what they would be for the farmer or other producer. More fundamentally, from the standpoint of the efficient use of scarce resources, speculation reduces the costs associated with risks for the economy as a whole. One of the important consequences, in addition to more people being able to sleep well at night because of having a guaranteed market for their output, is that more people find it worthwhile to produce things under risky conditions than would have otherwise. In other words, the economy can produce more soybeans because of soybean speculators, even if the speculators themselves know nothing about growing soybeans.

It is especially important to understand the interlocking mutual interests of different economic groups—the farmer and the speculator being just one example—and, above all, the effects on the economy as a whole, because these are things often neglected or distorted in the zest of the media for emphasizing conflicts, which is what sells newspapers and gets larger audiences for television news programs. Politicians likewise benefit from portraying different groups as enemies of one another and themselves as the saviors of the group they claim to represent.

When wheat prices soar, for example, nothing is easier for a demagogue than to cry out against the injustice of a situation where speculators sitting comfortably in their air-conditioned offices grow rich on the sweat of farmers toiling in the fields for months under a hot sun. The years when the speculators took a financial beating at harvest time, while the farmers lived comfortably on the guaranteed wheat prices paid by speculators, are of course forgotten.

Similarly, when an impending or expected shortage drives up prices, much indignation is often expressed in politics and the media about the higher retail prices being charged for things that the sellers bought from their suppliers when prices were lower. What things cost under earlier conditions is history; what the supply and demand are today is economics. During the early stages of the 1991 Persian Gulf War, for example, oil prices rose sharply around the world, in anticipation of a disruption of Middle East oil exports because of impending military action in the region. At this point, a speculator rented an oil tanker and filled it with oil purchased in Venezuela to be shipped to the United States. However, before the tanker arrived at an American port, the Gulf War was over sooner than anyone expected and oil prices fell, leaving the speculator unable to sell his oil for enough to recover his costs. Here too, what he paid in the past was history and what he could get now was economics.

From the standpoint of the economy as a whole, oil purchased at different times, under different sets of expectations, are the same when they enter the market today. There is no reason why they should be priced differently, if the goal is to allocate scarce resources in the most efficient way.

Time and Politics

Politics and economics differ radically in the way they deal with time. For example, when it becomes clear that the fares being charged on municipal buses are too low to permit these buses to be replaced as they wear out, the logical economic conclusion for the long run is to raise the fares. Politically, however, a politician who opposes the fare increase as "unjustified" may gain the votes of bus riders at the next election. Moreover, since all the buses are not going to wear out immediately, the consequences of holding down the fare will not appear all at once but will be spread out over time. It may be some years before enough buses start breaking down and wearing out, without adequate replacements, for the bus riders to notice that there now seem to be longer waits between buses and they do not arrive on schedule as often as they used to.

By the time the municipal transit system gets so bad that many people begin moving out of the city, taking the taxes they pay with them, so many years may have elapsed since the political bus fare controversy that few people remember it or see any connection between that controversy and their current problems. Meanwhile, the politician who won a municipal election by assuming the role of champion of the bus riders may now have moved on up to statewide office, or even national office, on the basis of his popularity. As a declining tax base causes deteriorating city services and neglected infrastructure, the erstwhile hero of the bus riders may even be able to boast that things were never this bad when he was a city official, and blame the current problems on the failings of his successors.

In economics, however, future consequences are anticipated in the concept of "present value." If, instead of fares being regulated by a municipal government, these fares were set by a private bus company operating in a free market, any neglect of financial provisions for replacing buses as they wear out would begin *immediately* to reduce the value of the bus company's stock. In other words, the present value of the bus company would decline as a result of the long-run consequences that were anticipated by investors concerned about the safety and profitability of their own money.

If a private bus company's management decided to keep fares too low to maintain and replace its buses as they wore out, perhaps deciding to pay themselves higher executive salaries instead of setting aside funds for the maintenance of their bus fleet, 99 percent of the public might still be unaware of this or its long-run consequences. But among the other one percent who would be far more likely to be aware would be those in charge of financial institutions that owned stock in the bus company, or were considering buying that stock or lending money to the bus company. For these investors, potential investors, or lenders examining financial records, the company's present value would be seen as reduced, long before the first bus wore out.

As in other situations, a market economy allows accurate knowledge to be effective in influencing decision-making, even if 99 percent of the population do not have that knowledge. In politics, however, the 99 percent who do not understand can create immediate political success for officials and policies that will turn out in the end to be harmful to society as a whole. It would of course be unreasonable to expect the general public to become financial experts or any other kind of experts. What may be more reasonable is to expect enough voters to see the dangers in letting economic decisions be made through political processes.

Time can turn economies of scale from an economic advantage to a political liability. After a business has made a huge investment in a fixed installation—a gigantic automobile factory, a hydroelectric dam, a skyscraper—the fact that this asset cannot be moved makes it a tempting target for high local taxation or for the unionization of employees who can shut it down with a strike and impose huge losses unless their demands are met. Where labor costs are a small fraction of the total costs of an enterprise with a huge capital investment, even a doubling of wages may be a price worth paying to keep a multi-billion dollar operation going. By contrast, an office—even the headquarters office of a national or international corporation—can much more readily be moved elsewhere, as New York discovered after its high taxes caused many of its big corporations to move their headquarters out of the city. With enough time, even many industries with huge fixed installations can change their regional distribution—not by physically moving existing dams, buildings, or other structures, but by not building any new ones in the unpromising locations where the old ones are, and by placing new and more modern structures and installations in states and localities with a better track record of treating businesses as economic assets, rather than economic prey.

A hotel cannot move across state lines, but a hotel chain can build their new hotels somewhere else. New steel mills with the latest technology can likewise be built elsewhere, while the old obsolete steel mill is closed down or phased out. As in the case of bus fares kept too low to sustain the same level and quality of service in the long run, here too the passage of time may be so long that few people connect the political policies and practices of the past with the current deterioration of the region into "rustbelt" communities with declining employment opportunities for its young people and a declining tax base to support local services.

Time and Foresight

Even though many government officials may not look ahead beyond the next election, individual citizens who are subjected to the laws and policies that officials impose nevertheless have foresight that causes many of these laws and policies to have very different consequences from those that were intended. For example, when tax rates are raised 10 percent, it may be assumed that tax revenues will also rise by 10 percent. But in fact more people may move out of the heavily taxed jurisdiction, or buy less of the heavily taxed commodity, so that the revenues received may be disappointingly far below what was estimated. The state of Alaska discovered this when it passed a law greatly increasing its tax rates on cigarette:

> The tax was to go into effect October 1, 1997. Smokers struck back by buying an astounding 175 million more cigarettes than usual in the three months before the tax deadline. Richard Watts of the Great Alaska Tobacco Company told the local papers that some smokers even bought sixty-carton cases—at $1,200 each—rather than pay the tax. As for Alaska's Department of Revenue, it saw its revenue go up in smoke: collections slowed 60 percent following the infamous increase date.

Conversely, when the federal tax rate on capital gains was lowered from 28 percent to 20 percent in 1997, it was assumed that revenues from the capital gains tax would fall below the $54 billion collected in 1996 and the $209 billion projected to be collected over the next four years, before the tax rate was cut. Instead, tax revenues *rose* after the capital gains tax rate was cut: $372 billion were collected in capital gains taxes over the next four years. People adjusted their behavior to a more favorable outlook for investments by increasing their investments, so that the new 20 percent tax rate on the returns from these increased investments amounted to more revenue than that produced by the old 28 percent tax rate. Instead of keeping their money in tax-exempt municipal bonds, for example, investors would now find it more advantageous to invest in producing real goods and services with a higher rate of return, now that lower tax rates enabled them to keep more of their gains. It was much the same story halfway around the world in India:

> Lower income taxes brought greater compliance and more revenues for the treasury. Direct taxes in 1995–96 accounted for 29 percent of revenues, compared to 19 percent in 1990–91. ·

Although it is common in politics and in the media to refer to government's "raising taxes" or "cutting taxes," this blurs a crucial distinction between tax *rates* and tax *revenues*. The government can change tax rates but the reaction of the public to these changes can result in either a higher or a lower amount of tax revenues being collected. Thus references to proposals for a "$500 billion tax cut" or a "$700 billion tax increase" are wholly misleading because all that the government can enact is a change in tax rates, whose actual consequences can be determined only after the fact.

The foresight of people subjected to various government policies can also cause results to differ from intentions when it comes to social policies. When money was appropriated by the U.S. government to help children with learning disabilities and psychological problems, the implicit assumption was that there was a more or less given number of such children. But the availability of the money created incentives for more children to be classified into these categories. Organizations running programs for such children had incentives to diagnose problem children as having the particular problem for which government money was available. Some low-income mothers on welfare even told their children to do badly on tests and act up in school, so as to add more money to their meager household incomes.

Where Third World governments have contemplated confiscation of land for redistribution to poor farmers, many years can elapse between the political campaign for redistribution of land and the time when it is actually done. During those years, the foresight of existing landlords is likely to lead them to neglect to maintain the property as well as they did when they expected to reap the long-terms benefits of investing time and money in weeding, draining, fencing and otherwise caring for the land. By the time the land actually reaches the poor, it may be much poorer land. As one development economist put it, land reform can be "a bad joke on those who can least afford to laugh."

The political popularity of threatening to confiscate the property of rich foreigners—whether land, factories, railroads or whatever—has led many Third World leaders to make such threats, even when they were too fearful of the economic consequences to actually carry out these threats. Such was the case in Sri Lanka in the middle of the twentieth century:

> Despite the ideological consensus that the foreign estates should be nationalized, the decision to do so was regularly postponed. But it remained a potent political threat, and not only kept the value of the shares of the tea companies on the London exchange low in relation to their dividends, but also tended to scare away foreign capital and enterprise.

In short, people have foresight, whether they are landowners, welfare mothers, investors, taxpayers or whatever. A government which proceeds as if the planned effect of its policies is the only effect often finds itself surprised or shocked because those subject to the policies react in ways that benefit or protect themselves, often with the side effect of causing the polices to produce very different results from what was planned.

Foresight takes many forms in many different kinds of economies. During periods of inflation, when people spend money faster, they also tend to hoard consumer goods and other assets, accentuating the imbalance between the reduced amount of real output available in the market and the increased amount of money available to purchase it. In other words, they anticipate future difficulties in finding goods that they will need or in having assets set aside for a rainy day, when money is losing its value too rapidly to fulfill that role as well. During the runaway inflation in the Soviet Union in 1991, both consumers and businesses hoarded:

> Hoarding reached unprecedented proportions, as Russians stashed hug supplies of macaroni, flour, preserved vegetables, and potatoes on their balconies and filled their freezers with meat and other perishable goods.

Business enterprises likewise sought to deal in real goods, rather than money:

> By 1991, enterprises preferred to pay each other in goods rather than rubles. (Indeed, the cleverest factory managers struck domestic and international barter deals that enabled them to pay their employees, not with rubles, but with food, clothing, consumer goods, even Cuban rum.

Both social and economic policies are often discussed in terms of the goals they proclaim, rather than the incentives they create. For many, this may be due simply to shortsightedness. For professional politicians, however, the fact that their time horizon is often bounded by the next election means that any goal that is widely accepted can gain them votes, while the long-run consequences come too late to be politically relevant, and the lapse of time can make the connection between cause and effect can be too difficult to prove without complicated analysis that most voters cannot or will not engage in.

In the private marketplace, however, experts can be paid to engage in such analysis and exercise such foresight. Thus the bond-rating services Moody's and Standard & Poor's downgraded California's state bonds in 2001, even though there had been no default and the state budget still had a surplus in its treasury. What Moody's and Standard & Poor's realized was that the huge costs of dealing with California's electricity crisis were likely to strain the state's finances for years to come, raising the possibility of a default on state bonds or a delay in payment, which amounts to a partial default. A year after these agencies had downgraded the state's bonds, it became public knowledge that the state's large budget surplus had suddenly turned into an even larger budget deficit—and many people were shocked by the news.

PART V:
THE NATIONAL
ECONOMY

Chapter 15

National Output

Just as there are basic economic principles which apply in particular markets for particular goods and services, so there are principles which apply to the economy as a whole. For example, just as there is a demand for particular goods and services, so there is an aggregate demand for the total output of the whole nation. Moreover, aggregate demand can fluctuate, just as demand for individual things can fluctuate. In the three years following the great stock market crash of 1929, the money supply in the United States declined by a staggering one-third. This meant that it was now impossible to continue to sell as many goods and hire as many people *at the old price levels*, including the old wage levels. If prices and wage rates had also declined immediately by one-third, then of course the reduced money supply could still have bought as much as before, and the same real output and employment could have continued. There would have been the same amount of real things produced, just with smaller numbers on their price tags, so that paychecks with smaller numbers on them could have bought just as much as before. In reality, however, a complex national economy can never adjust that fast or that perfectly, so there was a massive decline in total sales, with corresponding declines in production and employment.

Thus began the Great Depression of the 1930s, during which as many as one-fourth of all workers were unemployed and American corporations as a whole operated at a loss for two years in a row. U. S. Steel stock went from 261 3/4 to 21 1/4 and General Electric fell from 396 1/4 to 70 1/4 in 1932. General Motors stock, which peaked at 72 3/4 in 1929, hit bottom at 7 5/8. For the entire decade of the 1930s, unemployment averaged more than 18 percent. It was the greatest economic catastrophe in the history of the

United States. The fears, policies and institutions it generated were still evident more than half a century later.

THE FALLACY OF COMPOSITION

While some of the same principles which apply when discussing markets for particular goods, industries, or occupations may also apply when discussing the national economy, it cannot be assumed in advance that this is always the case. When thinking about the national economy, a special challenge will be to avoid what philosophers call "the fallacy of composition"—the mistaken assumption that what applies to a part applies automatically to the whole. For example, the 1990s were dominated by news stories about massive reductions in employment in particular American firms and industries, with tens of thousands of workers being laid off by some large companies and hundreds of thousands in some industries. Yet the rate of unemployment in the U.S. economy as a whole was the lowest in years during the 1990s, while the number of jobs nationwide rose to record high levels. What was true of the various sectors of the economy that made news in the media was not true of the economy as a whole.

The fallacy of composition threatens confusion in many aspects of the study of the national economy, because what is true of an individual or even an industry is not necessarily true for the economy. For example, any given individual who doubles the amount of money he or she has will be richer, but a nation cannot be made richer by printing twice as much money. That is because the price level will rise in the economy as a whole if there is twice as much money in circulation and the same amount of goods.

Another example of the fallacy of composition would be adding up all individual investments to get the total investments of the country. When individuals buy government bonds, that is an investment for those individuals. But, for the country as a whole, there are no more investment goods—office buildings, factories, hydroelectric dams, etc.—than if these bonds had never been purchased. What these individuals have purchased is a right to sums of money to be collected from future taxpayers. These individuals' additional assets are the taxpayers' additional liabilities, which cancel out for the country as a whole.

The fallacy of composition is not peculiar to economics. In a sports stadium, any given individual can see the game better by standing up but, if everybody stands up, everybody will not see better. In a burning building, any given individual can get out faster by running than by walking. But, if everybody runs, the stampede is likely to create bottlenecks at doors, preventing escapes by people struggling against one another to get out, causing some of these people to lose their lives needlessly in the fire. That is why there are fire drills, so that people will get in the habit of leaving in an emergency in an orderly way, so that more lives can be saved.

What is at the heart of the fallacy of composition is that it ignores *interactions* among individuals, which can prevent what is true for one of them from being true of them all.

Among the common economic examples of the fallacy of composition are attempts to "save jobs" in some industry threatened with higher unemployment for one reason or another. Any given firm or industry can always be rescued by a sufficiently large government intervention, whether in the form of subsidies, purchases of the firm's or industry's products by government agencies, or by other such means. The interaction that is ignored by those advocating such policies is that everything the government spends is taken from somebody else. The 10,000 jobs saved in the widget industry may be at the expense of 15,000 jobs lost elsewhere in the economy by the government's taxing away the resources needed to keep those other people employed.

We need only imagine what would have happened if the government had decided to "save jobs" in the typewriter industry when personal computers first appeared on the scene and began to take away customers from the typewriter manufacturers. If laws had been passed restricting the number of computers that could be sold, this would undoubtedly have saved the jobs of many people who manufactured typewriters or who produced typewriter ribbons, carbon paper, and other accessories. But there would have been fewer jobs created in the computer-manufacturing industry and in the many branches of the software industry. The fallacy is not in believing that jobs can be saved in given industries or given sectors of the economy. The fallacy is in believing that these are *net* savings of jobs for the economy as a whole.

OUTPUT AND DEMAND

One of the most basic things to understand about the national economy is how much its total output adds up to. We also need to understand the important role of money in the national economy, which was so painfully demonstrated in the Great Depression of the 1930s. The government is al-

most always another major factor in the national economy, even though it
may not be in particular industries. As in many other areas, the facts are relatively straightforward and not difficult to understand. What gets complicated are the misconceptions that have to be unravelled.

One of the oldest confusions about national economies is reflected in fears
that the growing abundance of output threatens to reach the point where it
exceeds what the economy is capable of absorbing. If this were true, then
masses of unsold goods would lead to permanent cutbacks in production,
leading in turn to massive and permanent unemployment. Such an idea has
appeared from time to time over more than two centuries, though usually not
among economists. However, a Harvard economist of the mid-twentieth
century named Seymour Harris seemed to express such views when he said:
"Our private economy is facing the tough problem of selling what it can produce." A popular, best-selling author of the 1950s and 1960s named Vance
Packard expressed similar worries about "a threatened overabundance of the
staples and amenities and frills of life" which have become "a major national
problem" for the United States."

Yet today's output is several times what it was when Professor Harris and
Mr. Packard expressed their worries, and many times what it was in the eighteenth and nineteenth centuries, when others expressed similar worries. Why
has this not created the problem that so many have feared for so long, the
problem of insufficient income to buy the ever-growing output that has been
produced?

First of all, while income is usually measured in money, real income is
measured by what that money can buy, how much real goods and services.
The national output likewise consists of real goods and services. The total
real income of everyone in the national economy and the total national output are one and the same thing. They do not simply happen to be equal at a
given time or place. They are necessarily equal because they are the same
thing looked at from different angles—that is, from the viewpoint of income
and that of output. The fear of a permanent barrier to economic growth,
based on output exceeding income, is as inherently groundless today as it was
in past centuries when output was a small fraction of what it is today.

What has lent an appearance of plausibility to the idea that total output
can exceed total income is the fact that both output and income fluctuate
over time, sometimes disastrously, as in the Great Depression of the 1930s.
At any given time, for any of a number of reasons, either consumers or businesses—or both—may hesitate to spend their income. Since everyone's income depends on someone else's spending, such hesitations can reduce

aggregate income and with it aggregate demand. So can mismanagement of the money supply by government officials. Moreover, when various government policies generate uncertainty and apprehensions, this can lead individuals and businesses to want to hold on to their money until they see how things are going to turn out.

When millions of people do this at the same time, that in itself can make things turn out badly. An economy cannot continue operating at full capacity if people are no longer spending and investing at full capacity, so cutbacks in production and employment may follow until things sort themselves out. How such situations come about, how long it will take for things to sort themselves out, and what policies are best to cope with these problems are all things on which different schools of economists may disagree. However, what economists in general agree on is that this situation is very different from the situation feared by those who foresaw a national economy glutted by its own growing abundance because people lack the income to buy it all.

MEASURING NATIONAL OUTPUT

The distinction between income and wealth that was made when discussing individuals in Chapter 9 applies also when discussing the income and wealth of the nation as a whole. A country's total wealth includes everything it has left from the past plus everything currently being produced. National output, however, is what is produced during a given year. Both are important in different ways for indicating how much is available for different purposes, such as maintaining or improving the people's standard of living, or for carrying out the functions of government, business, government or other institutions.

National output during a year can be measured in a number of ways. The most common measure today is the Gross Domestic Product (GDP), which is the sum total of everything produced within a nation's borders. An older and related measure, the Gross National Product (GNP) is the sum total of all the goods and services produced by the country's people, wherever they or their resources may be located. These two measures of national output are sufficiently similar that people who are not economists need not bother about the differences. For the United States, the difference between GDP and GNP is less than one percent.

The real distinction that must be made is between both these measures of national output during a given year—a *flow* of real income—versus the accumulated *stock* of wealth as of a given time. For example, at any given time, a country can live beyond its current production by using up part of its accumulated stock of wealth from the past. During World War II, for example, American production of automobiles stopped, so that factories which normally produced cars could instead produce tanks, planes and other military equipment. This meant that existing cars simply deteriorated, as did most refrigerators, apartment buildings and other parts of the national stock of wealth. Wartime government posters said:

> Use it up,
> Wear it out,
> Make it do,
> Or do without.

After the war was over, there was a tremendous increase in the production of cars, refrigerators, housing, and other parts of the nation's accumulated stock of wealth which had been allowed to wear down or wear out while production was being devoted to urgent wartime purposes. Both the fixed assets of businesses and the durable equipment of consumers grew much faster between 1947 and 1973 than they had during earlier or later decades of the twentieth century, as the nation's stock of durable assets that had been depleted during the war was replenished.

Just as national income does not refer to money or other paper assets, so national wealth does not consist of these pieces of paper either, but of the real goods and services that such things can buy. Otherwise, any country could get rich immediately just by printing more money. Sometimes national output or national wealth is added up by using the money prices of the moment, but most serious long-run studies measure output and wealth in real terms, taking into account price changes over time. This is necessarily an inexact process because the prices of different things change differently over time. In the century between 1900 and 2000, the real cost of electricity, eggs, bicycles, and clothing all declined in the United States, while the real cost of bread, beer, potatoes, and cigarettes all rose.

The Composition of Output

Prices are not the only things that change over time. The real goods and services which make up the national output also change. The cars of 1950 are not the same as the cars of the year 2000. The older cars did not have air-conditioning, seat belts, anti-lock brakes, or many other features that have been added over the years. So when we try to measure how much the production of automobiles has increased in real terms, a mere count of how many such vehicles there were in both time periods misses a huge qualitative difference in what we are defining as being the same thing— cars. This is true of housing as well. The average house at the end of the twentieth century was much larger, had more bathrooms, and was far more likely to have air conditioning and other amenities than houses that existed in the middle of that century. Merely counting how many houses there were at both times does not tell us how much the production of housing had increased. Just between 1983 and 2000, the median square feet in a new single-family house in the United States increased from 1,585 to 2,076.

While these are problems which can be left for professional economists and statisticians to try to wrestle with, it is important for others to at least be aware of these problems, so as not to be misled by politicians or media pundits who throw statistics around for one purpose or another.

Comparisons over Time

Over a period of generations, the goods and services which constitute national output change so much that statistical comparisons can become practically meaningless, because they are comparing apples and oranges. At the beginning of the twentieth century, the national output did not include any airplanes, television sets, computers or nuclear power plants. At the end of that century, national output did not include many typewriters, slide rules (once essential for engineers, before there were electronic calculators), or a host of equipment and supplies once widely used in connection with horses that formerly provided the basic transportation of the country.

What then, does it mean to say that the Gross National Product was X percent larger in the year 2000 than in 1900, when it consisted of very different things? It may mean something to say that output this year was 5 percent higher or 3 percent lower than it was last year because it consists of much the same things in both years. But the longer the time span involved, the more such statistics approach meaninglessness.

International Comparisons

The same problems which apply when comparing a given country's output over time can also apply when comparing the output of two very different countries at the same time. If some Caribbean nation's output consists largely of bananas and other tropical crops, while some Scandinavian country's output consists more of industrial products and crops more typical of cold climates, how is it possible to compare totals made up of such differing items? This is not just comparing apples and oranges, it may be comparing cars and sugar.

Statistical comparisons of incomes in Western and non-Western nations are affected by the same age differences that exist within nations. For example, the median ages in Afghanistan, Yemen, and Angola are all below twenty, while the median ages in Germany and Italy is about forty. Such huge age gaps overstate the real significance of some international differences in income. Just as nature provides—free of charge—the heat required to grow pineapples or bananas in tropical countries, while other countries would run up huge heating bills growing these same fruits in greenhouses, so nature provides free for the young many things that can be very costly to provide for older people.

Enormously expensive medications and treatments for dealing with the many physical problems that come with aging are all counted in statistics on a country's output, but fewer such things are necessary in a country with a younger population. Thus statistics on real income per capita overstate the difference in economic well-being between older Western nations and younger non-Western nations. If it were feasible to remove from national statistics all the additional wheelchairs, nursing homes, pacemakers, and medications ranging from Geritol to Viagra—all of which are ways of providing for an older population things which nature provides free to the young—then international comparisons of real income would more accurately reflect actual levels of economic well-being. After all, an elderly person in a wheelchair would gladly change places with a young person who does not need a wheelchair, and so cannot be said to be economically better off than the younger person by the amount that the wheelchair cost—even though that is what gross international statistical comparisons would imply.

One of the usual ways of making international comparison is to compare the total money value of outputs in one country versus another. However, this gets us into other complications created by official exchange rates between their respective currencies, which may or may not reflect the actual purchasing power of those currencies. Governments may set their official exchange rates anywhere they want, but that does not mean that the actual purchasing power of the money will be whatever they say it is. Country A may have more output per capita than Country B if we measure by official exchange rates, while it may be just the reverse if we measure by the purchasing power of the money. Surely we would say that Country B has the larger total value of output if it could purchase everything produced in country A and still have something left over.

As in other cases, the problem is not with understanding the basic economics involved. The problem is with confusion spread by politicians, the media and others trying to prove some point with statistics. For example, some have claimed that Japan has had a higher per capita income than the United States, using statistics based on official exchange rates of the dollar and the yen. But, in fact, the United States has significantly higher per capita income than Japan when measured by the purchasing power of the two countries' national outputs.

The average American's annual income could buy everything the average Japanese annual income buys and still have thousands of dollars left over. Therefore the average American has a higher standard of living than the average Japanese. Yet statistics based on official exchange rates may show the average Japanese earning thousands of dollars more than the average American in some years, leaving the false impression that the Japanese are more prosperous than Americans.

Another complication in comparisons of output between nations is that more of one nation's output may have been sold through the marketplace, while more of the other nation's output may have been produced by government and either given away or sold at less than its cost of production.

When too many automobiles have been produced in a market economy to be sold profitably, the excess cars have to be sold for whatever they will bring, even if that is less than they cost to produce. When the value of national output is added up, these cars are counted according to what they sold for. But, in an economy where the government provides many free or subsidized goods, these goods are valued at what it cost the government to produce them. These ways of counting exaggerate the value of government-provided goods and services, many of which are provided by government precisely because they would never cover their costs of production if sold in a free market economy.

Both capitalism and socialism can produce more of particular things than people want, but a capitalist economy reduces the value of the surplus goods and services, while a socialist economy counts them according to what they cost, whether or not those costs could be recovered from the consuming public. Given this tendency to overvalue the output of socialist economies relative to capitalist economies when adding up their respective Gross Domestic Products, it is all the most striking that capitalist economies still show higher per capita output.

Despite all the problems with comparisons of national output between very different countries or between time periods far removed from one another, Gross Domestic Product statistics provide a reasonable basis for comparing similar countries at the same time—especially when population size differences are taken into account by comparing Gross Domestic Product per capita. Thus when the data show that the Gross Domestic Product per capita in Norway in 2002 was double what it was in Portugal the same year, we can reasonably conclude that the Norwegians had a significantly higher standard of living.

Statistical Trends

One of the problems with comparisons of national output over time is the arbitrary choice of the year to use as the beginning of the time span. For example, one of the big political campaign issues of 1960 was the rate of growth of the American economy under the existing administration. Presidential candidate John F. Kennedy promised to "get America moving again" economically if he were elected, implying that the national economic growth rate had stagnated under the party of his opponent. The validity of this charge depended entirely on which year you chose as the year from which to begin counting.

The long-term average annual rate of growth of the Gross National Product of the United States had been about 3 percent per year. As of 1960, this growth rate was as low as 1.9 percent (since 1945) or as high as 4.4 percent (since 1958). Whatever the influence of the existing administration on any of this, whether it was doing a wonderful job or a terrible job depended entirely on the base year arbitrarily selected.

Many "trends" reported in the media or proclaimed in politics likewise depend entirely on which year has been chosen as the beginning of the trend. Crime has been going up if you measure from 1960 to the present, but down if you measure from 1990 to the present. It has been claimed that automobile fatality rates have declined since the federal government began imposing various safety regulations. This is true—but it is also true that automobile fatality rates were declining for decades before the federal government imposed any safety regulations. Is the continuation of a trend that existed long before a given policy was begun proof of the effectiveness of that policy?

National output data, like many other statistics, fluctuate over time. That makes it possible to say that the trends are going up or down, depending on which point in these fluctuations you choose as the base year from which to begin counting. Even in the absence of deliberate manipulation of trend data, honest confusion can lead to false conclusion. One of the first things taught in introductory statistics is that correlation is not causation. Unfortunately, it may also be one of the first things forgotten.

In some countries, especially in the Third World, so much economic activity takes place "off the books" that official data on national output miss much—if not most—of the goods and services produced in the economy. In all countries, work done domestically and not paid for in wages and salary—cooking food, raising children, cleaning the home—goes uncounted. This inaccuracy does not directly affect trends over time if the same percentage of economic activity goes uncounted in one era as in another. In reality, however, domestic economic activities have undergone major changes over time and vary greatly from one society to another.

For example, as more women have entered the work force, many of the domestic chores formerly performed by wives and mothers without generating any income statistics are now performed for money by child care centers, home cleaning services and restaurants or pizza-delivery companies. Because money now formally changes hands in the marketplace, rather than informally between husband and wife in the home,[1] today's statistics count as output things that did not get counted before. This means that national output trends reflect not only real increases in the goods and service being produced, but also the counting of things that were not counted before, even though they existed before.

The longer the time period being considered, the more the shifting of economic activities from the home to the marketplace makes the statistics not comparable. In centuries past, it was common for a family's food to be grown in its own garden or on its own farm, and this food was often preserved in jars by the family rather than being bought from stores where it was preserved in cans. Clothing was often home-made, as were some items of furniture and even wine might be fermented from the fruits grown by the family. In pioneering times in America, or in some Third World countries today, the home itself might have been constructed by the family or with the help of friends and neighbors. As these activities moved from the family to the mar-

---

[1] In times past, it was common in many working-class communities around the world for the husband to turn most of his pay over to his wife to spend for the family's needs, including her own. This pattern remained widespread in Japan at the end of the twentieth century. But such transactions went unrecorded.

ketplace, the money paid for them made them part of official statistics. This makes it harder to know how much of the statistical trends in output over time represent real increases in totals and how much of these trends represent differences in how much has been recorded or gone unrecorded.

Just as national output statistics can overstate increases over time, they can also understate these increases. In very poor Third World countries, increasing prosperity can look statistically like stagnation. One of the ravages of extreme poverty is a high infant mortality rate, as well as health risks to others from inadequate food or shelter. As Third World countries rise economically, one of the first consequences of higher income per capita is that more infants, small children, and frail old people are able to survive, now that they can afford better nutrition and medical care. This is particularly likely at the lower end of the income scale. But, with more poor people now surviving, both absolutely and relative to the more prosperous classes, a higher percentage of the country's population now consists of these poor people. Statistically, the averaging in of more poor people can understate the country's average rise in real income or can even make the average income decline statistically, even if every individual in the country has higher incomes than in the past.[2]

---

[2] Imagine a Third World country with 100 million people, one-fourth of whom average $1,000 a year in per capita income, another fourth average $2,000, another fourth $4,000 and the top fourth $5,000. Now imagine that (1) *everyone's* income rises by 20 percent and (2) the two poorest classes double in size as a result of reduced mortality rates, while the two top classes remain the same size. If you work out the arithmetic, you will see that per capita income for the country as a whole remains the same. Obviously, if the income had risen by less than 20 percent, per capita income would have *fallen*, even though each individual's income rose.

Chapter 16

Money and
the Banking System

Any commodity to be called "money" must be generally acceptable in exchange, and any commodity generally acceptable in exchange should be called money.

-IRVING FISCHER

Everyone seems to want money, but there have been particular times in particular countries when no one wanted money, because they considered it worthless. In reality, it was the fact that no one would accept money that made it worthless. When you can't buy anything with money, it becomes just useless pieces of paper or useless metal disks. In France during the 1790s, a desperate government passed a law prescribing the death penalty for anyone who refused to sell in exchange for money. What all this suggests is that the mere fact that the government prints money does not mean that it will in fact function as money. We therefore need to understand how money functions, if only to avoid reaching the point where it malfunctions.

THE ROLE OF MONEY

Many economies in the distant past functioned without money. People simply bartered their products and labor with one another. But these have usually been small, uncomplicated economies, with relatively few things to trade, because most people provided themselves with food, shelter and clothing, while trading with others for a limited range of amenities or luxuries.

Barter is awkward. If you produce chairs and want some apples, you certainly are not likely to trade one chair for one apple, and you may not want enough apples to add up to the value of a chair. But if chairs and apples can both be exchanged for something that can be subdivided into very small units, then more trades can take place, benefitting both chair-makers and apple-growers, as well as everyone else. All that people have to do is to agree on what will be used as an intermediary means of exchange and that means of exchange becomes money.

Some societies have used sea shells as money, others have used gold or silver, and still others have used special pieces of paper printed by their governments. In the early colonial era in British West Africa, bottles and cases of gin were sometimes used as money, often passing from hand to hand for years without being consumed. In a prisoner-of-war camp during the Second World War, cigarettes from Red Cross packages were used as money among the prisoners, producing economic phenomena long associated with money, such as interest rates and Gresham's law.[1]

What makes all these different things money is that people will accept them in payment for the goods and services which actually constitute real wealth. Money is equivalent to wealth for an individual only because other individuals will supply the real goods and services desired in exchange for that money. But, from the standpoint of the national economy as a whole, money is not wealth. It is just a way to transfer wealth or to give people incentives to produce wealth.

While money facilitates the production of real wealth—greases the wheels, as it were—this is not to say that its role is inconsequential. Wheels work much better when they are greased. When a monetary system breaks down for one reason or another, and people are forced to resort to barter, the clumsiness of that method quickly becomes apparent to all. In 2002, for example, the monetary system in Argentina broke down, leading to a decline in economic activity and a resort to barter clubs called *trueque*:

---

[1] Gresham law is that bad money drives good money out of circulation. In the P.O.W. camp, the least popular brands of cigarettes circulated as money, while the most popular brands were smoked.

This week the bartering club has pooled its resources to "buy" 220 pounds of bread from a local baker in exchange for half a ton of firewood the club had acquired in previous trades—the baker used the wood to fire his oven. . . . The affluent neighborhood of Palermo hosts a swanky *trueque* at which antique china might be traded for cuts of prime Argentine beef.

Although money itself is not wealth, an absence of a functioning monetary system can cause losses of real wealth, when transactions are reduced to the crude level of barter.

INFLATION

The national price level rises for the same reason that prices of particular goods and services rise—namely, that there is more demanded than supplied at a given price. When people have more money, they tend to spend more. Without a corresponding increase in the volume of output, the prices of existing output simply rises because the quantity demanded exceeds the quantity supplied at current prices and people bid against each other when there is a shortage.

Whatever the money consists of—sea shells, gold, or whatever—more of it in the national economy means higher prices. This relationship between the total amount of money and the general price level has been seen for centuries. When Alexander the Great began spending the captured treasures of the Persians, prices rose in Greece. Similarly, when the Spaniards removed vast amounts of gold from their colonies in the Western Hemisphere, price levels rose not only in Spain, but across Europe, because the Spaniards used much of their wealth to buy imports from other European countries. Sending their gold to those countries to pay for these purchases added to the total money supply across the continent.

None of this is hard to understand. Complications and confusion come in when we start thinking about such mystical and fallacious things as the "intrinsic value" of money or believe that gold somehow "backs up" our money or in some mysterious way gives it value.

For much of history, gold has been used as money by many countries. Sometimes the gold was used directly in coins or (for large purchases) in nuggets, gold bars or other forms. Even more convenient for carrying around were pieces of paper money printed by the government that were redeemable in gold whenever you wanted it redeemed. It was not only more convenient to carry around paper money, it was also safer than carrying large sums of money as metal that jingled in your pockets or was conspicuous in bags, attracting the attention of criminals.

The big problem with money created by the government is that those who run the government always face the temptation to create more money and spend it. Whether among ancient kings or modern politicians, this has happened again and again over the centuries, leading to inflation and many economic and social problems that flow from inflation. For this reason, many countries have preferred using gold, silver, or some other material that is inherently limited in supply, as money. It is a way of depriving governments of the power to expand the money supply to inflationary levels.

Gold has long been considered ideal for this purpose, since the supply of gold in the world cannot be increased rapidly. When paper money is convertible into gold whenever the individual chooses to do so, then the money is said to be "backed up" by gold. This expression is misleading only if we imagine that the value of the gold is somehow transferred to the paper money, when in fact the gold simply limits the amount of paper money that can be issued.

The American dollar was once redeemable in gold on demand, but that was ended back in 1933. Since then, we have simply had paper money, limited in supply only by what officials thought they could or could not get away with politically. To give some idea of the cumulative effects of inflation, a one-hundred-dollar bill would buy less in 1998 than a twenty-dollar bill bought in the 1960s. Among other things, this means that people who saved money in the 1960s had four-fifths of its value silently stolen from them over the next three decades.

Sobering as such inflation may be in the United States, it pales alongside levels of inflation reached in some other countries. "Double-digit inflation" during a given year in the United States creates political alarms, but various countries in Latin America and Eastern Europe have had periods when the annual rate of inflation was in four digits.

Since money is whatever we accept as money in payment for real goods and services, there are a variety of other things that function in a way very similar to money. Credit cards and checks are obvious examples. Mere promises may also function as money, serving to acquire real goods and services, when the person who makes the promises is highly trusted. IOUs from reliable merchants were once passed from hand to hand as money. What this means is that aggregate demand is created not only by the money issued by the government but also by credits originating in a variety of other sources.

What this also means is that a liquidation of credits, for whatever reason, reduces aggregate demand, just as if the official money supply had contracted.

Some banks used to issue their own currency, which had no legal standing, but which was nevertheless widely accepted in payment when the particular bank was regarded as sufficiently reliable and willing to redeem its currency in gold. In those times and places where bankers had more credibility than government officials, bank notes might be preferred to the official money printed by the government. Sometimes money issued by some other country is preferred to money issued by one's own. Beginning in the late tenth century, Chinese money was preferred to Japanese money in Japan. In twentieth century Bolivia, most of the savings accounts were in dollars in 1985, during a period of runaway inflation of the Bolivian peso.

Gold continues to be preferred to many national currencies, even though gold earns no interest, while money in the bank does. The fluctuating price of gold reflects not only the changing demands for it for making jewelry—the source of about 80 percent of the demand for gold—or in some industrial uses but also, and more fundamentally, these fluctuations reflect the degree of worry about the possibility of inflation that could erode the purchasing power of official currencies.

That is why a major political or military crisis can send the price of gold shooting up, as people dump their holdings of the currencies that might be affected and begin bidding against each other to buy gold, as a more reliable way to hold their existing wealth, even if it does not earn any interest or dividends. For example, when the World Trade Center in New York was destroyed on September 11, 2001, the price of gold rose from about $270 an ounce to nearly $290 in one day. On the eve of the war with Iraq in 2003, gold reached $385 an ounce, as people worried about what the economic impact of that war would be.

Conversely, long periods of prosperity with price stability are likely to see the price of gold falling, as people move their wealth out of gold and into other financial assets that earn interest or dividends and can therefore increase their wealth. The great unspoken fear behind this and many other transactions in the financial markets is the fear of inflation. Nor is this fear irrational, given how often governments of all types—from monarchies to democracies to dictatorships—have resorted to inflation, as a means of getting more wealth without having to directly confront the public with higher taxes.

Raising tax rates has always created political dangers to those who hold political power. Political careers can be destroyed when the voting public turns against those who raised their tax rates. Sometimes public reaction to higher taxes can range all the way up to armed revolts, such as those that led to the American war of independence from Britain. In addition to adverse political reactions to higher taxes, there can be adverse economic reactions. As tax rates reach ever higher levels, particular economic activities may be abandoned by those who do not find the net rate of return on these activities, after taxes, to be enough to justify their efforts. Thus many people abandoned agriculture and moved to the cities during the declining era of the Roman Empire, adding to the number of people needing to be taken care of by the government, at the very time when the food supply was declining because of those who had stopped farming.

In order to avoid the political dangers that raising tax rates can create, governments around the world have for thousands of years resorted to inflation instead. As John Maynard Keynes observed:

> There is no record of a prolonged war or a great social upheaval which has not been accompanied by a change in the legal tender, but an almost unbroken chronicle in every country which has a history, back to the earliest dawn of economic record, of a progressive deterioration in the real value of the successive legal tenders which have represented money.

If fighting a major war requires half the country's annual output, then rather than raise tax rates to 50 percent of everyone's earnings in order to pay for it, the government may choose instead to create more money for itself and spend that money buying war materiel. With half the country's resources being used to produce military equipment and supplies, civilian goods will become more scarce just as money becomes more plentiful. This changed ratio of money to civilian goods will lead to inflation as more money is bid for fewer goods and prices rise as a result.

Not all inflation is caused by war, though inflation has often accompanied military conflicts. Even in peacetime, governments have found many things to spend money on, including luxurious living by kings or dictators and numerous showy projects that have been common in both democratic and undemocratic governments. To pay for such things, using the government's power to create more money has often been considered easier and safer than raising tax rates. Put differently, inflation is in effect a hidden tax. The money that people have saved is robbed of part of its purchasing power, which is quietly transferred to the government that issues new money.

In the modern era of paper money, increasing the money supply is a relatively simple matter of turning on the printing presses. However, long before there were printing presses, governments were able to create more money by the simple process of reducing the amount of gold or silver in coins of a given denomination. Thus a French franc or a British pound might begin by containing a certain amount of precious metal, but coins later issued by the French or British government would contain less and less of those metals, enabling these governments to issue more money from a given supply of gold and silver. Since the new coins had the same legal value as the old, the purchasing power of them all declined as coins became more abundant.

More sophisticated methods of increasing the quantity of money have been used in countries with government-controlled central banks, but the net result is still the same: An increase in the amount of money, without a corresponding increase in the supply of real goods, means that prices rise—which is to say, inflation. Conversely, when output increased during Britain's industrial revolution in the nineteenth century, its prices declined because its money supply did not increase correspondingly.

Doubling the money supply while the amount of goods remains the same may more than double the price level, as the speed with which the money circulates increases when people lose confidence in its retaining its value. During the drastic decline in the value of the Russian ruble in 1998, a Moscow correspondent reported:

> Many are hurrying to spend their shrinking rubles as fast as possible while the currency still has some value.

Something very similar happened in Russia during the First World War and in the years after the revolutions of 1917. By 1921, the amount of currency issued by the Russian government was hundreds of times greater than the currency in circulation on the eve of the war in 1913—and the price level rose to *thousands* of times higher than in 1913. When the money circulates faster, the effect on prices is the same as if there were more money in circulation. When both things happen on a large scale simultaneously, the result is runaway inflation. During the last, crisis-ridden year of the Soviet Union in 1991, the value of the ruble fell so low that Russians used it for wallpaper and toilet paper, both of which were in short supply.

Perhaps the most famous inflation of the twentieth century occurred in Germany during the 1920s, when 40 marks were worth one dollar in July 1920 but it took more than 4 trillion marks to be worth one dollar by November 1923. People discovered that their life's savings were not enough to buy a pack of cigarettes. The German government had, in effect, stolen virtually everything they owned by the simple process of keeping more than 1,700 printing presses running day and night, printing money.

Here too, the circulation of money speeded up, causing the inflation to increase even more than the increase in the money supply. During the worst of the inflation, in October 1923, prices rose 41 percent *per day*. Workers were paid twice a day and some were allowed time off in the middle of the day to enable them to rush off to the stores to buy things before the prices rose yet again. In other cases, wives showed up at work at lunchtime to take their husband's pay and rush off to spend it before it lost too much value. Some have blamed the economic chaos and bitter disillusionment of this era for setting the stage for the rise of Adolf Hitler and the Nazis.

DEFLATION

While inflation has been a problem that is centuries old, at particular times and places deflation has also been devastating. As noted at the beginning of chapter 15, the money supply in the United States declined by one-third from 1929 to 1932, making it impossible for Americans to buy as many goods and services as before *at the old prices*. Prices did come down—the Sears catalog for 1931 had many prices lower than they had been a decade earlier—but some prices could not change because there were legal contracts involved.

Mortgages on homes, farms, stores, and office buildings all specified monthly mortgage payments in money terms. These terms might have been quite reasonable and easy to meet when the total amount of money in the economy was substantially larger, but now it was the same as if these payments had been arbitrarily raised—as in fact they were raised in real purchasing power terms. Many home-owners, farmers and businesses simply could not pay after the national money supply contracted—and therefore they lost the places that housed them. People with leases faced very similar problems, as it became increasingly difficult to come up with the money to pay the rent. The vast amounts of goods and services purchased on credit by businesses and individuals alike produced debts that were now harder to pay off than when the credit was extended in an economy with a larger money supply.

Those whose wages and salaries were specified in contracts—whether unionized workers or professional baseball players—were now legally entitled to more real purchasing power than when these contracts were originally signed. So were government employees, whose salary scales were fixed by law. But, while deflation benefitted these particular groups *if they kept their jobs*, the difficulty of paying them meant that many would lose their jobs. Similarly, banks that owned the mortgages which many people were struggling to pay were benefitted by receiving mortgage payments worth more purchasing power than before—*if they received the payments at all*. But so many people were unable to pay their debts that many banks began to fail. More than 9,000 banks suspended operations over a four year period from 1930 through 1933. Other creditors likewise lost money when debtors simply could not pay them.

Just as inflation tends to be made worse by the fact that people spend a depreciating currency faster than usual, in order to buy something with it before it loses still more value, so a deflation tends to be made worse by the fact that people hold onto money longer, especially during a depression, with widespread unemployment making everyone's job or business insecure. Not only was there less money in circulation during the downturn in the economy from 1929 to 1932, what money there was circulated more slowly, which further reduced demand for goods and services—which in turn reduced demand for the labor.

Theoretically, the government could have increased the money supply to bring the price level back up to where it had been before. The Federal Reserve System had been set up, nearly 20 years earlier during the Woodrow Wilson administration, to deal with changes in the nation's money supply. President Wilson explained that the Federal Reserve "provides a currency which expands as it is needed and contracts when it is not needed" and that "the powers to direct this system of credits is put into the hands of a public board of disinterested officers of the Government itself" to avoid control by bankers or other special interests. However, what a government can do theoretically is not necessarily the same as what it is likely to do politically or what its leaders understand intellectually.

Both liberal and conservative economists, looking back on the Great Depression of the 1930s, have seen the Federal Reserve System's monetary policies during that period as confused and counterproductive. Milton Friedman called the people who ran the Federal Reserve System in those years "inept" and John Kenneth Galbraith called them a group with "startling incompetence." For example, the Federal Reserve raised the interest rate in 1931, as the downturn in the economy was nearing the bottom, with businesses failing and banks collapsing all across the country, along with massive unemployment. Today, any student in Economics 1 who answered an exam question by saying that the way to get out of a depression is to raise the interest rate would be risking a zero for that answer, since higher interest rates reduce the amount of credit and therefore further reduce aggregate demand at a time when more demand is needed.

Nor were the presidents who were in office during the Great Depression any more economically sophisticated. Both Republican President Herbert Hoover and his Democratic successor, Franklin D. Roosevelt, thought that wage rates should not be reduced, so this way of adjusting to deflation was discouraged by the federal government—for both humanitarian and political reasons. The theory was that maintaining wage rates meant maintaining purchasing power, so as to prevent further declines in sales, output and employment. Unfortunately, this policy works only so long as people keep their jobs—and higher wage rates under given conditions mean lower employment. Therefore higher real wage rates per hour did not translate into higher aggregate earnings, on which higher aggregate demand depends. Both the Hoover administration and the Roosevelt administration applied the same reasoning—or lack of reasoning—to agriculture: The prices of farm products were to be kept up in order to maintain the purchasing power of farmers. President Hoover decided that the federal government should "give indirect support to prices which had seriously declined" in agriculture. President Roosevelt later institutionalized this policy in agricultural price support programs which led to mass destructions of food at a time of widespread hunger.

In short, misconceptions of economics were bipartisan. Nor were such misconceptions confined to the United States. Writing in 1931, John Maynard Keynes said of the British government's monetary policies that the arguments being made for those policies "could not survive ten minutes' rational discussion."

Monetary policy is just one of many areas in which it is not enough that the government could do things to make a situation better. What matters is what government is in fact likely to do, which can in many cases make the situation worse.

THE BANKING SYSTEM

We have already noted, in Chapter 12, one of the most important roles of a bank is serving as intermediaries to transfer savings from some people to others who need to borrow. Not only does this happen across generations, as discussed there, it happens also when money is lent to individuals and organizations of all sorts. A student just emerging from dental school seldom has enough cash on hand to buy all the equipment and supplies needed to get started as a dentist. Almost no one has enough cash on hand to buy a house and many must buy a car with installment payments. Typically, the seller of a home or an automobile receives the full price immediately, not from the buyer, but from some financial institution whom the buyer must repay in installments.

Modern banks, however, do more than simply transfer cash. Each individual bank may do that but the banking system as a whole does something more. It creates credits which, in effect, add to the money supply through what is called "fractional reserve banking." A brief history of how this practice arose may make the process clearer.

Goldsmiths have for centuries had to have some safe place to store the precious metal that they use to make jewelry and other items. Once they had established a vault or other secure storage place, other people often stored their own gold with the goldsmith, rather than take on the cost of creating their own secure storage facilities. In other words, there were economies of scale in storing gold in a vault or other stronghold, so goldsmiths ended up storing other people's gold, as well as their own.

Naturally, the goldsmiths gave out receipts entitling the owners to reclaim their gold whenever they wished to. Since these receipts were redeemable in gold, they were in effect "as good as gold" and circulated as if they were money, buying goods and services as they were passed on from one person to another. From experience, goldsmiths learned that they seldom had to redeem all the gold that was stored with them at any given time. If a goldsmith felt confident that he would never have to redeem more than one-third of the gold that he held for other people at any given time, then he could lend out the other two-thirds and earn interest on it. Since the receipts for gold and two-thirds of the gold itself were both in circulation at the same time, the goldsmiths were, in effect, adding to the total money supply.

In this way, there arose two of the major features of modern banking—(1) holding only a fraction of the reserves needed to cover deposits and (2) adding to the total money supply. Since all the depositors are not going to want their money at one time, the bank lends most of it to other people, in order to earn interest on those loans. Some of this interest they share with the depositors by paying interest on their bank accounts. Again, with the depositors writing checks on their accounts while part of the money in those accounts is also circulating as loans to other people, the banking system is in effect adding to the national money supply, over and above the money printed by the government.

One of the reasons this system worked was that the whole banking system has never been called upon to actually supply cash to cover all the checks written by depositors. Instead, if the Acme Bank receives a million dollars worth of checks from its depositors, who received these checks from people whose accounts are with the Zebra Bank, the Acme bank does not ask the Zebra Bank for the million dollars. Instead, the Acme Bank balances these checks off against whatever checks were written by its own depositors and ended up in the hands of the Zebra Bank. For example, if Acme bank depositors had written $1,200,000 worth of checks to businesses and individuals who then deposited those checks in the Zebra Bank, then Acme Bank would just pay the difference. This way, only $200,000 is needed to settle more than two millions dollars' worth of checks that had been written on accounts in the two banks.

Both banks could keep just a fraction of their deposits in cash because all the checks written on all the banks required just a fraction of the total amounts on those checks to settle the differences between banks. Moreover, since all depositors would not want their money in cash at the same time, a relatively small amount of hard cash would permit a much larger amount of credits created by the banking system to function as money in the economy, expanding the aggregate demand beyond the money issued by the government.

This system, called "fractional reserve banking," worked fine in normal times. But it was very vulnerable when many depositors wanted hard cash at the same time. While most depositors are not going to ask for their money at the same time under normal conditions, there are special situations where more depositors will ask for their money than the bank can supply from the cash it has kept on hand. Usually, this would be when the depositors fear that they will not be able to get their money back. At one time, a bank robbery could cause depositors to fear that the bank would have to close and therefore they would all run to the bank at the same time, trying to withdraw their money before the bank collapsed. If the bank had only one-third as much money available as the total depositors were entitled to and one-half of the depositors asked for their money, then the bank ran out of money and collapsed, with the remaining depositors losing everything. The money taken by the bank robbers was often far less damaging than the run on the bank that followed.

The bank may be perfectly sound in the sense of having enough assets to cover its liabilities, but these assets cannot be instantly sold to get money to pay off the depositors. A building owned by a bank is unlikely to find a buyer instantly when the bank's depositors start lining up at the teller's window, asking for their money. Nor can a bank instantly collect all the money due them on 30-year mortgages. Such assets are not considered to be "liquid" because they cannot be readily turned into cash.

More than time is involved when evaluating the liquidity of assets. You can always sell a diamond for a dime—and pretty quickly. It is the degree to which an asset can be converted to money without losing its value that makes it liquid or not. American Express traveler's checks are liquid because they can be converted to money at their face value at any American Express office. A Treasury bond that is due to mature next month is almost as liquid, but not quite, even though you may be able to sell it as quickly as you can cash a traveler's check, but no one will pay the full face value of that Treasury bond today.

Because a bank's assets cannot all be liquidated at a moment's notice, anything that could set off a run on a bank could cause that bank to collapse. Not only would many depositors lose their savings, the nation's total money supply could suddenly decline, if this happened to enough banks at the same time. After all, part of the monetary demand consists of credits created by the banking system during the process of lending out money. When that credit disappears, there is no longer enough demand to buy everything that was being produced—at least not at the prices that had been set when the money supply was larger. This is what happened during the Great Depression of the 1930s, when thousands of banks in the United States collapsed and the total money supply of the country contracted by one-third.

In order to prevent a repetition of this catastrophe, the Federal Deposit Insurance Corporation was created, guaranteeing that the government would reimburse depositors whose money was in an insured bank when it collapsed. Now there was no longer a reason for depositors to start a run on a bank, so very few banks collapsed, and there was less likelihood of a sudden and disastrous reduction of the nation's total money supply.

While the Federal Deposit Insurance Corporation is a sort of firewall to prevent bank failures from spreading throughout the system, a more fine-tuned way of trying to control the national supply of money and credit is through the Federal Reserve System. The Federal Reserve is a central bank run by the government to control all the private banks. It has the power to tell the banks what fraction of their deposits must be kept in reserve, with only the remainder being allowed to be lent out. It also lends money to the banks, which the banks can then re-lend to the general public. By setting the interest rate on the money that it lends to the banks, the Federal Reserve System indirectly controls the interest rate that the banks will charge the general public. All of this has the net effect of allowing the Federal Reserve to control the total amount of money and credit in the economy as a whole, to one degree or another.

Because of the powerful leverage of the Federal Reserve System, public statements by the chairman of the Federal Reserve Board are scrutinized by bankers and investors for clues as to whether "the Fed" is likely to tighten the money supply or ease up. An unguarded statement by the chairman of the Federal Reserve Board, or a statement that is misconstrued by financiers, can set off a panic in Wall Street that causes stock prices to plummet. Or, if the Federal Reserve Board chairman sounds upbeat, stock prices may soar—to unsustainable levels that will ruin many people when the prices come back down. Given such drastic repercussions, which can affect financial markets around the world, Federal Reserve Board chairmen over the years have learned to speak in highly guarded and Delphic terms that often leave listeners puzzled as to what they really mean. What *BusinessWeek* magazine said of Federal Reserve chairman Alan Greenspan could have been said of many of his predecessors in that position: "Wall Street and Washington expend megawatts of energy trying to decipher the delphic pronouncements of Alan Greenspan."

In assessing the role of the Federal Reserve, as well as any other organs of government, a sharp distinction must be made between their stated goals and their actual performance or effect. The Federal Reserve System was established in 1914 as a result of fears of such economic consequences as deflation and bank failures. Yet the worst deflation and the worst bank failures in the country's history occurred after the Federal Reserve was established. The financial crises of 1907, which helped spur the creation of the Federal Reserve System, was dwarfed by the financial crises associated with the stock market crash of 1929 and the Great Depression of the 1930s.

Chapter 17

The Role of Government

You know, doing what is right is easy. The problem is knowing what is right.

—President Lyndon B. Johnson

A modern market economy cannot exist in a vacuum. Market transactions take place within a framework of rules and require someone with the authority to enforce those rules. Government not only enforces its own rules but also enforces contracts and other agreements and understandings among the numerous parties in the economy. Sometimes government also sets standards, defining what is a pound, a mile, or a bushel. And to support itself, governments must also collect taxes, which in turn affect economic decision-making by those affected by those taxes.

Beyond these basic functions, which virtually everyone can agree on, governments can play more expansive roles, all the way up to directly owning and operating all the farms and industries in a nation. Controversies have raged around the world, for more than a century, on the role that government should play in the economy. For much of the twentieth century, those who favored a larger role for government were clearly in the ascendancy. Russia, China, and others in the Communist bloc of nations were at one extreme, but democratic countries like Britain, India, and France also had their governments take over ownership of various industries and tightly control the decisions made in other industries that were allowed to remain privately owned. Wide sections of the political, intellectual and even business communities have often been in favor of this expansive role of government.

During the 1980s, however, the tide began to turn the other way, toward reducing the role of government. This happened first in Britain and the United States, and then such trends spread rapidly through the democratic countries and were climaxed by the collapse of Communism in the Soviet bloc. As a 1998 study put it:

> All around the globe, socialists are embracing capitalism, governments are selling off companies they had previously nationalized, and countries are seeking to entice back multinational corporations that they had expelled just two decades earlier.

Experience—often bitter experience—had more to do with such changes than any new theory or analysis. However, in order to understand basic economics, it is not necessary to enter into these controversies. Here we can examine the basic functions of government that virtually everyone can agree on and explain why those functions are important for the allocation of scarce resources which have alternative uses.

The most basic function of government is to provide a framework of law and order, within which the people can engage in whatever economic and other activities they choose, making such mutual accommodations and agreements among themselves as they choose. There are also certain activities which generate significant costs and benefits that extend beyond those individuals who engage in these activities. Here government can take account of these costs and benefits when the marketplace does not.

The individuals who work for government in various capacities tend to respond to the incentives facing them, just as people do in corporations, in families, and in other human institutions and activities. Government is neither a monolith nor simply the public interest personified. To understand what it does, its incentives and constraints must be taken into account, just as the incentives and constraints of the marketplace must be for those who engage in market transactions.

LAW AND ORDER

Where government restricts its economic role to that of an enforcer of laws and contracts, some people say that such a policy amounts to "doing nothing." However, what is called "nothing" has often taken centuries to achieve—namely, a reliable framework of laws, within which economic activity can flourish, and without which even vast riches in natural resources may go unused and the people remain much poorer than they need to be.

Like the role of prices, the role of a reliable framework of laws may be easier to understand by observing what happens in places where that framework does not exist. Countries whose governments are ineffectual, arbitrary, or corrupt can remain poor despite an abundance of natural resources, because neither foreign nor domestic entrepreneurs want to risk the kinds of large investments needed to develop natural resources into products that bring increased prosperity.

A classic example is the African nation of Congo, rich in minerals but poor in every other way. Here is the scene encountered at the airport in its capital city of Kinshasa:

> Kinshasa is one of the world's poorest cities, so unsafe for arriving crews that they get shuttled elsewhere for overnight stays. Taxiing down the scarred tarmac feels like driving over railroad ties. Managers charge extra to turn on the runway lights at night, and departing passengers can encounter several layers of bribes before boarding.

Bolivia is another Third World country where law and order has broken down:

> The media are full of revelations about police links to drug trafficking and stolen vehicles, nepotism in the force, and the charging of illegal fees for services. Officers on meagre salaries have been found to live in mansions.

In poor countries where middle class or wealthy people are targets of widespread violence by criminals or ideologues, costly and extraordinary precautions are necessary for personal safety. Thus fenced and gated private developments with their own security guards are widespread in Brazil, where there is also a large market for armor-plated cars. Private spending on security in Brazil is estimated to substantially exceed public spending on police, and private security guards outnumber policemen by three to one.

Whatever the merits or demerits of particular laws, someone must administer those laws—and how efficiently or how honestly that is done can make a huge economic difference. The phrase "the law's delay" goes back at least as far as Shakespeare's time. Such delay imposes costs on those whose investments are idled, whose shipments are held up, and whose ability to plan their economic activities is crippled by red tape and slow-moving bureaucrats.

Moreover, bureaucrats' ability to create delay often means an opportunity for them to collect bribes to speed things up—all of which adds up to higher costs of doing business. That in turn means higher prices to consumers, and correspondingly lower standards of living for the country as a whole.

A study by the World Bank concluded that "across countries there is evidence that higher levels of corruption are associated with lower growth and lower levels of per capita income." In India, for example, as an Indian business executive put it, the entrepreneur there "has to bribe from twenty to forty functionaries if he is serious about doing business."

During czarist Russia's industrialization in the late nineteenth and early twentieth centuries, one of the country's biggest handicaps was the widespread corruption in the general population, in addition to the corruption that was rampant within the Russian government. Foreign firms which hired Russian workers and even Russian executives made it a point *not* to hire Russian accountants. This corruption continued under the Communists and has become an international scandal in the post-Communist era. One study pointed out that the stock of a Russian oil company sold for about one percent of what the stock of a similar oil company would sell for in the United States because "the market assumes that Russian oil companies will be systematically looted by insiders." Nor is this corruption confined to the industrial or commercial sector. According to a report from *The Chronicle of Higher Education*'s Moscow correspondent in 2002:

> It costs between $10,000 and $15,000 in bribes merely to gain acceptance into well-regarded institutions of higher learning in Moscow, the daily newspaper *Izvestia* has reported . . . At Astrakhan State Technical University, about 700 miles south of Moscow, three professors were arrested after allegedly inducing students to pay cash to ensure good grades on exams. . . . Over all, Russian students and their parents annually spend at least $2 billion—and possibly up to $5 billion—in such "unofficial" educational outlays, the deputy prime minister, Valentina Matviyenko, said last year in an interview.

In a country's economy, bribes are not simply a cost to companies doing business in that particular country. They are a deterrent to other companies that are deciding where to invest and where to avoid—and the loss of those investments can be a much bigger cost to the economy than the bribes themselves. As *The Economist* magazine put it: "For sound economic reasons, investors and international aid agencies are increasingly taking the level of bribery and corruption into account in their investment and lending."

It is not just corruption but also sheer bureaucracy which can stifle economic activity. Even one of India's most spectacularly successful industrialists, Aditya Birla, found himself forced to look to other countries in which to expand his investments, because of India's slow-moving bureaucrats:

> With all his successes, there were heartbreaks galore. One of them was the Mangalore refinery, which Delhi's bureaucrats took eleven years to clear—a record even by the standards of the Indian bureaucracy. While both of us were waiting for a court to open up at the Bombay Gymkhana one day, I asked Aditya Birla what had led him to invest abroad. He had no choice, he said, in his deep, unaffected voice. There were too many obstacles in India. To begin with, he needed a license, which the government would not give because the Birlas were classified as "a large house" under the MRTP [Monopolies and Restrictive Trade Practices] Act. Even if he did get one miraculously, the government would decide where he should invest, what technology he must use, what was to be the size of the plant, how it was to be financed—even the size and structure of his public issue. Then he would have to battle the bureaucracy to get licenses for the import of capital goods and raw materials. After that, he faced dozens of clearances at the state level—for power, land, sales tax, excise, labor, among others. "All this takes years, and frankly, I get exhausted just thinking about it."

This head of 37 companies with combined sales in the billions of dollars—someone capable of creating many much-needed jobs in India—ended up producing fiber in Thailand, which he converted to yarn in his factory in Indonesia, exporting the yarn to Belgium, where it was woven into carpets—which were then exported to Canada. All the jobs, incomes, business opportunities, and taxes from which India could have benefited were lost because of the country's own bureaucracies.

The Framework of Laws

For fostering economic activities and the prosperity resulting from them, laws must be reliable, above all. If the application of the law varies with the whims of kings or dictators, with changes in democratically elected governments, or with the caprices or corruption of appointed officials, then the risks surrounding investments rise, and consequently the amount of investing is likely to be less than purely economic considerations would produce in a market economy under a reliable framework of laws.

One of the major advantages that enabled nineteenth-century Britain to become the first industrialized nation was the dependability of its laws. Not only could Britons feel confident when investing in their country's economy, without fear that their earnings would be confiscated, or dissipated in bribes, or the contracts they made voided for political reasons, so could foreigners doing business or making investments in Britain. For centuries, the reputation of British law for dependability and impartiality attracted investments and entrepreneurs from continental Europe, as well as skilled immigrants and refugees, who helped create whole new industries in Britain. In short, both the physical capital and the human capital of foreigners contributed to the development of the British economy from the medieval era, when it was one of the more backward economies in Western Europe, to a later era, when it became one of the most advanced, setting the stage for Britain's industrial revolution that led the world into the industrial age.

In other parts of the world as well, a framework of dependable laws encouraged both domestic and foreign investment, as well as attracting immigrants with skills lacking locally. In Southeast Asia, for example, the imposition of European laws under the colonial regimes of the eighteenth and nineteenth centuries replaced the powers of local rulers and tribes. Under these new frameworks of laws—often uniform across larger geographical areas than before, as well as being more dependable at a given place—a massive immigration from China and a smaller immigration from India brought in people whose skills and entrepreneurship created whole industries and transformed the economies of countries throughout the region.

European investors also sent capital to Southeast Asia, financing many of the giant ventures in mining and shipping that were often beyond the resources of the Chinese and Indian immigrants, as well as beyond the resources of the indigenous peoples. In colonial Malaya, for example, the tin mines and rubber plantations which provided much of the country's export earnings were financed by European capital and worked by laborers from China and India, while most local commerce and industry were in the hands of the Chinese, leaving the indigenous Malays largely spectators at the modern development of their own economy.

While impartiality is a desirable quality in laws, even laws which are discriminatory can still promote economic development, if the nature of the discrimination is spelled out in advance, rather than taking the form of biased, unpredictable, and corrupt decisions by judges, juries, and officials. The Chinese and Indians who settled in the European colonial empires of Southeast Asia never had the same legal rights as Europeans there, nor the same rights as the indigenous population. Yet whatever rights they did have could be relied upon and therefore served as a basis for the creation of Chinese and Indian businesses in the region.

Similarly in the Ottoman Empire, Christians and Jews never had the same rights as Moslems. Yet, during the flourishing centuries of that empire, the rights which Christians and Jews did have were sufficiently dependable to enable them to prosper in commerce, industry, and banking to a greater extent than the Moslem majority. Moreover, their economic activities contributed to the prosperity of the Ottoman Empire as a whole. Similar stories could be told of the Lebanese minority in colonial West Africa, Indians in colonial Fiji, German immigrants in Brazil, and other minority groups in other countries who prospered under laws that were dependable, even if not impartial.

Dependability is not simply a matter of the government's own treatment of people. It must also prevent some people from interfering with other people, so that criminals and mobs do not make economic life risky and thereby stifle the economic development required for prosperity. Governments differ in the effectiveness with which they can enforce their laws in general, and even a given government may be able to enforce its laws more effectively in some places than in others. For centuries during the Middle Ages, the borderlands between English and Scottish kingdoms were not effectively controlled by either country and so remained lawless and economically backward. Mountainous regions have often been difficult to police, whether in the Balkans, the Appalachian region of the United States, or elsewhere. Such places have likewise tended to lag in economic development and to attract few outsiders and little outside capital.

Today, high-crime neighborhoods and neighborhoods subject to higher than normal rates of vandalism or riots similarly suffer economically from a lack of law and order. Some businesses simply will not locate there. Those that do may be less efficient or less pleasant than businesses in other neighborhoods, where such substandard businesses would be unable to compete. The costs of additional security devices inside and outside of stores, as well as security guards in some places, all add to the costs of doing business and are reflected in the higher prices of goods and services purchased by people in high-crime areas, even though most people in such areas are not criminals.

Property Rights

One of the most misunderstood aspects of law and order are property rights. While these rights are cherished as personal benefits by those fortunate enough to own a substantial amount of property, what matters from the standpoint of economics is how property rights affect the allocation of scarce resources which have alternative uses. Property rights need to be assessed in terms of their economic effects on the well-being of the population at large. This is ultimately an empirical question which cannot be settled on the basis of assumptions or rhetoric.

What is different with and without property rights? One small but telling example was the experience of a delegation of American farmers who visited the Soviet Union. They were appalled at the way various agricultural produce was shipped, carelessly packed and with spoiled fruit or vegetables left to spread the spoilage to other fruits and vegetables in the same sacks or boxes.[1] Coming from a country where individuals owned agricultural produce as their private property, American farmers had no experience with such gross carelessness and waste, which would have caused somebody to lose much money needlessly in the United States, and perhaps go bankrupt. In the Soviet Union, the loss was even more painful, since the country often had trouble feeding itself, but there were no property rights to convey these losses directly to the produce handlers and shippers who caused it.

In a country without property rights, or with the food being owned "by the people," there was no given individual with sufficient incentives to ensure that this food did not spoil needlessly before it reached the consumers. Those who handled the food in transit were paid salaries, which were fixed independently of how well they did or did not safeguard the food. In theory at least, closer monitoring of produce handlers could have reduced the spoilage. But monitoring is not free. The human resources which go into monitoring are themselves among the scarce resources which have alternative uses. Moreover, monitoring raises the further question: Who will monitor the monitors? The Soviets tried to deal with this problem by having Communist Party members honeycombed throughout the society to report on derelictions of duty and violations of law. However, the widespread corruption and inefficiency found even under Stalinist totalitarianism suggest the limita-

---

[1] Similar practices were followed at a Soviet factory which produced metal pipes. Ordinary pipes were coated with oil to prevent corrosion, while stainless steel pipes were supposed to be kept away from oil because it ruined them. But the workers not only packed both kinds of pipes together, they even walked on top of stainless steel pipes with their oil-covered boots. The reason was that the authorities measured output in terms of railroad carloads of pipes that were shipped. Since there were not enough stainless steel pipes to fill a railroad car, they were lumped in with the ordinary pipes that were coated with oil.

tions of official monitoring, as compared to automatic self-monitoring by property owners.

No one has to stand over an American farmer and tell him to take the rotten peaches out of a basket before they spoil the others, because those peaches are his private property and he is not about to lose money if he doesn't have to. *Property rights create self-monitoring*, which tends to be both more effective and less costly than third-party monitoring. Most Americans do not own any agricultural land or agricultural crops, but they have more and better food available at lower prices than in countries where there are no property rights in agricultural land or its produce, and where much food may spoil needlessly as a result.

The only animals threatened with extinction are animals not owned by anybody. Colonel Sanders was not about to let chickens become extinct. Nor will McDonald's stand idly by and let cows become extinct. Likewise, it is things not owned by anybody (air and water, for example) which are polluted. In centuries past, sheep were allowed to graze on unowned land—"the commons," as it was called—with the net result that land on the commons was so heavily grazed that it had little left but patchy ground and the shepherds had hungry and scrawny sheep. But privately owned land adjacent to the commons was usually in far better condition. Similar neglect of unowned land occurred in the Soviet Union. According to Soviet economists, "forest areas that are cut down are not reseeded," though it would be financial suicide for a lumbering company to let that happen on their own property in a capitalist economy.

All these things, in different ways, illustrate the value of private property *to the society as a whole*, including people who own no private property, but who benefit from the greater economic efficiency it creates, which translates into a higher standard of living for the country as a whole.

Despite a tendency to think of property rights as special privileges for the rich, many property rights are actually more valuable to people who are not rich—and such property rights have often been infringed or violated for the benefit of the rich. Although the average rich person, by definition, has more money than the average person who is not rich, in the aggregate the non-rich population often has far more money. This means, among other things, that many properties owned by the rich would be bid away from them by the greater purchasing power of the non-rich, if unrestricted property rights prevailed in a free market. Thus land occupied by mansions located on huge estates would pass through the market to entrepreneurs who would build smaller and more numerous homes or apartment buildings—all for the use of people with more modest incomes, but with more money in the aggregate.

Someone once said, "It doesn't matter whether you are rich or poor, so long as you have money." This was meant as a joke but it has very serious implications. In a free market, the money of ordinary people is just as good as the money of the rich—and in the aggregate, there is more of it. The individually less affluent need not directly bid against the more affluent. Entrepreneurs or their companies, using their own money or money borrowed from banks and other financial institutions, can acquire mansions and estates, and replace them with middle-class homes and apartment buildings for people of modest incomes. This would of course change the communities in ways the rich might not like, however much others might like to live in the resulting newly developed communities. Wealthy people have often forestalled such transfers of property by getting laws passed to *restrict* property rights in a variety of ways. For example, various affluent northern California communities have required land to be sold only in lots of one acre or more per house, thereby pricing such land and homes beyond the reach of most people and thus neutralizing the greater aggregate purchasing power of less affluent people. Zoning boards, "open space" laws, historical preservation agencies and other organizations and devices have also been used to severely limit the sale of private property for use in ways not approved by those who wish to keep things the way they are in their communities.

The effectiveness of these laws infringing or negating property rights has been shown, not only by the maintenance of existing communities in their existing character, often with negligible population growth despite rising employment in the area, but also by the rapid increase in home prices as more people bid for a relatively unchanged number of homes, leaving those who lose out in this local competition to have to live farther away from their jobs.

Using many political and legal devices to prevent the unfettered sale of property rights from transferring land and transforming communities, Palo Alto, California—adjacent to Stanford University—had its home prices increase approximately four-fold in one decade, while its population actually declined in the face of increasing employment around them in Silicon Valley. In San Mateo County, another affluent area in northern California, more than half the land is legally off-limits as "open space," likewise causing home prices to skyrocket and keeping the less affluent from being able to live in the area.

One symptom of this is that the number of blacks living in San Mateo County actually declined by 10,000 people between the 1990 census and the

2000 census, even though the overall population of the county increased by 50,000 people. Similar patterns of a declining black population while the total population increased also appeared in nearby San Francisco County and Marin County, both similarly affluent counties with similar restrictive land use policies.

By infringing or negating property rights, affluent and wealthy property owners are able to keep out people of average or low incomes and, at the same time, increase the value of their own property by ensuring its growing scarcity relative to increasing employment in the area. Some even acquire a sense of moral superiority in doing so, demonizing the intermediaries who seek to transfer land to new uses. "Developer" is as much of a dirty word among those protecting the status quo in California as "profits" were to India's socialist Prime Minister Nehru.

While strict adherence to property rights would allow landlords to evict tenants at will, the economic incentives are for them to do just the opposite—to try to keep their apartments as fully rented and as continuously occupied as possible, so long as the tenants pay their rent and behave themselves. Only when rent control or other restrictions on their property rights are enacted are landlords likely to do otherwise. Under rent control and tenants rights laws, landlords have been known to try to harass tenants into leaving, whether in New York or in Hong Kong.

Under stringent rent control and tenants rights laws in Hong Kong, landlords were known to sneak into their own buildings late at night to vandalize the premises, in order to make them less attractive or even unlivable, so that tenants would move out and the empty building could then be torn down legally, to be replaced by something more lucrative as commercial or industrial property. This of course was by no means the purpose or intention of those who had passed rent control laws in Hong Kong. But it illustrates again the importance of making a distinction between intentions and effects—and not just as regards property rights laws. In short, incentives matter and property rights need to be assessed economically in terms of the incentives created by their existence, their modifications, or their elimination.

The powerful incentives created by a profit-and-loss economy depend on the profits being private property. When government-owned enterprises in the Soviet Union made profits, those profits were not their private property but belonged to "the people"—or, in more mundane terms, could be taken by the government for whatever purposes higher officials chose to spend them on. Soviet economists Schmelev and Popov pointed out and lamented the adverse effects of this on incentives:

But what justifies confiscating the larger part—sometimes 90–95 percent—of enterprises' profits, as is being done in many sectors of the economy today? What political or economic right—ultimately what human right—do ministries have to do that? Once again we are taking away from those who work well in order to keep afloat those who do nothing. How can we possibly talk about independence, initiative, rewards for efficiency, quality, and technical progress?

Of course, the country's leaders could continue to *talk* about such things, but destroying the incentives which exist under property rights meant that there was a reduced chance of achieving these goals. Because of an absence of property rights, those who ran enterprises that made profits "can't buy or build anything with the money they have" which represent "just figures in a bank account with no real value whatever without permission from above" to use that money. In other words, success does not lead to expansions of successful enterprises or contraction of unsuccessful ones, as it does in a market economy.

While government officials in the United States cannot arbitrarily confiscate profits as directly as Soviet officials could, American legislators can pass laws imposing costs on private enterprises, thereby causing profits to be reduced—and incentives to be changed. In California, for example, the state legislature passed a law requiring landlords to give elderly tenants a year's notice before evicting them and to pay up to $3,000 to each tenant evicted, to help with relocation costs. This legislation was intended to deal with the danger of mass evictions by landlords who were losing money under rent control in places like San Francisco, and who wanted to stop renting.

Since this legislation went into effect on January 2, 2000, owners of cheap hotels in San Francisco evicted many elderly tenants during December 1999, in order to escape these impending costs of shutting down their hotels. Here again, the goals of the law were very different from the consequences— which, in this case, caused many poor and elderly single men to be thrown out on the streets during the Christmas season, in a city with a severe housing shortage and the highest rents in the country. Far more anger and indignation were directed at the hotel owners than at those who had passed such legislation. Yet, in the absence of attempts to confiscate profits through both rent control laws and laws on evictions, the ordinary incentives of property rights and a free market would have caused the hotel owners to want to keep all the tenants they could.

Social Order

Order includes more than laws and the government apparatus that administers laws. It also includes the honesty, reliability and cooperativeness of the people themselves. Honesty and reliability can vary greatly between one country and another. As a knowledgeable observer put it: "While it is unimaginable to do business in China without paying bribes, to offer one in Japan is the greatest faux pas."

Honesty and reliability can also vary widely among particular groups within a given country, and that also has economic repercussions. Some insular groups rely upon their own internal social controls for doing business with fellow group members whom they can trust. One such group are the Marwaris of India, whose business networks were established in the nineteenth century and extended beyond India to China and Central Asia, and who "transacted vast sums merely on the merchant's word." But "doing business among strangers," as *The Economist* puts it, "is not easy" in India. Yet that is an essential part of a successful modern mass economy, which requires cooperation among far more people than can possibly know each other personally. As for the general level of reliability among strangers in India, *The Economist* reported:

> If you withdraw 10,000 rupees from a bank, it will probably come in a brick of 100-rupee notes, held together by industrial strength staples that you must struggle to prise open. They are there to prevent someone from surreptitiously removing a few notes. On trains, announcements may advise you to crush your empty mineral-water bottles lest someone refill them with tap water and sell them as new. . . . Any sort of business that requires confidence in the judicial system is best left alone.

Where neither the honesty of the general population nor the integrity of the legal system can be relied upon, economic activities are inhibited. At the same time, groups whose members can rely on each other, such as the Marwaris, have a great advantage in competition with others, in being able to secure mutual cooperation in economic activities that extend over distances and time—activities that would be far more risky for others in such societies and still more so for strangers.

Like the Marwaris, Hasidic Jews in New York's jewelry business often give consignments of jewels to one another and share the sales proceeds on the basis of verbal agreements among themselves. The extreme social isolation of the Hasidic community from the larger society, and even from other Jews, makes it very costly for anyone who grows up in that community to disgrace his family and lose his own standing, as well as his own economic and social relationships, by cheating on an agreement with a fellow Hasidim.

It is much the same story halfway around the world, where the overseas Chinese minority in various southeast Asian countries make verbal agreements among themselves, without the sanction of the local legal system. Given the unreliability and corruption of some of these post-colonial legal systems, the ability of the Chinese to rely on their own social and economic standards gives them an economic advantage over their indigenous competitors who lack an equally reliable and inexpensive way of making transactions. The costs of doing business are thus less for the Chinese than for Malay, Indonesian or other businesses in the region, giving the Chinese competitive advantages. This ability to rely on others within the group or family has likewise been a factor in the remarkable success of the Palanpuri Jains in India, who are the leading diamond suppliers there and who also control half the world's supply of uncut diamonds. Indeed, these Jains have begun to displace Jews in Antwerp, where about 90 percent of the world's uncut diamonds and half of its polished diamonds are sold.

Although businesses in some American communities must incur the extra expense of heavy grates for protection from theft and vandalism while closed and security guards for protection while open, businesses in other American communities have no such expenses and are therefore able to operate profitably while charging lower prices. Rental car companies can park their cars in lots without fences or guards in some communities, while in other places it would be financial suicide to do so. But, in those places where rare car thefts from unguarded lots cost less than paying guards and maintaining fences would cost, then rental car agencies—and other businesses—can flourish in such communities.

In short, honesty is more than a moral principle. It is also a major economic factor. While government can do little to create honesty, in various ways it can either support or undermine the traditions on which honest conduct is based. This it can do by what it teaches in its schools, by the examples set by public officials, or by the laws that it passes. These laws can create incentives toward either moral or immoral conduct. Where laws create a situation where the only way to avoid ruinous losses is by violating the law, the government is in effect reducing public respect for laws in general and rewarding dishonest behavior. Advocates of rent control, for example, often point to examples of villainy among landlords to demonstrate the need for both rent control itself and related tenants' rights legislation. However, rent control laws can widen the difference between the value of a given apartment building to honest owners and dishonest owners. Where the cost of legally mandated services is high enough to equal or exceed the amount of rent permitted under the law, the value of a building to an honest landlord can become zero or even negative. Yet, to a landlord who is willing to violate the law and save money by neglecting required services, or who accepts bribes from prospective tenants, the building may still have some value.

Where something has different values to different people, it tends to move through the marketplace to its most valued use, which is where the bids will be highest. In this case, dishonest landlords can easily bid apartment buildings away from honest landlords, some of whom may be happy to escape the bind that rent control puts them in. Landlords willing to resort to arson may find the building most valuable of all, if they can sell the site for commercial or industrial use after burning the building down, thereby getting rid of both tenants and rent control. As one study found:

> In New York City, landlord arsons became so common that the city responded with special welfare allowances. For a while, burned-out tenants were moved to the top of the list for coveted public housing. That then gave *tenants* an incentive to burn down the buildings in which they lived—which they did, often moving television sets and furniture out onto the sidewalk before starting the fire.

Those who create incentives toward widespread dishonesty by promoting laws which make honest behavior financially impossible are often among the most indignant at the dishonesty—and the least likely to regard themselves as in any way responsible for it. Arson is just one of the forms of dishonesty promoted by rent control laws. Shrewd and unscrupulous landlords have made virtually a science out of milking a rent-controlled building by neglecting maintenance and repairs, defaulting on mortgage payments, falling behind in the payment of taxes, and then finally letting the building become the property of the city, while they move on to repeat the same destructive process with other rent-controlled buildings.

Without rent control, the incentives facing landlords are directly the opposite—that is, to maintain the quality of the property, in order to attract tenants, and to safeguard it against fire and other sources of dangers to the survival of the building. In short, complaints against landlords' behavior by rent control advocates can be valid, even though few of these advocates see any connection between rent control and a declining moral quality in people who become landlords. When honest landlords stand to lose money under rent control, while dishonest landlords can still make a profit, it is virtually inevitable that the property will pass from the former to the latter.

Rent control laws are just one of a number of severe restrictions which can make honest behavior too costly for many people, and which therefore promote widespread dishonesty. Bureaucratic delays in many countries such as India virtually ensure that bribery will become widespread when the costs of these delays become greater than the costs of the bribes. The Prohibition era in the United States during the 1920s made widespread violation of the bans against alcoholic beverages so common as to become almost respectable among the general public, quite aside from the boost that it gave to organized crime. It is common in Third World countries for much—sometimes most—economic activity to take place "off the books," which is to say illegally, because oppressive levels of bureaucracy and red tape make legal operation too costly for most people to afford.

When laws and policies make honesty increasingly costly, then government is, in effect, promoting dishonesty. Such dishonesty can extend then beyond the particular laws and policies in question to a more general habit of disobeying laws, to the detriment of the whole economy and society.

EXTERNAL COSTS AND BENEFITS

Economic decisions made through the marketplace are not always better than decisions that governments can make. Much depends on whether those market transactions accurately reflect both the costs and the benefits which result. Under some conditions, they do not.

When someone buys a table or a tractor, the question as to whether it is worth what it cost is answered by the actions of the purchaser who made the decision to buy it. However, when an electric utility company buys coal to burn to generate electricity, a significant part of the cost of the electricity-generating process is paid by people who breathe the smoke that results from the burning of the coal and whose homes and cars are dirtied by the soot. Cleaning, repainting and medical costs paid by these people are not taken into account in the marketplace, because these people do not participate in the transactions between the coal producer and the utility company.

Their costs are called "external costs" by economists because such costs fall outside the parties to the transaction that creates these costs. External costs are therefore not taken into account in the marketplace, even when these are very substantial costs, which can extend beyond monetary losses to include bad health and premature death.

While there are many decisions that can be made more efficiently through the marketplace than by government, this is one of those decisions that can be made more efficiently by government than by the marketplace. Clean air laws can reduce harmful emissions by legislation and regulations. Clean water laws and laws against disposing of toxic wastes where they will harm people can likewise force decisions to be made in ways that take into account the external costs that would otherwise be ignored by those transacting in the marketplace.

By the same token, there may be transactions that would be *beneficial* to people who are not party to the decision-making, and whose interests are therefore not taken into account. The benefits of mud flaps on cars and trucks may be apparent to anyone who has ever driven in a rainstorm behind a car or truck that was throwing so much water or mud onto his windshield as to dangerously obscure vision. Even if everyone agrees that the benefits of mud flaps greatly exceed their costs, there is no feasible way of buying those benefits in a free market, since you receive no benefits from the mud flaps that you buy and put on your own car, but only from mud flaps that other people buy and put on their cars and trucks. These are "external benefits." Here again, it is possible to obtain collectively through government what cannot be obtained individually through the marketplace, simply by having laws passed requiring all cars and trucks to have mud flaps on them.

Some benefits are indivisible. Either everybody gets these benefits or nobody gets them. Military defense is one example. If military defense had to be purchased individually through the marketplace, then those who felt threatened by foreign powers could pay for guns, troops, cannon and all the other means of military deterrence and self-defense, while those who saw no dangers could refuse to spend their money on such things. However, the level of military security would be the same for both, since supporters and non-supporters of military forces are intermixed in the same society and exposed to the same dangers from enemy action.

Given the indivisibility of the benefits, even some citizens who fully appreciate the military dangers, and who consider the costs of meeting those dangers to be fully justified by the benefits, might still feel no need to spend their own money for military purposes, since their individual contribution would have no serious effect on their own individual security, which would depend primarily on how much others contributed. In such a situation, it is entirely possible to end up with inadequate military defense, even if everyone understands the cost of effective defense and considers the benefits worth it.

By collectivizing this decision and having it made by government, an end result can be achieved that is more in keeping with what most people want than if those people were allowed to decide individually what to do. Even among free market advocates, few would suggest that each individual should buy military defense in the marketplace. In short, there are things that government can do more efficiently than individuals because external costs or external benefits make individual decisions, based on individual interests, a less effective way of weighing costs and benefits to the whole society.

INCENTIVES AND CONSTRAINTS

Government is of course inseparable from politics, especially in a democratic country, so a distinction must made and kept in mind between what a government *can* do to make things better than they would be in a free market and what it is in fact *likely* to do under the influence of political incentives and constraints. The distinction between what the government can do and what it is likely to do can be lost when we think of the government as simply an agent of society or even as one integral performer. In reality, the many individuals and agencies within a national government have their own separate interests, incentives, and agendas, to which they may respond far more often than they respond to either the public interest or to the policy agendas set by political leaders. Even in a totalitarian state such as the Soviet Union, different branches and departments of government had different interests that they pursued, despite whatever disadvantages this might have for the economy or the society. For example, industrial enterprises in different ministries avoided relying on each other for equipment or resources, if at all possible. Thus an enterprise located in Vladivostok might order equipment or natural resources that it needed from another enterprise under the same ministry located in Minsk, thousands of miles away, rather than depend on getting what they needed from another enterprise located nearby in Vladivostok that was under the control of a different ministry. Thus materials might be needlessly shipped thousands of miles eastward on the overburdened Soviet railroads, while the same kinds of materials were also being shipped westward on the same railroads by another enterprise in another ministry.

Such economically wasteful cross-hauling was one of many inefficient allocations of scarce resources due to the political reality that government is not a monolith, even in a totalitarian society. In democratic societies, where innumerable interest groups are free to organize and influence different branches and agencies of government, there is even less reason to expect that the government will follow one coherent policy, much less a policy that would be followed by an ideal government representing the public interest.

Under popularly elected government, the political incentives are to do what is popular, even if the consequence are worse than the consequences of doing nothing, or doing something that is less popular. As an example of what virtually everyone now agrees was a mistaken policy, the Nixon administration in 1971 created the first peacetime nationwide wage controls and price controls in the history of the United States. Among those at the meeting where this fateful decision was made was internationally renowned economist Arthur F. Burns, who argued strenuously against the policy being considered—and was over-ruled. Nor were the other people present economically illiterate. The president himself had long resisted the idea of wage and price controls and had publicly rejected the idea just eleven days before doing an about-face and accepting it. Inflation had created mounting pressures from the public and the media to "do something."

With a presidential election due the following year, the administration could not afford to be seen as doing nothing while inflation raged out of control. However, even aside from such political concerns, the participants in this meeting were "exhilarated by all the great decisions they had made" that day, according to a participant. Looking back, he later recalled "that more time was spent discussing the timing of the president's speech than how the economic program would work." There was particular concern that, if his speech were broadcast in prime time, it would cause cancellation of the very popular television program *Bonanza*, leading to public resentments. Here is what happened:

Nixon's speech—despite the preemption of *Bonanza*—was a great hit. The public felt that the government was coming to its defense against the price gougers . . . During the next evening's newscasts, 90 percent of the coverage was devoted to Nixon's new policy. The coverage was favorable. And the Dow Jones Industrial Average registered a 32.9 point gain—the largest one-day increase up to then.

In short, the controls were a complete success politically. As for their economic consequences:

Ranchers stopped shipping their cattle to the market, farmers drowned their chickens, and consumers emptied the shelves of supermarkets.

In short, artificially low prices led to supplies being reduced while the demands of consumers increased. For example, more American cattle began to be exported, mostly to Canada, instead of being sold in the price-controlled U.S. market. Thus price controls produced essentially the same results under the Nixon administration as they had produced in the Roman Empire under Diocletian, in the Soviet Union under the Communists, in Ghana under Nkhrumah, and in numerous other times and places where such policies had been tried before. Nor was this particular policy unique politically in how it was conceived and carried out. Veteran economic adviser Herbert Stein observed, 25 years after the Nixon administration meeting at which he had been present, "failure to look ahead is extremely common in government policy making."

Another way of saying the same thing is that political time horizons tend to be much shorter than economic time horizons. Before the full economic consequences of the wage and price control policies became widely apparent, Nixon had been re-elected with a landslide victory at the polls. There is no "present value" factor to force political decision-makers to take into account the long-run consequences of their current decisions.

One of the important fields neglected as a result of the short political time horizon is education. As a writer in India put it, "No one bothers about education because results take a long time to come." This is not peculiar to India. With fundamental educational reform being both difficult and requiring years to show end results, it is politically much more expedient for elected officials to demonstrate immediate "concern" for education by voting to spend increasing amounts of the taxpayers' money on it, even if that leads only to more expensive incompetence.

The constraints within which government policy-making operates are as important as the incentives. Important and beneficial as a framework of rules of law may be, what that also means is that many matters must be dealt with categorically, rather than incrementally. The application of categorical laws prevents the enormous powers of government from being applied at the discretion or whim of individual functionaries, which would invite both corruption and arbitrariness. However, there are many things which require discretionary incremental adjustments, as noted in Chapter 4, and for these things categorical laws can be difficult to apply or can produce counterproductive results. For example, while prevention of air pollution and water pollution are widely recognized as legitimate functions of government, which can achieve more economically efficient results than those of the free market, doing so through categorical laws can create major problems. Despite the political appeal of categorical phrases like "clean water" and "clean air," there are in fact no such things, never have been, and perhaps never will be. Moreover, there are diminishing returns in removing impurities from water or air. A study of environmental risk regulation cited a former administration of the Environmental Protection Agency on this:

> A former EPA administrator put the problem succinctly when he noted that about 95 percent of the toxic material could be removed from waste sites in a few months, but years are spent trying to remove the last little bit. Removing that last little bit can involve limited technological choice, high cost, devotion of considerable agency resources, large legal fees, and endless argument.

Reducing truly dangerous amounts of impurities from water or air may be done at costs that most people would agree were quite reasonable. But, as higher and higher standards of purity are prescribed by government, in order to eliminate ever more minute traces of ever more remote or more questionable dangers, the costs escalate out of proportion. Even if removing 98 percent a given impurity costs twice as much as eliminating 97 percent, and removing 99 percent costs ten times as much, the political appeal of categorical phrases like "clean water" may be just as potent when the water is already 99.9 percent pure as when it was dangerously polluted.

Depending on what the particular impurity is, minute traces may or may not pose a serious danger. But political controversies over impurities in the water are unlikely to be settled at a scientific level when passions can be whipped up in the name of non-existent "clean water." No matter how pure the water becomes, someone can always demand the removal of more impurities. And, unless the public understands the logical and economic implications of what is being said, that demand can become politically irresistible, since no public official wants to be known as being opposed to clean water.

It is not even certain that reducing extremely small amounts of substances that are harmful in larger amounts reduces risks at all. For example, although high doses of saccharin have been shown to increase the rate of cancer in laboratory rats, very low doses seem to *reduce* the rate of cancer in these rats. This is similar to research findings that, although a large intake of alcohol shortens people's lifespan, very modest amounts of alcohol—like one glass of wine or beer per day—tend to reduce life-threatening conditions like hypertension. If there is some threshold amount of a particular substance required before it becomes harmful, that makes it questionable whether spending vast amounts of money to try to remove that last fraction of one percent from the air or water is going to make the public safer by even a minute amount. It also raises questions about basing categorical policies on laboratory tests which conclude, for example, that saccharin is dangerous to humans because great amounts of it cause cancer in laboratory rats.

The same principle applies in many other contexts, where minute traces of impurities can produce major political and legal battles—and consume millions of tax dollars with little or no net effect on the health or safety of the public. For example, one legal battle raged for a decade over the impurities in a New Hampshire toxic waste site, where these wastes were so diluted that children could have eaten some of the dirt there for 70 days a year without any significant harm—if there had been any children playing there, which there were not. As a result of spending more than nine million dollars, the level of impurities was reduced to the point where children could have safely eaten the dirt there 245 days a year. Moreover, without anything being done at all, both parties to the litigation agreed that more than half the volatile impurities would have evaporated by the year 2000. Yet hypothetical dangers to hypothetical children kept the issue going.

With environmental safety, as with other kinds of safety, some forms of safety in one respect create dangers in other respects. California, for example, required a certain additive to be put into all gasoline sold in that state, in order to reduce the air pollution from automobile exhaust fumes. However, this new additive tended to leak from filling station storage tanks and automobile gas tanks, polluting the ground water in the first case and leading to more automobile fires in the second. Similarly, government-mandated air bags in automobiles, introduced to save lives in car crashes, have themselves killed small children.

These are all matters of incremental trade-offs to find an optimal amount and kind of safety, in a world where being categorically safe is as impossible as achieving 100 percent clean air or clean water. Incremental trade-offs are made all the time in individual market transactions, but it can be politically suicidal to oppose demands for more clean air, clean water or automobile safety. Therefore saying that the government *can* improve over the results of individual transactions in a free market is not the same as saying that it *will* in fact do so. Among the greatest external costs imposed in a society can be those imposed politically by legislators and officials who pay no costs whatever, while imposing billions of dollars in costs on others, in order to respond to political pressures from advocates of particular interests or ideologies.

By the same token, while external costs are not automatically taken into account in the marketplace, this is not to say that there may not be some imaginative ways in which they can be. In Britain, for example, ponds or lakes are often privately owned, and these owners have every incentive to keep them from becoming polluted, since a clean body of water is more attractive to fishermen or boaters who pay for its use. Similarly with shopping malls: Although maintaining clean, attractive malls with benches, rest rooms and security personnel costs money that the mall owners do not collect from the shoppers, a mall with such things attracts more customers, and so the rents charged the individual storeowners can be higher because a location in such malls is more valuable than in a mall without such amenities.

In short, while externalities are a serious consideration in determining the role of government, they do not simply provide a blanket justification or a magic word which automatically allows economics to be ignored and politically attractive goals to be pursued without further ado. Both the incentives of the market and the incentives of politics must be weighed when choosing between them on any particular issue.

Just as we must keep in mind a sharp distinction between the goals of a particular policy and the actual consequences of that policy, so we must keep in mind a sharp distinction between the purpose for which a particular governmental power was created and the purposes for which that power can be used. For example, President Franklin D. Roosevelt took the United States off the gold standard in 1933 under presidential powers created during the First World War to prevent trading with enemy nations. Though that war had been over for more than a dozen years and we no longer had any enemy nations, the power was still there to be used for wholly different purposes.

Powers do not expire when the crises that created them have passed. Nor does the repeal of old laws have a high priority among legislators. Still less are institutions likely to close up on their own when the circumstances that caused them to be created no longer exist. For example, during the depths of the Great Depression of the 1930s, when money was in short supply, the Reconstruction Finance Corporation was created to lend money to American banks and businesses, in order to try to maintain production and employment. Yet the RFC continued in existence for years after the depression was history and the economy was going through a boom, with money in such abundant supply as to create inflation.

When the RFC was finally closed down by Congress in 1953, the blow was softened politically by creating a "temporary" agency called the Small Business Administration to do some of the things that the RFC had been doing, but only for small and presumably struggling enterprises. Just a few years later, however, the SBA was made permanent—and then grew by leaps and bounds in the decades ahead. Despite its rationale of helping small "mom and pop" businesses, SBA's loans seldom went to such businesses and in fact concentrated on businesses of some substantial size—in one extreme case, a business with 30,000 employees and annual sales of nearly a billion dollars. Far from helping small businesses get started, it was helping a failed big business to drag out its death throes for a few more years with the taxpayers' money. Whatever Congress or the voters may have thought when they supported the creation of this agency, once it was in existence it responded to an ever-changing variety of political pressures and opportunities, taking on roles never contemplated when it was created.

Chapter 18

An Overview

The economic principles involved in discussions of the national economy are not overly complicated but two crucial misconceptions need to be guarded against: (1) the fallacy of composition and (2) assessing economic activity as if it were a zero-sum game, in which what is gained by some is lost by others.

There are also sometimes misconceptions of the nature of government, leading to unrealistic demands being made on it and hasty denunciations of the "stupidity" or "irrationality" of government officials when those demands are not met.

ZERO-SUM THINKING

The notion that what is gained by some must be lost by others is seldom explicitly expressed. Rather, it is implicit in much discussion—and even laws and policies—dealing with labor-management relations, landlord-tenant relations, or the relations among classes or ethnic groups. Zero-sum thinking also dominates much discussion of international trade, as will become painfully clear in Chapter 19.

Minimum wage laws, for example, are often advocated by those who see themselves as taking the side of the workers against their employers, when in fact the employers may end up less harmed by such laws than are the workers themselves, whose unemployment can deprive them of both current income and the human capital that work experience could build up for them and enable them to earn higher incomes in the future. Similarly, rent control often ends up harming both tenants and landlords, though in different ways.

Landlords are unlikely to end up living homeless on the streets, though some former tenants may, given that homelessness is particularly prevalent in cities with strong rent control laws.

Individuals who stand in the relationship of employer and employee, or landlord and tenant, would never have entered into such relationships in the first place unless both sides expected to become better off than they would have been if they had not entered into these relationships. In other words, it is not a zero-sum activity. That is why anything which reduces such relationships is likely to be harmful to both parties—a fact often overlooked by those who think in terms of taking sides.

Zero-sum thinking is especially misleading in countries where wealth is growing. Discussions of the relative shares going to different social groups are often illustrated by pie-charts showing who gets how big a slice of the nation's income. But the actual economic well-being of all these groups— their per capita real income—is often far more dependent on how big the whole pie is rather than how one group's slice compares to another group's slice. As noted in Chapter 9, even when the share of national income going to the lowest fifth declined, the per capita real income of people in that quintile rose by thousands of dollars.

Those who are preoccupied with relative shares often show little or no interest in the growth of wealth. That is, they not only fail to pay much attention to the statistics on the growth of national wealth, more fundamentally they show little or no interest in which conditions or which policies would enhance the prospects for such growth and which policies might impede that growth. They tend to view economic policies largely, if not solely, in terms of how these policies will affect the internal distribution of income, rather than its over-all growth.

Internationally, zero-sum thinking has led some nations to keep out foreign investors, for fear that these investors would carry off part of the national wealth. Similar thinking has led to popular resentments of various immigrant minorities who send money back to their families in the countries that they came from, because this has been seen as exporting part of the national wealth to another country. Like much zero-sum thinking, this depends on blindly disregarding the *creation* of wealth. Neither investors nor immigrants simply come into a country and share its pre-existing wealth. They create additional wealth. Part of this additional wealth goes to the population of the country to which they have moved and part goes to themselves and their families, wherever these might be located. But the host country population loses nothing on net balance and typically gains.

If the kind of thinking which would lead people to believe otherwise seems primitive or illogical, that is not to say that it has not prevailed among peoples and rulers in many lands. Some poor nations in Asia, Africa, and Latin America have kept out foreign investments that were desperately needed, for fear of losing wealth that the foreigners would carry away. Accusations of exporting the host country's wealth were made against the overseas Chinese in Southeast Asia for generations, while in fact the Chinese were creating whole industries that never existed before in these countries and adding to their wealth. Zero-sum thinking and a disregard of the creation of wealth have often gone together in countries around the world.

THE FALLACY OF COMPOSITION

Just as the assumption of a zero-sum process may be implicit, rather than explicit, so is the assumption that what is true of a part is true of the whole— that is, the fallacy of composition. The fallacy in the fallacy of composition comes from ignoring the *interactions* which prevent what is true of a part from automatically being true of the whole. Because a national economy involves many complex interactions among millions of individuals, businesses and other organizations, what is true for some of them need not be true for the economy as a whole.

Not only may the fates of particular parts of an economy differ from the fate of the economy as a whole, to some extent it is inevitable that parts of the economy suffer from the progress of the whole. How are the new technologies, the new industries, and the new ways of distributing products to get the resources they need, except by taking capital, labor and other factors of production away from other parts of the economy?

Automobiles, trucks, and tractors displaced horses from their historically large role in transportation and farming in twentieth century America, thereby freeing up all the resources required to feed and maintain vast numbers of horses. Workers were also displaced from agriculture as farming methods became more efficient. One of the key factors in the growth of industrial output during the twentieth century was the ever-growing availability of workers displaced from agriculture. How else could modern industries have gotten all the millions of workers needed to fill their factories, except by taking them from the farms?

Those who lament the passing of the family farm often see no connection between that and the greater outpouring of goods and services from industry and commerce that created a rising standard of living for millions of people. Nothing is easier for the media or for politicians than to present "human interest" stories about someone whose family has been farming for generations and who has now been forced out of the kind of life they knew and loved by the impersonal economic forces of the marketplace. What is forgotten is that these "impersonal" forces represent benefits to consumers who are just as much persons as the producers who have been arbitrarily selected as the focus of the discussion. The temptation is always there to try to "solve" the problem of those whose plight has been singled out for attention, without regard for the repercussions on others elsewhere.

The constant shifting of resources which has contributed to American prosperity was often thwarted for decades in India, which followed policies which made it virtually impossible to fire workers or to shut down certain enterprises. Such government restrictions and controls contributed to India's poverty—by an amount estimated at hundreds of dollars per capita annually. In a poor country, that is a very serious loss.

An observer of the Indian economy said: "I sometimes wonder how we could have gone so wrong when we had such brilliant economists." The short answer is that power trumps knowledge—and for nearly half a century the supreme power in India was in the hands of people committed to a government-controlled economy. Efforts by economists to point out what was wrong with the policies being followed were essentially exercises in futility. Some of India's top economists, including a Nobel Prize winner, simply left the country.

THE ROLE OF GOVERNMENT

Too often there has been a tendency to regard government as a monolithic decision-maker or as the public interest personified. But different elements within the government respond to different outside constituencies and are often in opposition to one another for that reason, as well as because of jurisdictional frictions among themselves. Many things done by government officials in response to the incentives and constraints of the situations in which they find themselves may be described as "irrational" by observers but are often more rational than the assumption that these officials represent the public interest personified. Politicians like to come to the rescue of particular industries, professions, classes, or racial or ethnic groups from whom voting and financial support can be expected—and to represent the benefits to these groups as net benefits to the country. Such tendencies are not confined to any given country but can be found in modern democratic states around the world. As a writer in India put it:

> Politicians lack the courage to privatize the huge, loss-making public sector be-cause they are afraid to lose the vote of organized labor. They resist dismantling subsidies for power, fertilizer, and water because they fear the crucial farm vote. The won't touch food subsidies because of the massive poor vote. They will not remove thousands of inspectors in state governments, who continuously harass private businesses, because they don't want to alienate government servants' vote bank. Meanwhile, these giveaways play havoc with state finances and add to our disgraceful fiscal deficit. Unless the deficit comes under control, the na-tion will not be more competitive, nor will the growth rate rise further to 8 or 9 percent, which is what is needed to create jobs and improve the chances of the majority of our people to actualize their capabilities in a reasonably short time.

While such problems may be particularly acute in India, they are by no means confined to India. In 2003, the Congress of the United States passed a farm subsidy bill—with bipartisan support—that is estimated to cost the average American family more than $4,000 over the next decade in inflated food prices.

The very different incentives facing government enterprises tend to result in very different ways of carrying out their functions, compared to the way things are done in a free market economy. After banks were nationalized in India in 1969, uncollectible debts rose to become 20 percent of all loans out-standing. Efficiency also suffered: An Indian entrepreneur reported that "it takes my wife half an hour to make a deposit or withdraw money from our local branch." Moreover, government ownership and control led to political influence in deciding to whom bank loans were to be made:

> I once chanced to meet the manager of one of the rural branches of a national-ized bank . . . He was a sincere young man, deeply concerned, and he wanted to unburden himself about his day-to-day problems. Neither he nor his staff, he told me, decided who qualified for a loan. The local politicians invariably made this decision. The loan takers were invariably cronies of the political bosses and did not intend to repay the money. He was told that such and such a person was to be treated as a "deserving poor." Without exception, they were rich.

The nationalization of banks in India was not simply a matter of transfer-ring ownership of an enterprise to the government. This transfer changed all the incentives and constraints from those of the marketplace to those of pol-itics and bureaucracy. The proclaimed goals, or even the sincere hopes, of those who created this transfer often meant much less than the changed in-centives and constraints.

In the United States, political control of banks' investment decisions has been less pervasive but has nevertheless changed the directions that invest-ments have taken from what they would be in a free market. The Commu-nity Investment Act, for example, requires banks to put a certain percentage of their investments into communities designated by govern-ment as being especially "needing" investments. Since there is no objective measure of "need," this amounts to directing investments where politicians want it to go.

As an entrepreneur in India put it: "Indians have learned from painful ex-perience that the state does not work on behalf of the people. More often than not, it works on behalf of itself." So do people in other walks of life. The problem is that this fact is not always recognized and people look to govern-ment to right wrongs and fulfill desires to an extent that may not always be possible.

The tragic bungling of economic policy by American presidents of both political parties, as well as by officials of the Federal Reserve System, during the Great Depression of the 1930s has sobering implications for those who regard government as a force to save the economy from the imperfections of the marketplace. Markets are indeed imperfect, as everything human is im-perfect. But "market failure" is not a magic phrase that automatically justifies government intervention, because the government can also fail—or can even make things worse.

Ironically, people are often more clear in their thinking about sports than about policies that have a more serious effect on their lives. When a home run slugger strikes out (as most of them do with some frequency), he is not automatically taken out of the game and a pinch hitter sent in. After all, pinch-hitters can also strike out, and they may not be as likely to hit a home run. Although it was fashionable at one time to represent the Roosevelt ad-ministration as having rescued the United States from the Great Depression of the 1930s, all previous American depressions had come and gone without significant government action—and prosperity had returned much more quickly in earlier times. Presidents Hoover and Roosevelt both tried to use the powers of the federal government to restore the economy—something previous presidents had not done. However good the intentions of these two presidents, economists and other scholars who have studied that era in depth have increasingly concluded that they made matters worse.

Whatever the merits or demerits of government economic policies, in the United States or in other countries around the world, the market alternative is very new as history is measured, and the combination of democracy and a free market still newer and rarer. As an observer in India put it:

> We tend to forget that liberal democracy based on free markets is a relatively new idea in human history. In 1776 there was one liberal democracy—the United States; in 1790 there were 3, including France; in 1848 there were only 5; in 1975 there were still only 31. Today 120 of the world's 200 or so states claims to be democracies, with more than 50 percent of the world's population residing in them (although Freedom House, an American think tank, counts only 86 countries as truly free).

ECONOMIC MEASUREMENT

Because a national economy includes such a huge mixture of ever-changing goods and services, merely measuring the rate of inflation is much more chancy than confident discussions of statistics on the subject might indicate. As already noted, cars and houses have changed dramatically over the years. If the average car today costs X percent more than it used to, does that mean that there has been X percent inflation or that most of that change has represented higher prices paid for higher quality and additional features? No one calls it inflation when someone who has been buying Chevrolets in years past begins to buy Cadillacs and pays more money for them. Why then call it inflation when a Chevrolet begins to have features that were once reserved for Cadillacs and its costs rise to levels once charged for Cadillacs?

Another source of inaccuracy in measuring inflation is in the things that are included and not included in the statistics used to create an index of inflation, such as the Consumer Price Index. Everything cannot be included in an index, both because of the enormous time and money this would require and because "everything" itself changes over time with the creation of new products and the disappearance of old ones. Instead, the prices of a collection of commonly purchased items are followed over the years, measuring how much those particular prices rise or fall.

The problem with this is that what is commonly used depends on prices. Within living memory, television sets were so expensive that only rich people could afford them. So were air-conditioned cars and portable computers. At that time, no one would have dreamed of including such rare luxuries in a price index to measure the cost of living of the average American. Only after their prices fell to a fraction of what they once were did such items become commonplace possessions. What this means is that the price indexes missed all the *falling* prices of such things in the years before they became widely used, while counting all the *rising* prices of other things that were already widely used. In short, these indexes were biased upward in their estimates of inflation.

Because government policies and private contracts were often based on the cost of living, as measured by these indexes, huge sums of money changed hands across the country, as a result of exaggerated estimates of inflation. Social Security recipients, for example, received billions of dollars in cost-of-living increases in their pension checks because of an inflation that was in part a statistical artifact, rather than a real increase in the prices of buying what they had always bought. This was a factor in creating an official panel of distinguished scholars to revise the indexes. But, no matter how distinguished the individuals or how conscientiously they worked, the task they were attempting could never achieve precision, even if it could be made more realistic than it was.

When considering particular markets for particular products, we are dealing with familiar concrete things, whether hamburgers or hotels, busses or barbecues. But when discussing national output as a whole, which consists of innumerable very different things that can only be added up abstractly, there is much more room for confusion by some and manipulation of that confusion by others.

The money supply and the banking system are key features of the national economy. Like so many other things, banking looks easy from the outside—simply take in deposits and lend much of it out, earning interest in the process and sharing some of that interest with the depositors to keep them putting their money into the banks. Yet we do not want to repeat the mistake that Lenin made in grossly under-estimating the complexity of business in general.

At the beginning of the twenty-first century, some post-Communist nations were having great difficult creating a banking system that could operate in a free market. In Albania and in the Czech Republic, for example, banks were able to receive deposits but were stymied by the problem of how to lend out the money to private businesses in a way that would bring returns on their investment. The London magazine *The Economist* reported that "the legal infrastructure is so weak" in Albania that the head of a bank there "is afraid to make any loans." Here we see again the problem of property rights discussed in the previous chapter. Even though another Albanian bank made loans, it found the collateral it acquired from a defaulting borrower was "impossible to sell." An Albanian bank with 83 percent of the country's deposits made no loans at all, but bought government securities instead, earning a low but dependable rate of return. What this means for the country's economy as a whole, *The Economist* reported, is that "capital-hungry enterprises are robbed of a source of finance."

In the post-Communist Czech Republic, lending was more generous—and losses much larger. Here the government stepped in to cover losses and the banks shifted their assets into government securities, as in Albania. As with Britain in earlier centuries, foreigners have been brought in to run financial institutions that the people of the country were having great difficulty running.

Whether such problems will sort themselves out over time—and how much time?—as private enterprises acquire track records and private bankers acquire more experience, while the legal system adapts to a market economy after the long decades of a Communist economic and political regime, is obviously a question for the Czechs and the Albanians. However, their experience again illustrates the fact that one of the best ways of understanding and appreciating an economic function is by seeing what happens when that function does not exist or malfunctions.

Understanding political functions can be as much of a challenge as understanding economic functions. What is especially challenging is deciding which things should be done through the economic system and which things should be done through the political system. While some decisions are clearly political decisions and others are clearly economic decisions, there are large areas where choices can be made through either process. Both the government and the marketplace can supply housing, transportation, education and many other things. For those decisions that can be made either politically or economically, it is necessary not only to decide which particular outcome would be preferred but also which process offers the best prospect of actually reaching that outcome. This in turn requires understanding how each process works in practice under their respective incentives and constraints.

The public can express their desires either through choices made in the voting booth or choices made in the marketplace. However, political choices are offered less often and are binding until the next election. Moreover, the political process offers "package deal" choices, where one candidate's whole spectrum of positions on economic, military, environmental, and other issues must be accepted or rejected as a whole in comparison with another candidate's spectrum of positions on the same issues. The voter may prefer one candidate's position on some of these issues and another candidate's position on other issues, but no such choice is available on election day. By contrast, consumers make their choices in the marketplace every day and can buy one company's milk and another company's cheese, or ship some packages by Federal Express and other packages by United Parcel Service. Then they can change their minds a day or a week later and make wholly different choices.

As a practical matter, virtually no one puts as much time and close attention into deciding whether to vote for one candidate rather than another as is usually put into deciding whether to buy one house rather than another—or perhaps even one car rather than another. Perhaps more important, the public usually buys finished results in the marketplace but can choose only among competing promises in the political arena. In the marketplace, the strawberries or the house that you are considering buying are right before your eyes when you make your decision, while the policies that a candidate promises to follow must be accepted more or less on faith—and the eventual consequences of those policies still more so. Speculation is just one aspect of a market economy but it is of the essence of elections. On the other hand, each voter has the same single vote on election day, whereas consumers have very different amounts of dollars to vote with in the marketplace. However, these dollar differences may even out somewhat over a lifetime, as the same individual moves from one income bracket to another over the years, but the differences are there as of any given time.

The influence of wealth in the marketplace makes many prefer to move decisions into the political arena, on the assumption that this is a more level playing field. However, among the things that wealth buys is more and better education, as well as more leisure time that can be devoted to political activities and the mastering of legal technicalities. All this translates into a disproportionate influence of wealthier people in the political process, while the fact that those who are not rich often have more money in the aggregate than those who are may give ordinary more weight in the market than in the political or legal arena.

PART VI:
THE INTERNATIONAL
ECONOMY

Chapter 19

International Trade

> ... *the same people who can be clearheaded and sensible when the subject is one of domestic trade can be incredibly emotional and muddleheaded when it becomes one of foreign trade.*
>
> —HENRY HAZLITT

When discussing the historic North American Free Trade Agreement of 1993 (NAFTA), the *New York Times* said:

> Abundant evidence is emerging that jobs are shifting across borders too rapidly to declare the United States a job winner or a job loser from the trade agreement.

Posing the issue in these terms committed the central fallacy in many discussions of international trade—assuming that one country must be a "loser" if the other country is a "winner." But international trade is not a zero-sum contest. Both sides must gain or it would make no sense to continue trading. Nor is it necessary for government officials or experts to determine whether both sides are gaining. Most international trade, like most domestic trade, is done by millions of individuals, each of whom can determine whether the item purchased is worth what it cost and is preferable to what is available from others.

As for jobs, before the free-trade agreement was passed, there were dire predictions of "a giant sucking sound" as jobs would be sucked out of the United States to Mexico and other countries with lower wage rates after the free-trade agreement went into effect. In reality, the number of American jobs *increased* after the agreement and the unemployment rate in the United States fell over the next seven years from more than seven percent down to four percent, the lowest level seen in decades. Before NAFTA was passed, Congressman David Bonior of Michigan warned: "If the agreement with Mexico receives congressional approval, Michigan's auto industry will eventually vanish." But what actually happened was that employment in the automobile industry increased by more than 100,000 jobs over the next six years.

Such results clearly surprised many people. But it should not have surprised anyone who understood economics.

Let's go back to square one. What happens when a given country, in isolation, becomes more prosperous? It tends to buy more because it has more to buy with. And what happens when it buys more? There are more jobs created for workers producing the additional goods and services.

Make that two countries and the principle remains the same. There is no *fixed* number of jobs that the two countries must fight over. If they both become more prosperous, they will both tend to create more jobs. The only question is whether international trade tends to make both countries more prosperous.

In the case of the post-NAFTA years, jobs increased by the millions in Mexico—at the same time when jobs were increasing by the millions in the United States.

The basic facts about international trade are not difficult to understand. What is difficult to untangle are all the misconceptions and jargon which so often clutter up the discussion. The great U.S. Supreme Court Justice Oliver Wendell Holmes said, "we need to think things instead of words." Nowhere is that more important than when discussing international trade, where there are so many misleading and emotional words used to describe and confuse things that are not very difficult to understand in themselves.

For example, the terminology used to describe an export surplus as a "favorable" balance of trade and an import surplus as an "unfavorable" balance of trade goes back for centuries. At one time, it was widely believed that an import surplus impoverished a nation because the difference between imports and exports had to be paid in gold, and the loss of gold was seen as a loss of national wealth. However, as early as 1776, Adam Smith's classic *The*

Wealth of Nations argued that the real wealth of a nation consists of its goods and services, not its gold supply. Too many people have yet to grasp this, even in the twenty-first century.

If the goods and services available to the American people are greater as a result of international trade, then Americans are wealthier, not poorer, regardless of whether there is a "deficit" or a "surplus" in the international balance of trade. As for gold, India had the world's largest supply of gold in 2003, but no one considered it the world's richest nation. Indeed, it is one of the poorest.

Incidentally, during the Great Depression of the 1930s, the United States had an export surplus—a "favorable" balance of trade—in every year of that disastrous decade. What may be more relevant is that both imports and exports were sharply lower than they had been during the prosperous decade of the 1920s. This reduction in international trade was a result of rising tariff barriers in countries around the world, as nations attempted to save jobs in their own domestic economies, during a period of widespread unemployment, by keeping out international trade.

Such policies have been regarded by many economists as needlessly worsening and prolonging the worldwide depression. The last thing needed when national income is going down is a policy that makes it go down faster, by denying consumers the benefits of being able to buy what they want at the lowest price available.

Slippery words can make bad news look like good news and vice versa. For example, the much-lamented international trade deficit of the United States narrowed by a record-breaking amount in the spring of 2001, as *BusinessWeek* magazine reported under the headline: "A Shrinking Trade Gap Looks Good Stateside." However, this happened while the stock market was falling, unemployment was rising, corporate profits were down, and the total output of the American economy went down. The supposedly "good" news on international trade was due to reduced imports during shaky economic times. Had the country gone into a deep depression, the international trade balance might have disappeared completely, but fortunately Americans were spared that much "good" news.

Just as the United States had a "favorable" balance of trade every year of the Great Depression of the 1930s, it became a record-breaking "debtor nation" during the booming prosperity of the 1990s. Obviously, such words cannot be taken at face value as indicators of the well-being of a country. We will need to examine what they mean in context in this chapter and the next.

THE BASIS FOR INTERNATIONAL TRADE

While international trade takes place for the same reason that other trades take place—because both sides gain—it is necessary to understand just why both countries gain, especially since there are so many politicians and journalists who muddy the waters with claims to the contrary.

The reasons why countries gain from international trade are usually grouped together by economists under three categories: absolute advantage, comparative advantage, and economies of scale.

Absolute Advantage

It is obvious why Americans buy bananas grown in the Caribbean. Bananas can be grown much more cheaply in the tropics than in places where greenhouses and other artificial means of maintaining warmth would be necessary. In tropical countries, nature provides free the warmth that people have to provide by costly means in cooler climates, such as that of the United States.

Therefore it pays Americans to buy bananas grown in the tropics, rather than grow them at higher costs within the United States.

Sometimes the advantages that one country has over another, or over the rest of the world, are extreme. Growing coffee, for example, requires a peculiar combination of climatic conditions—warm but not too hot, nor with sunlight beating down on the plants directly all day, nor with too much moisture or too little moisture, and in some kinds of soils but not others. Putting together these and other requirements for ideal coffee-growing conditions drastically reduces the number of places that are best suited for producing coffee. It has not been uncommon for more than half the coffee in the entire world to be grown in Brazil—and in just one region of Brazil, at that. This does not mean that other countries cannot grow coffee. It is just that the amount and quality of coffee that most countries could produce would not be worth the resources it would cost, when more and better coffee can be bought from Brazil at a lower cost.

These are examples of what economists call "absolute advantage"—one country, for any of a number of reasons, can produce some things cheaper or better than another. Those reasons may be due to climate, geography, or the mixture of skills in their respective populations. Whatever the reason may be in each particular case, absolute advantage means that one country can simply produce a given product more cheaply or better than another. Foreigners who buy that country's products benefit from the lower costs, while the country itself obviously benefits from the larger market for its products and sometimes from the fact that part of the inputs needed to create the product are free, such as warmth in the tropics or rich nutrients in the soil in various places around the world.

There is another more subtle, but at least equally important, reason for international trade. This is what economists call "comparative advantage."

Comparative Advantage

To illustrate what is meant by comparative advantage, suppose that one country is so efficient that it is capable of producing *anything* more cheaply than a neighboring country. Is there any benefit that the more efficient country can gain from trading with its neighbor?

Yes.

Why? Because being able to produce *anything* more cheaply is not the same as being able to produce *everything* more cheaply. When there are scarce resources which have alternative uses, producing more of one product means producing less of some other product. The question is not simply how much it costs, in either money or resources, to produce chairs or television sets in one country, but how many chairs it costs to produce a television set, when resources are shifted from producing one product to producing the other. If that trade-off is different between two countries, then the country that can get more television sets by foregoing the production of chairs can benefit from trading with the country that gets more chairs by not producing television sets. A numerical example can illustrate this point.

Even if the United States could produce anything more efficiently than Canada, it could still benefit by not producing some things and importing them from Canada instead. For example, assume that an average American worker produces 500 chairs a month, while an average Canadian worker produces 450, and that an American worker can produce 200 television sets a month while a Canadian worker produces 100. The tables below illustrate what the output would be under these conditions if both countries produced both products versus each country producing only one of these products. In both tables we assume the same respective outputs per worker and the same total number of workers—500—devoted to producing these products in each country:

PRODUCTS	AMERICAN WORKERS	AMERICAN OUTPUT	CANADIAN WORKERS	CANADIAN OUTPUT
chairs	200	100,000	200	90,000
television sets	300	60,000	300	30,000

With both countries producing both products, under the conditions specified, their combined output would come to a grand total of 190,000 chairs and
90,000 television sets per month from a grand total of a thousand workers.

What if the two countries specialize, with the United States putting all its
chair-producing workers into the production of television sets instead, and
Canada doing the reverse? Then *with the very same output per worker* as before in each country, they can now produce a larger grand total of the two
products from the same thousand workers:

PRODUCTS	AMERICAN WORKERS	AMERICAN OUTPUT	CANADIAN WORKERS	CANADIAN OUTPUT
chairs	0	0	500	225,000
television sets	500	100,000	0	0

Without any change in the productivity of workers in either country, the
total output is now greater from the same number of workers, that output
now being 100,000 television sets instead of 90,000 and 225,000 chairs instead of 190,000. That is because each country now produces where it has a
comparative advantage, whether or not it has an absolute advantage. Economists would say that the United States has an "absolute advantage" in producing both products but that Canada has a "comparative advantage" in
producing chairs. That is, Canada loses fewer television sets by shifting re-

sources to the production of chairs than the United States would lose by such a shift. Under these conditions, Americans can get more chairs by producing television sets and trading them with Canadians for chairs, instead of by producing their own chairs directly at the expense of labor and other resources that could have gone into producing something where their advantage was greater. Conversely, Canadians can get more television sets by producing chairs and trading them for American-made television sets.

Only if the United States produced everything more efficiently than Canada *by the same percentage for each product* would there be no gain from trade because there would then be no comparative advantage. This is virtually impossible to find in the real world. Similar principles apply on a personal level in everyday life. Imagine, for example, that you are an eye surgeon and that you paid your way through college by washing cars. Now that you have a car of your own, should you wash it yourself or should you hire someone else to wash it—even if your previous experience allows you to do the job in less time than the person you hire? Obviously, it makes no sense to you financially, or to society in terms of over-all well-being, for you to be spending your time sudsing down an automobile instead of being in an operating room saving someone's eyesight. In other words, even though you have an "absolute advantage" in both activities, your comparative advantage in treating eye diseases is far greater.

The key to understanding both individual examples and examples from international trade is the basic economic reality of scarcity. The surgeon has only 24 hours in the day, like everyone else. Time that he is spending doing one thing is time taken away from doing something else. The same is true of countries, which do not have an unlimited amount of labor, time, or other resources, and so must do one thing at the cost of not doing something else. That is the very meaning of economic costs—*foregone alternatives*, which apply whether the particular economy is capitalist, socialist, feudal, or whatever—and whether the transactions are domestic or international.

Even if Silicon Valley companies are capable of producing computers or software more cheaply than companies in Taiwan, the same engineers and technicians cannot be doing both things at the same time. If Silicon Valley companies exceed their Taiwanese counterparts in efficiency more in the production of software than of computers, then it pays for the software to be produced in the United States and the hardware to be produced in Taiwan.

Both countries can have more of both things by specializing and trading with one another.

Comparative advantage is not just a theory but a very important fact in the history of many nations. It has been more than a century since Great Britain produced enough food to feed its people. Britons have been able to get enough to eat only because the country has concentrated its efforts on producing those things in which it has had a comparative advantage, such as manufacturing, shipping, and financial services—and using the proceeds to buy food from other countries. British consumers ended up better fed and with more manufactured goods than if the country grew enough of its own food to feed itself. Since the real cost of anything that is produced are the other things that could have been produced with the same efforts, it would cost the British too much industry and commerce to transfer enough resources into agriculture to become self-sufficient in food. They are better off getting food from some other country whose comparative advantage is in agriculture, *even if that other country's farmers are not as efficient as British farmers.*

Such a trade-off is not limited to industrialized nations. When cocoa began to be grown on farms in West Africa, which ultimately produced over half of the world's supply, African farmers there reduced the amount of food they grew, in order to earn more money by planting cocoa trees on their lands, instead of food crops. As a result, their earnings enabled them to live off food produced elsewhere. This food included not only meat and vegetables grown in the region, but also imported rice and canned fish and fruit, the latter items being considered to be luxuries at the time.

Economies of Scale

While absolute advantage and comparative advantage are the key reasons for benefits from international trade, they are not the only reasons. Sometimes a particular product requires such huge investment in machinery and in developing a specialized labor force that the resulting output can be sold at a low enough price to be competitive only when some enormous amount of output is produced, because of economies of scale, as discussed in Chapter 6.

It has been estimated that the minimum output of automobiles needed to achieve an efficient cost per car is somewhere between 200,000 to 400,000 automobiles per year. Producing in such huge quantities is not a serious problem in a country of the size and wealth of the United States, where General Motors produced more than half a million Chevrolets in 2000. But, in a country with a much smaller population—Australia, for example—there is no way to sell enough cars within the country to be able to develop and produce automobiles from scratch to sell at prices low enough to compete with automobiles produced in much larger quantities in the United States or Japan. The largest number of cars of any given make sold in Australia is only about half of the quantity needed to reap all the cost benefits of economies of scale. While the number of automobiles owned per capita is very similar in Australia and in the United States, there are more than a dozen times as many Americans as there are Australians.

Even those cars which have been manufactured in Australia have been developed in other countries—Toyotas and Mitsubishis from Japan and Ford and General Motors cars from the United States. They are essentially Australian-built Japanese or American cars, which means that companies in Japan and the United States have already paid the huge engineering and other costs of developing these vehicles. But the Australian market is not large enough to achieve sufficient economies of scale to produce Australian automobiles from scratch at a cost that would enable them to compete in the market with imported cars. Although Australia is a modern prosperous country, with output per person similar to that of Great Britain and higher than that in Canada, its small population limits its total purchasing power to less than one-seventh that of Japan and one-twentieth of that of the United States.

Exports enable some countries to achieve economies of scale that would not be possible from domestic sales alone. Some business enterprises make most of their sales outside their respective countries' borders. For example, the Dutch retailer Royal Ahold is the world's largest food distributor and has more than two-thirds of its sales outside of the Netherlands, with two-thirds of its profit coming from the United States, although it also owns hundreds of stores in Argentina, Brazil, and other countries as well. The Swedish retailer Hennes & Mauritz has more than four-fifths of its sales outside of Sweden. Heineken likewise does not have to depend on the small Holland market for its beer sales, since it sells beer in 170 other countries. Toyota, Honda, and Nissan all earn most of their profits in North America. Small countries like South Korea and Taiwan depend on international trade to be able to produce many products on a scale far exceeding what can be sold domestically.

In short, international trade is necessary for many countries to achieve economies of scale that will enable them to sell at prices that can compete with the prices of similar products in the world market. For some products requiring huge investments in machinery and research, only a very few large and prosperous countries could reach the levels of output needed to repay all these costs from domestic sales alone. International trade creates greater efficiency by allowing more economies of scale around the world, even in countries whose domestic markets are not large enough to absorb all the output of mass production industries, as well as by taking advantage of each country's absolute or comparative advantages.

As in other cases, we can sometimes understand the benefits of a particular way of doing things by seeing what happens when they are done differently. For many years, India encouraged small businesses and maintained barriers against imports that could compete with them. However, the lifting of import restrictions at the end of the twentieth century and the beginning of the twenty-first century changed all that. As the *Far Eastern Economic Review* put it:

> The nightmare of the Indian toy industry comes in the form of a pint-sized plastic doll. It's made in China, sings a popular Hindi film song, and costs about 100 rupees ($2). Indian parents have snapped it up at markets across the country, leaving local toy companies petrified. Matching the speed, scale and technology involved in the doll's production—resulting in its rock-bottom price—is beyond their abilities. . . . In areas such as toys and shoes, China has developed huge economies of scale while India has kept its producers artificially small.

The economic problems of toy manufacturers in India under free trade are overshadowed by the far more serious problems created by previous import restrictions which forced hundreds of millions of people in a very poor country to pay needlessly inflated prices for a wide range of products because of policies protecting small-scale producers from the competition of larger producers at home and abroad. Fortunately, decades of such policies were finally ended in India in the last decade of the twentieth century.

INTERNATIONAL TRADE RESTRICTIONS

While there are many advantages to international trade for the world as a whole and for countries individually, like all forms of greater economic efficiency, at home or abroad, it displaces less efficient ways of doing things. Just as the advent of the automobile inflicted severe losses on the horse-and-buggy industry and the spread of giant supermarket chains drove many small neighborhood grocery stores out of business, so imports of things in which other countries have a comparative advantage create losses of revenue and jobs in the corresponding domestic industry. Despite offsetting economic gains that typically far outweigh the losses, politically it is almost inevitable that there will be loud calls for government protection from foreign competition through various restrictions against imports. Many of the most long-lived fallacies in economics have grown out of attempts to justify these international trade restrictions. Although Adam Smith refuted most of these fallacies more than two centuries ago, as far as economists are concerned, such fallacies remain politically alive and potent today.

Some people argue, for example, that wealthy countries cannot compete with countries whose wages are much lower. Poorer countries, on the other hand, may say that they must protect their "infant industries" from competition with more developed industrial nations until the local industries acquire the experience and know-how to compete on even terms. In all countries, there are complaints that other nations are not being "fair" in their laws regarding imports and exports. A frequently heard complaint of unfairness, for example, is that some countries "dump" their goods on the international market at artificially low prices, losing money in the short run in order to gain a larger market share that they will later exploit by raising prices after they achieve a monopolistic position.

In the complexities of real life, seldom is any argument right 100 percent of the time or wrong 100 percent of the time. When it comes to arguments for international trade restrictions, however, most of the arguments are fallacious most of the time. Let us examine them one at a time, beginning with the high-wage fallacy.

The High-Wage Fallacy

In a prosperous country such as the United States, a fallacy that sounds very plausible is that American goods cannot compete with goods produced by low-wage workers in poorer countries, some of whom are paid a fraction of what American workers receive. But, plausible as this may sound, both history and economics refute it. Historically, high-wage countries have been exporting to low-wage countries for centuries. The Dutch Republic was a leader in international trade for nearly a century and a half—from the 1590s to the 1740s—while having some of the highest-paid workers in the world. Britain was the world's greatest exporter in the nineteenth century and its wage rates were much higher than the wage rates in many, if not most, of the countries to which it sold its goods. Conversely, India has had far lower wage rates than those in more industrialized countries like Japan and the United States, but India restricted imports of automobiles and other products made in Japan and the United States because India's domestic producers could not compete in price or quality with such products. After an easing of restrictions on international trade, even the leading Indian industrial firm, Tata, has had to be concerned about imports from China, despite the higher wages of Chinese workers:

> . . . the Tata group set up a special office to educate the different parts of its sprawling business empire on the possible fallout from the removal of import restrictions. Jiban Mukhopadhyay, economic adviser to the group's chairman, heads the operation. In his desk drawer he keeps a silk tie bought on a trip to China. Managers who attend the company's WTO [World Trade Organization] workshop are asked to guess its price. "It's only 85 rupees," he points out. "A similar tie made in India would cost 400 rupees."

Economically, the key flaw in the high-wage argument is that it confuses wage rates with labor costs—and labor costs with total costs. Wage rates are measured per hour of work. Labor costs are measured per unit of output. Total costs include not only the cost of labor but also the cost of capital, raw materials, transportation, and other things needed to produce output and bring the finished product to market.

When workers in a prosperous country receive wages twice as high as workers in a poorer country and produce three times the output per hour, then it is the high-wage country which has the lower labor costs per unit of output. That is, it is cheaper to get a given amount of work done in the more prosperous country simply because it takes less labor, even though individual workers are paid more for their time. The higher-paid workers may be more efficiently organized and managed, or have far more or better machinery to work with, or work in companies or industries with greater economies of scale. Often transportation costs are lower in the more developed country, so that total costs of delivering the product to market are less.

There are, after all, reasons why one country is more prosperous than another in the first place—and often that reason is that they are more efficient at producing and delivering output, for any of a number of reasons. In short, higher wage rates per unit of time are not the same as higher costs per unit of output. It may not even mean higher labor costs per unit of output—and of course labor costs are not the only costs.

An international consulting firm determined that the average labor productivity in the modern sectors in India is 15 percent of labor productivity in the United States. In other words, if you hired an average Indian worker and paid him one-fifth of what you paid an average American worker, it would cost you *more* to get a given amount of work done in India than in the United States. Paying 20 percent of what an American worker makes to someone who produces only 15 percent of what an American worker produces would increase your labor costs.

Labor costs are only part of the story. The cost of capital and management are a considerable part of the cost of many products. In some cases, capital costs exceed labor costs, especially in industries with high fixed costs, such as electric utilities and telephone companies, both of which have huge investments in transmission lines that carry their services into millions of homes. A prosperous country usually has a greater abundance of capital and, because of supply and demand, capital tends to be cheaper there than in poorer countries where capital is more scarce and earns a correspondingly higher rate of return.

The history of the beginning of the industrialization of Russia under the czars illustrates how the supply of capital affects the cost of capital. When Russia began a large-scale industrialization program in the 1890s, foreign investors could earn a return of 17.5 percent per year on their investments—until so many invested in Russia that the rate of return fell below 5 percent by 1900. Poorer countries with high capital costs would have difficulty competing with richer countries with lower capital costs, even if they had a real advantage in labor costs, which they often do not.

Against this background, it may be easier to understand why dire predictions of a "giant sucking sound" as American jobs would drawn to Mexico in the wake of the North American Free Trade Agreement of 1993 turned out to be completely wrong. Given the economic realities, it is by no means surprising that the number of American jobs increased and the unemployment rate in the United States fell to record lows, while the number of jobs in Mexico also increased by millions. Both countries gained for the same reasons that countries have gained from international trade for centuries—absolute advantage, comparative advantage, and economies of scale.

At any given time, it is undoubtedly true that some industries will be adversely affected by competing imported products, just as they are adversely affected by every other source of cheaper or better products. These other sources of greater efficiency are at work all the time, forcing industries to modernize, downsize or go out of business. Yet, when this happens because of foreigners, it can be depicted politically as a case of our country versus theirs, when in fact it is the old story of domestic special interests versus consumers.

During periods of high unemployment, politicians are especially likely to be under great pressure to come to the rescue of particular industries that are losing money and jobs, by restricting imports that compete with them. One of the most tragic examples of such restrictions occurred during the world-wide depression of the 1930s, when tariff barriers and other restrictions went up around the world. The net result was that world exports in 1933 were only one-third of what they had been in 1929. Just as free trade provides economic benefits to all countries simultaneously, so trade restrictions reduce the efficiency of all countries simultaneously, lowering standards of living, without producing the increased employment that was hoped for.

In 1933, twenty distinguished American economists made a public appeal for reductions in tariffs, but without any effect on the existing or subsequent U.S. administrations. To politicians, 20 votes do not amount to much in a country the size of the United States. At any given time, a protective tariff or other import restriction may provide immediate relief to a particular industry and thus gain the political and financial support of corporations and labor unions in that industry. But, like many political benefits, it comes at the expense of others who may not be as organized, as visible, or as vocal. Economists have long blamed international trade restrictions around the world for needlessly prolonging the worldwide depression of the 1930s. But not only do economist have relatively few votes, many voters know little about economics. Many disastrous policies in many places and times have resulted from these two facts.

"Infant Industries"

One of the arguments for international trade restrictions that economists have long recognized as valid, in theory at least, is that of protecting "infant industries" *temporarily* until they can develop the skill and experience necessary to compete with long-established foreign competitors. Once this point is reached, the protection (whether tariffs, import quotas, or whatever) can be taken away and the industry allowed to stand or fall in the competition of the marketplace. In practice, however, a new industry in its infancy seldom has enough political muscle—employees' votes, employers' campaign contributions, local governments dependent on their taxes—to get protection from foreign competition. On the other hand, an old, inefficient industry that has seen better days may well have some political muscle left and obtain enough protectionist legislation or subsidies from the government to preserve itself from extinction at the expense of the consumers, the taxpayers, or both.

National Defense

Even the greatest advocates of free trade are unlikely to want to depend on imports of military equipment and supplies from nations that could turn out at some future time to be enemy nations. Therefore domestic supplies of munitions and weapons of war have been supported in one way or another, in order to assure that those suppliers will be available in the event that they are needed to provide whatever is required for national defense.

One of the rare cases in history where a people did depend on potential enemies for military supplies occurred in colonial America, where the indigenous American Indians obtained guns and ammunition from the European settlers. When warfare broke out between them, the Indians could win most of the battles and yet lose the war when they began to run out of bullets, which were available only from the white settlers. Since guns and bullets were products of European civilization, the Indians had no choice but to rely on that source. But countries that do have a choice almost invariably prefer having their own domestic suppliers of the things that are essential to their own national survival. Unfortunately, the term "essential to national defense" can be—and has been—stretched to include products only tangentially related to military necessity. Such products can acquire protection from international competition under a national defense label for purely self-serving reasons. In short, while the argument for international trade restrictions for the sake of national defense can be valid, whether it is or is not valid for a particular industry in a particular country at a particular time depends on the actual circumstances of that industry, that country, and that time.

"Dumping"

A common argument for government protection against a competitor in other countries is that the latter is not competing "fairly" but is instead "dumping" its products on the market at prices below their costs of production. The argument is that this is being done to drive the domestic producers out of business, letting the foreign producer take over the market, after which prices will be raised to monopolistic levels. In response to this argument, governments have passed "anti-dumping" laws, which ban, restrict, or heavily tax the products of foreign companies declared to be guilty of this practice.

Everything in this argument depends on whether or not the foreign producer is in fact selling goods below their costs of production. As already noted in Chapters 6 and 7, determining production cost is not easy in practice, even for a firm operating within the same country as the government agencies that are trying to determine its costs. For government officials in Europe to try to determine the production costs of a company located in Southeast Asia is even more problematical, especially when they are simultaneously investigating many dumping charges involving many other companies scattered around the world. All that is easy is for domestic producers to bring such charges when imports are taking away some of their customers.

Given the virtual impossibility of determining whether imported goods are in fact being sold below their costs of production, thousands of miles away and in very different economic conditions, officials in charge of administering anti-dumping laws may rely on whether an imported good is being sold for less abroad than it sells for in its country of origin, or they may simply hazard a guess as to whether it is being sold below cost. Since this whole procedure is being carried out in response to complaints from domestic producers, the path of least resistance politically is to declare that dumping has occurred.

But here, as elsewhere, the seemingly simple concept of "cost" becomes much more complex in practice. Since there are economies of scale, the Thai producer's costs when selling huge numbers of mountain bikes in Europe were unlikely to be as high as the costs of other producers selling much smaller numbers of mountain bikes within Thailand, where there was far less demand for such a luxury item from a poorer and smaller population. Indeed, this Thai producer's own costs of selling small numbers of mountain bikes in Thailand were likely to be higher per bike than the costs of selling vast numbers of them in large orders to Europe. To sell bikes in Europe for less than bicycle producers charged in Thailand did not necessarily mean selling below the cost of producing bikes for the huge European market.

This situation was not unique. The European Union has applied anti-dumping laws against bed linen from Egypt, antibiotics from India, footwear from China, microwave ovens from Malaysia, and monosodium glutamate from Brazil, among other products from other places. Nor is the European Union unique. The United States has applied anti-dumping laws to steel from Japan, aluminum from Russia, and golf carts from Poland, among other products. Without any serious basis for determining the costs of producing these thing, U.S. government agencies rely on "the best information available"—which is often supplied by those American businesses that are trying to keep out competing foreign products.

Whatever the theory behind anti-dumping laws, in practice they are part of the arsenal of protectionism for domestic producers, at the expense of domestic consumers. Moreover, even the theory is not without its problems. Dumping theory is an international version of the theory of "predatory pricing," whose problems are discussed in Chapter 23. Predatory pricing is a charge that is easy to make and hard to either prove or disprove, whether domestically or internationally. Where the political bias is toward accepting the charge, it does not have to be proven.

Kinds of Restrictions

Tariffs are taxes on imports which serve to raise the prices of those imports and thus enable domestic producers to charge higher prices for competing products than they could in the face of cheaper foreign competition. Import quotas likewise restrict foreign companies from competing on even terms with domestic producers. Although tariffs and quotas may have the same economic end results, these effects are not equally obvious to the public. Thus, while a $10 tariff on imported widgets may enable the domestic producers of widgets to charge $10 more than they could otherwise, without losing business to foreign producers, a suitable quota limitation on imported widgets can also drive up the price of widgets by $10 through its effect on supply and demand. In the latter case, however, it is by no means as easy for the voting public to see and quantify the effects. What that can mean politically is that a quota restriction which raises the price of widgets by $15 may be as easy for elected officials to pass as a tariff of $10.

Sometimes this approach is buttressed by claims that this or that foreign country is being "unfair" in its restrictions on imports from the United States. But the sad fact is that virtually all countries impose "unfair" restrictions on imports, usually in response to internal special interests. However, here as elsewhere, choices can only be made among alternatives actually available. Other countries' restrictions deprive both them and us of some of the benefits of international trade. If we do the same in response, it will deprive both of us of still more benefits. If we let them "get away with it," this will minimize the losses on both sides.

Even more effective disguises for international trade restrictions are health and safety rules applied to imports—rules which often go far beyond what is necessary for either health or safety. Mere red tape requirements can also grow to the point where the time needed to comply adds enough costs to be prohibitive, especially for perishable imports. If it takes a week to get your strawberries through customs, you may as well not ship them. All these measures, which have been engaged in by many countries around the world, share with import quotas the political advantage that it is hard to quantify precisely their effect on consumer prices, however large that effect may be.

CHANGING CONDITIONS

Over time, comparative advantages change, causing international production centers to shift from country to country. For example, when the computer was a new and exotic product, much of its early development and production took place in the United States. But, after the technological work was done that turned computers into a widely used product that many people knew how to produce, the United States retained its comparative advantage in the development of computer software design, but the machines themselves could now easily be assembled in poorer countries overseas—and were. Even computers sold within the United States under American brand names were often manufactured in Asia.

The computer software industry in the United States could not have expanded so much and so successfully if most American computer engineers and technicians were tied down with the production of machines that could have been just as easily be produced in some other country. Since the same American labor cannot be in two places at one time, it can move to where its comparative advantage is greatest only if the country "loses jobs" where it has no comparative advantage. That is why the United States could have unprecedented levels of prosperity and rapidly growing employment at the very times when media headlines were regularly announcing lay-offs by the tens of thousands in some industries and by the hundreds of thousands in others.

Desperate attempts to salvage their wrong predictions have led some to assert that the new jobs were only low-wage jobs "flipping hamburgers" and the like. But assertions are not facts. If Americans in general were losing higher-paid jobs and being forced to take lower-paid jobs, how then could the American standard of living have continued to rise, as data in chapter 9 showed? In reality, when the shifting of low-skill jobs to other countries enables an American company to become more profitable, it can then afford to hire Americans for higher-skill jobs. It is not a zero-sum game when there is more total wealth available after the shift.

While it is undoubtedly true that some particular individuals, or even many employees of some particular firms or industries, may have lost ground during the transition, we cannot commit "the fallacy of composition" and assume that what is true for some is true in general. The rise in the general level of real income in the United States means that the gains have clearly outstripped the losses. But, where those who lose jobs are organized, their complaints carry more political weight.

When the number of jobs in the American steel industry was cut from 340,000 to 125,000 during the decade of the 1980s, that had a devastating impact and was big economic and political news. It also led to a variety of laws and regulations designed to reduce the amount of steel imported into the country to compete with domestically produced steel. Of course, this reduction in supply led to higher steel prices within the United States and therefore higher costs for all other American industries that were producing objects made of steel, ranging from automobiles to oil rigs. With American manufacturers paying more than a hundred dollars more per ton of steel, and having to recover such increased costs from increased prices charged the consumers, all these products were at a disadvantage in competing with similar foreign-made products, both within the United States and in international markets.

It has been estimated that the gain in domestic American steel production due to import restrictions led to a net loss in the production of domestic American steel products as a whole. In other words, American industry as a whole was worse off, on net balance, as a result of the import restrictions on steel.

Nor were workers any better off after import restrictions were imposed in order to "save jobs." When new restrictions were placed on steel imports in 2002, the *Wall Street Journal* estimated that "Illinois would lose five jobs for every one protected, Ohio three for every one and Pennsylvania and Indiana, two for every one." In short, states in which the production of steel and steel products is concentrated stood to lose jobs, on net balance, as a result of policies designed to save jobs by putting restrictions on the importation of foreign steel. A later study confirmed a net loss of American jobs from steel tariffs.

While such steel import restrictions made no sense economically, they made sense politically to those in Washington responsible for creating these restrictions. From a political standpoint, what matters is not what works out best for the country over all. What matters is how vocal and how much political muscle one sector has relative to another. Such economically short-sighted and nationally counterproductive policies are by no means confined to the steel industry or to the United States.

Regardless of the particular industry or the particular country, if a million new and well-paying jobs are created in companies scattered all across the country as a result of international free trade, that carries less weight politically than if half a million jobs are lost in one industry where labor unions and employer associations are able to raise a clamor. When the million new jobs represent a few dozen jobs here and there in innumerable businesses scattered across the nation, there is not enough concentration of economic interest and political clout in any one place to make it worthwhile to mount a comparable counter-campaign. Therefore laws are often passed restricting international trade for the benefit of some concentrated and vocal con-stituency, even though these restrictions may cause far more losses of jobs nationwide.

Chapter 20

International
Transfers of Wealth

Transfers of wealth among nations take many forms. Individuals and businesses in one country may simply invest directly in the business enterprises of another country. Alternatively, they may put their money in another country's banks, which will in turn makes loans to individuals and enterprises, so that this is indirect foreign investment. Yet another option is to buy the bonds issued by a foreign government.

In addition to investments of various kinds, there are remittances from people living in foreign countries back to family members in their countries of origin. In 2001, for example, more than $9 billion in remittances were sent back to Mexico from the United States and more than $23 billion was sent back to Latin America and the Caribbean as a whole. Nor is this a new phenomenon. Back in the nineteenth and early twentieth centuries, remittance from Chinese immigrants in the United States made the localities from which they had come in China visibly more prosperous than other regions. Similarly, remittances from Japanese Americans during that same era helped build up Hiroshima to the point where it became a major industrial center—and therefore a military target for the first atomic bomb.

In centuries past, imperial powers simply transferred vast amounts of wealth from the nations they conquered. Alexander the Great looted the treasures of the conquered Persians. Spain took gold and silver by the ton from the conquered indigenous peoples of the Western Hemisphere and forced some of these indigenous peoples into mines to dig up more. Julius Caesar was one of many Roman conquerors to march in triumph through the eternal city, displaying the riches and slaves he was bringing back from his victories abroad. In more recent times, both prosperous nations and international agencies have transferred part of their wealth to poorer countries under the general heading of "foreign aid."

None of this is very complicated—so long as we remember Justice Oliver Wendell Holmes' admonition to "think things instead of words." When it comes to international trade and international transfers of wealth, the things are relatively straightforward, but the words are often slippery and misleading.

INTERNATIONAL INVESTMENTS

Theoretically, investments might be expected to flow from where capital is abundant to where it is in short supply, much like water seeking its own level. In a perfect world, wealthy nations would invest much of their capital in poorer nations, where capital is more scarce and would therefore offer a higher rate of return. However, in the highly imperfect world that we live in, that is by no means what usually happens. For example, out of a worldwide total of $9 trillion in international bank loans and deposits in 2001, only about $700 billion went to poor countries—*less than one percent*. Out of $12 trillion in international investment securities, only about $600 billion went to poor countries, an even smaller fraction of one percent. In short, rich countries tend to invest in other rich countries.

There are reasons for this, just as there are reasons why some countries are rich and others poor in the first place. The biggest deterrent to investing in any country is the danger that you will never get your money back. Investors are wary of unstable governments, whose changes of personnel or policies create risks that the conditions under which the investment was made can change—the most drastic change being confiscation or "nationalization." Widespread corruption is another deterrent to investment, as it is to economic activity in general. Countries high up on the international index of corruption, such as Nigeria or Russia, are unlikely to attract international investments on a scale that their natural resources or other economic potential might justify. Conversely, the top countries in terms of having low levels of corruption are all prosperous countries, mostly European or European-offshoot nations plus Japan and Singapore. As noted in Chapter 17, the level of honesty has serious economic implications.

Even aside from confiscation and corruption, many poorer countries "do not let capital come and go freely," according to *The Economist*. Where capital cannot get out easily, it is less likely to go in, in the first place. It is not these countries' poverty, as such, that deters investments. When Hong Kong was a British colony, it began very poor and yet grew to become an industrial powerhouse, at one time having more international trade than a vast country like India. Massive inflows of capital helped develop Hong Kong, which operated under the security of British laws, had low tax rates, and allowed some of the freest flows of capital and trade anywhere in the world.

Simple and straightforward as the basic principles of international transfers of wealth may be, words and accounting rules can make them seem more complicated. If Americans buy more Japanese goods than the Japanese buy American goods, then Japan gets American dollars to cover the difference. Since the Japanese are not just going to collect these dollars as souvenirs, they usually turn around and invest them in the American economy. In most cases, the money never leaves the United States. The Japanese simply buy investment goods—Rockefeller Center, for example—rather than consumer goods. American dollars are worthless to the Japanese if they do not spend them on something. In gross terms, international trade has to balance. But it so happens that the conventions of international accounting count imports and exports in the "balance of trade," but not things which don't move at all, like Rockefeller Center. However, accounting conventions and economic realities can be very different things.

In some years, the best-selling car in America has been a Honda or a Toyota, but no automobile made in Detroit has ever been the best-selling car in Japan. The net result is that Japanese automakers receive many millions of dollars in American money and Japan usually has a net surplus in its trade with the United States. But what do the makers of Hondas and Toyotas do with all that American money? One of the things they do is build factories in the United States, employing thousands of American workers to manufacture their cars closer to their customers, so that Honda and Toyota do not have to pay the cost of shipping cars across the Pacific Ocean. Their American employees have been paid sufficiently high wages that they have repeatedly voted against joining labor unions in secret ballot elections. On July 29, 2002, the ten millionth Toyota was built in the United States. Looking at *things*, rather than words, there is little here to be alarmed about. What alarms people are the words and the accounting rules which produce numbers to fit those words.

A country's total output consists of both goods and services—houses and haircuts, sausages and surgery—but the international trade balance consists only of physical goods that move. The American economy produces more services than goods, so it is not surprising that the United States imports more goods than it exports—and exports more services than it imports. American know-how and American technology are used by other countries around the world and these countries of course pay the U.S. for these services. For example, most of the personal computers in the world run on operating systems created by the Microsoft Corporation. But foreign payments to Microsoft and other American companies for their services are not counted in the international balance of trade, since trade includes only goods.

This is just an accounting convention. Yet the American "balance of trade" is reported in the media as if this partial picture were the whole picture and the emotionally explosive word "deficit" sets off alarms. Yet there is often a substantial surplus earned by the United States from its services, which are omitted from the trade balance. In the year 2000, for example, the United States earned $38 billion from royalty and license fees alone, and more than $278 billion from all the services it supplied to other countries. That is more than double the Gross Domestic Product of Norway.

When you count all the money and resources moving in and out of a country for all sorts of reasons, then you are talking about the international "balance of payments"—regardless of whether the payments were made for goods or services. While this is not as misleading as the balance of trade, it is still far from being the whole story, and it has no necessary connection with the health of the economy. Ironically, one of the rare balance of payments surpluses for the United States in the late twentieth century was followed by the 1992 recession. Nigeria has had years of international trade surpluses and is one of the poorest countries in the world. This is not to say that countries with trade surpluses or payments surpluses are at an economic disadvantage. It is just that these numbers, by themselves, do not necessarily indicate either the prosperity or the poverty of any economy.

According to the accounting rules, when people in other countries invest in the United States, that makes the U.S. a "debtor" to those people, because Americans owe them the money that they sent to U.S., since it was not sent as a gift. When people in many countries around the world feel more secure in putting their money in American banks or investing in American corporations, rather than relying on their own banks and corporations, then vast sums of money from overseas find their way to the United States. Foreigners invested $12 billion in American businesses in 1980 and this rose over the years until they were investing more than $200 billion annually by 1998. Looked at in terms of *things*, there is nothing wrong with this. It created more jobs for American workers and created more goods for American consumers, as well as providing income to foreign investors. Looked at in terms of *words*, however, this was a growing debt to foreigners.

The more prosperous and secure the American economy is, the more foreigners are likely to want to send their money to the United States and the higher the annual American balance of payments "deficits" and accumulated international "debt" rises. Hence it is not at all surprising that the long prosperity of the U.S. economy in the 1990s was accompanied by record levels of international deficits and debts. The United States was where the action was and this was where many foreigners wanted their money to be, in order to get in on the action. By the end of 2001, the United States was approximately $1.3 trillion in debt to foreigners, including international institutions. While this was largely a result of American prosperity, this is not to say that things cannot be different for other prosperous countries with different circumstances.

Some other prosperous countries invest more abroad than foreign countries invest in them. Switzerland, for example, had a net investment of $300 billion in other countries—which was larger than the Swiss Gross Domestic Product. None of this means that there is something wrong with Switzerland's being a creditor nation. Everything depends on the particular circumstances, opportunities, and constraints facing each country. Vast sums of money come into Switzerland as a major international financial center and, if they cannot find enough good investments within their own small country, it makes perfect sense for them to invest much of this money in other countries. The point here is that neither deficits nor surpluses are inevitable consequences of either prosperity or poverty and neither word, by itself, tells much about the condition of a country's economy.

The word "debt" covers very different kinds of transactions, some of which may in fact present problems and some of which do not. Every time you deposit a hundred dollars in a bank, that bank goes a hundred dollars deeper into debt, because it is still your money and they owe it to you. Some people might become alarmed if they were told that the bank in which they keep their life's savings was going deeper and deeper into debt every month. But such worries would be completely uncalled for, if the bank's growing debt means only that many other people are also depositing their pay checks in that same bank.

On the other hand, if you are simply buying things on credit, then that is a debt that you are expected to pay—and if you run up debts that are beyond your means of repayment, you can be in big trouble. However, a bank is in no trouble if someone deposits millions of dollars in it, even though that means going millions of dollars deeper in debt. On the contrary, the bank officials would probably be delighted to get millions of dollars, from which they can make more loans and earn more interest.

For most of its history, the United States has been a debtor nation—and has likewise had the highest standard of living in the world. One of the things that helped develop the American economy and changed the United States from a small agricultural nation to an industrial giant was an inflow of capital from Western Europe in general and from Britain in particular. These vast resources enabled the United States to build canals, factories and transcontinental railroads to tie the country together economically. As of the 1890s, for example, foreign investors owned about one-fifth of the stock of the Baltimore & Ohio Railroad, more than one-third of the stock of the New York Central, more than half the stock of the Pennsylvania Railroad and nearly two-thirds of the stock of the Illinois Central.

Obviously, foreign investors would never have sent their money to America unless they expected to get it back with interest and dividends. Equally obviously, American entrepreneurs would never have agreed to pay interest and dividends unless they expected these investments to produce big enough returns to cover these payments and still leave a profit for the American enterprises.

This all worked out largely as planned, for generations on end. But this meant that the United States was officially a debtor nation for generations on end. Only as a result of lending money to European governments during the First World War did the United States become a creditor nation. Since then, the U.S. has been both, at one time or another. But these have been accounting details, not determinants of American prosperity or problems.

While foreign investments played a major role in the development of particular sectors of the American economy, especially in the early development of industry and infrastructure, there is no need to exaggerate its over-all importance, even in the nineteenth century. For the American economy as a whole, it has been estimated that foreign investment financed about 6 percent of all capital formation in the United States in the nineteenth century. Railroads were exceptional and accounted for an absolute majority of foreign investments in the stocks and bonds of American enterprises.

Neither the domestic economy nor the international economy is a zero-sum process, where some must lose what others win. Everyone can win when investments create a growing economy. There is a bigger pie, from which everyone can get bigger slices. The massive infusion of foreign capital contributed to making the United States the leading industrial nation by 1913, when it produced more than one-third of all the manufactured goods in the world. Despite fears in some countries that foreign investors would carry off much of their national wealth, leaving the local population poorer, there is probably no country in history from which foreigners have carried away more vast amounts of wealth than the United States. By that reasoning, Americans ought to be some of the poorest people in the world, instead of having the world's highest standard of living. The reason for that prosperity is that economic transactions are not a zero-sum activity.

In some less fortunate countries, the same words used in accounting—especially "debt"—may have a very different economic reality behind them. For example, when exports will not cover the cost of imports and there is no high-tech know-how to export, the government may borrow money from some other country or from some international agency, in order to cover the difference. These are genuine debts and causes for genuine concern. But the mere fact of a large trade deficit or a large payments deficit does not by itself create a crisis, though political and journalistic rhetoric can turn it into something to alarm the public.

Deficits and debts are accounting concepts. What matters economically is what is done with the resources involved. Even the biggest and richest corporations have debts, since they sell bonds as well as stocks. As far as accounting is concerned, debts are debts. But that is why economics differs from accounting—and why the facts often differ greatly from what is said in politics and the media.

OTHER TRANSFERS

Even in an era of international investments in the trillions of dollars, other kinds of transfers of wealth among nations remain significant. These include remittances, foreign aid, and transfers of human capital in the form of the skills and entrepreneurship of emigrants.

Remittances

Emigrants working in foreign countries often send money back to their families to support them. During the nineteenth and early twentieth centuries, Italian emigrant men were particularly noted for enduring terrible living conditions in various countries around the world, and even skimping on food, in order to send money back to their families in Italy. Most of the people fleeing the famine in Ireland during the 1840s traveled across the Atlantic with their fares paid by remittances from members of their families already living in the United States. The same would be true of Jewish emigrants from Eastern Europe to the United States in later years.

By the late twentieth century, there were so many emigrants working in so many countries abroad, and sending money home, that their remittances exceeded all the foreign aid from all the government agencies in the world combined. Most of Pakistan's international trade deficit was covered by remittances from Pakistanis working abroad and Jordan received more money from Jordanians living overseas than it did from all its exports.

At one time, overseas Chinese living in Malaysia, Indonesia and other Southeast Asian nations were noted for sending money back to their families in China. Politicians and journalists in these countries often whipped up hostility against the overseas Chinese by claiming that such remittances were impoverishing their countries for the benefit of China. In reality, the Chinese created many of the enterprises—and sometimes whole industries—in these Southeast nations. What they were sending back to China was a fraction of the wealth they had created and added to the wealth in the countries where they were now living.

Similar charges were made against the Lebanese in West Africa, the Indians and Pakistanis in East Africa, and other groups around the world. The underlying fallacy in each case was due to ignoring the wealth created by these groups, so that the countries to which they immigrated had more wealth—not less—as a result of these groups being there. Sometimes the hostility generated against such groups has led to their leaving these countries or being expelled, often followed by economic declines after their departure.

Emigrants and Immigrants

From the standpoint of the economy as a whole, money is not wealth, as we have seen in other economic contexts. People are one of the biggest sources of wealth. Whole industries have been created and economies have been transformed by immigrants—or have collapsed after emigrants took their skills with them and left. After the Moriscoes—Moorish Christians—were expelled from Spain in the early sixteenth century, a Spanish cleric asked: "Who will make our shoes now?" This was a question that might better have been asked *before* the Moriscoes were expelled, especially since this particular cleric had supported the expulsions.

Historically, it has not been at all unusual for a particular ethnic or immigrant group to create or dominate a whole industry. German immigrants created the leading beer breweries in the United States in the nineteenth century, and most of the leading brands of American beer in the twenty-first century are produced in breweries created by people of German ancestry. China's most famous beer—Tsingtao—was also created by Germans and there are German breweries in Australia, Brazil, and Argentina.

There were no watches manufactured in London until Huguenots fleeing France took watch-making skills with them to England and Switzerland, making both these nations among the leading watch-makers in the world. Conversely, France faced increased competition in a number of industries which it had once dominated, because the Huguenots who had fled persecution in France opened up competing businesses in surrounding countries. One of the most striking examples of a country's losses due to those who emigrated was that of Nazi Germany, whose anti-Semitic policies led many Jewish scientists to flee to America, where they played a major role in making the United States the first nation with an atomic bomb. Thus Germany's ally Japan then paid an even bigger price for policies that led to massive Jewish emigration from Nazi-dominated Europe.

One of the vital sources of the skills and entrepreneurship behind the rise of first Britain, and later the United States, to the position of the leading industrial and commercial nation in the world were the numerous immigrant groups who settled in these countries, often to escape persecution or destitution in their native lands. The woolen, linen, cotton, silk, paper, and glass industries were revolutionized by foreign workers and foreign entrepreneurs in England, while the Jews and the Lombards developed British financial institutions. The United States, as a country populated overwhelmingly by immigrants, had even more occupations and industries created or dominated by particular immigrant groups. The first pianos built in colonial America were built by Germans—who also pioneered in building pianos in czarist Russia, England, and France—and firms created by Germans continued to produce the leading American pianos, such as Steinway and Schnabel, in the twenty-first century.

Perhaps to an even greater degree, the countries of Latin America have been dependent on immigrants—especially immigrants from countries other than the conquering nations of Spain and Portugal. According to the distinguished French historian Fernand Braudel, it was these immigrants who "created modern Brazil, modern Argentina, modern Chile." Among the foreigners who have owned or directed more than half of particular industries in particular countries have been the Lebanese in West Africa, Greeks in the Ottoman Empire, Germans in Brazil, Indians in Fiji, Britons in Argentina, Belgians in Russia, Chinese in Malaysia, and many others. Nor is this all a thing of the past. Four-fifths of the doughnut shops in California are owned by people of Cambodian ancestry and more than half the doctors in Britain were born outside of Britain.

It would be misleading, however, to assess the economic impact of immigration solely in terms of its positive contributions. Immigrants have also brought diseases, crime, internal strife, and terrorism. Nor can all immigrants be lumped together. When only two percent of immigrants from Japan to the United States go on welfare, while 46 percent of the immigrants from Laos do, there is no single pattern that applies to all immigrants. There are similar disparities in crime rates and in other both negative and positive factors that immigrants from different countries bring to the United States and to other countries in other parts of the world. Everything depends on which emigrants you are talking about, which countries you are talking about and which periods of history.

Imperialism

Plunder of one nation or people by another has been all too common throughout human history.

Although imperialism is one of the ways in which wealth can be transferred from one country to another, there are also non-economic reasons for imperialism which have caused it to be persisted in, even when it was costing the conquering country money on net balance. Military leaders may want strategic bases, such as the British base at Gibraltar or the American base at Guantanamo Bay in Cuba. Nineteenth century missionaries urged the British government toward acquiring control of various countries in Africa where there was much missionary work going on—such urgings often being opposed by chancellors of the exchequer, who realized that Britain would never get enough money out of these poor countries to repay the costs of establishing and maintaining a colonial regime there.

Some private individuals like Cecil Rhodes might get rich in Africa, but the costs to the British taxpayers exceeded even Rhodes' fabulous fortune. Modern European imperialism in general was much more impressive in terms of territories controlled than in terms of economic significance. When European empires were at their peak in the early twentieth century, Western Europe was less than 2 percent of the world's land area but it controlled more than another 40 percent in overseas empires. However, most major industrial nations sent only trivial percentages of their exports or investments to their conquered colonies in the Third World and received imports that were similarly trivial compared to what these industrial nations produced themselves or purchased as imports from other industrial countries.

At the height of the British Empire in the early twentieth century, the British invested more in the United States than in all of Asia and Africa put together. Quite simply, there was more wealth to be made from rich countries than from poor countries. For similar reasons, throughout most of the twentieth century the United States invested more in Canada than in all of Asia and Africa put together. Only the rise of prosperous Asian industrial nations in the latter part of the twentieth century attracted more American investors to that part of the world. As of 2001, the United States had several times as much invested in a small country like the Netherlands than in the whole vast continent of Africa.

Perhaps the strongest evidence against the economic significance of colonies in the modern world is that Germany and Japan lost all their colonies and conquered lands as a result of their defeat in the Second World War—and both countries reached unprecedented levels of prosperity thereafter. A need for colonies was a particularly effective political talking point in pre-war Japan, which had very few natural resources of its own. But, after its dreams of military glory ended with its defeat and devastation, Japan simply bought whatever natural resources it needed from those countries that had them.

Imperialism has often caused much suffering among the conquered peoples. But, in the modern industrial world at least, imperialism has seldom been a major source of international transfers of wealth.

While investors have tended to invest in more prosperous nations, making both themselves and these nations wealthier, some people have depicted investments in poor countries as somehow making the latter even poorer. The Marxian concept of "exploitation" was applied internationally in Lenin's book *Imperialism*, where investments by industrial nations in non-industrial countries were treated as being economically equivalent to the looting done by earlier imperialist conquerors. Tragically, however, it is in precisely those less developed countries where little or no foreign investment has taken place that poverty is at its worst. Similarly, those poor countries with less international trade as a percentage of their national economies have had lower economic growth rates than poor countries where international trade plays a larger economic role. Indeed, during the decade of the 1990s, these latter countries had declining economies, while those more "globalized" countries had growing economies.

Wealthy individuals in poor countries often invest in richer countries, where their money is safer from political upheavals and confiscations. Ironically, poorer countries are thus helping richer industrial nations to become still richer. Meanwhile, under the influence of theories of economic imperialism which depicted international investments as being the equivalent of imperialist looting, governments in many poorer countries pursued policies which discouraged investments from being made there by foreigners. By the late twentieth century, however, the painful economic consequences of such policies had become sufficiently apparent to many people in the Third World that some governments—in Latin America and India, for example—began moving away from such policies, in order to gain some of the benefits received by other countries which had risen from poverty to prosperity with the help of foreign investments. Economic realities had finally broken through ideological beliefs, though generations had suffered needless deprivations before basic economic principles were finally accepted.

Many economic fallacies are due to conceiving of economic activity as a zero-sum contest, in which what is gained by one is lost by another. This in turn is often due to ignoring the fact that wealth is *created* in the course of economic activity. If payments to foreign investors impoverished a nation, then the United States would be one of the most impoverished nations in the world, because foreigners took nearly $270 billion out of the American economy in 2001—which was more than the Gross Domestic Product of Egypt or Malaysia. Since most of this money consisted of earnings from assets that foreigners owned in the United States, Americans had already gotten the benefits of the additional wealth that those assets had helped create, and were simply sharing part of that additional wealth with those abroad who had contributed to creating it.

Foreign Aid

What is called "foreign aid" are transfers of wealth from foreign governmental organizations, including international agencies, to the governments of poorer countries. The term "aid" assumes *a priori* that such transfers will in fact aid the poorer countries' economies to develop. In some cases it does, but in other cases foreign aid simply enables the existing politicians in power to enrich themselves through graft and to dispense largess in politically strategic ways to others who help to keep them in power. Because it is a transfer of wealth to governments, as distinguished from investments in the private sector, foreign aid has encouraged many countries to set up government-run enterprises that have failed.

Perhaps the most famous foreign aid program was the Marshall Plan, which transferred wealth from the United States to various countries in Western Europe after the end of World War II. It was far more successful than later attempts to imitate it by sending foreign aid to Third World countries. Western Europe's economic distress was caused by the devastations of the war. Once the people were fed and the infrastructure rebuilt, Western Europe simply resumed the industrial way of life which they had achieved— indeed, pioneered—before. That was wholly different from trying to create all the industrial skills that were lacking in poorer, non-industrial nations. What needed to be rebuilt in Europe was physical capital. What needed to be created in much of the Third World was more human capital. The latter proved harder to do, just as the vast array of skills needed in a modern economy had taken centuries to create in Europe.

Even massive and highly visible failures and counterproductive results from foreign aid have not stopped its continuation and expansion. The vast sums of money dispensed by foreign aid agencies such as the International Monetary Fund and the World Bank give the officials of these agencies enormous influence on the governments of poorer countries, regardless of the success or failure of the programs they suggest or impose as preconditions for receiving the money. In short, there is no economic bottom line to determine which actions, policies, organizations or individuals could survive the weeding out process that takes place through competition in the marketplace.

In addition to the "foreign aid" dispensed by international agencies, there are also direct government-to-government grants of money, shipments of free food, and loans which are made available on terms more lenient than those available in the financial markets and which are periodically "forgiven," allowed to default, or "rolled over" by being repaid from the proceeds of new and larger loans. Thus American government loans to the government of India and British government loans to a number of Third World governments have been simply cancelled, converting these loans into gifts.

Sometimes a richer country takes over a whole poor society and heavily subsidizes it, as the United States did in Micronesia. So much American aid poured in that many Micronesians abandoned economic activities on which they had supported themselves before, such as fishing and farming. If and when Americans decide to end such aid, it is not at all certain that the skills and experience that Micronesians once had will remain widespread enough to allow them to become self-sufficient again.

Beneficial results of foreign aid are more likely to be publicized by the national or international agencies which finance these ventures, while failures are more likely to be publicized by critics, so the net effect is not immediately obvious. One of the leading development economists of his time, the late Professor Peter Bauer of the London School of Economics, argued that, on the whole, "official aid is more likely to retard development than to promote it." Whether that controversial conclusion is accepted or rejected, what is more fundamental is that terms like "foreign aid" not be allowed to insinuate a result which may or may not turn out to be substantiated by facts and analysis.

Many Third World countries have considerable internal sources of wealth which are not fully utilized for one reason or another—and this wealth often greatly exceeds whatever foreign aid such countries have ever received. In many poorer countries, much—if not most—economic activity takes place "off the books" or in the "underground economy" because the costs of red tape, corruption, and bureaucratic delays required to obtain legal permission to run a business or own a home put legally recognized economic activities beyond the financial reach of much of the population. These people may operate businesses ranging from street vending to factories or build homes for themselves or others, without having any of this economic activity legally recognized by their governments.

According to *The Economist* magazine, in a typical African nation, only about one person in ten works in a legally recognized enterprise or lives in a house that has legally recognized property rights. In Egypt, for example, an estimated 4.7 million homes have been built illegally. In Peru, the total value of all the real estate that is not legally covered by property rights has been estimated as more than a dozen times larger than all the foreign direct investments ever made in the country in its entire history. Similar situations have been found in India, Haiti, and other Third World countries.

The economic consequences of these legal bottlenecks in many countries can be profound because they prevent many existing enterprises, representing vast amounts of wealth in the aggregate, from developing beyond the small scale in which they start. Many giant American corporations began as very humble enterprises, not very different from those which abound in Third World countries today. Levi's, Macy's, Saks, and Bloomingdale's all began as peddlers, for example. While such businesses may get started with an individual's own small savings or perhaps with loans from family or friends, eventually their expansion into major corporations usually requires the mobilization of the money of innumerable strangers willing to become investors. But the property rights system which makes this possible has not been as accessible to ordinary people in Third World countries as it has been to ordinary people in the United States.

An American bank that is unwilling to invest in a small business may nevertheless be willing to lend money to its owner in exchange for a mortgage on his home—but the home must first be legally recognized as his property. After the business becomes a major success, other strangers may lend money on its growing assets or invest directly as stockholders. But all of this too hinges on a system of dependable and accessible property rights, which is capable of mobilizing far more wealth internally than is ever likely to be transferred from other nations or from international agencies like the World Bank or the International Monetary Fund.

THE INTERNATIONAL MONETARY SYSTEM

Wealth may be transferred from country to country in the form of goods and services, but by far the greatest transfers are made in the form of money. Just as a stable monetary unit facilitates economic activity within a country, so international economic activity is facilitated when there are stable relationships between one country's currency and another's. It is not simply a question of the ease or difficulty of converting dollars into yen or francs at a given moment. A far more important question is whether an investment made in the United States, Japan, or France today will be repaid a decade or more from now in money of the same purchasing power.

Where currencies fluctuate relative to one another, anyone who engages in any international transactions becomes a speculator. Even a tourist who buys souvenirs in Mexico will have to wait until the credit card bill arrives to discover how much the item they paid 30 pesos for will cost them in U.S. dollars. It can turn out to be either more or less than they thought. Where millions of dollars are invested overseas, the stability of the various currencies is urgently important. It is important not simply to those whose money is directly involved, it is important in maintaining the flows of trade and investment which affect the material well-being of the general public in the countries concerned.

During the era of the gold standard, which began to break down during the First World War and ended during the Great Depression of the 1930s, various nations made their national currencies equivalent to a given amount of gold. An American dollar, for example, could always be exchanged for a fixed amount of gold from the U. S. government. Both Americans and foreigners could exchange their dollars for a given amount of gold. Therefore any foreign investor putting his money into the American economy knew in advance what he could count on getting back if his investment worked out. No doubt that had much to do with the vast amount of capital that poured into the United States from Europe and helped develop it into the leading industrial nation of the world.

Other nations which made their currency redeemable in fixed amounts of gold likewise made their economies safer places for both domestic and foreign investors. Moreover, their currencies were also automatically fixed relative to the dollar and other currencies from other countries that used the gold standard. As Nobel Prizewinning monetary economist Robert Mundell put it, "currencies were just different names for particular weights of gold." During that era, financier J. P. Morgan could say, "money is gold, and nothing else."

Various attempts at stabilizing international currencies against one another have followed the disappearance of the gold standard. Some nations have made their currencies equivalent to a fixed number of dollars, for example. Various European nations have joined together to create their own international currency, the Euro, and the Japanese yen has been another stable currency widely accepted in international financial transactions. At the other extreme have been various South American countries, whose currencies have fluctuated wildly in value, with double- and triple-digit inflation not being unknown.

These monetary fluctuations have had repercussions on such real things as output and employment, since it is difficult to plan and invest when there is much uncertainty about what the money will be worth, even if the investment is successful otherwise. The economic problems of Argentina and Brazil have been particularly striking in view of the fact that both countries are richly endowed with natural resources and have been spared the destruction of wars that so many other countries on other continents have suffered in the course of the twentieth century.

With the spread of electronic transfers of money, reactions to any national currency's change in reliability can be virtually instantaneous. Any government that is tempted toward inflation knows that money can flee from their economy literally in a moment. The discipline this imposes is different from that once imposed by a gold standard, but whether it is equally effective will only be known when future economic pressures put the international monetary system to a real test.

As in other areas of economics, it is necessary to be on guard against emotionally loaded words that may confuse more than they clarify. One of the terms widely used in discussing the relative values of various national currencies are "strong" and "weak." Thus, when the euro was first introduced as a monetary unit in the European Union countries, its value fell from $1.18 to 83 cents and it was said to be "weakening" relative to the dollar. Later it rose again, to reach $1.16 in early 2003, and was then said to be "strengthening." Words can be harmless if we understand what they do and don't mean, but misleading if we take their connotations at face value.

One thing that a "strong" currency does not mean is that the economies that use that currency are necessarily better off. Sometimes it means the opposite. A "strong" currency means that the prices of exports from countries that use that currency have risen in price to people in other countries. Thus the rise in value of the euro in 2003 has been blamed by a number of European corporations for falling exports to the United States, as the prices of their products rose in dollars, causing fewer Americans to buy them. Meanwhile, the "weakening" of Britain's pound sterling had opposite effects. *BusinessWeek* magazine reported:

> Britain's hard-pressed manufacturers love a falling pound. So they have warmly welcomed the 11% slide in sterling's exchange rate against the euro over the past year. . . . As the pound weakens against the euro, it makes British goods more competitive on the Continent, which is by far their largest export market. And it boosts corporate profits when earnings from the euro zone are converted into sterling.

Just as a "strong" currency is not always good, it is not always bad either. In the countries that use the Euro, businesses that borrow from Americans find the burden of that debt to be less and easier to repay when fewer Euros are needed to repay dollars. When Norway's krona rose in value relative to Sweden's krone, Norwegians living near the border of Sweden crossed over and saved 40 percent buying a load of groceries in Sweden. The point here is simply that words like "strong" and "weak" currencies by themselves tell us little about the economic realities, which have to be looked at directly and specifically, rather than by relying on the emotional connotations of words.

ZERO-SUM THINKING

Lurking in the background of much confused thinking about international trade and international transfers of wealth is an implicit assumption of a zero-sum contest, where some can gain only if others lose. Thus, for example, some have claimed that multinational corporations profit by "exploiting" workers in the Third World. If so, it is hard to explain why the vast majority of American investments in other countries go to richer countries, not poorer countries. More than four-fifths of all U.S. direct investment in other countries in the year 2000 went to high-income countries, such as Canada, Japan, and Western European nations. Another 18 percent went to middle-income countries like Brazil, Indonesia, Mexico, and Thailand. That left just one percent invested in low-income countries such as those in sub-Saharan Africa or in the less developed parts of Asia.

Why are profit-seeking companies investing far more where they will have to pay high wages to workers in affluent industrial nations, instead of low wages to "sweatshop" labor in the Third World? Why are they passing up supposedly golden opportunities to "exploit" the poorest workers? Exploitation may be an intellectually convenient, emotionally satisfying, and politically expedient explanation of income differences between nations or between groups within a given nation, but it does not have the additional feature of fitting the facts about where profit-seeking enterprises invest their money. Moreover, even within poor countries, the very poorest people are typically those with the least contact with multinational corporations, often because they are located away from the ports and other business centers.

American multinational corporations alone have provided employment to more than 30 million people worldwide. But, given their international investment patterns, few of those jobs are likely to be in the poorest countries where they are most needed. In some relatively few cases, a multinational corporation may in fact invest in a Third World country, where the local wages are sufficiently lower to compensate for the lower productivity of the workers and/or the higher costs of shipping in a less developed transportation system and/or the bribes that have to be paid to government officials to operate in many such countries.

Various reformers or protest movements of college students and others in the affluent countries may then wax indignant over the low wages and "sweatshop" conditions in these Third World enterprises. However, if these protest movements succeed politically in forcing up the wages and working conditions in these countries, the net result can be that even fewer foreign companies will invest in the Third World and fewer Third World workers will have jobs. Since multinational corporations typically pay about double the local wages in poor countries, the loss of these jobs is likely to translate into more hardship for Third World workers, even as their would-be benefactors in the West congratulate themselves on having ended "exploitation."

Chapter 21

An Overview

Free trade may have wide support among economists, but its support among the public at large is considerably less. An international poll conducted by *The Economist* magazine found more people in favor of protectionism than of free trade in Britain, France, Italy, Australia, Russia, and the United States. Part of the reason is that the public has no idea how much protectionism costs and how little net benefit it produces. It has been estimated that all the protectionism in the European Union countries put together saves no more than a grand total of 200,000 jobs—at a cost of $43 billion. That works out to about $215,000 for each job saved.

In other words, if the European Union permitted 100 percent free international trade, every worker who lost his job as a result of foreign competition could be paid $100,000 a year in compensation and the European Union countries would still come out ahead. Alternatively, the displaced workers could simply go find other jobs. Whatever losses they might encounter in the process do not begin to compare with the staggering costs of keeping them working where they are. That is because the costs are not simply their salaries, but the even larger costs of producing in less efficient ways.

The costs of protectionism can be measured not only in money but also in the number of jobs lost by industries adversely affected by the protection given to one particular industry. When there were 160,000 workers in the American steel industry when tariffs were imposed for their protection and 9 million workers in industries using steel, it can hardly be surprising that there were net losses of jobs from these tariffs.

Only part of the problem of getting the general public to understand international trade is due to their not having the facts. Another part is their not having enough knowledge of economics to withstand the barrage of self-serving arguments put out by many in business, labor, and agriculture, who wish to escape the consequences of having to compete in the marketplace with foreign producers. When American steel producers have higher production costs per ton than their German, Japanese, Brazilian and South Korean rivals, it is easier to ask the U.S. government for protection from foreign competitors than to try to reduce their own high costs of production.

Another reason for public support for protectionism is that many economists do not bother to answer either the special interests or those who oppose free trade for ideological reasons, since the arguments of both have essentially been refuted long ago and are now regarded in the economics profession as beneath contempt. But this has only allowed vehement and articulate spokesmen to have a more or less free hand to monopolize public opinion, which seldom hears more than one side of the issue. One of the few leading economists to bother answering protectionist arguments has been MIT's internationally renowned economist, Professor Jagdish Bhagwati, who agreed to a public debate against Ralph Nader. Here was his experience:

> Faced with the critics of free trade, economists have generally reacted with contempt and indifference, refusing to get into the public arena to engage the critics in battle. I was in a public debate with Ralph Nader on the campus of Cornell University a couple of years ago. The debate was in the evening, and in the afternoon I gave a technical talk on free trade to the graduate students of economics. I asked, at the end, how many were going to the debate, and not one hand went up. Why, I asked. The typical reaction was: why waste one's time? As a consequence, of the nearly thousand students who jammed the theater where the debate was held, the vast majority were anti-free traders, all rooting for Mr. Nader.

Because the buzzword "globalization" has been coined to describe the growing importance of international trade and global economic interdependence, many tend to see international trade and international financial transactions as something new—allowing both special interests and ideologues to play on the public's fear of the unknown. However, the term "globalization" also covers more than simple free trade among nations. It includes institutional rules governing the reduction of trade barriers and the movements of money. Among the international organizations involved in creating these rules are the World Bank, the International Monetary Fund, and the World Trade Organization. These rules are legitimate subjects of controversy, though these are not all controversies about free trade, as such. One of the severest critics of the Inter-

national Monetary Fund, for example, has been Nobel Prize-winning economist Joseph Stiglitz, who favors free trade but attacks the specific rules imposed by the IMF when making loans to poor countries.

THE ROLE OF TRADE

Americans have not had to pay nearly as much attention to international
trade as people in other countries, such as Britain or Holland, whose
economies have been more dependent on such trade for centuries. Still,
American overseas trade has been growing in recent years, not only absolutely but also as a percentage of the U.S. economy. The ratio of the total
international trade of the United States—combining exports and imports—
to the total output of the American economy was just 8 percent in 1950 but
was 26 percent by 2000. Moreover, even in the past, the modest share of international economic transactions in the American economy was nevertheless significant in transforming the United States from a predominantly
agricultural nation into a major industrial power.

In addition to the large foreign investments that went into creating leading American railroads in the late nineteenth century, as noted in chapter 20,
even earlier—in the 1820s and 1830s—foreign purchasers of state bonds financed the digging of canals, the construction of urban public works, and the
creation of banks in the United States. Later, in the post-Civil War period,
foreign investments financed 15 percent of all the net capital formation in
the United States from 1869 to 1875. In short, while international trade and
international financial transactions have not played as large or as visible a
role in the economy of the United States as in the economies of some other
countries, that role has not been negligible.

International trade is basically a further extension of the division of functions that marks every modern economy. There was a time, not many centuries ago, when farm families provided themselves with food, shelter, and
even clothing made with their own hands. They grew their own fruits and
vegetables, raised their own livestock to provide meat, milked their own cows
and even made their own cheese. Homespun clothing was common as well
on the American frontier. A remarkable degree of economic self-sufficiency
is possible, even at the level of the individual family. But that only raises the
question: Why did this way of doing things die out? Why did people begin
to purchase all these things from other people who specialized in producing
particular goods?

The answer is of course that specialists could produce better products at lower costs. But, so long as family farms were isolated—that is, could receive specialized products only with high transportation costs added—a self-sufficient way of life made sense. But, once the transportation system was able to bring a wheat farmer numerous consumer products at affordable prices, and to carry his wheat to market at lower cost, it made more sense for the family to spend their time growing more wheat, instead of making homespun clothing, because they could buy their clothing with what they earned from selling more wheat, and still have something left over. Everything depends on whether the time and efforts required to produce their own clothing directly would yield more clothing in the end if put into growing wheat to sell.

That same principle applies not only to clothing but to other products as well—and regardless of whether those products are produced within the same national borders or on the other side of the world. That is the basis for international trade. Although this is often described as trade between nations, it is in fact trade between individuals. Each individual decides whether what is bought is worth it, in the light of other options available. Each Frenchman decides for himself whether he wants to see a movie made in Hollywood and each person in Singapore decides whether to buy a camera made in Germany or Japan.

International trade is not a zero-sum contest between nations, but a wide array of voluntary transactions between individuals living in different countries, who must all gain if these transactions are to continue. International trade is just one more way of getting more output from scarce resources which have alternative uses.

Just as trade restrictions such as the American Hawley-Smoot tariffs of the 1930s damaged the already ailing U.S. economy of the Great Depression, the North American Free Trade Agreement of 1993 helped enhance the prosperity of the 1990s, creating more jobs and reducing unemployment to record low levels, despite the cries of protectionists that NAFTA would lead to a massive flight of jobs from America to low-wage countries elsewhere.

The growth of international trade and international finance over the years is one sign of the benefits it produces. This growth has generally exceeded the growth of the national economies involved, so that international transactions have become a larger proportion of all transactions. Even an economy like that of the United States, where international trade played a relatively small role at one time, has seen its international component rising, both in trade and in investment in and from other economies.

Third World countries and formerly Communist countries which once severely restricted their international economic transactions have increasingly
opened up their economies to the international economy. The term "globalization" has been used to describe this process of expanded international
commerce and investment, though there has long been much global economic activity by particular countries and enterprises. The British, for example, built the first railroads in many countries, from India to Argentina and
from Australia to West Africa. The leading manufacturer of agricultural machinery in czarist Russia was the American firm International Harvester.
During the colonial era in East Africa, entrepreneurs from India were so
dominant in the economy that rupees became the common currency in the
region. In short, "globalization" is a new name for an old phenomenon, but
one that has become even more important in recent times.

Globalization undoubtedly harms some businesses and industries and
costs some people their jobs. But so do any other ways of creating greater efficiency in the allocation of scarce resources which have alternative uses. Opponents of free trade try to depict it as harmful to the society as a whole, and
appeal to a sense of "us" against "them," as if other countries are in some way
making Americans worse off by selling them things that they want to buy.

Like anything else that allows goods and services to be produced more
cheaply or better, international trade benefits the consumers while reducing
profits and employment among those who produce more costly or obsolete
products. Protecting the less efficient producer makes no more sense internationally than it does domestically. Whatever jobs are saved in either case do
not represent net savings for the economy as a whole, but only the saving of
some jobs by sacrificing others, along with sacrificing the consumer. When
particular jobs and businesses succumb to more efficient competition,
whether domestic or international, resources which have alternative uses can
go to those alternative uses and thus add to the national output. It is not a
zero-sum game. Conversely, preventing such transfers saves relatively few
jobs at very high costs per job, as in the European Union countries, or saves
jobs in one industry at the expense of more jobs in other industries, as in the
case of the American steel tariffs.

International trade is one way of sharing in the advantages that other
countries have in producing particular products. Together with international
investments, this is also a way to share in the technology and organizational
advances made in other countries, as well as in agricultural produce transplanted from other parts of the world, such as the rubber transplanted to
Malaysia and the cocoa transplanted to Ghana—with each of these countries

becoming the world's leading producer of their respective transplanted products at one time.

Perhaps the most important international transplants have been human beings. The vast majority of the populations of the Western Hemisphere have been transplanted, mostly from Europe, but also from Asia and Africa. With them have come widespread changes in the prevalent technology of the hemisphere, as well as changes in political and other ideas. Nor has this transfer of "human capital" stopped in later centuries. The 1990 U.S. Census revealed that there were more than two and a half million highly educated people from Third World countries living in the United States, not counting students. Meanwhile, 40 percent of all emigrants from the Philippines were college educated.

THE ROLE OF INTERNATIONAL INVESTMENT

The transfer of wealth internationally through market transactions allocates the resources of the world in much the same way that such transfers allocate resources domestically. In both cases, it is like water seeking its own level. If investments with a given degree of risk are paying off at a higher rate in Taiwan than in Sweden, then American, British or German capital will flow to Taiwan and not to Sweden, thereby raising the level of productivity in the world as a whole and raising standards of living internationally. Money and the resources it represents become, as it were, citizens of the world.

Such economic benefits are often not welcome politically, however. While comparative advantage and free trade allow all nations to share in the world prosperity promoted by free movements of resources, not all industries within all nations prosper. Those sectors of particular economies that are unable to match the competition in efficiency not only stand to lose money and jobs, they may even be threatened with bankruptcy and extinction. Seldom will they go quietly. Representatives of industries and regions that stand to lose business and jobs because of international competition are almost certain to seek restrictions on imported goods or resources which threaten their particular well-being, however beneficial such international transactions may be to the population as a whole.

International movements of goods and investments also restrict the range of options available to particular governments. As noted in Chapter 16, governments have for centuries transferred wealth from the people to themselves by the simple process of issuing inflationary amounts of money and spending the newly created money for whatever the government wanted to finance. With free international movements of wealth—at instantaneous speeds with computerized financial transactions—money and the resources they represent tend to be transferred out of countries whose governments are conducting such clandestine confiscations.

Other economically counterproductive policies tend likewise to cause domestic wealth to flow out of a country and foreign wealth to stop coming in. Thus it was a matter of concern to India when the private financial rating agency Standard and Poor's downgraded the rating of the country's currency in August 2001 because of what *The Economist* magazine called the "shaky finances" of India's government. In California as well, that state's bonds were sharply downgraded by both Moody's and Standard and Poor's, even though the state had a record surplus in its budget, because both these rating agencies recognized that the policies being followed would soon turn that state's huge surplus into a huge deficit—as it did.

Both businessmen and politicians who suffer from the operation of free international trade and wealth transfers have every reason to represent their own problems as disadvantages to the country as a whole. No small part of the confusion surrounding international trade has its origins in their attempts to mobilize political support to stop international trade from causing them problems. Such attempts have been going on for centuries, in countries around the world. Most economists today reject most of their arguments, and the economics profession has rejected most of these arguments since 1776, when Adam Smith rebutted them in *The Wealth of Nations*.

There are special circumstances in which special interferences with free international trade can in fact be beneficial—national defense being one obvious example—but that is very different from saying that most of interferences that are advocated are likely to be beneficial.

Political leaders have far more control when wealth flows into their countries in the form of "foreign aid"—that is, transfers from national or international agencies to governments—rather than as private investments to private individuals or businesses. But receiving wealth from abroad via the marketplace would require satisfying foreign investors that a project was likely to succeed and that the local legal and political system was one they could rely on when time came to take their earnings out or to take their whole investment out if they wished.

Showy projects with only a political pay-off for the government—a sports stadium, a glitzy plaza, or a national airline in a country without enough passengers to enable it to pay for itself—can all be financed by foreign aid, but are unlikely to be financed by international investors risking their own money. Moreover, government officials can be more generous with themselves and their followers and favorites when it comes to appropriating foreign aid money for personal use, including putting it in Swiss banks. Third World countries often have ruins or remnants of failed projects financed by foreign aid, like these in the African nation of Niger:

> The relics of many high-minded, high-tech development projects litter Niger like the dinosaur bones occasionally discovered beneath the shifting sands. Sophisticated irrigation systems that work well with First World maintenance turned into rusted pipes in Niger. The European cows that were supposed to improve milk production keeled over in the heat.

The availability of foreign aid reduces the necessity for a country to restrict its investments to economically viable projects or to reduce its level of corruption. Far more wealth may be available internationally for the economic development of a poor country through private international investors than through foreign aid, and yet that country's government may prefer to receive a smaller amount through foreign aid, since government officials themselves benefit more from this smaller amount than from a larger amount of wealth that would have preconditions which negatively affect these officials' well-being, even if private investment would enhance the economic well-being of their country as a whole.

In short, countries with inefficient economies and corrupt governments are far more likely to receive foreign aid than to receive investments from people who are risking their own money. Put differently, the availability of foreign aid reduces the necessity for a country to restrict its investments to economically viable projects or to reduce its level of corruption.

An intermediary form of wealth transfer is an investment from private sources that is guaranteed by their own government, which stands ready to reimburse them with taxpayers' money should their overseas investment prove unprofitable or the profits uncollectible. Thus when the Mexican government was on the verge of defaulting on its loans from American banks in 1996, the American government lent them the money to pay off these banks and other investors. Obviously, if these banks had been forced to take huge losses, they would have become more wary of risky investments in the future and in other countries. As we have seen in other contexts, losses play as important a role in the economy as profits, though they are not nearly as popular. Artificially preventing losses is reducing incentives to allocate resources efficiently.

The periodic "forgiveness" of loans to Third World countries likewise reduces incentives for the governments of these countries to use the loans in ways that contribute to the growth of national wealth, from which the loans could be paid off. The only clear beneficiaries of such "forgiveness," aside from Third World political leaders who escape responsibility, are those people in wealthier donor countries who feel a sense of *noblesse oblige*. But the subsidizing of political irresponsibility has heavy costs that fall ultimately on the peoples of the poorer countries.

The sums of money received in foreign aid are dwarfed by the sums of money available for investment internationally in countries with responsible and dependable governments. Moreover, as noted in Chapter 20, vast sources of untapped capital already exist within Third World countries themselves, in the form of economic assets which cannot be turned into financial assets because of the inaccessibility of property rights for most people in those countries. In short, the internal institutions and policies which inhibit international transfers of private investment to poor countries also inhibit the mobilization of investments based on existing assets within those countries.

These assets also include human capital, which may be as under-utilized as the country's physical assets. Many Third World countries contain entrepreneurial minority groups—Chinese minorities in various Southeast Asian countries, Lebanese in West Africa, Indians in East Africa and Fiji—who have been subjected to discriminatory restrictions on their economic activities or have even been expelled or forced out by hostile public or governmental actions. Painful as the losses suffered by members of these minorities are when forced to leave countries where they were born, the losses suffered by the countries themselves after such groups have left have been a major factor in the continuing poverty of some Third World nations. For example, whole sectors of the Ugandan economy collapsed after 50,000 Indians and Pakistanis were forced to leave the country in the 1970s.

Indigenous human capital may also leave because the political and institutional climate offers far less opportunity for individuals to advance economically than the opportunities available in some foreign countries. India, for all its poverty, has for centuries been an exporter of entrepreneurs, who have created thriving enterprises from the Caribbean to the South Pacific and from Russia to Africa. Today, computer engineers from India are a major force in America's Silicon Valley and Indians are 10 percent of all anesthesiologists in the United States.

Despite a vision of helpless Third World countries, whose economic rise is possible only through transfers of foreign aid and foreign know-how from more prosperous and more industrially advanced countries, many Third World nations have within themselves both physical assets and human assets far exceeding any that they are likely to receive from other countries. This is not to say that it would be easy politically to reform the policies and institutions which hold back internal economic development in the Third World. What is easy politically is to accept foreign aid and use it to help keep existing political leaders in power, whether or not the foreign aid has any significant effect on the economic condition of the country as a whole.

Enormous amounts of wealth created in "underground" economies in the Third World provide evidence of the entrepreneurship already present in these countries, even if the legal systems in these countries impede this wealth from being mobilized for larger corporate development, such as occurs in Western countries or in some Asian nations such as Japan. Often there have been entrepreneurial minorities in Third World countries who have been responsible for much, if not most, of the development of modern economic sectors in those countries. The Chinese have played this role in Malaysia, Indonesia and other Southeast Asian nations, Indians and Pakistanis did the same in East Africa and the Lebanese in West Africa. In past eras, Armenians played this role in parts of the Russian and Ottoman Empires, and the Jews in much of Eastern Europe.

Without exception, the success of these minorities has been resented and this resentment has in many cases led politically to their persecution or expulsion. In addition to the tragedies inflicted on these minorities, the economic impact of their departures has been a loss to the countries in which they have not been allowed to contribute what they could. Very few Third World countries have been devoid of the human capital—indigenous or otherwise—needed for economic development. West Africa, for example, became the world's leading grower and exporter of cocoa as a result of the planting and growing of this crop by innumerable African small farmers, even though cocoa was not indigenous to Africa.

During the twentieth century, many poor countries spent decades keeping out foreign products, foreign investments, and multinational corporations, for fear of being exploited. This meant that they had to produce for themselves many products that were available at lower prices in the world market, as well as products that could have been produced more cheaply within their own borders by foreign companies using more advanced technology and industrial experience. People in poor countries were thus denied not only the benefits of a greater abundance of goods, but also opportunities to become familiar with more advanced technology and modern organizational practices that would enable them to create and manage such enterprises themselves. An analysis of 2,700 firms in East Asia by the National Bureau of Economic Research concluded that "firms in which foreigners have a substantial ownership share have markedly higher productivity than those that are domestically owned." More productivity means higher standards of living.

The poorer the country, the less could they afford to forego opportunities for a higher standard of living. Eventually, by the late twentieth century, many Third World governments finally realized their mistake, but whole generations had had their economic well-being needlessly sacrificed in the meantime. Partly this change in policy was made because these governments had observed the dramatic economic improvements in once-poor countries like South Korea and Taiwan, which opted to participate heavily in global markets, as compared to the relative stagnation in countries like India and some Latin American nations which did not. However, the history of Western nations in centuries past could have revealed similar lessons.

While Britain was the nation that led the world into the industrial age, nevertheless in earlier pre-industrial centuries, Britain was much like Third World countries today. It exported raw materials such as wool and imported manufactured products from more advanced nations on the continent of Europe. Britain's financial institutions were run by foreigners and whole British industries, such as watch-making and piano-manufacturing, were created by immigrants and expatriates. It was only after centuries of learning from others that Britain was ready to take its place at the head of technological and organizational advances in the world economy. Japan went through a similar phase in the late nineteenth and early twentieth centuries.

PART VII: SPECIAL
ECONOMIC ISSUES

Chapter 22

"Non-Economic" Values

While economics offers many insights and makes it easier to see through some popular notions that sound good but will not stand up under scrutiny, economics has also acquired the name "the dismal science" because it pours cold water on many otherwise attractive and exciting—but fallacious—notions about how the world can be arranged. One of the last refuges of someone whose pet project or theory has been exposed as economic nonsense is to say: "Economics is all very well, but there are also *non-economic* values to consider." Presumably, these are supposed to be higher and nobler concerns that soar above the level of crass materialism.

Of course there are non-economic values. In fact, there are *only* non-economic values. Economics is not a value in and of itself. It is only a way of weighing one value against another. Economics does not say that you should make the most money possible. Many professors of economics could themselves make more money in private industry. Anyone with a knowledge of firearms could probably make more money working as a hit man for organized crime. But economics does not urge you toward such choices.

Adam Smith, the father of laissez-faire economics, gave away substantial sums of his own money to less fortunate people, though he did so with such discretion that this fact was discovered only after his death, when his personal records were examined. Henry Thornton, one of the great monetary economists of the nineteenth century and a banker by trade, regularly gave away more than half his annual income before he got married and had a family to support—and he continued to give large donations to humanitarian causes afterwards, including the anti-slavery movement.

The first public libraries in New York City were not established by the government but by industrial entrepreneur Andrew Carnegie, who also established the foundation and the university that bear his name. John D. Rockefeller likewise established the foundation that bears his name and the University of Chicago, as well as creating many other philanthropic enterprises. Halfway around the world, the Tata Institute in Bombay was established by the country's leading industrialist, J. R. Tata. In eighteenth century Britain, canals were built with donations from businessmen.

The United States, which has come to epitomize capitalism in the eyes of many people around the world, is unique in having hundreds of colleges, hospitals, foundations, scholarship funds, libraries, museums and other institutions created by the donations of private individuals, many of these being individuals who earned money in the market place and then devoted much of it—sometimes most of it—to helping others. *BusinessWeek* magazine in 2002 listed numerous entrepreneurs who had donated hundreds of millions of dollars each—and some, billions—to philanthropy. The market as a mechanism for the allocation of scarce resources among alternative uses is one thing; what one chooses to do with the resulting wealth is another.[1]

What lofty talk about "non-economic values" usually boils down to is that some people do not want their own particular values weighed against anything. If they are for saving Mono Lake or preserving some historic building, then they do not want that weighed against the cost—which is to say, ultimately, against all the other things that might be done instead with the same resources. For such people, there is no point considering how many Third World children could be vaccinated against fatal diseases with the money that is spent saving Mono Lake or preserving a historic building. We should vaccinate those children *and* save Mono Lake *and* preserve the historic building—as well as doing innumerable other good things, according to this way of looking at the world.

To people who think (or rather, react) in this way, economics is at best a nuisance that stands in the way of doing what they have their hearts set on

---

[1]Back in the 1960s, Professor George J. Stigler of the University of Chicago, already one of the leading economists of his day and destined to become a Nobel Prize winner, used to sell reprints of an article by Frank Knight to his graduate students for 25 cents each. It is very unlikely that either Stigler or Knight did this for the money. Rather, it was a way to allocate copies of the reprints— of which there was not an unlimited supply— so that they went to those students who actually wanted to read them, rather than to all those who would have taken them if they had been handed out free of charge.

doing. At worst, economics is seen as a needlessly narrow, if not morally warped, way of looking at the world.

Such condemnations of economics are due to the fundamental fact that economics is the study of the use of scarce resources which have alternative uses. We might all be happier in a world where there were no such constraints to force us into choices and trade-offs that we would rather not face. But that is not the world that human beings live in—or have ever lived in, during thousands of years of recorded history.

In the world that people live in, and are likely to live in for centuries to come, trade-offs are inescapable. Even if we refuse to make a choice, circumstances will make choices for us, as we run out of resources for many important things that we could have had, if only we had taken the trouble to weigh alternatives.

MARKETS AND GREED

"Greed" is seldom defined. Virtually everyone would prefer to get a higher price for what he sells and pay a lower price for what he buys. Would you pay a dollar for a newspaper that was available for fifty cents? Or offer to work for half of what an employer was willing to pay you? Would adding a string of zeros to prices or salaries change the principle or the definition of greed? It is hard to see why it should. But, if everybody is greedy, then the word is virtually meaningless. If it refers to people who desire far more money than most others would aspire to, then the history of most great American fortunes—Ford, Rockefeller, Carnegie, etc.—suggests that the way to amass vast amounts of wealth is to figure out some way to provide goods and services at *lower* prices, not higher prices.

Back in the nineteenth century, Richard Sears was ferociously determined to overtake Montgomery Ward, the world's largest retailer at that time, and worked tirelessly for incredible hours toward that end, sometimes taking risks that bordered on the reckless. Sears sought out every way of cutting costs, so that he could undercut Ward's prices, and every way of attracting customers away from all his rivals. He did all this, not because he did not have enough money to live on, but because he wanted more—and he wanted his company to be number one. If that is our definition of "greed," then he was greedy. More important, in this case as in many others, it was precisely such greed that led to *lower* prices. That was how Sears overtook Montgomery Ward and replaced it as the leading retailer in the country at the beginning of the twentieth century. In later years, that is how Wal-Mart over-took Sears.

Those who condemn greed may espouse "non-economic values." But lofty talk about "non-economic values" too often amounts to very selfish attempts to have one's own values subsidized by others, obviously at the expense of those other people's values. A typical example of this appeared in a letter to *Editor & Publisher* magazine, written by a newspaper columnist who criti-cized "the annual profit requirements faced by newspapers" due to "the de-mands of faceless Wall Street financial analysts who seem, from where I sit, insensitive to the vagaries of newspaper journalism."

Despite the rhetorical device of describing some parties to a transaction in less than human terms ("faceless Wall Street analysts"), they are all people and they all have their own interests, which must be mutually reconciled in one way or another, if those who supply the money that enables newspapers to operate are to be willing to continue to do so. Although people who work on Wall Street may control millions of dollars each, this is not all their own personal money by any means. Much of it comes from the savings, or the money paid into pension funds, by millions of other people, many of whom have very modest incomes.

If "the vagaries of newspaper journalism" make it difficult to earn as high a return on investments in newspapers or newspaper chains as might be earned elsewhere in the economy, why should workers whose pension funds will be needed to provide for their old age subsidize newspaper chains by accepting a lower rate of return on money invested in such corporations? Since many editors and columnists earn much more than some of the people whose pay-ments into pension funds supply newspapers with the money to operate, it would seem especially strange to expect people with lower incomes to be subsidizing people with higher incomes—teachers and mechanics, for exam-ple, subsidizing editors and reporters.

Why should financial analysts, as the intermediaries handling pension funds and other investments from vast numbers of people, betray those peo-ple who have entrusted their savings to them by accepting less of a return from newspapers than what is available from other sectors of the economy? If good journalism—however defined—results in lower rates of return on the money invested in newspaper chains, whatever special costs of newspa-per publishing are responsible for this can be borne by any of a number of people who benefit from newspapers. Readers can pay higher prices, colum-nists, editors and reporters can accept lower salaries, advertisers can pay higher rates.

Why should the sacrifice be forced onto mechanics, nurses, teachers, etc., around the country whose personal savings and pension funds provide the money that newspaper chains acquire by selling corporate stocks and bonds? Why should other sectors of the economy that are willing to pay more for the use of these funds be deprived of such resources for the sake of one particular sector?

The point here is not how to solve the problems of the newspaper industry. The point is to show how differently things look when considered from the standpoint of allocating scarce resources which have alternative uses. This fundamental economic reality is obscured by emotional rhetoric that ignores the interests and values of many people by summarizing them via unsympathetic intermediaries such as "insensitive" financial analysts, while competing interests are expressed in idealistic terms, such as journalistic quality. Financial analysts may be as sensitive to the people they are serving as others are to the very different constituencies they represent.

Both in the private sector and in the government sector, there are always values that some people think worthy enough that other people should have to pay for them—but not that they should have to pay for them themselves. Nowhere is the weighing of some values against other values obscured more often by rhetoric than when discussing government policies. Taxing away what other people have earned, in order to finance one's own moral adventures via social programs, is often depicted as a humanitarian endeavor, while allowing others the same freedom and dignity as oneself, so that they can make their own choices with their own earnings, is considered to be pandering to "greed." Greed for power is no less dangerous than greed for money, and has shed far more blood in the process. Political authorities have often had "non-economic values" that were devastating to the general population.

Does a free market, as a mechanism for mutual accommodation, facilitate greed as it facilitates the fulfillment of people's other desires? It certainly does not prevent greed, though it does exact a quid pro quo—providing others with something that they want, in order to get them to part with their money. A more relevant question, however, is whether other economic systems, including those founded on altruistic and egalitarian principles, actually end up with less greed than an economic system that depends on prices to allocate scarce resources.

Although socialist systems, including the Communist variety, began as attempts to apply egalitarian principles, examples of sacrificing the well-being millions of people for the well-being of those with political power abounded in the Soviet Union and the Communist bloc in general. At the purely economic level, the ruling *nomenklatura* of the U.S.S.R. had separate stores in which only they were eligible to make purchases, as well as other government-supported facilities to which they alone had access. These were of course the best stores, with the most abundant supplies of the commodities most in demand. In addition, the housing, medical care and other facilities open to Communist Party bosses was likewise the best. The rhetoric of equality—egalitarian terms like "comrade" and "people's democracy"—was no match for the reality of greed, especially when that greed could use the power of a totalitarian state, instead of having to supply others' desires in order to earn their money.

Even in a democratic country like India, the era of massive government controls over the economy—lasting for nearly half a century, from independence in 1947 to the beginning of the last decade of the twentieth century—was an era of massive corruption of both high officials and innumerable petty bureaucrats, whose permissions were necessary to do virtually all of the ordinary things that people do at will in a free market economy. Pervasive bribery was only part of that cost. The inefficiencies created by intrusive bureaucratic controls have been estimated to have cost the economy vast amounts of lost production that would have made the average Indians' income hundreds of dollars a year higher. In one of the poorest countries in the world, where malnutrition was a serious problem for many, such a loss meant far more than whether the average American's annual income was a few hundred dollars more or less.

Greed can flourish under very different economic systems. The only real question is: What are its actual consequences under these systems? Where the desire for a fortune can be satisfied by finding ways to lower prices and thereby expand the market for one's output, that is very different from a system where that same desire is more readily fulfilled by imposing political power. In other words, greed is not the product of one particular economic system, but something that all economic, political, and social systems have to cope with in one way or another.

People who deplore greed often show a disdain for wealth. Although a disdain for wealth is often admired, only those who already have a certain amount of wealth can afford to disdain any further pursuit of it. Wealth means options and who would want fewer options? More important, from the standpoint of society as a whole, wealth is the only thing that can prevent poverty. Yet many people who claim to be concerned about poverty show remarkably little interest in how wealth is generated or which policies make it harder or easier to create more.

One of the special variations on the theme of greed is that some businesses are guilty of "charging all that the traffic will bear." Often such statements are made, not simply as a moral condemnation, but as a causal explanation of prices that are considered to be "too high" for one reason or another. If widgets have been selling for five dollars apiece for some time and suddenly the price rises to eight dollars, then the explanation that is offered may be that the widget manufacturers are now charging all that the traffic will bear.

As a causal explanation, this immediately raises a question: Why were they not charging all that the traffic would bear before? Chances are that they were. It is just that the traffic would not bear more than five dollars before and will now bear eight. Therefore what needs to be understood is a causal explanation of what has changed, if widget manufacturers were charging all that the traffic would bear both times.

It is not just businesses that charge all that the traffic will bear. The very people who are making this accusation would seldom agree to work for half of their present salaries—or even three-quarters of their present salaries. They are charging what the traffic will bear for their work. And if someone else offers to pay them twice what they are currently earning, it is very unlikely that they will continue working for their current employer, unless that employer matches the offer.

Strictly speaking, a business is unlikely to charge literally all that the traffic will bear. If General Motors is selling a certain automobile for $25,000, it could probably still sell some to real devotees of that particular car if they doubled the price to $50,000. But, although the traffic would bear a price of $50,000, sales would probably be so reduced that GM would not make as much money as they would by charging $25,000. However, we can take the expression "charging what the traffic will bear" as meaning simply maximizing total profits. What we really need to understand are the implications of saying that higher prices are due to profit maximizing. We also need to understand the consequences of trying to stop it.

During the California electricity crisis of 2000–2001, for example, as the wholesale price of electricity suddenly shot up far above what they had been, some electricity generating companies were accused of charging whatever the traffic would bear. Why would the traffic bear higher electricity prices in 2000 and 2001 than before? Not surprisingly, it had to do with supply and demand.

As the price of the fuels used to generate electricity rose, so did the cost of generating a given amount of electricity. Whereas the price of natural gas delivered to electric utilities in California was only $2.70 per million British thermal units (BTUs) in 1998–1999, by the summer of 2000 the price had nearly doubled to $5.00 per million BTUs. This was part of a nationwide increase in natural gas prices, as a result of a cold winter after several mild winters, thereby causing more natural gas to be used for heating than in the previous years. In the meantime, the international oil cartel raised the price of petroleum, which is also used to generate electricity. Moreover, this all happened while a west coast drought reduced the amount of water passing over hydroelectric dams, thereby generating less electricity than usual.

Meanwhile, on the demand side, Pacific coast winters were colder than usual and summers were hotter than usual in California and Nevada. This meant that more electricity was being used for heating in the winter and for cooling in the summer. In short, there was a reduction in the quantity of electricity available at a given cost and an increase in the quantity of electricity demanded at existing prices. A price rise under these conditions is hardly surprising.

Unfortunately, most members of the general public were unaware of these factors behind the suddenly rising prices, and so were resentful and became receptive to those who blamed the price increases on power companies' charging what the traffic would bear. If this were just a philosophical issue, it would have no economic implications. But when the political consequences included price "caps" placed on electricity sold to western states, that in turn led to economic consequences.

When there was more electricity demanded than supplied at government-controlled prices in the western states, power generators had a choice of where to sell their output, just as a landlord has a choice of which of the surplus applicants to rent his apartments to under rent control. Not surprisingly, they sold their electricity to states not covered by the price controls. In other words, California and other western states received less electricity than they would have received if the electricity-generating companies had been allowed to charge what the traffic would bear.

Had the price controls been nationwide, then California would no doubt have received a larger share of the electricity being generated in other states. However, it is doubtful whether the total amount of electricity generated nationwide would have remained unchanged. More likely, less electricity would have been produced nationwide when its price was held down artificially nationwide, and more shortages and blackouts would have occurred across the country, instead of only in California and Nevada.

Electricity is only an example. The same principle applies much more widely. To say that the traffic will bear a higher price is to say that the quantity demanded—of electricity, widgets, cameras, or whatever—exceeds the quantity supplied at the current price. Price controls under these conditions virtually guarantee that the shortage will not be corrected. Focusing on the seller's "greed" neither explains what caused the shortage nor offers any way of ending it.

SAVING LIVES

Perhaps the strongest arguments for "non-economic values" are those involving human lives. Many highly costly laws, policies, or devices designed to safeguard the public from lethal hazards are defended on grounds that "if it saves just one human life" it is worth whatever it costs. Powerful as the moral and emotional appeal of such pronouncements may be, they cannot withstand scrutiny in a world where scarce resources have alternative uses.

One of those alternative uses is saving other human lives in other ways. Few things have saved as many lives as the simple growth of wealth. An earthquake powerful enough to kill a dozen people in California will kill hundreds of people in some less affluent country and thousands in a Third World nation. Greater wealth enables California buildings, bridges, and other structures to be built to withstand far greater stresses than similar structures can withstand in poorer countries. Those injured in an earthquake in California can be rushed far more quickly to far more elaborately equipped hospitals with larger numbers of more highly trained medical personnel. This is just one of innumerable ways in which wealth saves lives.

There have been various calculations of how much of a rise in national income saves how many lives. Whatever the correct figure may be—X million dollars to save one life—anything that prevents national income from rising that much has, in effect, cost a life. If some particular safety law, policy, or device costs 5X million dollars, either directly or in its inhibiting effect on economic growth, then it can no longer be said to be worth it "if it saves just one human life" because it does so at the cost of 5 other human lives. There is no escaping trade-offs, so long as resources are scarce and have alternative uses.

"UNMET NEEDS"

One of the most common—and certainly one of the most profound—misconceptions of economics involves "unmet needs." Politicians, journalists, and academicians are almost continuously pointing out unmet needs in our society that should be supplied by some government program or other. Most of these are things that most of us wish our society had more of.

What is wrong with that? Let us go back to square one. If economics is the study of the use of scarce resources which have alternative uses, then it follows that there will always be unmet needs. Some particular desires can be singled out and met 100 percent, but that only means that other desires will be even more unfulfilled than they are now.

Anyone who has driven in most big cities will undoubtedly feel that there is an unmet need for more parking spaces. But, while it is both economically and technologically possible to build cities in such a way as to have a parking space available for anyone who wants one, anywhere in the city, at any hour or the day or night, does it follow that we should do it?

The cost of building vast new underground parking garages, or of tearing down existing buildings to create parking garages above ground, or of designing new cities with fewer buildings and more parking lots, would all be astronomically costly. What other things are we prepared to give up, in order to have this automotive heaven? Fewer hospitals? Less police protection? Fewer fire departments? Are we prepared to put up with even more unmet needs in these areas? Maybe some would give up public libraries in order to have more places to park. But, whatever choices are made and however it is done, there will still be more unmet needs elsewhere, as a result of meeting an unmet need for more parking spaces.

We may differ among ourselves as to what is worth sacrificing in order to have more of something else. The point here is more fundamental: Merely demonstrating an unmet need is not sufficient to say that it should be met—not when resources are scarce and have alternative uses.

In the case of parking spaces, what might appear to be cheaper, when measured only in government expenditures, would be to restrict or forbid the use of private automobiles in cities, adjusting the number of cars to the number of existing parking spaces, instead of vice-versa. Moreover, passing and enforcing such a law would cost a tiny fraction of the cost of greatly expanding the number of parking spaces. But this saving in government expenditures would have to be weighed against the vast private expenditures currently devoted to the purchase, maintenance, and parking of automobiles in cities. Obviously these expenditures would not have been undertaken in the first place if those who pay these prices did not find the benefits to be worth it to them.

To go back to square one again, *costs are foregone opportunities*, not government expenditures. Forcing thousands of people to forego opportunities for which they have willingly paid vast amounts is a cost that may far outweigh the savings from not having to build more parking spaces or do the other things necessary to accommodate cars in cities. None of this says that we should have either more or fewer parking spaces in cities. What it says is that the way this issue—and many others—is presented makes no sense in a world of scarce resources which have alternative uses. That is a world of trade-offs, not solutions—and whatever trade-off is decided upon will still leave unmet needs.

So long as we respond gullibly to political rhetoric about unmet needs, we will arbitrarily choose to shift resources to whatever the featured unmet need of the day happens to be and away from other things. Then, when another politician—or perhaps even the same politician at a later time—discovers that robbing Peter to pay Paul has left Paul worse off, and now wants to help him meet his unmet needs, we will start shifting resources in another direction. In short, we will be like a dog chasing his tail in a circle and getting no closer, no matter how fast he runs.

This is not to say that we have the ideal trade-offs already and should leave them alone. Rather, it says that whatever trade-offs we make should be seen from the outset as trade-offs—not meeting unmet needs.

The very word "needs" arbitrarily puts some desires on a higher plane than others, as categorically more important. But, however urgent it may be to have *some* food and some water, in order to sustain life itself, nevertheless—beyond some point—both become not only unnecessary but even counter-productive and dangerous. Widespread obesity among Americans shows that food has already reached that point and anyone who has suffered the ravages of flood (even if it is only a flooded basement) knows that water can reach that point as well. In short, even the most urgent needs remain needs only within a given range. We cannot live half an hour without oxygen, but even oxygen beyond some concentration level can promote the growth of cancer and has been known to make newborn babies blind for life. There is a reason why hospitals do not use oxygen tanks willy-nilly.

In short, nothing is a "need" categorically, regardless of how urgent it may be to have at particular times and places and in particular amounts. Unfortunately, most laws and government policies apply categorically, if only because of the dangers in leaving every official to become a petty despot in interpreting what these laws and policies mean and when they should apply. In this context, calling something a "need" categorically is playing with fire. Many complaints that some basically good government policy has been applied stupidly may fail to address the underlying problem of categorical laws in an incremental world. There may not have been any intelligent way to apply categorically a policy designed to meet desires whose benefits vary incrementally and ultimately cease to be benefits.

By its very nature, as a study of the use of scarce resources which have alternative uses, economics is about incremental trade-offs—not about "needs" or "solutions." That may be why economists have never been as popular as politicians who promise to solve our problems and meet our needs.

WHAT IS "WASTE"?

Although efficiency is what economics is all about, there are many false notions as to what constitutes "efficiency." Some think that it can be reduced to output per man-hour or to more miles per gallon or larger crops per acre. It cannot.

Efficiency is inescapably bound up with what people want—and at what cost. Even an apparently scientific question like the efficiency of an automobile engine rests ultimately on what you want the car to do. Otherwise, all automobile engines are 100 percent efficient, in the sense that all the energy they get from gasoline is used, whether in moving the car forward, overcoming internal friction in the engine, shaking the car body randomly, generating heat that is radiated out into the air, etc. It is only after you define what you want as moving the car forward that the efficiency of different engines can be compared in terms of what percentage of their power is used for that particular purpose.

When a third party defines efficiency for other people, that often conflicts with what those other people prefer in their own individually differing circumstances. For example, there have been many laments about Americans using gasoline in "wasteful" ways during the 1980s and 1990s, as contrasted with their more "fuel-efficient" behavior in the 1970s. But the reason for the change was that the real price of gasoline was lower in the 1980s and 1990s, reflecting large increases in both the immediate supply and the known reserves of petroleum in the world. Consumers were responding to the changing realities conveyed by prices, rather than to the fashionable but unsubstantiated alarms conveyed by words in the media and in politics.

During the 1970s, an international oil cartel—the Organization of Petroleum Exporting Countries (OPEC)—deliberately cut back on petroleum production, disrupting economies around the world. In the United States, government price controls turned a minor adjustment into a major shortage.

By the 1990s, new discoveries of petroleum deposits and the weakening of the OPEC cartel had the world awash in oil, with the real price of gasoline hitting an all-time low.

It is not wasteful to increase one's use of resources that have become more abundant. That is precisely what is supposed to happen in a price-coordinated economy because that is the most efficient behavior, with efficiency being defined as the most effective way of satisfying people's desires. Waste is no more objectively definable than its opposite, efficiency. The arbitrary assumption that it is serves only to let third parties impose their definitions on other people, who obviously would not be doing the things that observers define as wasteful if they themselves did not see matters differently.

Chapter 23

Myths About Markets

There are so many myths about markets that only a sample can be presented here. Because the underlying logic of these misconceptions is seldom spelled out, making that logic plain can seem like an exercise in satire. For example, many people argue as if businesses can set prices by an act of will, as if economic activity is a zero-sum process, in which what is gained by some is lost by others, and as if those who favor free market competition are pro-business. All these are demonstrably false beliefs. So is the so-called "trickle-down theory." There is also much confusion about morality and markets.

MORALITY AND MARKETS

The market is as moral or immoral as the people in it. So is the government. The fact that we call one set of people "the market" and another set of people "society" does not mean that the moral or other imperfections of first set of people automatically justify having the second set of imperfect people over-ruling their decisions. Like economics, the market is not some separate entity with its own values. It is people making their own individual choices and their mutual accommodations.

Once it was fashionable to contrast the selfishness of the isolated individual in a market economy with cooperative actions among people with a more communal spirit under various forms of socialism. One reason such rhetorical or ideological fashions no longer have the same effectiveness is the actual track record of socialist systems in practice. What also needs to be considered is the track record of market economies in creating widespread cooperation among people through individual incentives. Such cooperation does not even stop at national borders.

The Indian software company Wipro creates and maintains computer systems for the American hardware chain Home Depot and, through the magic of the electronic revolution, telephone calls made by British customers to Harrod's department store in London are answered by Indians living near Delhi. Fires in the oil fields of the Middle East have been put out by a company in Texas that specializes in putting out oil fires. More than half the life insurance on people in the Philippines, Malaysia and Singapore is provided by insurance companies in other countries. Britain's hot-selling automobile, the Mini Cooper, is made with engines from Brazil, sheet metal from Germany and various other parts manufactured in Czechoslovakia. In the international diamond center in Antwerp, Hasidic Jews and Jains from India dominate the industry and interact socially as well. As the *Wall Street Journal* reported:

> In Antwerp, Jews and Indians have come to be so embedded in each other's lives that many of the Indian dealers speak Hebrew and Yiddish. Most traditional Indian weddings have a special kosher section. After a devastating earthquake in the Indian state of Gujarat in 2001, Jewish diamond traders raised thousands of dollars for humanitarian aid.

Is cooperation any less because the incentives behind it are the individual benefits of the participants?

Despite the painful facts of history, the idea persists in many places that political decisions are more moral than decisions made through the marketplace. Writers for the *San Francisco Chronicle* referred to "how amoral the marketplace can be" when explaining why the water supply owned by the city of Stockton could not be entrusted to private enterprise. "Water is too life-sustaining a commodity to go into the marketplace with," they quoted the mayor of Stockton as saying. Yet, every day, life-sustaining food is supplied through private enterprises, as are many life-saving medicines. The net result is that people in most market economies are less likely to suffer from malnutrition than from obesity—just the opposite of what happens in countries where political authorities control food—and most new life-saving medicines are developed in market economies, notably that of the United States. As for privately run water systems, they already exist in Argentina. *The Economist* reported on the results of privatization:

Connections to the water and sewerage networks rose, especially among poorer households: most richer households were already hooked up . . . Before privatisation really go under way, in 1995, child mortality rate were falling at much the same pace in municipalities that eventually privatised and those that did not. After 1995, the fall accelerated in privatising municipalities . . . The fall was concentrated in deaths from infectious and parasitic diseases, the sort most likely to be affected by water quality and availability. Death from other causes did not decline.

In Britain as well, the privatized water supply in England has lower water bills, higher quality drinking water, less leakage, and a sewage disposal system that complies with environmental regulations a higher percentage of the time than those in Scotland, where the government runs the water system. Empirical consequences, however, often matter less than deeply ingrained beliefs and attitudes. Whether in urgent or less urgent matters, many believe that those with political power are better qualified to make moral decisions than are the private parties directly concerned. Such attitudes are international. An entrepreneur in India reported his experience with a government minister there:

I had argued that lowering the excise duty would lower consumer prices of shampoos, skin creams, and other toiletries, which in turn would raise their demand. The tax revenues would thus rise, although the tax rate might be lower. Indian women did not need lipsticks and face creams, felt the minister. I replied that all women wanted to look pretty.

"A face cream won't do anything for an ugly face. These are luxuries of the rich," he said. I protested that even a village girl used a paste of haldi so that she could look pretty.

"No, it's best to leave a face to nature," he said impatiently.

"Sir," I pleaded, "how can you decide what she wants? After all, it is her hard-earned money."

"Yes, and I don't want her wasting it. Let her buy food. I don't want multinational companies getting rich selling face cream to poor Indians."

The idea that third party observers can impose morally better decisions often includes the idea that they can define what are "luxuries of the rich," when it is precisely the progress of free market economies which has turned luxuries of the rich into common amenities of people in general, including the poor. Within the twentieth century, automobiles, telephones, refrigerators, television sets, air-conditioners, and personal computers all went from being luxuries of the rich to being common items across the spectrum of Americans and among millions of people in many other market economies.

In the nineteenth century, a President of the United States was criticized for spending the government's money to install such a luxury item as a bathtub in the White House. In past centuries, even such things as oranges, sugar, and cocoa were luxuries of the rich in Europe. Not only do third party definitions of what is a luxury of the rich fail to account for such changes, the stifling of free markets by third parties enables such things to remain exclusive luxuries longer than they would otherwise.

PRICES

There seem to be almost as many myths about prices as there are prices. For example, it is common to hear that the same thing is sold at very different prices by different sellers. While this can happen, usually this involves defining things as being "the same" when in fact they are not. Other myths include the notion that "greedy" sellers are responsible for rising prices or that "predatory" businesses destroy competition by selling below cost and bankrupting their rivals, so that they can then raise prices to monopolistic levels afterward. While these are only a small sample, looking at them closely may illustrate how easy it is to create a plausible-sounding myth and get it accepted by many otherwise intelligent people, who simply do not bother to scrutinize the logic or the evidence.

Different Prices for the "Same" Thing

Physically identical things are often sold for different prices, usually because of accompanying conditions that are quite different. As noted in Chapter 6, two airline passengers sitting side by side in the same plane may have paid very different fares because one bought a guaranteed reservation, while the other was a standby who got on board when there happened to be space available. What they really bought were two very different probabilities of getting on board that plane. Only in retrospect did they end up with the same thing—but people do not act in retrospect. As of the time they acted, they bought very different things. Similarly, someone who wins an automobile with a $20 lottery ticket can end up with the same car for which someone else paid $20,000. But one bought a low probability of getting a car and the other bought a virtual certainty. The car they ended up with may be the same but what they bought was not the same.

Goods sold in attractively decorated stores with polished and sophisticated sales staffs, as well as easy return policies, are likely to cost more than the physically identical products sold in a stark warehouse store with a no-refund policy. Christmas cards can usually be bought for much lower prices on December 26th than on December 24th, even though the cards are physically identical to what they were when they were in great demand before Christmas.

A consumer magazine in northern California compared the total cost of buying the identical set of food items of the same brands in various stores in their area. These total costs ranged from $80 in the least expensive store to $125 in the most expensive. Indeed, they ranged from $98 to $103 at three different Safeway supermarkets.

Part of the reason for the variations in price was the variation in the cost of real estate in the different communities—the store with the lowest prices being located in less expensive Fremont and the one with the highest prices being located in San Francisco, which has had the highest real estate prices of any major city in the country. The cost of the land on which the stores sat was different and these costs had to be recovered from the prices charged the stores' customers.

Another reason is the cost of inventory. The cheapest store had only 49 percent of the items in stock at a given time, while all three Safeway stores had more than three-quarters of the items in stock. In other words, going to different stores meant having different probabilities of finding what you wanted. It was like the difference between buying reserved seats on an airplane versus being a standby. Cost differences reflected differences in availability, which is to say, differences in the costs of maintaining inventory, even when the particular commodities were physically the same. It also meant differences in the costs measured in the time that customer would have to spend going from store to store to find all the items on a grocery shopping list.

Mistakes or miscalculations may sometimes cause the same thing to be sold for different prices under comparable conditions temporarily, but competition usually makes this a passing phenomenon. When customers go where prices are lower, those whose prices are higher have little choice but to lower their prices, if they are not offering some offsetting advantages along with the same physical product. Where there are permanently different prices for things that are truly the same, the higher-price seller usually ends up going out of business for lack of customers.

"Predatory" Pricing

One of the popular myths that has become part of the tradition of anti-trust law is "predatory pricing." According to this theory, a big company that is out to eliminate its smaller competitors and take over their share of the market will lower its prices to a level that dooms the competitor to unsustainable losses and forces it out of business. Then, having acquired a monopolistic position, it will raise its prices—not just to the previous level, but to new and higher levels in keeping with its new monopolistic position. Thus, it recoups its losses and enjoys above-normal profits thereafter, at the expense of the consumers.

One of the most remarkable things about this theory is that those who advocate it seldom provide concrete examples of when it ever actually happened. Perhaps even more remarkable, they have not had to do so, even in courts of law, in anti-trust cases.

Both the A & P grocery chain in the 1940s and the Microsoft Corporation in the 1990s were accused of pursuing such a practice in anti-trust cases, but without a single example of this process having gone to completion. Instead, their current low prices (in the case of A & P) or the inclusion of a free Internet browser in Windows software (in the case of Microsoft) have been interpreted as directed toward that end—though not with having actually achieved it. Since it is impossible to prove a negative, the accused company cannot disprove that it was pursuing such a goal, and the issue simply becomes a question of whether those who hear the charge choose to believe it. But this is more than just a theory without evidence. It is something that it makes little or no economic sense.

A company that sustains losses by selling below cost to drive out a competitor is following a very risky strategy. The only thing it can be sure of is losing money initially. Whether it will ever recover enough extra profits to make the gamble pay off in the long run is problematical. Whether it can do so and escape the anti-trust laws is even more problematical—and these laws can lead to millions of dollars in fines and/or the dismemberment of the company. But, even if our would-be predator manages somehow to overcome these problems, it is by no means clear that eliminating all existing competitors will mean eliminating competition.

Even when a rival firm has been forced into bankruptcy, its physical equipment and the skills of the people who once made it viable do not vanish into
thin air. A new entrepreneur can come along and acquire both—perhaps at
low distress sale prices for both the physical equipment and the unemployed
workers, enabling the new competitor to have lower costs than the old and
hence be a more dangerous rival.

As an illustration of what can happen, back in 1933 *The Washington Post*
went bankrupt, though not because of predatory pricing. In any event, this
bankruptcy did not cause the printing presses, the building, or the reporters
to disappear. All were acquired by publisher Eugene Meyer, at a price that
was less than one-fifth of what he had bid unsuccessfully for the same newspaper just four years earlier. In the decades that followed, under new ownership and management, *The Washington Post* grew to become the largest
newspaper in the nation's capital, while its rivals disappeared one by one, until it was the only major newspaper in town by 1978. By the early twenty-
first century, *The Washington Post* had one of the five largest circulations in
the country.

Bankruptcy can eliminate particular owners and managers, but it does not
eliminate competition in the form of new people, who can either take over
an existing bankrupt enterprise or start their own new business from scratch
in the same industry. Destroying a particular competitor without destroying
competition can be an expensive endeavor, with little prospect of recouping
the losses by subsequent monopoly profits.

BRAND NAMES

Brand names are often thought to be just ways of being able to charge a
higher price for the same product by persuading people through advertising
that there is a quality difference, when in fact there is no such difference. In
other words, brand names are considered to be useless things from the standpoint of the consumer's interests. As India's Prime Minister Nehru once
asked, "Why do we need nineteen brands of toothpaste?"

In reality, brand names serve a number of purposes from the standpoint of
the consumer. Brands are a way of economizing on scarce knowledge, and of
forcing producers to compete in quality and price.

When you drive into a town you have never seen before and want to get
some gasoline for your car or to eat a hamburger, you have no direct way of

knowing what is in the gasoline that some stranger at the filling station is putting into your tank or what is in the hamburger that another stranger is cooking for you to eat at a roadside stand that you have never seen before. But, if the filling station's sign says Chevron and the restaurant's sign says McDonald's, then you don't worry about it. At worst, if something terrible happens, you can sue a multi-billion-dollar corporation. You know it, the corporation knows it, and the local dealer knows it. That is what reduces the likelihood that something terrible will happen.

On the other hand, imagine if you pull into a no-name filling station in some little town and the stranger there puts something into your tank that messes up your engine or—worse yet—if you eat a no-name hamburger that sends you to the hospital. Your chances of suing the local business owner successfully (perhaps before a jury of his friends and neighbors) may be considerably less. Moreover, even if you should win, the chances of collecting enough money to compensate you for all the trouble you have been put through is more remote.

Brand names are not guarantees. But they do reduce the range of uncertainty. If a hotel sign says Hyatt Regency, chances are you will not have to worry about whether the bed sheets in your room were changed since the last person slept there. If the camera you buy is a Nikon, it is unlikely to jam up the first time you wind the film. Even if you stop at a dingy and run-down little store in a strange town, you are not afraid to drink a soda they sell you, if it is a bottle or can of Coca Cola or Seven-Up. Imagine, however, if the owner of this unsavory little place mixed you a soda at his own soda fountain. Would you have the same confidence in drinking it?

Like everything else in the economy, brand names have both benefits and costs. A hotel with a Hyatt Regency sign out front is likely to charge you more for the same size and quality of room, and accompanying service, than you would pay in some comparable, locally-run, independent hotel *if you knew where to look*. Someone who regularly stops in this town on business trips might well find a locally-run hotel that is a better deal. But it is as rational for you to look for a brand name when passing through for the first time as it is for the regular traveller to go where he knows he can get the same things for less.

Since brand names are a substitute for specific knowledge, how valuable they are depends on how much knowledge you already have about the particular product or service. Someone who is very knowledgeable about photography might be able to safely get a bargain on an off-brand camera or lens, or even a second-hand camera or lens. But that same person might be well advised to stick to well known brands of new stereo equipment, if his knowledge in that field falls far short of his expertise in photography.

Many critics of brand names argue that the main brands "are all alike." Even when that is so, the brand names still perform a valuable function. All the brands may be better than they would have to be if the product were sold under anonymous or generic labels. Both Kodak and Fuji film have to be better than they would have to be if boxes simply said "Film," without any reference to the manufacturer. But, when film is sold with brand names on the boxes, Kodak knows that it will lose millions of dollars in sales if it falls behind Fuji in quality and Fuji knows that it will lose millions if it falls behind Kodak. When United Parcel Service first began to compete with Federal Express in overnight deliveries, UPS announced that it would deliver packages by 3 PM the next day. Federal Express immediately announced that it would deliver them by 10:30 AM—which both companies subsequently did.

Brands have not always existed. They came into existence and then survived and spread for a reason. In eighteenth century England, for example, only a few luxury goods, such as Chippendale furniture, were known by their manufacturer's brand name. It was an innovation when Josiah Wedgwood put his name on chinaware that he sold and which ultimately became world famous for its quality and appearance.

In nineteenth century America, most food processors did not put brand names on the food that they sold—a situation which allowed adulteration of food to flourish. When Henry Heinz entered this business and sold unadulterated processed food, he identified his products with his name, reaping the benefits of the reputation he established among consumers, which allowed his company to expand rapidly and an array of new processed foods bearing his name to be readily accepted by the public. In short, the rise of brands promoted better quality by allowing consumers to distinguish and choose, and forcing producers to take responsibility for what they made, reaping rewards when it was good and losing customers when it was not.

Quality standards for hamburgers, milk shakes and French fries were all revolutionized in the 1950s and 1960s by McDonald's, whose methods and machinery were later copied by some of their leading competitors. But the whole industry's standards became higher because McDonald's spent millions of dollars researching the growing, storage and processing of potatoes, in addition to making unannounced visits to its potato suppliers, as it did to its suppliers of hamburger meat, in order to ensure that its quality specifications were being followed, while its huge buying power forced dairies to supply a higher quality of milk shake mix that McDonald's demanded. After all this was done, some might say in later years that leading hamburger chains were "all alike," but they were all better because McDonald's could first reap the rewards of having its brand name identified in the public mind with higher quality products than they had previously been used to in hamburger stands.

Even when the various brands of a product are made to the same formula by law, as with aspirin, quality control is promoted when each producer of each bottle of aspirin is identified than when the producer is anonymous. Moreover, the best-known brand has the most to lose if some impurity gets into the aspirin during production and causes anyone injury or death. This is especially important with foods and medicines.

McDonald's not only has to meet the standards set by the government, it has to meet the standards set by the competition of Wendy's and Burger King. If Campbell's soup were identified on the label only as "soup"—or "Tomato Soup," "Clam Chowder," etc.—the pressures on all canned soup producers to maintain both safety and quality would be less.

In countries where there are no brand names, or where there is only one producer created or authorized by the government, the quality of the product or service tends to be notoriously low. During the days of the Soviet Union, the country's only airline, Aeroflot, became the epitome of bad service and rudeness to passengers. After the dissolution of the Soviet Union, a new privately financed airline began to have great success, in part because its passengers appreciated being treated like human beings for a change. The management of the new airline declared that its employment policy was that it would not hire anyone who had ever worked for Aeroflot.

Similarly, one of the reasons for the great success of McDonald's in Moscow—the largest McDonald's in the world, with lines of people waiting to get into it—is that it was being compared to the previous bad quality of service in Soviet restaurants, not to Wendy's or Burger King.

Competition in the marketplace affects not only price but quality. Brand names make the competitors responsible for both.

THE ROLE OF PROFITS

Business and the Market

Those who favor government intervention in the economy often depict those who prefer free competition as pro-business apologists. This has been profoundly wrong for at least two centuries. Adam Smith, the eighteenth-century father of free-market economics, was so scathingly critical of businessmen that it would be impossible to find a single favorable reference to them in his 900-page classic, *The Wealth of Nations*.[1] Instead, Smith warned against "the clamour and sophistry of merchants and manufacturers." Any suggestions about laws and policies coming from such people, he said, ought to be "carefully examined, not only with the most scrupulous, but with the most suspicious attention." In the nineteenth century, the next great classical economist in the free-market tradition, David Ricardo, spoke of businessmen as "notoriously ignorant of the most obvious principles" of economics. Knowing how to run a business is not the same as understanding the larger and very different issues involved in knowing how the economy as a whole affects the population as a whole. Skepticism about the business community has remained part of the tradition of free-market economists throughout the twentieth century as well, with Milton Friedman's views being very similar to those of Adam Smith on this point.

Free market competition has often been opposed by the business community, from Adam Smith's time to our own. It was business interests which promoted the pervasive policies of government intervention known as "mercantilism" in the centuries before Smith and others made the case for ending such interventions and establishing free markets. Then, after free market principles had gained wider acceptance in the nineteenth and twentieth centuries, business leaders were of course prepared to invoke those principles for political reasons, whenever it suited their particular purposes of the moment. But business leaders and organizations have proven equally willing to seek government intervention to keep out foreign competition, bail out failing corporations and banks, and receive billions of dollars in agricultural subsidies, ostensibly for the sake of saving family farms, but in reality going disproportionately to large agricultural corporations.

When President Richard Nixon imposed the first peacetime wage and price controls in 1971, he was publicly praised by the chairman of General Motors, and cooperation with these policies was urged by the National Association of Manufacturers and the U. S. Chamber of Commerce. Businesses themselves have pushed for laws making it harder for outside investors to take over a corporation and replace its management. Business leaders are not

---

[1]When I taught economics, I used to offer to give an A to any student who could find a favorable reference to businessmen in *The Wealth of Nations*. None ever did.

wedded to a free market philosophy or any other philosophy. They promote their own self-interest any way they can, like other special interest groups. Economists and others who are in fact supporters of free markets have known that for at least two centuries.

As noted in earlier chapters, the efficient uses of scarce resources by the economy as a whole depends on a system that features both profits and losses. Businesses are interested only in the profit half. If they can avoid losses by getting government subsidies, tariffs and other restrictions against imports, or domestic laws that stifle competition in various agricultural products, they will do so. Losses, however, are essential to the process that shifts resources to those who are providing what consumers want at the lowest prices—and away from those who are not.

The American computer industry is a classic example. Over a period of more than a decade, the prices of computers declined by an average of more than 30 percent *annually*. Meanwhile, the advances in computer chip design led to a 30 percent annual increase in the power to process millions of pieces of information per second. Yet, during this incredible era of progress, some computer companies have operated at huge losses, while others have profited greatly. Data General lost $59 million dollars in one year, UNISYS lost $436 million and IBM lost $18 billion in two years. Resources were shifting to other firms that were providing more of what the consumers wanted at lower prices. Symbolic of these changes is that Microsoft's Bill Gates, once just a subcontractor to IBM, became the richest man in America while IBM was losing billions of dollars and laying off more than 100,000 employees. It was all part of the same process.

Much the same story could be told of the airline industry. Between the last year of federal regulation in 1977 and twenty years later in 1997, the average air fare dropped by 40 percent and the average percentage of seats filled on planes rose from 56 percent to 69 percent, while more passengers than ever were carried more safely than ever. Meanwhile, many airlines went bankrupt. That was the cost of greater efficiency. It has been estimated that, during the era of federal regulation, government intervention in the market had caused costs and fares to be 50 percent higher than they would have been in a free market. When the protection of federal regulation was removed, those airlines which could not survive with lower fares and rising fuel costs went out of business.

Even people who understand the need for competition, and for both profits and losses, nevertheless often insist that it should be "fair" competition. But this is a slippery word that can mean almost anything. For many years, there were federal "fair trade" laws designed to prevent chain stores from selling merchandise below list price and thus driving smaller sellers out of business. With international trade likewise, there are those who say that they are for free trade, provided that it is "fair" trade. Here too, it means artificially keeping prices higher than they would be in the absence of government intervention, so that companies with higher costs of doing business can survive. Like discussions of fairness in other contexts besides economics, this kind of reasoning ignores the costs imposed on third parties—in this case, the consumers who pay needlessly high prices to keep less efficient businesses operating, using scarce resources which have more valuable alternative uses.

Some people consider it a valid criticism of corporations that they are "just in business to make profits." By this kind of reasoning, workers are just working to earn their pay. In the process, however, they produce all the things that give their contemporaries the highest standard of living the world has known. What matters is not the motivation but the results. In the case of business, the real question is: What are the *preconditions* for earning a profit?

One preconditions is that profit-seeking corporations cannot squander scarce resources the way Soviet enterprises did. Corporations operating in a market economy have to pay for all their inputs—whether labor, raw materials, or electricity—and they have to pay as much as others are willing to bid for them. Then they have to sell their own end product at a price as low as their competitors are charging. If they fail to do both, they fail to make a profit. And if they keep on failing to make a profit, either the management will be replaced or the whole business will be replaced by some competitor who is more efficient.

Sometimes the charge is made that profits are short-run gains, with the implication that they come at the expense of longer-term considerations. But future values are reflected in the present value of a business' assets. A factory that runs full blast to make a profit today, while neglecting the maintenance and repair of its machinery will immediately see a decline in the value of its property and of its stockholders' stock. It is in the *absence* of a profit-and-loss economy that there are few incentives to maintain the long-run productivity of an industrial enterprise or a collective farm, as in the Soviet Union. What happens to the enterprise after the current management's tenure is over is of little concern in a system where there are no profits and no present values to influence decisions.

Non-Profit Organizations

We have seen that the role of profit-seeking businesses is better understood when they are recognized as profit-and-loss businesses, with all the pressures and incentives created by these dual potentialities. By the same token, what are called "non-profit organizations" can be better understood when they are seen as non-profit *and non-loss* institutions—that is, institutions which operate free of the constraints of a bottom line.

This does not mean that non-profit organizations have unlimited money. It does mean that, with whatever money they do have, non-profit organizations are under very little pressure to achieve their institutional goals to the maximum extent possible with the resources at their disposal. Those who supply those resources include the general public, who cannot closely monitor what happens to their donations or their taxes, and those whose money provided the endowments—$13 billion at Harvard, for example—that help finance non-profit institutions. Much or most of these endowments were left by people who are now dead, who cannot monitor at all.

What would be called "losses" in other kinds of enterprises are called "deficits" in non-profit organizations and serve as reasons given when seeking donations or government subsidies to cover shortfalls. Non-profit organizations have additional sources of income, including fees from those who use their services, such as visitors to museums and audiences for symphony orchestras. These fees are in fact the main source of the more than half a trillion dollars in revenue received annually by non-profit organizations in America. However, these fees do not cover the full costs of their operation—which is to say, the recipients are receiving goods and services that cost more than these recipients are paying and some are receiving them free. Such subsidized beneficiaries cannot impose the same kind of economic discipline as the customers of a profit-and-loss business who are paying the full cost of everything they get.

Under these conditions, the goals of those individuals who happen to be in charge of a non-profit institution at a given time can be substituted for the institution's ostensible goals or the goals of their donors or founders. It has been said, for example, that Henry Ford and John D. Rockefeller would turn over in their graves if they knew what kinds of things are being financed today by the foundations which bear their names. While that is ultimately unknowable, it is known that Henry Ford II resigned from the board of the Ford Foundation in protest against what the foundation was doing with the money left by his grandfather. More generally, it is now widely recognized how difficult it is to establish a foundation to serve a given purpose and expect it to stick to that purpose after the money has been contributed and the donors are dead.

Academic institutions, hospitals and foundations are usually non-profit organizations in the United States, although non-profit institutions cover a wide range and can also engage in activities normally engaged in by profit-seeking enterprises, such as selling Sun Kist oranges or publishing *The Smithsonian* magazine. In whatever activities they engage, non-profit organizations are not under the same pressures to get "the most bang for the buck" as are enterprises in which profit and loss determine their survival. This effects efficiency, not only in the narrow financial sense, but also in the broader sense of achieving avowed purposes. Colleges and universities, for example, can become disseminators of particular ideological views that happen to be in vogue ("political correctness") and restrictors of alternative views, even though the goals of education would be better served by exposing students to a range of contrasting and contending ideas.

Two centuries ago, Adam Smith pointed out how academics running colleges and universities financed by endowments can run them in self-serving ways, being "very indulgent to one another," so that each academic would "consent that his neighbour may neglect his duty, provided he himself is allowed to neglect his own." Widespread complaints today that professors neglect teaching in favor of research, and sometimes neglect both in favor of leisure or other activities, suggest that the underlying principle has not changed much in more than two hundred years. Tenure guaranteeing lifetime appointments are common in non-profit colleges and universities, but are practically unknown in businesses that must meet the competition of the marketplace.

This is only one of the ways in which the employment policies of non-profit organizations have more latitude than those of enterprises that operate in the hope of profit and under the threat of losses. Before World War II, hospitals were among most racially discriminatory of American employers, even though their avowed purposes would have been better served by hiring the best-qualified doctors, even when those doctors happened to be black or Jewish. Non-profit foundations were also among the most racially discriminatory institutions at that time.

The same was true of the academic world, where the first black professor was not hired at a major university until 1940, not long after the first Jewish professor received tenure at Columbia University, which was already more than 150 years old at the time. It was only in the postwar era, with racial attitudes beginning to change in the wake of the horrors of the Nazi Holocaust, that either blacks or Jews began to have more widespread access to positions in non-profit organizations.

None of this should suggest that non-profit organizations are oblivious to money. It is just that the purposes for which the money is spent may be quite different from the purposes for which it was donated. Non-profit organizations can be very eager to get more money, and some even skirt the boundaries of the law to do so. In 1999, for example, non-profit organizations took in about $500 million from sellers of commercial products who were allowed to say or suggest in their advertisements that some foundation or other non-profit organization was favorable toward these products. Commercial endorsements by these tax-exempt organizations are illegal, but denials that these commercial tie-ins were endorsements have usually kept law enforcement officials at bay.

The American Medical Association, for example, collected $600,000 for allowing its logo to be displayed in advertisements for a pharmaceutical drug. Another non-profit organization, The American Cancer Society, pulled in more than a million dollars the same year for allowing the use of its name and logo in advertisements for commercial products, even though it claims that it does not endorse anything. Looked at from the other side, American Express has paid hundreds of millions of dollars to a variety of non-profit organizations for advertising tie-ins.

The fact that some organizations' income is called profit and other organizations' income is not does not change anything economically, however much it may suggest to the unwary that one institution is greedy and the other is not. Many heads of non-profit organizations receive far more money in salary than the average owner of a store or a restaurant receives in profits. It is not uncommon for presidents of leading American universities to receive more than half a million dollars a year in income—and for college football coaches to receive even more.

What changes incentives and constraints is the fact that the money received by a profit-and-loss business comes directly from those who use its goods and services, while the money received by a non-profit organization comes primarily from subsidized beneficiaries, from donors and—indirectly—from the taxpayers who pay the additional taxes made necessary by the tax exemptions of non-profit organizations. That gives the managers of non-profit organization far more room to do what they want, rather than what either the public wants or what their deceased donors wanted when these organizations were set up.

The fact that a non-profit organization can provide its services free or below cost virtually assures a market for its output, without being forced to produce that output at the lowest cost. Indeed, the very nature of the output itself can be changed to meet the preferences of the non-profit officials, among other indulgences that are possible with money donated by people who are unlikely to monitor performance as closely as stockholders or financiers who specialize in corporate takeovers. Despite a tendency in the media to treat non-profit organizations as disinterested, those non-profits which depend on continuing donations from the public have incentives to be alarmists, in order to scare more money out of their contributors.

"TRICKLE DOWN" THEORY

There have been many economic theories over the centuries, accompanied by controversies among different schools of economists. But one of the most politically prominent economic theories today is one that has never existed among economists—the "trickle down" theory.[2]

People who are politically committed to policies of redistributing income and who tend to emphasize the conflicts between business and labor, rather than their mutual interdependence, often accuse those opposed to them of believing that benefits must be given to the wealthy in general or to business in particular, in order that these benefits will eventually "trickle down" to the masses of ordinary people. But no recognized economist of any school of thought has ever had any such theory or made any such proposal. It is a straw man. It cannot be found in even the most voluminous and learned histories of economic theories.

Proposals to reduce taxes on capital gains, for example, are often opposed politically by saying that those who make such proposals believe in a "trickle down" theory of economics. In reality, economic processes work in the directly opposite way from that depicted by those who imagine that profits first benefit business owners and that benefits only belatedly trickle down to workers.

---

[2]A writer in India refers to those promoting a change from government planning to a freer market as people who have "blind faith in the 'trickle-down' theory of distributing the benefits of economic growth among different socio-economic groups in the country." But free market economics is not about "distributing" anything to anybody. It is about letting people earn whatever they can from voluntary transactions with other people.

When an investment is made, whether to build a railroad or to open a new restaurant, the first money is spent hiring people to do the work. Without that, nothing happens. Even when one person decides to operate a store or hamburger stand without employees, that person must first pay somebody to deliver the goods that are going to be sold. Money goes out first to pay expenses and then comes back as profits later—if at all. The high rate of failure of new businesses makes painfully clear that there is nothing inevitable about the money coming back.

Even with successful and well-established businesses, years may elapse between the initial investment and the return of earnings. From the time when an oil company begins spending money to explore for petroleum to the time when the first gasoline resulting from that exploration comes out of a pump at a filling station, a decade may have passed. In the meantime, all sorts of employees have been paid—geologists, engineers, refinery workers, truck drivers. It is only afterwards that profits begin coming in. Only then are there any capital gains to tax. The real effect of a reduction in the capital gains tax is that it opens the prospect of greater *future* net profits and thereby provides incentives to make *current* investments.

Nor is the oil industry unique. No one who begins publishing a newspaper expects to make a profit—or even break even—during the first year or two. But reporters and other members of the newspaper staff expect to be paid every payday, even while the paper shows only red ink on the bottom line. Amazon.com began operating in 1994 but its first profits did not appear until the last quarter of 2001, after the company lost a total of $2.8 billion over the years. Even a phenomenally successful enterprise like the McDonald's restaurant chain ran up millions of dollars in debts for years before it saw the first dollar of profit. Indeed, it teetered on the brink of bankruptcy more than once in its early years. But the people behind the counter selling hamburgers were paid regularly all that time.

In short, the sequence of payments is directly the opposite of what is assumed by those who talk about a "trickle-down" theory. The workers must be paid first and then the profits flow upward later—if at all.

Chapter 24

Parting Thoughts

We shall not grow wiser before we learn that much that we have done was very foolish.

—F. A. HAYEK

Sometimes the whole is greater than the sum of its parts. In addition to whatever you may have learned in the course of this book about particular things such as prices, commodity speculation, or international trade, you may also have acquired a more general skepticism about many of the glittering words and fuzzy phrases that are mass produced by the media, by politicians, and by others.

You may no longer be as ready to believe those who talk about things selling "below their real value" or about how terrible it is for the United States to be "a debtor nation." Statements and statistics about "the rich" and "the poor" may not be uncritically accepted any more. Nor should you find it mysterious that so many places with rent control laws also have housing shortages.

However, no listing of economic fallacies can be complete, because the fertility of the human imagination is virtually unlimited. New fallacies are being conceived, or misconceived, while the old ones are still being refuted. The most that can be hoped for is to reveal some of the more common fallacies and promote both skepticism and an analytical approach that goes beyond the emotional appeals which sustain so many harmful and even dangerous economic fallacies in politics and in the media.

This should include a more careful use and definition of words, so that statements about how countries with high wages cannot compete in international trade with countries which have low wages do not escape scrutiny because of verbal confusion. High *wage rates per unit of time* are very different from high *labor costs per unit of output*, since countries with high wage rates per unit of time often have lower labor costs per unit of output, as a result of having more output per worker. Similarly sloppy use of terms often occurs in media and political discussions of taxation. For example, the growing federal deficits of the 1980s in the United States have often been blamed on the "tax cuts" early in that decade. But, although *tax rates per dollar of income* were cut, the *total tax revenues* of the federal government were higher in every year of the 1980s than in any previous year in the history of the country, as a result of incomes growing by more than the tax rates were cut. It was increased spending which led to growing deficits—a fact concealed by sloppy use of the word "taxes," which can refer to either individual tax rates or the total tax revenues of the government.

Many economic fallacies depend upon not thinking beyond the initial consequences of particular policies. Restricting the importation of foreign steel will indeed save jobs in the domestic steel industry, but its repercussions on the prices and sales of other domestic products made with higher-priced domestic steel can easily cost far more jobs than those that were saved.

In wartime, when military forces absorb many resources which would normally go into producing civilian products, there is often an understandable desire to ensure that such basic things as food continue to be available to the civilian population, especially those with low incomes. Thus price controls may be imposed on bread and butter, but not on champagne and caviar. However right this may seem, when you look only at the initial consequences, the picture changes drastically when you follow the subsequent repercussions.

If the prices of bread and butter are kept lower than they would be if determined by supply and demand in a free market, then producers of bread and butter tend to end up with lower rates of profit than producers of champagne and caviar, who remain free to charge "whatever the traffic will bear," since no one regards these things as essential. However, because all producers compete for labor and other scarce resources, this means that producers of champagne and caviar are in a more advantageous position to gain such resources, at the expense of producers of bread and butter, than they would have been in a free market without price controls. Shifting resources from the production of bread and butter to the production of champagne and caviar is one of the repercussions that escapes notice when we fail to think beyond the initial stage of consequences of economic policies.[1]

The importance of economic principles extends beyond things that most people think of as economics. For example, those who worry about the exhaustion of petroleum, iron ore, or other natural resources often assume that they are discussing the amount of physical stuff in the earth. But that assumption changes radically when you realize that statistics on "known reserves" of these resources may tell us more about the interest rate and the costs of exploration than about how much of the resource remains underground. Some communities may decide to restrict how tall local buildings will be allowed to be built, without any thought that this has economic implications which can result in much higher rents being charged. These are just some of a whole range of problems and issues which, on the surface, might not seem like economic matters, but which nevertheless look very different after understanding basic economic principles.

One of the recurring themes in our consideration of various policies and institutions, in a diverse range of countries around the world, has been the distinction between the *goals* of these policies and institutions versus the *incentives* they create. The importance of that distinction extends beyond the particular things discussed in this book—and, indeed, beyond economics. Nothing is easier than to proclaim a wonderful goal. Legislation "to relieve the distress of the German people" gave dictatorial powers to Adolf Hitler, leading to more distress and disaster than the German people—and many other peoples—had ever experienced before.

What must be asked about any goal is: What specific things are going to be done in the name of that goal? What does the particular legislation or policy reward and what does it punish? What constraints does it impose? Looking to the future, what are the likely consequences of such incentives and constraints? Looking back at the past, what have been the consequences of similar incentives and constraints in other times and places? As the distinguished British historian Paul Johnson put it:

> The study of history is a powerful antidote to contemporary arrogance. It is humbling to discover how many of our glib assumptions, which seem to us

---

[1]For similar reasons, rent control tends to shift resources from the production of ordinary housing for ordinary people toward the production of luxury housing for the affluent and wealthy.

novel and plausible, have been tested before, not once but many times and in innumerable guises; and discovered to be, at great human cost, wholly false.

We have seen some of those great human costs—people going hungry in Russia, despite some of the richest farmland on the continent of Europe, people sleeping on cold sidewalks during winter nights in New York, despite far more boarded-up housing units in the city than it would take to shelter them all. A desperate government in eighteenth-century France decreed the death penalty for anyone who refused to accept the money that the revolutionary leaders had issued, in utter ignorance or disregard of economics.

Some of the economic policies which have led to counterproductive or even catastrophic consequences in various countries and in various periods of history might suggest that there was unbelievable stupidity on the part of those making these decisions—which, in democratic countries, might also imply unbelievable stupidity on the part of those who voted for them. But this is not so. While the economic analysis required to understand these issues may not be particularly difficult to grasp, one must first stop and think about them in an economic framework. When people do not stop and think through certain issues, it does not matter whether those people are geniuses or morons, because the quality of the thinking that they *would have* done is a moot point.

In addition to the role of incentives and constraints, one of our other central themes has been the role of *knowledge*. In free market economies, we have seen giant multi-billion-dollar corporations fall from their pinnacles, some all the way to bankruptcy and extinction, because their knowledge of changing circumstances, and the implications of those changes, lagged behind that of upstart rivals. What is important is not that A & P succumbed to Safeway or White Castle to McDonald's, but that knowledge and insights proved decisive in market competition. The public benefitted from that, by getting what it wanted at lower prices, because some business decisions were based on a clearer understanding of the economic realities of the times and circumstances.

In centrally planned economies, we have seen the planners overwhelmed by the task of trying to set literally millions of prices and keep changing those prices in response to innumerable and often unforeseeable changes in circumstances. It was not remarkable that they failed so often. What was remarkable was that anyone had expected them to succeed, given the vast amount of knowledge that would have had to be marshalled and mastered in one place by one set of people to make such an arrangement work. Lenin was only one of many theorists over the centuries who imagined that it would be easy to run economic activities—and the first to encounter directly the economic and social catastrophes to which that belief led, as he himself admitted.

Given the decisive advantages of knowledge and insight in a market economy, even when this knowledge and insight are in the minds of people born and raised in poverty, like J. C. Penney or F. W. Woolworth, we can see why market economies have outperformed other economies that depend on ideas originating within a narrow elite of birth or ideology. While market economies are often thought of as money economies, they are still more so knowledge economies, for money can always be found to back new insights, technologies and organizational methods that work, even when these innovations were created by people initially lacking in money, whether Henry Ford, Thomas Edison, David Packard, Ray Kroc, or others. Capital is always available under capitalism, but knowledge and insights are rare and precious under any system.

Knowledge can be bought and sold in a free market, like anything else. Writers, athletes, and entertainers have agents, whose knowledge increases the earning power of those they represent. Operators of hotel, restaurant, or other franchises exchange their particular knowledge of local conditions for the franchisers' general knowledge of how to run such businesses and market them to the public. At one time, young people who lacked both money and knowledge could purchase the knowledge they needed by exchanging their own unpaid labor for experience that would enable them to get on the economic ladder and eventually move up that ladder as far as their abilities would take them. Laws, policies, and adverse public opinion have largely closed that avenue of advancement for the poor, though people whose initial productivity is great enough to make them employable at pay scales set by minimum wage laws or union contracts can still purchase knowledge and experience by working for less than they might get elsewhere, in order to move from apprentices to journeymen in skilled trades or from interns to physicians in medicine.

Knowledge should not be narrowly conceived as the kind of information in which intellectuals and academics specialize. We should not be like the depiction of the famous scholar Benjamin Jowett, master of Balliol College at Oxford, who inspired this verse:

> My name is Benjamin Jowett.
>   If it's knowledge, I know it.
> I am the master of this college,
>   What I don't know isn't knowledge.

In reality, there is much that the intelligentsia do not know that is vital knowledge in the functioning of an economy. It may be easy to disdain the kinds of highly specific knowledge and implications which are often economically decisive by asking, for example: How much knowledge does it take to fry a hamburger? Yet McDonald's did not become a multi-billion-dollar corporation, with thousands of outlets around the world, for no reason—not with so many rivals trying desperately and unsuccessfully to do the same, and some even failing to make enough money to stay in business. Anyone who studies the history of this franchise chain[2] will be astonished at the amount of detailed knowledge, insights, organizational and technological innovation, financial improvisation, all-out efforts and desperate sacrifices that went into creating an enormous economic success from selling just a few mundane food products.

Nor was McDonald's unique. All sorts of businesses—from Sears to Intel and from Honda to the Bank of America—had to struggle upward from humble beginnings to ultimately achieve wealth and security. In all these cases, it was the knowledge that was built up over the years—the human capital—which ultimately attracted the financial capital to make ideas become a reality. The other side of this is that, in countries where the mobilization of financial resources is made difficult by deficiencies in property rights laws, those at the bottom have fewer ways of getting the capital needed to back their entrepreneurial endeavors. More important, the whole society loses the benefits it could gain from what these stifled entrepreneurs could contribute to the economic rise of the nation.

Success is only part of the story of a free market economy. Failure is at least as important a part, though few want to talk about it and none want to experience it. When the same resources—whether land, labor, steel, or petroleum—can be used by different firms and different industries to produce different products, the only way for the successful ideas to become realities is to take resources away from other uses that turn out to be unsuccessful, or which have become obsolete after having had their era of success. Economics is not about "win-win" options, but about often painful choices in the allocation of scarce resources which have alternative uses. Success and failure are not isolated good fortunes and misfortunes, but inseparable parts of the same process.

---

[2]For example, John F. Love, *McDonald's: Behind the Arches.*

All economies—whether capitalism, socialism, feudalism or whatever—are essentially ways of cooperating in the production and distribution of goods and services, whether this is done efficiently or inefficiently, voluntarily or involuntarily. Naturally, individuals and groups want their own particular contributions to the process to be better rewarded, but their complaints or struggles over this are a sideshow to the main event of complementary efforts which produce the output on which all depend. Yet invidious comparisons and internecine struggles are the stuff of social melodrama, which in turn is the lifeblood of the media and politics, as well as for portions of the intelligentsia.

By portraying cooperative activities as if they were zero-sum contests—whether in employer-employee relations or in international trade or other cooperative endeavors—those with the power to impose their misconceptions on others through words or laws can create a negative-sum contest, in which all are worse off. A young worker who is destitute of both knowledge and money would today find it virtually impossible to purchase the knowledge that was vital to a future career by working long hours for no pay, as many did it times past—including F. W. Woolworth, who by this means rose from poverty to become one of the richest man of his times in retailing.

Those with a zero-sum vision who have seen property rights as mere special privileges for the affluent and the rich have helped erode or destroy such rights, or have made them practically inaccessible to the poor in Third World countries, thereby depriving the poor of one of the mechanisms by which people from backgrounds like theirs have risen to prosperity in other times and places.

However useful economics may be for understanding many issues, it is not as emotionally satisfying as more personal and melodramatic depictions of these issues often found in the media and in politics. Dry empirical questions are seldom as exciting as political crusades or moral pronouncements. But they are questions that must be asked, if we are truly interested in the well-being of others, rather than in excitement or a sense of moral superiority for ourselves. Perhaps the most important distinction is between what sounds good and what works. The former may be sufficient for purposes of politics or moral preening, but not for the economic advancement of people in general or the poor in particular. For those who are willing to stop and think, basic economics provides some tools for evaluating policies and proposals in terms of their logical implications and empirical consequences.

If this book has contributed to that end, then it has succeeded in its mission.

QUESTIONS

PART I: PRICES AND MARKETS

1. Can there be a growing scarcity without a growing shortage—or a growing shortage without a growing scarcity? Explain with examples.

2. Can a decision be economic, if there is no money involved? Why or why not?

3. Can there be surplus food in a society where people are hungry? Explain why or why not.

4. When a country goes from having a housing shortage to having a housing surplus, within a time period too short for any new housing to have been built, what has probably happened?

5. Which of the following are—or are not—affected by price controls that limit how high the product's price can go: (a) the quantity supplied, (b) the quantity demanded, (c) the quality of the product, (d) a black market for the product, (e) the supply of auxiliary services that usually go with the product, (f) efficiency in the allocation of resources or (g) the average level of honesty among those who sell or rent the product. Explain in each case.

6. Building ordinary housing and luxury housing involves using many of the same resources, such as bricks, pipes, and construction labor. How does the allocation of these resources between ordinary housing and luxury housing tend to change after rent control laws are passed?

7. Are prices usually higher or lower in low-income neighborhoods. Why? Include among prices the interest rate on money borrowed and the cost of getting paychecks cashed. If you were considering opening a business in a low-income neighborhood, would you expect to make a

higher or a lower rate of profit there than you would receive if you opened the same business in a middle-class or affluent neighborhood? Which kind of business is more likely to locate in each kind of neighborhood—a highly successful supermarket chain or a small independent business run by recent immigrants with a limited knowledge of English? Why would each kind of business tend to locate in one place but not the other?

8. When a government institution or program produces counterproductive results, is that a sign of irrationality on the part of those who run that particular institution or program?

9. We all consider some things more important than others. Why then can there be a problem when some official government policy establishes "national priorities"?

10. We tend to think of costs as the money we pay for things. But does that mean that there would be no costs in a primitive society that did not yet use money or in a modern cooperative community, where people collectively produce the goods and services they use and do not charge each other for them?

11. Adam Smith had a high opinion of capitalism, despite his low opinion of capitalists. How does this relate to the difference between systemic causation and intentional causation?

12. Why do American manufacturers of computers or television sets tend to have them transported by others while Chinese manufacturers tend to transport them themselves?

13. Explain how a fighter pilot's combat experience is a scarce resource which has alternative uses—and the consequences of allocating that resource in different ways.

14. Because most basic economic principles are relatively straightforward and not difficult to understand, they are often dismissed as too "simplistic" to explain the complexities of the real world. Critique that belief.

15. How can you put a price on music or health?

PART II: INDUSTRY AND COMMERCE

1. What are some of the reasons why some of the biggest and most profitable businesses have declined into obscurity or even bankruptcy?

2. How and why can Toyota manufacture cars with only enough inventory of parts to last an hour, while Soviet industries had nearly enough inventory to last for a year?

3. In some industries, the four or five top firms may make the great majority of the sales in the whole industry. Moreover, that may be true for decades on end. Does this then mean that there is a lack of competition in this industry?

4. How did the movement of population from rural to urban America affect the economics of retail selling in the early twentieth century? How did the later movement of population from urban to suburban America in the second half of the twentieth century affect the economics of department stores, grocery stores, and hamburger restaurants? Explain with examples.

5. Why is it that General Motors can make millions of automobiles, without making a single tire to go on them, while Soviet enterprises not only tended to make all their own components, but sometimes even made the bricks for the buildings in which they operated?

6. How did diseconomies of scale in agriculture affect the way tractor drivers plowed fields in the Soviet Union? What if agricultural enterprises had been privately owned and the tractor drivers were plowing their own fields? Would the work have been done differently and would the farm be likely to be as large? Explain why.

7. Any given individual's knowledge is extremely limited, under any economic or political system. How does the effect of this limitation differ in an economy coordinated by prices than in an economy coordinated by central planners?

8. Advertising, even when it is successful, is often considered to be a benefit only to those who advertise, but of no benefit to consumers, who have to pay the cost of the advertisements in the higher price of the products they buy. Critique this view.

9. What can and should be done for companies lagging behind while the rest of the economy is moving ahead?

10. Why are retired people able to get much lower priced travel rates—on cruise ships, for example—than most other people?

11. Why is the perennial desire to "eliminate the middleman" perennially frustrated?

12. After the A & P grocery chain cut its profit margins on the goods it sold, back in the early twentieth century, its rate of profit on its investment rose well above the national average. Why?

PART III: WORK AND PAY

1. What have been some of the economic and social consequences of the substitution of machine power for human strength, as a result of industrialization, and the growing importance of knowledge, skills, and experience in a high-tech economy?

2. Would you expect the average hammer to drive more nails per year in a richer country or a poorer country? Would you expect the average worker to produce more output per hour in a richer country or a poorer country? Explain the reasons in each case.

3. Some studies have attempted to determine how employment has changed in the wake of a minimum wage increase by surveying individual firms to find out how their employment has changed, and then adding up the results. What is the problem with this procedure?

4. How can per capita income be increasing by 50 percent over a period of years, while average family income and average household income remain almost stationary over those same years?

5. When the difference in income between the top and bottom brackets increases, does that necessarily mean that a given set of individuals are falling further behind another given set of individuals?

6. Would a country in transition between a communist economy and a capitalist economy, such as China, tend to have more equality of income or less, compared to an economy that was continuing to be communist or continuing to be capitalist?

7. Although maximum wage laws existed long before minimum wage laws, only the latter are common today. However, in those special cases where there have been maximum wage laws—as under wage and price controls during World War II, for example, what effects would such laws have on the allocation of scarce resources—and on discrimination against minorities and women?

8. Does inequality of income tend to be greater or less in the long run than in the short run? Greater or less than inequalities in consumption? Why

do many statistics about "the rich" and "the poor" include people who are neither rich nor poor in reality?

9. A *New York Times* columnist once used per capita income statistics to judge the economic performance of the administration of President Lyndon Johnson and, in later years, used household income statistics to judge the economic performance of the administration of President Ronald Reagan. Which set of statistics would tend to make the economic progress of the country look better and why?

10. A government official in India said: "I don't want multinational companies getting rich selling face cream to poor Indians." What does that statement imply?

PART IV: TIME AND RISK

1. Does it make economic sense for a ninety-year-old man, with no heirs, to plant trees that will take 20 years to grow to maturity and bear fruit?

2. Why do insurance companies buy insurance from a re-insurance company? How does this affect the allocation of scarce resources which have alternative uses?

3. Why may the statistics on the known reserves of a natural resource provide a misleading picture of how much of that resource there is in the ground?

4. "Insurance principles often conflict with political principles." Explain why, with examples.

5. How does commodity speculation differ from gambling? What is the effect of commodity speculation on output? On the allocation of scarce resources which have alternative uses?

6. Why does it pay an insurance company or a commodity speculator to offer a deal in which they guarantee to pay a given sum of money to someone under given circumstances? And why does it pay for that person to accept the offer?

7. Why would a bus company owned or controlled by the government charge fares too low to replace existing buses as they wear out? What if the executives of a privately owned and privately controlled bus company decided to divert part of the money they received from bus fares toward paying themselves higher salaries, instead of setting aside

enough money to replace buses as they wear out? What would happen to the value of the stock in their company and how would the stockholders be likely to react?

8. Many poor countries have confiscated businesses or land owned by wealthy foreign companies. Why has this seldom made the poor country more prosperous?

9. Those who favor increases in tax rates are often disappointed that the additional revenue turns out to be less than they expected. Conversely, those who fear that cuts in tax rates will substantially reduce the government's revenues have often been surprised to find the government's revenues rising. Explain why.

10. Why does it make sense for an individual driver to get insurance on his automobile? Why then doesn't Hertz buy insurance for its automobiles?

PART V: THE NATIONAL ECONOMY

1. Does the presence or absence of property rights make any difference to people who own no property? For example, are tenants affected economically by whether the community in which they rent apartments or houses allows unbridled property rights or reduces those property rights through zoning laws, open space laws, height restrictions on buildings, or rent control laws? Explain how people who own no property are affected.

2. During the Great Depression of the 1930s, both Republican President Herbert Hoover and his successor, Democratic President Franklin D. Roosevelt, tried to keep up the prices of goods and labor. What was the economic problem with these policies?

3. During a period of inflation, does money circulate faster or slower—and why? What are the consequences? What do you suppose happens during a period of deflation—and what are the consequences then?

4. During an all-out war, how can a country's military plus civilian consumption add up to more than its output, without borrowing from other countries?

5. "Under both capitalism and socialism, the scarcity of knowledge is the same, but the way these different economies deal with it can be quite different." Explain.

6. "The nationalization of banks in India was not simply a matter of transferring ownership of an enterprise to the government. This transfer changed all the incentives and constraints from those of the marketplace to those of politics and bureaucracy." Explain what consequences followed and why.

7. Even if detailed statistics are available, why is it difficult to compare the national output at the beginning of the twentieth century with the national output at the beginning of the twenty-first century, and say by what percentage it has increased? Why is it hard even to say how much prices for particular goods have increased from one century to another?

8. Why would an Albanian bank, with 83 percent of the country's deposits, refuse to make any loans? And what were the consequences for the Albanian economy?

9. In a free country, people can express their desires either through the political system or through the marketplace. What difference does it make which one they choose? Explain why the end results are, or are not, likely to be any different.

10. Since "money talks" in the marketplace, why would rich people want to shift some decisions out of the marketplace and have them settled politically or by courts? (Hint: housing is a classic example.)

PART VI: THE INTERNATIONAL ECONOMY

1. If laws restrict the importation of a particular foreign product, in order to protect the jobs of domestic workers who produce that product, how is it possible that this can end up reducing domestic employment?

2. Britain began importing farm products at a time when its own farmers were more efficient than the foreign farmers whose products it was importing. How could this be beneficial to Britain? How did this effect the international allocation of scarce resources which have alternative uses?

3. What are the three most important benefits of international trade? Explain each in terms of its effect on the efficient allocation of scarce resources which have alternative uses.

4. Why might the government of a Third World country prefer to receive a smaller amount of money as foreign aid, rather than a larger amount of money as private investment?

5. What is meant by a "favorable balance of trade"? Why was it considered favorable? Is it also favorable to producing prosperity in the economy?

6. When foreigners annually take more wealth out of the U.S. economy than the Gross Domestic Product of Egypt or Malaysia, how can that fail to make Americans poorer?

7. What *economic* difference does it make when the level of honesty in one country is very different from that in another country?

8. In the absence of restrictions on international trade, would low-wage countries tend to take jobs away from high-wage countries through lower production costs that would allow them to sell at lower prices? Explain.

9. The United States has often been a "debtor nation" owing more to people in other countries than people in other countries owe to Americans, while Switzerland has often been a "creditor nation," to whom others owe more to the Swiss than the Swiss owe to others. What tends to lead to this difference and is it economically beneficial or harmful to Americans or Swiss?

10. What were the causes and effects of a large worldwide decline in international trade in the 1930s compared to the 1920s?

PART VII: SPECIAL ECONOMIC ISSUES

1. Costly safety devices or policies have often been defended on grounds that "if it saves just one life, it is worth it." What is the problem with that reasoning?

2. What are some of the reasons why different prices are charged for things that are physically identical?

3. Some people respond to economic analysis by saying, "But there are also *non-economic* values to consider." Discuss.

4. What is the point of having different brands of the same product if in fact all the brands are of pretty much the same quality and sell for about the same price? What would happen in this situation if laws did away with brands, so that each producer could only identify what the product was, but not who made it?

5. How have business entrepreneurs usually been seen by free market economists over the past two centuries? How have businesses seen the free market?

6. Explain how the presence or absence of the profit motive affects an organization's likelihood of achieving the purpose for which it was created, to the maximum extent possible with the resources at its disposal.

7. What are the problems with the "trickle-down theory"?

8. For about a century—from the 1770s to the 1870s—most of the leading economists believed that the relative prices of goods reflected their relative costs of production, especially the amount of labor they required. What are some of the problems with that theory?

9. When fighting a war leads to a diversion of a substantial amount of resources from civilian to military purposes, most people would be more concerned to see that the poor could still get bread than that the rich could still get caviar. Why then not put price controls on bread but not on caviar?

10. Nobel Prize economist F. A. Hayek said: "We shall not grow wiser before we learn that much that we have done was very foolish." What do you consider to be the three most foolish policies discussed in this book? Would you have considered those policies foolish before reading *Basic Economics*?

SOURCES

It is neither possible nor necessary to document the source of every statement made in this book. However, there are some key facts which some readers may want to check out or to explore further. Rather than clutter the text with footnotes, in a book intended for the general public, the citations are listed here in an informal way that should nevertheless make it possible to find the original sources.

CHAPTER 1: WHAT IS ECONOMICS?

The article about middle-class Americans began on the front page of Section 3 of the *New York Times* of August 1, 1999 and was written by Louis Uchitelle. The statement that Marxist economist Oskar Lange did not differ fundamentally from Milton Friedman on certain basic propositions and procedures can be verified by reading Oskar Lange, "The Scope and Method of Economics," in the *Review of Economic Studies* (1945–1946), pages 19–32, and comparing that with Milton Friedman's essay "The Methodology of Positive Economics" in his book *Essays in Positive Economics*.

CHAPTER 2: THE ROLE OF PRICES

The quoted statistics and analysis about the Soviet economy are from a book titled *The Turning Point: Revitalizing the Soviet Economy* by two Soviet economists, Nikolai Shmelev and Vladimir Popov, especially pages 128, 130–131, 141, 181. The quote from Friedrich Engels is from his preface to the first German edition of *The Poverty of Philosophy* by Karl Marx, where Marx himself makes similar comments in the text, though not in as lucid language as that used by Engels. Information on Ghana and the Ivory Coast is from a book by W. L. Alpine and James Picket, *Agriculture, Liberalisation and Economic Growth in Ghana and Côte D'Ivoire:1968–1990*, published in Paris in 1996 by the Organisation for Economic Co-Operation and Development. South Korea's surpassing of India, after starting from a similar economic level, was mentioned on page 222 of *The Commanding Heights* by Daniel Yergin and Joseph Stanislaw. India's relaxation of government controls over its economy was reported in the distinguished British magazine, *The Economist*, June 2, 2001, page 13. The use of food and electricity in an Israeli kibbutz, before and after prices were charged for them, is discussed on pages 332 and 333 of *Heaven on Earth: the Rise and Fall of Socialism* by Joshua Muracchik, published in 2002 by Encounter Books. The relationship between housing prices and population changes in upstate New York was described on page 70 of an article titled "Down-and-Out Upstate," by Jerry Zremski in the Autumn 1999 issue of *City Journal*, published by the Manhattan Institute, a think tank in New York.

CHAPTER 3: PRICE CONTROLS

The fact that the housing shortage in the United States occurred when there was no change in the ratio of housing to people is from a book titled *Roofs or Ceilings?* by two economists later destined to win Nobel Prizes, Milton Friedman and George J. Stigler. The book itself has long been out of print, but excerpts from it were included in a collection of writings titled *Rent Control: Costs and Consequences*, edited by Robert Albon and published in 1980 by an Australian think tank, The Centre for Independent Studies, located in Sydney. This particular statement occurs on page 16. The data on housing in San Francisco after the 1906 earthquake are on pages 5 and 6. The facts about rent control in Sweden are from a different article in the same book, "The Rise, Fall and Revival of Swedish Rent Control" by Sven Rydeenfelt. The lack of building in Melbourne under Australian rent control is mentioned on page 125 in another article. The age of rent-controlled housing in San Francisco is from page 61 of *San Francisco Housing DataBook*, a 2001 study commissioned by the city and produced by consultants called Bay Area Economics. Facts about the effects on rent control in Britain, France, Germany, and the Netherlands are from *Rent Control in North America and Four European Countries* by Joel F. Brenner and Herbert M. Franklin, published by Mercury Press, pages 4, 9, and 69. The withdrawal of rental units after the imposition of rent control in Toronto was mentioned on page 21 of *Zoning, Rent Control and Affordable Housing* by William Tucker, published by the Cato Institute, a think tank in Washington. Many of the facts about rent control and homelessness in the United States are from *The Excluded Americans* by William Tucker (especially pages 19, 162, 275 and Chapter 19, which discusses various elite celebrities living in rent-controlled apartments). The comment from the *New York Times* is from page 40 of an article by John Tierney in their Sunday magazine section of May 4, 1997, titled "At the Intersection of Supply and Demand." The fact that nearly half the rent-controlled apartments in San Francisco had only one tenant is from page 21 of *San Francisco Housing DataBook*, cited above. The paradox of higher rents in rent-controlled cities is from another study by William Tucker, "How Rent Control Drives Out Affordable Housing," *Policy Analysis* paper number 274, published by the Cato Institute. The decline of the housing stock under rent control in

Washington is cited in an article by Thomas Hazlett in a book titled *Resolving the Housing Crisis*, published in 1982 by a San Francisco think tank, the Pacific Institute for Public Policy Research. San Francisco's experience under rent control is from a study whose results were reported on page 13 of the *San Francisco Weekly* of January 30, 2002 in an article titled "Legends in Our Own Minds," by Matt Smith. Data on the number of buildings taken over by the city government in New York can be found on page 99 of *The Homeless* by Christopher Jencks, published by Harvard University Press in 1994. The fact that building resumed in various Massachusetts communities after the state banned local rent control laws can be found in *Rude Awakenings* by Richard W. White, Jr., published in 1992 by ICS Press in San Francisco. Soviet economists' comments on the gasoline shortage in the United States are from page 89 of *The Turning Point* by Nikolai Shmelev and Vladimir Popov. Information on the amounts of gasoline sold during the 1970s gasoline shortages are from "Gas Crisis in New York: One Fact, Many Notions," *New York Times*, July 29, 1979, p. 30; Stephen Chapman, "The Gas Line of '79," *The Public Interest*, Summer 1980, page 47 and American Petroleum Institute, *Basic Petroleum Data Book: Petroleum Industry Statistics*, Vol. IV, No. 3 (September 1984), Section VII, Table 8. The postwar meat shortage in the United States under price controls is discussed on pages 58 and 59 of *Prices and Price Controls* published by the Foundation for Economic Education, Inc., in Irvington-on-Hudson, New York. The agricultural price support program in general is covered in Chapter 1 of *The Structure of American Industry* by Walter Adams and James Brock. The surpluses of wheat and rice created by India's agricultural price support program were reported on page 63 of the *Far Eastern Economic Review* of December 6, 2001, in an article titled "The Problems of Plenty" by Joanna Slater. Information on the effects of price supports in the sugar industry are from a front-page article in the *New York Times* of May 6, 2001 titled "Sugar Rules Defy Free-Trade Logic." Inflated prices of lamb, butter, and sugar in the European Union were reported in *The Economist*, June 9, 2001, page 70, in an article titled "Special Report: Agricultural Trade." The statement that every cow in the European Union gets more subsidies per day than most Africans have to live on is from page A12 of the January 7, 2003 issue of the *Wall Street Journal* in a column titled "Fight Poverty, Not Patents" by Carl Bildt. The costs of the 2002 American farm subsidy bill were estimated in the August 29, 2002 issue of *National Review* in an article titled "Twisting 'The Facts,'" by Brian Riedl. The fact that 85 percent of Mexico's agricultural subsidies go to the top 15 percent of farmers is from page A13 of the *Wall Street Journal* of March 5, 2003. Data on the costs of European Union agricultural subsidies in general in 2002 are from page 33 of *The Economist* of October 5, 2002, under the title "Scandalous." The effects of price control on the use of medical care is discussed in detail in Chapter 3 of *Applied Economics* by Thomas Sowell. The passage describing the cause and effect of price controls during a seventeenth-century local food shortage in Italy is from page 381 of *The Formation of National States in Western Europe*, edited by Charles Tilly and published by the Princeton University Press in 1975. Discussions of the effects of price controls in besieged sixteenth-century Antwerp, as well as the eighteenth-century and nineteenth-century local food shortages in India are from pages 33 and 34 of *Forty*

Centuries of Wage and Price Controls by Robert L. Schuettinger and Eamonn F. Butler, published by the Heritage Foundation, a Washington think tank, in 1979. London's newspaper *The Guardian* reported the story of the British girl who received a breast implant in its November 9, 1998 issue, page 6, under the title, "Girl, 12, to Get Breast Implant." The 10,000 people in Britain who had waited 15 months or more for surgery were reported in *The Economist* magazine of London on page 55 of its April 13, 2002 issue. The British woman whose cancer surgery was postponed until it had to be cancelled because the cancer had become inoperable during the long delays was mentioned in *The Economist* of November 24, 2001, on page 52.

CHAPTER 4: AN OVERVIEW

The quotes from a Japanese fighter pilot in World War II are from pages 125 and 217 of *Samurai* by Suburo Sakai, 1963 Ballantine Books edition. The quotes from Frederick Engels and Adam Smith are from, respectively, page 476 of *Selected Correspondence* by Karl Marx and Frederick Engels and page 423 of the Modern Library edition of *The Wealth of Nations* by Adam Smith. The relative costs for security in inner city and suburban shopping malls were discussed on page 251 of *America in Black and White* by Stephan Thernstrom and Abigail Thernstrom. Comparisons of bombing and rent control as means of destroying housing appear on pages 422 and 425 of an article by Walter Block titled "Rent Control" in *The Fortune Encyclopedia of Economics*, edited by David Henderson. India's increased wheat supply after price controls were eased was discussed on pages 131 and 132 of *India Unbound* by Gurcharan Das, published in 2001 by Alfred A. Knopf. The economic problems of the rich "black earth" country of Russia are discussed in Frank Viviano, "Russian Farmland Withers on the Vine: Politics, Mind-set Keep Nation on a Diet of Imports," *San Francisco Chronicle*, October 19, 1998, p. A1 and in Andrew Higgins, "Food Lines," *Wall Street Journal*, October 1998, pp. A1 ff. The steel manufacturer whose equipment automatically shifted from oil to natural gas was mentioned in a front page story by Steve Liesman and Jacob M. Schlesinger titled, "Blunted Spike: The Price of Oil Has Doubled This Year; So Where's the Recession?" in the December 13, 1999 issue of the *Wall Street Journal*. Former food-exporting countries which become unable to feed themselves are mentioned in innumerable places, including *Modern Times* by Paul Johnson, pages 724–727 of the 1992 edition. Russian exports of wheat under the czar are shown on page 62 of *The Turning Point* by Soviet economists Nikolai Shmelev and Vladimir Popov. For a painfully enlightening examination of the media's inability to understand basic economic principles during the gasoline crises of the 1970s, and their resulting susceptibility to irrational explanations of what was happening, see Thomas W. Hazlett, *TV Coverage of the Oil Crises: How Well Was the Public Served?* (Washington: The Media Institute,1982). The changing views of the *Washington Post* on oil rationing can be seen by comparing their editorials in the November 25, 1973 issue and the June 15, 1980 issue. California's subsidized water for farmers is discussed on pages A1 and A6 of the May 30,

1991 issue of *The Wall Street Journal* under the title "Big Farmers in West Get Subsidized Water Despite Drought Crisis," by Charles McCoy. The effects of subsidized water to farmers in India were reported on page 14 of *The Economist* of June 2, 2001, under the title, "Grim Reapers."

CHAPTER 5: THE RISE AND FALL OF BUSINESSES

The epigraph is from page 52 of the May 27, 2002 issue of *Fortune* magazine. Information on the number of A & P stores in 1929 is from pages 89 and 90 of the April 14, 2003 issue of *Fortune*. The fact that 38 companies dropped off the list of the Fortune 500 in just one year is from page F–22 of the same issue. The decline of Japan's Mizuho bank was reported on page C1 of the May 8, 2003 issue of the *Wall Street Journal* in a news story titled "Mizuho's Fate May Rest on a Japan Bailout." The changing profitability of Japanese manufacturers of compact disc players was mentioned on page 45 of the *Far Eastern Economic Review* of November 28, 2002, in an article titled "Picturing the Future" by Ben Dolven. Sony's shift from large losses to large profits was discussed on page 63 of the March 1, 2003 issue of *The Economist*, in an article titled "The Complete Home Entertainer?" A similar change in profitability at General Motors was discussed on page 52 of the February 20, 2003 issue of *BusinessWeek* in an article titled "Rick Wagoner's Game Plan" by David Welch. The historical sketches of various businesses are based on information from a variety of sources, including innumerable newspaper and magazine articles, as well as books such as *New and Improved: The Story of Mass Marketing in America* written by Richard S. Tedlow and *Brand New: How Entrepreneurs Earned Consumers' Trust from Wedgwood to Dell* by Nancy F. Koehn, both published by the Harvard Business School Press (in 1996 and 2001, respectively), *Forbes Greatest Business Stories of All Time* by Daniel Gross and the editors of *Forbes* magazine, *Masters of Enterprise* by H. W. Brands, *Empire Builders* by Burton W. Folsom, Jr., *The First Hundred Years are the Toughest: What We Can Learn for the Century of Competition Between Sears and Wards* by Cecil C. Hoge, Sr. *A & P* by M. A. Adelman, *The Rise and Decline of the Great Atlantic & Pacific Tea Company* by former A & P executive William L. Walsh and *Made in America* by Sam Walton. The declining circulation of New York City newspapers is from a story on page E5 of the *New York Times* of November 18, 1990, written by Frank J. Prial and titled, "Suburban Sprawl Also Applies to the Circulation of Newspapers." Statistics on newspaper circulations in 2003 are from *Editor & Publisher*, May 12, 2003, page 4. The fact that Smith-Corona made over half the typewriters and word processors sold in North America in 1989 is from the March 5, 1990 issue of *HFD-The Weekly Home Furnishings Newspaper*, in an article titled "Smith Corona's Market Share is Growing," by Manning Greenberg. The quote about the Soviet economy is from an article by Robert Heilbroner titled "Socialism" in *The Fortune Encyclopedia of Economics*, p. 164. On the misallocation of gasoline, see Stephen Chapman, "The Gas Lines of '79," *The Public Interest*, Summer 1980, page 47; Steven Rattner, "Gas Crisis: Experts Find Mixture of Causes,"

New York Times, January 24, 1979, p. A1 ff; Pranay B. Gupte, "U. S. to Allow Shift of Some Gas Stocks to Urban Sections," *New York Times*, June 30, 1979, pp. A 1 ff. On the 3,000 pages of regulations and subsequent "clarifications," see the story by Rattner listed above. On the lack of gasoline shortages in the United States during the 1967 Arab oil embargo, see Thomas W. Hazlett, *TV Coverage of the Oil Crises*, pp. 14–15. The dire predictions that ending price controls on oil would cause skyrocketing gasoline prices are quoted in Werner Meyer, "Snake Oil Salesmen," *Policy Review*, Summer 1986, pp. 74–76, *passim*. On gasoline prices reaching an all-time low, see "Gas is Cheap. But Taxes are Rising," *Consumer Research*, August 1994, pp. 28–29. The firing of Montgomery Ward executives who urged expansion into suburban malls is mentioned on page 153 of *The New York Times Century of business*, edited by Floyd Norris and Christine Blackman, and published in the year 2000 by McGraw-Hill. The big New York department stores' initial rejection of credit cards is mentioned on page 204 of the same book. The fact that some companies made more profit from their own credit cards than from the rest of their business is from page 38 of the March 17, 2003 issue of *Fortune* magazine. The founding of the Bank of Italy is discussed on page 28 of *A.P. Giannini: Banker of America* by Felice A. Bonadio, published in 1994 by the University of California Press.

CHAPTER 6: THE ROLE OF PROFITS—AND LOSSES

The report on the competition between Wal-Mart and Kroger's is from page B1 of the *Wall Street Journal* of May 27, 2003, under the title "Price War in Aisle 3." Information and comments on the Ambassador automobile in India are from *The Economist* of February 22, 1997, under the title, "Make Us Competitive—But Not Yet" and from page 14 of the December 30, 1997 issue of the London newspaper *The Independent*. The story of the microchip, including Intel's risking its corporate survival for the sake of research, is discussed on pages 247–248, 254, 259–262 of *Forbes Greatest Business Stories of All Time*, edited by Daniel Gross, et al and published in 1996 by John Wiley & Co. Advanced Micro Device's billion-dollar losses while trying to gain market share from Intel were reported on pages 66–67 of the March 10, 2003 issue of *BusinessWeek*. The fact that 120 out of the top 500 companies in America made losses in 2002 was reported on page 199 of the April 4, 2003 issue of *Fortune* magazine under the title "Honey, I Shrunk the Profits" by Ann Harrington. Data on corporate profit rates in the American economy are from pages 46 and 49 of *The Illustrated Guide to the American Economy* by Herbert Stein and Murray Foss, third edition, published in 1999 by the AEI Press for the American Enterprise Institute, a Washington think tank. The statistic that the largest manufacturer of automobiles in the United States in 1896 produced just six cars is from *The American Car Dealership* by Robert Genat, page 7. The fact that Fortune 500 companies averaged just pennies of profit on each dollar of revenue is from page 197 of the April 4, 2003 issue of *Fortune* under the title "Honey, I Shrunk the Profits." Data on economies and diseconomies of scale in the automobile and beer industries are from pages 76, 77, 131 and 145 of *The Structure of American Industry*, 9th edition, by Walter Adams and James Brock, published by Prentice-Hall. Data on the relative costs of airlines are from page B3 of the *New York Times* of April 27, 2002 in a news story that began on page B1 under the title "U.S. Airways Ready to Test Federal Loan Program" by Edward Wong. The survey of airline quality was published in the May 14, 2001 issue of *BusinessWeek* on page 14. The quotation from the Indian entrepreneur is from page 266 of *India Unbound* by Gurcharan Das. Data and comments on the efficiency of Soviet enterprises are from *The Turning Point* by Soviet economists Nikolai Shmelev and Vladimir Popov. The practices of Soviet tractor drivers are discussed on page 184 of *The Age of Delirium: The Decline and Fall of the Soviet Union* by David Satter, published in 1996 by Yale University Press. Howard Johnson's pioneering in restaurant franchising is discussed on page 51 of *Fast Food: Roadside Restaurants in the Automobile Age* by John A. Jakle & Keither A. Sculle, published by Johns Hopkins University Press in 1999. A news story about fancy hotels renting rooms for less than the price at more modest hotels was in the *Wall Street Journal* of July 19, 2001, on page B1 under the title, "Deluxe Travel at Discount Prices," by Melanie Trottman. A similar story appeared in the same newspaper on August 10, 2001, pages W1 and W9, under the title "Peak Season, Off-Peak Prices," by Jesse Drucker. The discussions and analysis of middlemen in West Africa are from pages 22 through 27 of *West African Trade* by P.T. Bauer, published by Cambridge University Press in 1954. Gunnar Myrdal's opposite conclusions are from page 89 of his book *Asian Drama*, abridged edition, published in 1972 by Vintage Books. Soviet enterprises' tendency to make things for themselves, rather than get them from specialized producers, is discussed on pages 160–161 of *The Red Executive* by David Granick. Chinese firms that supplied their own transportation services are discussed on pages 28–31 of the *Far Eastern Economic Review* of July 25, 2002 under the title, "The Perils of Delivering the Goods," written by Ben Dolven. The huge inventories in the Soviet Union, compared to those in Japan or the United States, were discussed on pages 133 to 137 of *The Turning Point* by Shmelev and Popov. The inventory practices of the Chrysler division of DaimlerChrylser were reported on page B2 of the March 15, 2003 issue of the *New York Times* under the title, "Uncertain Economy Hinders Highly Precise Supply System," by Daniel Altman. American retailers' deductions from the bills of manufacturers who do not meet delivery specifications were reported in the *New York Times* of August 17, 2001, under the title, "Send It Right The First time," by Constance L. Hays.

CHAPTER 7: BIG BUSINESS AND GOVERNMENT

The government of India's restrictions on businesses' output were discussed on pages 99, 174 and 175 of *India Unbound* by Gurcharan Das, published in 2001 by Alfred A. Knopf. The differing costs of producing electricity to run a dishwasher at different times are discussed on page 112 of the March 26, 2001 issue of *BusinessWeek*, in a column titled "How to Do Deregulation Right" by Peter Coy. Riots in India over electricity rates are mentioned on page 46 of an article titled "Impossible India's Improbable Chance" by David Gardner in the book *The World in 2001*, published by the British magazine, *The Economist*. Data on the trucking industry are from pages 435 and 436 of an article by Thomas G. Moore titled "Trucking Deregulation" in *The Fortune Encyclopedia of Economics*. Data on airlines are from pages 380 and 381 of an article in the same book by Alfred E. Kahn titled "Airline Deregulation." The fact that more imported than American-made portable electric typewriters were sold in the United States in the 1980s was mentioned in on page 71 of the April 26, 1982 issue of *US News & World Report* in an article titled "When Japanese Set Their Sights on Typewriters," *US News & World Report* by Michael Doan. The division of air and rail traffic between Madrid and Seville was shown on page 267 of *Industries in Europe*, edtied by Peter Johnson. The economics effects of India's Monopolies and Restrictive Trade Practices Act and its repeal in 1991 are discussed in *India Unbound*, pages 159–170, 183–184, 220, 263–264. The city of Munich's switching its computers from using Microsoft Windows to using Linux was reported in *The Times* of London under the headline "Need to Know" by Tom Bawden, Ingrid Mansell and Neejam Verjee (downloaded from the Internet).

CHAPTER 8: AN OVERVIEW

Forbes magazine's report on Toyota's costs and profits is from page 75 of an article that began on page 72 of the April 14, 2003 issue, under the title "The 'OOF' Company," by Robyn Meredith and Jonathan Fahey. The comparison of the number of labor hours per car produced by General Motors and Toyota are from pages 54 and 58 of the February 10, 2003 issue of *BusinessWeek*, in an article titled "Rich Wagoner's Game Plan" by David Welch. The historical information about the A & P grocery chain is from *The Rise and Decline of the Great Atlantic & Pacific Tea Company* by William I. Walsh. The information on the McDonald's restaurant chain is from *Fast Food* by John A. Jakle and Keith Sculle, pages 58 and 146–147, from *McDonald's: Behind the Golden Arches*, revised edition (1995), by John H. Love, Chapters 1–3, and from *Masters of Enterprise: From John Jacob Astor and J. P. Morgan to Bill Gates and Oprah Winfrey* by H. W. Brands, published in 1999 by The Free Press 1999, page 222. The number of McDonald's restaurants in countries around the world is from page 70 of *The Economist* of November 3, 2001. McDonald's first quarter of losses as a public corporation was reported in the December 18, 2002 final edition of the *Washington Post* on page EO3, under the title "Down Day on Wall Street Reflects Trouble at Retailers, McDonald's." The characterization of McDonald's "savage price war" with Burger King if from the December 22, 2002 on-line edition of the *Washington Post*, which is also the source of the data on the amount of McDonald's losses. *The Economist*'s comment on McDonald's top management was on page 59 of its April 12, 2003 issue, under the title, "Did Somebody Say a Loss?" Examples of the kinds of detailed information about hotel services and amenities provided by trade association data can be found in *2001 Lodging Survey: Lodging*

Services, Facilities, and Trends, published by the American Hotel & Lodging Foundation in Washington, D.C. Data on American profits as a percentage of national output (Gross Domestic Product) are from page 65 of *The Economist* of December 8, 2001, under the title "What Doth It Profit?" The quotation about service differences in India are from page 112 of *India Unbound* by Gurcharan Das and the comment on India's bank tellers is from *The Economist* of February 22, 1997, in an article titled, "India's Companies Will Become Worldclass Only When They Are Forced to Compete." The McDonald's practice of making unannounced inspections of the suppliers of their hamburger meat and the potatoes used for French fries is from page 130 and 131 of *McDonald's* by John F. Love. Kroc's insistence on stringent cleanliness inside, outside and around each restaurant is detailed on pages 142 to 144 and 147. Henry J. Heinz's competitive advantages from selling unadulterated horseradish are discussed on pages 52 and 53 of *Brand New: How Entrepreneurs Earned Consumers' Trust from Wedgwood to Dell* by Nancy F. Koehn, published in 2001 by the Harvard Business School Press. Woolworth's early travails are recounted in the first three chapters of *Remembering Woolworth's* by Karen Plunkett-Powell. Information on the decline of urban newspapers and the rise of suburban papers is from Frank J. Prial, "Suburban Sprawl Also Applies to the Circulation of Newspapers," *New York Times*, November 18, 1990, p. E5. Lenin's estimate of how easy it was to run an enterprise was from his book *The State and Revolution*, written on the eve of the Bolshevik revolution. His later change of mind is from "The Fight to Overcome the Fuel Crisis," "The Role and Functions of Trade Unions Under the New Economic Policy," "Five Years of the Russian Revolution and the Prospects of the World Revolution," and "Ninth Congress of the Russian Communist Party (Bolsheviks)," all quoted from the 1951 edition of *Selected Works* by V. I. Lenin, published in Moscow by the Foreign Languages Publishing House. The U.S. Supreme Court decision with the narrow definition of the market for shoes was *Brown Shoe Co. v. United States*, 370 U.S. 294 (1962). The decline in the number of pay telephones was reported in the May 14, 2001 issue of *BusinessWeek* on page 16.

CHAPTER 9: PRODUCTIVITY AND PAY

Comparisons of labor productivity in Japanese-owned and Chinese-owned cotton mills in China are from page 47 of *The Rise of "The Rest"* by Alice Amsden, published in 2001 by Oxford University Press. Comparisons of American-owned manufacturing firms in Britain and British-owned manufacturing firms were made on page 52 of the October 12, 2002 issue of *The Economit* under the title, "Blame the Bosses." Data on Americans' changing incomes between 1975 and 1991 are from pages 8 and 22 of the 1995 *Annual Report* of the Federal Reserve Bank of Dallas. Earlier studies indicating similar patterns include *Years of Poverty, Years of Plenty* by Greg Duncan et al, published by the University of Michigan Press. Similar changes in individual incomes in continental European countries were reported on page 5 of *Poor Statistics: Getting the Facts Right About Poverty in Australia* by Peter Saunders, published in April 2002 by the Centre for Independent Studies in Sydney. Similar data on incomes in Britain and New Zealand were reported on page 32 of *Poverty and Benefit Dependency* by David Green, published in 2001 by the New Zealand Business Roundtable, and similar data from Canada appeared in an article titled "Time Reveals the Truth about Low Incomes," by Jason Clemens & Joel Emes, which appeared on pages 24–26 of the Summer 2001 issue of *Fraser Forum*, published by the Fraser Institute in Vancouver, British Columbia, Canada. Data on American household incomes in 2001 are from page 16 of Section 4 of the January 12, 2003 issue of the *New York Times* in an article titled "Defining the Rich in the World's Wealthiest Nation" by David Leonhardt, beginning on page 1 of that section. Changes in the composition of the 400 richest Americans are from pages 80 and 81 of the September 30, 2002 issue of *Forbes* magazine in an article by William P. Barrett titled "The March of the 400." The data showing 64 million people in the top 20 percent of American households and 39 million in the bottom 20 percent are from page 11 of *Income Inequality: How Census Data Misrepresent Income Distribution* by Robert Rector and Rea S. Hederman, published by the Heritage Foundation in Washington. The misleading claim that income quintiles divide the country into five equal parts was made on page 48 of *Economics Explained* by Robert Heilbroner and Lester Thurow. Data on numbers of heads of household working in high-income and low-income households in 2000 are from Table HINC–06 from the Current Population Survey, downloaded from the Bureau of the Census web site. The fact that the top 10 percent of American income earners worked less than the bottom 10 percent in the late nineteenth century, and just the reverse in the early twenty-first century is from page 92 of *Saving Capitalism from the Capitalists* by Rajan and Zingales. The fact that household income rose by just 6 percent between 1969 and 1996, while per capita real income rose by 51 percent over that same span is calculated from statistics on pages C–6 and C–33 of the Census Bureau's *Current Population Reports*, P–60–203, whose individual title is *Measuring 50 Years of Economic Change*. The misguided remark from the *Washington Post* is from page 34 of its September 7, 1998 issue, in an article titled "The Rich Get Richer, and So Do the Old," by Barbara Vobejda. No doubt it was reprinted from a recent issue of the regular daily *Washington Post*. The fact that 3.5 percent of American households have a net worth of one million dollars or more, and that 80 percent of American millionaires inherited nothing, are from page 3 of *The Millionaire Next Door* by Thomas J. Stanley and William D. Danko. The fact that the real income of those who had been in the bottom 20 percent in 1975 was by 1991 higher than the real income of the average American in 1991 is from page 14 of the 1995 *Annual Report* of the Federal Reserve Bank of Dallas. The falling income share and rising real income of households in the bottom 20 percent is documented on page 19 of *Money Income in the United States: 2001*, which is one of the Current Population Reports, number P60–218, published by the Census. The upward shift in the peak earning years during the last half of the twentieth century was reported on page 16 of the 1995 *Annual Report* of the Federal Reserve Bank of Dallas. The fact that women who worked continuously earned slightly more than men who did the same is from page 103 of "The Economic Role of Women," *The Economic Report of the President, 1973*, published by the U.S. Government Printing Office. The differences between the earnings of women with and without children are from page 15 of a valuable compendium of data on women in the economy titled *Women's Figures*, 1999 edition, written by Diana Furchtgott-Roth and Christine Stolba and published by the American Enterprise Institute, a Washington think tank. Data on male predominance in work-related deaths are from the same source, page 33. Comparison of the incomes of black, white, and Hispanic males of the same age and IQ are from page 323 of *The Bell Curve* by Richard Herrnstein and Charles Murray. The comparison of the incomes of Maoris with those of other New Zealanders of comparable age, skill, and literacy is quoted from page 43 and 44 of *Poverty and Benefit Dependency* by David Green. The number of Americans working in the Soviet Union is from page 11 of *The Turning Point* by Nikolai Shmelev and Vladimir Popov. Violations of apartheid laws by employers in South Africa are discussed on pages 152 and 153 of *Capitalism and Apartheid* by Merle Lipton. Violations of these laws by home builders in Johannesburg are discussed on page 164 of *Apartheid: A History* by Brian Lapping. Violations of the residential aspects of the apartheid laws are discussed on pages 112 and 113 of *South Africa's War Against Capitalism* by Walter E. Williams—a black American economist who himself violated these laws by living in an area set aside for whites. The round-the-clock use of trucks in mid-twentieth century West Africa is discussed on pages 14 and 15 of *West African Trade* by P.T. Bauer. Data on the average life of capital equipment in the Soviet Union and in the United States are from pages 145–146 of *The Turning Point* by Nikolai Shmelev and Vladimir Popov.

CHAPTER 10: CONTROLLED LABOR MARKETS

The fact that the average American has nine jobs between the ages of 18 and 35 is from page 79 of *Savings Capitalism from the Capitalists* by Rahhuram G. Rajan and Luigi Zingales. The effects of job security for NATO's military personnel were reported in a front-page article in the *Wall Street Journal* of February 3, 2003, under the title "How the Armies of Europe Let Their Guard Down," by Philip Shiskin. The effect of minimum wages in reducing the employment of workers in general in various countries, and the employment of younger and less skilled workers in particular, is discussed on pages 33, 34, and 335 of *What Future for New Zealand's Minimum Wage Law*, based on a study done by ACIL Economics and Policy, Pty. Ltd., and published by the New Zealand Business Roundtable. Similar conclusions for the United States are found in *Youth and Minority Unemployment*, written by Walter E. Williams and published in 1977 by the Hoover Institution Press. The unemployment rate in Switzerland in February 2003 was reported on page 100 of March 15, 2003 issue of *The Economist*. The quote from the *Wall Street Journal* about the unemployment rate in Hong Kong in 1991 was from page C 16 of the January 16, 1991 issue. New government-mandated benefits for workers in Hong Kong and the higher unemployment rates after China took control are mentioned on page 45 of *Country Commerce: Hong Kong*, a report released in December 2002 by The Economist Intelligence Unit, based in New York and affiliated with the London magazine, *The Economist*. The effect of informal minimum wages in West Africa are discussed on pages 18 and 19 of *West African Trade*, written by Professor P. T. Bauer of the London School of Economics and published in 1954 by Cambridge University Press. The use of minimum wage laws to promote racial discrimination is discussed on page 14 of *Youth and Minority Unemployment* by Walter Williams and on page 50 of *The Japanese Canadians* by Charles H. Young and Helen R. Y. Reid. The effects of minimum wages on the employment of black teenagers is discussed in *Youth and Minority Unemployment* by Walter E. Williams. Data on American automobile production and employment are from *Motor Vehicle Facts & Figures: 1997*, published by the American Automobile Manufacturers Association and from pages 19 and 20 of an article by Christopher J. Singleton titled "Auto Industry Jobs in the 1980s: A Decade of Transition," which appeared in the U. S. Department of Labor's *Monthly Labor Review* for February 1992. Data on the decline of unionization is available from many sources, one being an article by Richard A. Ryan titled "Labors Gains Undercut by Lingering Problems," which appeared in *The Detroit News* of July 25, 1999. The amount of hours of labor used per automobile produced by American and Japanese auto makers is from page 69 of the April 21, 2003 issue of *BusinessWeek* magazine in an article by David Weeks beginning on page 68 and titled, "Pick Me as Your Strike Target! No, Me!"

CHAPTER 11: AN OVERVIEW

Data on wages and salaries as a share in national income are from page 104 of "Structural Changes: Regional and Urban" by Carol E. Heim in *The Cambridge Economic History of the United States*, Volume III: *The Twentieth Century*, edited by Stanley L. Engerman and Robert E. Gallman, published in the year 2000 by Cambridge University Press. The fact that nearly half the billionaires in the world are in the United States is from page 132 of the March 17, 2003 issue of *Forbes* magazine. Information on China's income inequalities are from "Income Distribution in China: To Each According to His Abilities," *The Economist*, June 2, 2001, pages 39 and 45. Data on regional differences in poverty rates in India are from page 7 of a special section on India in *The Economist* of June 2, 2001. The examples of social mobility in India are discussed on pages 187–195, 207–210, 244–254 *India Unbound* by Gurcharan Das. The economist who wrote of the "winner-take-all" effect of motion pictures and recorded music was Professor Robert Shiller of Yale, writing in *The Economist* of March 22, 2003 on page 70 under the title, "Risk Management for the Masses." The laments of R. H. Tawney and others about widespread public acceptance of inequality can be found in Chapter II of his book *Equality*. The fact that most American living below the official poverty line owned a microwave oven and a videocassette recorder in 1994 is from page 22 of the 1995 *Annual Report* of the Federal Reserve Bank of Dallas. The stories of the great American fortunes created by Carnegie, Ford, Vanderbilt, etc., are widely available in numerous books but the stories of similar individuals in India are from pages 187–195, 207–210, 246–248 of *India Unbound* by Gurcharan Das. The falling percentage share of American income by families in the bottom quintile and the rising real incomes of such families are shown in data on page 21 of the U.S. Bureau of the Census publication *Money Income in the United States: 2000*, Current Population Reports P60–213.

CHAPTER 12: INVESTMENT AND SPECULATION

The experience of the Tata and Birla enterprises in India are from page 93 of *India Unbound* by Gurcharan Das. The statement that businesses in India must break laws in order to operate is from page 143 of the same book. The numerous government regulations in India are discussed on page 94. India's freeing up its economy is discussed on page 29 and the rising foreign investment that followed is discussed on page 220. The disastrous speculation in silver by the Hunt brothers is covered on pages 249–250 of *The New York Times Century of Business*, edited by Floyd Norris and Christine Bockelmann and published in the year 2000 by McGraw-Hill. The speculation of Henry Heinz that led to bankruptcy is discussed in *Brand New* by Nancy F. Koehn, pages 321. The prediction of *The Economist* magazine that the price of oil was heading downward appeared on page 23 of the May 4, 1999 issue under the title, "The Next Shock?" The ability of Dell computers to operate with only enough inventory to last for five days was reported in the May 14, 2001 issue of *BusinessWeek* on page 38B. The downgrading of California's state bonds in 2001 was covered in many places, including page A3 of the April 25, 2001 issues of *The Wall Street Journal*. The buying up of future payments due to accident victims in installments by paying a lump sum is discussed in an article beginning on the front page of the *Wall Street Journal* of February 25, 1998 titled "Thriving Industry Buys Insurance Settlements from Injured Plaintiffs." Statistics on the purchase of annuities are from page 65 of *U.S. News & World Report*, October 22, 2001, in an article titled "Betting on A Long Life" by Leonard Wiener. Twentieth century energy consumption and the growth of known reserves of various metals are discussed on pages 40 and 41 of an article by William J. Baumol and Sue Anne Blackman titled "Natural Resources" in *The Fortune Encyclopedia of Economics*. Statistics on the known reserves of petroleum in 1950 and in 2000 are from Section II, Table 1 of *Basic Petroleum Data Book*, Vol. XXI, No. 1 (February, 2001), published by the American Petroleum Institute. Data on the reserves of copper are from pages 12 and 13 of *A Poverty of Reason* by Wilfred Beckerman, published by the Independent Institute. The bet between Julian Simon and Paul Ehrlich was covered in the *New York Times* of December 2, 1990, Section VI, page 52, in an article by John Tierney titled "Betting The Planet." The experiences of F. W. Woolworth are from *Remembering Woolworth's* by Karen Plunkett-Powell, pages 19 to 20 and 31 to 33. The fact that the cost of finding oil had fallen by two-thirds between 1977 and 1998 is based on U. S. Department of Energy statistics quoted on page 42 of *Julian Simon and the Triumph of Energy sustainability* by Fred L. Smith, Jr., published in 2000 by the American Legislative Exchange Council. The estimate that some Russian oil could be extracted for less than two dollars a barrel is from page 88 of the May 13, 2002 issue of *Fortune* magazine, in an article titled "Russia Pumps It Up" by Bill Powell.

CHAPTER 13: RISKS AND INSURANCE

Comparisons of the interest rates in Mexico, Brazil, and the United States are based on data in a graph on page 68 of the June 29, 2002 issue of *The Economist* in an article titled "Spreading Risk." Short-term interest rates in Hong Kong, Russia, and Turkey were reported on page 98 of the May 3, 2003 issue of *The Economist*. Rates of return on venture capital are from page C1 of the *Wall Street Journal* of April 29, 2002 in a story titled "Venture Firms Face Backlash from Investors," written by Lisa Bransten. Information on the current value of a dollar invested in gold, stocks, and bonds in 1801 is from an article titled "Now What?" in the September 21, 1998 *Forbes Global Business & Finance*, pages 20–21. Data on real rates of return on stocks and bonds from the 1930s to the end of the twentieth century are from *The Economist*, May 5, 2001, page 7 of a special section titled "Global Equity Markets: The Rise and Fall." The comment on academic institutions losing money in the stock market is from the *Wall Street Journal* of October 13, 1998, page C1. News of the former Yahoo CEO who sold his stock, just before it rose dramatically in price, is from page 75 of the February 4, 2002 issue of *BusinessWeek*. The fact that the 400 richest Americans lost $80 billion in one year was reported on pages 80 and 81 of the September 30, 2002 issue of *Forbes* magazine, under the title, "The March of the 400," by William P. Barrett. The discussion of mutual funds draws on two articles from page R1 of the April 9, 2001 issue of the *Wall Street Journal*: Jonathan Clements, "Seven Reasons to Index—and to Avoid Playing Those Favorites" by Jonathan Clements and "Index Funds: 25 Years in Pursuit of the Average," by Karen Damato. The fact that mutual funds as a whole lost money between early 1998 and early 2003 is from an article titled "Five Years of Feast and Famine" by Theo Francis in the *Wall Street Journal* of June 2, 2003, beginning on page R1. The one exception is covered on the same page of the same issue under the title "Survivor: How One Fund Avoids Losses," by Ian McDonald. Information on the number of insurance companies in the United States and their assets is from pages 507 and 508 of the Bureau of the Census publication *Statistical Abstract of the United States:2000*. Data on the percentage of current premium income that is paid out in current claims by Allstate and State Farm insurance companies is from page C10 of the January 2, 2003 issue of the *New York Times* in an article beginning on page C1 titled "Colossus; at the Accident Scene" by Jerry Guidera. The proportion of life insurance companies' income from premiums and investments is from page 81 of *Life Insurers Fact Book: 2000*, published by the American Council of Life Insurers, located in Washington, D. C. Data on varying motor vehicle death rates by age are from page 109 of *The Insurance Information Institute Fact Book 2001*. The quotation from a City Attorney in Oakland who complained that it was unfair to charge people different automobile insurance premiums based on where they lived was from page B1 of the *San Francisco Chronicle* of May 30, 2003 under the titled "Car Insurance Rates Hit" by Carolyn Said. The use of global positioning systems by insurance companies looking for their policy-holders in the wake of natural disaster is from the *New York Times* of January 18, 1999, section, C, page 8. The title of the story is "Media; Sweetheart, Give Me a Reboot" and it was written by Dylan Loeb McClain. The Indian government's tardiness in responding to a cyclone is discussed on page 535 of Indian economist Barun S. Mitra's article, "Dealing with Natural Disaster: Role of the Market," in the December 2000 issue of *Journal des Economistes et des Etudes Humaines*. The financial problems of government pension plans in Europe Union countries are discussed on pages 5 and 6 of a special section within the February 16, 2002 issue of *The Economist*, in an article titled "Snares and Delusions." The special section is titled "Time to Grow Up." The quotation about Brazil's government pension plan is from page 36 of the April 5, 2003 issue of *The Economist* in an article titled "Lula's Great Pension Battle." The New Zealand poll on the likelihood of receiving government pensions is cited on page 71 of the April-May 2003 issue of *Policy Review*, in an article titled "Market Reform: Lessons from New Zealand" by Rupert Darwall.

CHAPTER 14: AN OVERVIEW

The epigraph is from a column titled "Economic Profit vs. Accounting Profit" by Robert L. Bartley on page A17 of the *Wall Street Journal* of June 2, 2003. Smokers' responses to higher taxes on cigarettes in Alaska are discussed on page 37 of *The Greedy Hand: How Taxes Drive Americans Crazy and What to Do About It* by Amith Shlaes, published by Random House in 1999. Data on increased revenue after a reduction in the capital gains tax are from *The Wall Street Journal* of May 14, in an article on page A18 by Arthur Laffer, Lawrence Kudlow, and Stephen Moore, titled "Real Relief: A Capital-Gains Tax Cut." The quotation about rising tax revenues after a tax rate cut in India is from page 200 of *India Unbound* by Gurcharan Das. The comment on the negative effects of anticipations of land reform is from *Development Without Aid* by Melvyn B. Krauss. The economic consequences of political threats to nationalize the tea plantations in Sri Lanka were discussed on page 832 of Volume II of *Asian Drama: An Inquiry into the Poverty of Nations* by Gunnar Myrdal, first printing published in 1968 by the Pantheon division of Random House. Hoarding by Russian consumers and business enterprises during the 1991 inflation was discussed on pages 7 and 10 to 11 of *Kapitalizm: Russia's Struggle to Free Its Economy* by Rose Brady, published by Yale University Press in 1999. The downgrading of California's state government bonds by Standard & Poor's was reported on the front page of the April 25, 2001 issue of the *San Francisco Chronicle*, under the headline: "S&P Lowers California's Bond Rating" by Kathleen Pender and Moody's downgrading was reported in the *Sacramento Bee* of November 22, 2001, under the title "Credit-Rating Service Lowers California Bond Rating Again" by John Hill.

CHAPTER 15: NATIONAL OUTPUT

The fact that the money supply in the United States declined by more than one-third from 1929 to 1932 is based on the monumental National Bureau of Economic Research study *A Monetary History of the United States: 1867–1960* by Milton Friedman and Anna Jacobson Schwartz, published by Princeton University Press in 1963, page 352. Data on the unemployment rate during the Great Depression of the 1930s is from page 196 of an article titled "Great Depression" by Robert J. Samuelson, published in the *Fortune Encyclopedia of Economics*. Data on the fall in prices of various corporate stocks from 1929 to 1932 are from page 76 of *Since Yesterday: The 1930s in America* by Frederick Lewis Allen, published in 1986 in the Perennial Library edition by Harper & Row. The fears of a glutted market expressed by Seymour Harris and Vance Packard are quoted from the latter's book *The Waste Makers*, pages 7 and 19. The accelerated growth of durable equipment owned by both businesses and consumers after the Second World War is documented on page 17 of the April 2000 issue of the *Survey of Current Business*. The rises and falls in the real prices of various American consumer goods between the years 1900 and 2000 are shown on page 91 of the December 23, 2000 issue of *The Economist*. Data on the increased square footage of new houses between 1983 and 2000 are from page 29 of *Housing Market Statistics*, November 2001 issue, published by the National Association of Home Builders. Differences between the average per capita incomes in Japan and the United States, when measured by official exchanges rates rather than by the actual purchasing power of the yen and the dollar, is discussed on page 6 of the third edition of *The Illustrated Guide to the American Economy* by Herbert Stein and Murray Foss, published by the American Enterprise Institute. The Gross Domestic Product of Norway and Portugal in 2002 were reported on page 100 of the March 15, 2003 issue of *The Economist*.

CHAPTER 16: MONEY AND THE BANKING SYSTEM

The use of gin as currency in British West Africa was mentioned on page 233 of *The Economic Revolution in British West Africa* by Allan McPhee, second edition published by Frank Cass, Ltd. in 1971. The use of cigarettes as money in a prisoner-of-war camp during World War II was described by an economist who was one of those prisoners of war in an article in the November 1945 issue of *Economica* titled "The Economic Organization of a P.O.W. Camp," by R. A. Radford. The quote about Argentineans' resort to barter during the Argentine monetary crisis of 2002 was from page A4 of the *Los Angeles Times* of May 6, 2002, in a story that began on page A1 under the title "Where To Swap Till You Drop," by Hector Tobar. The fact that a hundred-dollar bill in the 1990s had less purchasing power than a twenty-dollar bill in the 1960s is from page 47 of an article titled "Going Underground," written by Peter Brimelow and published in the September 21, 1998 issue of *Forbes*

Global Business and Finance. The fact that Chinese money was once preferred to Japanese money in Japan is from page 150 of a book titled *Money* by Jonathan Williams. The fact that most savings accounts in Bolivia were in dollars during that country's runaway inflation is from page 210 of an article titled "Hyperinflation," written by Michael K. Salemi and published in *The Fortune Encyclopedia of Economics*, where the German hyperinflation of the 1920s is also discussed on page 208. The estimate that 80 percent of the demand for gold comes from the jewelry industry is from the *Wall Street Journal* of October 8, 2002, in a story titled "Hoarders Drive Up Gold, Despite Slump in Jewelry Sales," by Peter A. McKay. The rising price of gold on the day that the World Trade Center in New York was attacked by terrorists was shown on page 69 of *The Economist* of September 15, 2001 and its price on the eve of the 2003 war with Iraq is from page 33 of the January 28, 2003 issue of London's *Financial Times.* The quotation from John Maynard Keynes is from page 86 of 1952 printing of his *Essays in Persuasion.* The fact that German workers were paid twice a day during this period is from pages 450–451 of *Germany: 1866–1945* by Gordon A. Craig. The haste of Russians to spend their rubles during that country's inflation was in a news story from the front page of the *Christian Science Monitor* of August 31, 1999. The reporter was Judith Matloff and the title of the story was "Russians Replay 'Bad Old Days'." Data on the 1921 inflation in the Soviet Union is from page 6 of *The Turning Point* by Nikolai Shmelev and Vladimir Popov. Russians using rubles for wallpaper and toiler paper in 1991 was reported on page 11 of *Kapitalizm: Russia's Struggle to Free Its Economy* by Rose Brady, published by Yale University Press in 1999. The slowing circulation of money in the United States, along with the declining amount of money in the years following the stock market crash of 1929 is spelled out on pages 302 to 305 of *A Monetary History of the United States* by Milton Friedmand and Anna Jacobson Schwartz. President Woodrow Wilson's statement about the powers and structure of the Federal Reserve System was quoted on page 3 of *A History of the Federal Reserve* by Allan H. Meltzer. The remarkable agreement of both liberal and conservative economists in the United States on the confused and counterproductive monetary policies of the Federal Reserve during the Great Depression of the 1930s can be found by comparing the accounts in *The Great Crash* by John Kenneth Galbraith (especially his comment on page 27 of the 1997 edition) and in *A Monetary History of the United States* by Milton Friedman and Anna J. Schwartz, where this point is discussed on pages 407–419. The upward shift in the Federal Reserve's discount rate in 1931 is shown on page 304 of the latter book and the collapse of thousands of American banks during the Great Depression is mentioned on page 351. President Herbert Hoover's use of the federal government to try to prevent agricultural prices from falling is mentioned on pages 50 and 52 of the third volume of his *Memoirs.* John Maynard Keynes' comment on the monetary policy of the British government in 1931 are from page 283 of his *Essays in Persuasion,* 1952 printing. *Business Week* magazine's comment on Federal Reserve chairman Alan Greenspan was on page 45 of the June 16, 2003 issue.

CHAPTER 17: THE ROLE OF GOVERNMENT

The epigraph by President Lyndon B. Johnson is quoted from page 181 of *The Johnson Years: The Difference He Made* by Robert L. Hardesty, published in 1993 by the Lyndon Baines Johnson Library. The comment on the changing role of government in economies around the world is from page 10 of a 1990 book that goes into that subject at length—*The Commanding Heights*, written by Daniel Yergin and Joseph Stanislaw and published by Simon & Schuster. The account of the airport at Kinshasa, Congo, is from page A1 of the April 30, 2002 issue of *The Wall Street Journal*, in a story titled "Kinshasa is Poor, Scary and a Boon For Air France" by Daniel Michaels. Police corruption in Bolivia was reported on page 37 of the May 4, 2002 issue of *The Economist* under the title "Policing the Police." The cost of private security in Brazil was reported in *The Economist* of August 18, 2001 in an article on page 28 titled "Bullet-Proof in Alphaville." The reluctance of foreign companies to use Russian accountants during the czarist era is mentioned on page 187 of *Pioneers for Profit* by John P. McKay. The comment on bribes in India is from page 202 of *India Unbound* by Gurcharan Das, published in 2001 by Alfred A. Knopf. The comment about the looting of Russian oil companies is from page 57 of *Saving Capitalism from the Capitalists* by Raghuram G. Rajan and Luigi Zingales. Bribery in Russian universities was reported in the April 18, 2002 issue of *The Chronicle of Higher Education*, in a story titled "Reports of Bribe-Taking at Russian Universities Have Increased, Authorities Say," by Bryon MacWilliams. The fact that both businesses and international aid agencies are taking the level of bribery and corruption into consideration when deciding where to invest and lend is mentioned on page 65 of the March 2, 2002 issue of *The Economist*. The comment by Aditya Birla on the problems created by India's bureaucracy are from page 183 of *India Unbound* by Gurcharan Das. The comment by Soviet economists on the cutting down of forests without reseeding them is from page 109 of *The Turning Point* by Shmelev and Popov. The ingenious devices used by many affluent northern California, communities to prevent development are explored in articles in *Land Use and Housing on the San Francisco Peninsula: 1982 Annual*, edited by Thomas M. Hagler and published by the Stanford Environmental Law Society. Complaints about the confiscation of the profits of Soviet enterprises by the government of the U.S.S.R. are from page 261 of *The Turning Point* by Nikolai Shmelev and Vladimir Popov. Evictions of elderly tenants from cheap hotels in San Francisco in December 1999 were covered in front page stories in the *San Francisco Examiner* on December 21, 1999 and January 14, 2000. The comment on bribes in China and Japan is from page 42 of *The Character of Nations* by Angelo Codevilla. The ability of the Marwaris of India to rely on each other's word in business is mentioned on page 143 of *India Unbound* by Gurcharan Das. The role of Jains and Jews in the Antwerp international diamond center was discussed in a story beginning on page B1 of the May 27, 2003 issue of the *Wall Street Journal*. The story of how unscrupulous landlords exploit and destroy rent-controlled apartment buildings is told on page 43 of *Zoning, Rent Control and Affordable Housing* by William Tucker and in *The Ecology of Housing Destruction* by Peter D. Salins. The story of the genesis and consequences of President Nixon's wage and price controls is from pages 60 to 64 of *The Commanding Heights* by Daniel Yergin and Joseph Stanislaw and from an essay by Herbert Stein in the *Wall Street Journal* of August 25, 1996, page A 12. The comment that educational results "take a long time to come" is from page 313 of *India Unbound* by Gurcharan Das. The mention of a former EPA administrator's conclusions about removing toxic material is from page 11 of *Breaking the Vicious Cycle: Towar Effective Risk Regulation* by Stephen Breyer. The effects of small and large doses of saccharin on cancer in laboratory rats is from an article beginning on page 54 of the June 9, 2003 issue of *Fortune* magazine, titled "A Little Poison Can Be Good for You" by David Tripp. The costly cleanup of a toxic waste site in New Hampshire is discussed on pages 11 and 12 of *Breaking the Vicious Cycle* by Stephen Breyer. The bad effects of the gasoline additive MTBE on ground water has been discussed in many places, including the *San Francisco Chronicle* of August 19, 2001 in a front page story titled "Congress Not told of MTBE Dangers," by William Carlson. Examples of private market ways of taking externalities into account are found in an article titled "Public Goods and Externalities" by Tyler Cowen in *The Fortune Encyclopedia of Economics*, edited by David R. Henderson. Franklin D. Roosevelt's use of presidential powers created during the First World War to take the United States off the gold standard is mentioned on page 86 of *The New York Times Century of Business*. The sketch of the evolution of the Small Business Administration is from pages 5 and 7 of *Big Government and Affirmative Action: The Scandalous History of the Small Business Administration* by Jonathan J. Bean, published in 2001 by the University of Kentucky Press.

CHAPTER 18: AN OVERVIEW

Examples of various policies in India are from *India Unbound* by Gurcharan Das. The argument that government policy worsened, rather than alleviated, the Great Depression can be found in *A Monetary History of the United States* by Milton Friedman and Anna J. Schwartz, pages 407–419, in Paul Johnson's *A History of the American People*, pages 737–760 and in *Out of Work* by Richard K. Vedder and Lowell E. Gallaway, pages 89–97, 137–146. The quote about favors to special interests by India's government is from page 318 of *India Unbound* by Gurcharan Das. The quote about how new and rare free market democracies are in from page 317 of the same book. The problems of Albanian and Czech banks in the post-Communist era were reported in *The Economist* of April 28, 2001 on pages 77 and 78.

CHAPTER 19: INTERNATIONAL TRADE

The epigraph by Henry Hazlitt is from page 87 of *Economics in One Lesson* by Henry Hazlitt. The comment from the *New York Times* about whether the United States was a "job winner" or a "job loser" from freer trade was from an article by

Louis Uchitelle titled "Nafta and Jobs," which appeared in the November 14, 1993 issue, on the first page of section 4. The declining unemployment rate in the United states from 1993 to 2000 is shown on page 26 of a special supplement in the June 29, 2002 issue of *The Economist* under the title "Present at the Creation." Congressman Bonior's warning and the facts to the contrary are both from page 3 of a study titled *Trade Liberalization: The North American Free Trade Agreement's Economic Impact on Michigan*, published in December 1999 by The Mackinac Center, a think tank in Michigan. The increase of jobs in Mexico was reported on page A13 of the *Wall Street Journal* of March 5, 2003 and the simultaneous increase of jobs in the United States was reported on page 364 of *The Economic Report of the President*, February 2002. Justice Holmes' statement, "we need to think things instead of words" is from page 293 of *Collected Legal Papers* by Oliver Wendell Holmes. The fact that India had the world's largest supply of gold was reported on page 70 of the March 15, 2003 issue of *The Economist* under the title "Forseeing the Future," a story beginning on page 69. The American export surpluses during the 1930s and its lower total international trade in that decade compared to the 1920s can be calculated from data on page 864 of the U.S. Bureau of the Census publication, *Historical Statistics of the United States: Colonial Times to 1970*. The record-breaking reduction in the international trade deficit of the United States in the spring of 2001 was reported on page 35 of *BusinessWeek*'s May 7, 2001 issue under the title, "A Shrinking Trade Gap Looks Good Statewide." The West African example of comparative advantage among cocoa farmers is from page 68 of *The Economic Revolution in British West Africa* by Allan McPhee, published originally in 1926 and reprinted in 1971 by Frank Cass & Co., Ltd. The estimate of economies of scale in automobile production are from page 76 of *The Structure of American Industry*, ninth edition, by Walter Adams and James Brock, published in 1995 by Prentice-Hall. Pages 97 and 104 of the same book discusses job losses in the American steel industry and the job losses in the U.S. economy as a whole from trying to protect jobs in the steel industry. Data on production of Chevrolets in 2000 is from page 4 of *Ward's Motor Vehicle Facts & Figures: 2002*, published by Ward's Communications in Southfield, Michigan. Information on automobile production in Australia is from pages 59 and 81 *Ward's Automotive Yearbook*, 59th edition, published in 1997. Data on Australian and American populations and purchasing power in Australia are from pages 22, 24, 62, and 102 of *Pocket World in Figures 2001*, published by *The Economist*. Reports on the Dutch and Swedish international retailers is from "Shopping All Over the World," in *The Economist* of June 19, 1999, page 60 and information on Royal Ahold's stores in Latin America is from a *New York Times* article beginning on page W1 of the April 4, 2003 issue under the title "Royal Ahold to Sell Its South American Businesses." The fact that Toyota, Honda, and Nissan all earn most of their profits in North America is from page W1 of the October 31, 2002 issue of the *New York Times*, in a news story by Ken Belson titled "Slowdown? Don't Tell Toyota Motor." An example of how job shifts abroad lead to production changes domestically can be seen in a *Wall Street Journal* story by Joel Millman titled "Job Shift to Mexico Lets U.S. Firms Upgrade," which appeared in the November 15, 1999, page A 28. Information on China's toy exports to India, and on the Tata group's response to other Chinese exports are from pages 48 and 49 of the May 3, 2001 issue of *Far Eastern Economic Review*, in an article titled, "No More Fun and Games" by Joanna Slater and Nayan Chanda. Holland's position as a leading international trade nation from the 1590s to the 1740s was discussed on page 2 of *The Dutch Republic* by Jonathan Israel and the high wages of Dutch workers was discussed on pages 88–93 of *An Economic and Social History of the Netherlands 1800–1920* by Michael Wintle. Data on labor productivity in India and the United States are from page 65 of the September 8, 2001 issue of *The Economist*, under the title "Unproductive." The declining rates of return on capital invested in czarist Russia as the amount invested increased during its early industrialization are from page 139 of *Pioneers for Profit* by John P. McKay. The fact that world exports in 1933 were one-third of what they were in 1929 is from page 83 of *Against the Dead Hand* by Brink Lindsey. The 1933 public appeal by American economists to reduce tariffs is reproduced on pages 300 and 301 of *Economics and the Public Welfare: A Financial and Economic History of the United States, 1914–1939*, second edition, written by Benjamin M. Anderson and published in 1979 by the Liberty Fund in Indianapolis. Examples of the application of anti-dumping laws in the European Union are from pages 29 to 32 of *The Race to the Top: The Real Story of Globalization* written by Tomas Larsson and published by the Cato Institute. The application of American anti-dumping laws is discussed on pages 173 and 174 of *Globalization and Its Discontents* by Joseph E. Stiglitz. The *Wall Street Journal*'s estimates of job losses from steel import restrictions are from page A14 of the March 4, 2002 issue.

CHAPTER 20: INTERNATIONAL TRANSFERS OF WEALTH

Data on remittances from the United States to Mexico and Latin America are from page 23 of the January 11, 2003 issue of *The Economist*. Data on international investments are from page 6 of a special section of *The Economist* of May 3, 2003, that section being titled "A Cruel Sea of Capital." The production of the ten millionth Toyota in the United States was reported on page W1 of the October 31, 2002 issue of the *New York Times*, in a story titled "Slowdown? Don't Tell Toyota Motor," by Ken Belson. Data on payments earned by the United States from royalty and license fees from other countries are from page 77 of the December 2001 issue of *Survey of Current Business*, a publication of the U.S. Department of Commerce, and data on payments earned for all services supplied to other countries are from page 49 of the November 2001 issue of the same publication. The fact that a balance of payments surplus preceded the 1992 recession is from page D–20 of the December 1999 issue of the *Survey of Current Business*. The $1.3 trillion total international debt of the United States at the end of 2001 was reported on page 14 of the July 2002 issue of *Survey of Current Business* and the $300 billion foreign investments of Switzerland was from page 99 of the December 7, 2002 issue of *The Economist*. Data on foreign ownership of American railroads in the nineteenth century are from page 195 of *The History of Foreign Investment in the United States to 1914*, written by Mira

Wilkins and published by Harvard University Press. Information on the over-all amount foreign investment in nineteenth-century America, and on the railroads' majority share of foreign investment in American stocks and bonds are from pages 463 and 466 of "U. S. Foreign Financial Relations in the Twentieth Century" by Barry Eichengreen in *The Cambridge Economic History of the United States*, Volume III: *The Twentieth Century*, edited by Stanley L. Engerman and Robert L. Gallman, and published in the year 2000 by Cambridge University Press. Information on Americans producing more on than one-third of all the manufactured goods in the world in 1913 is from page 142 of *The History of Foreign Investment in the United States to 1914*, cited above. The Spanish cleric who supported expulsion of the Moriscoes was quoted on page 795 of *The Mediterranean World in the Age of Philip II*, Vol. II, by Fernand Braudel, 1973 English translation. The role of foreigners in various British industries and in finance is discussed on page xiv of *Alien Immigrants to England* by W. Cunningham and on pages 325–340 of *The Persecution of Huguenots and French Economic Development: 1680–1720* by Warren C. Scoville. The statement by Fernand Braudel that immigrants created modern Brazil, Argentina, and Chile is from page 440 of his book *A History of Civilization*. The economic role of the Lebanese in Africa is discussed on page 309 of "Lebanese Emigration in General," by R. Bayley Winder, which appeared in Vol IV (1961–62) of *Comparative Studies in Society and History*. The economic role of the Greeks in the Ottoman empire is discussed on pages 262–263 and 266 of "The Transformation of the Economic Position of the *Millets* in the Nineteenth Century," by Charles Isawi, which appeared in Volume I (*The Central Lands*) of *Christians and Jews in the Ottoman Empire: The Functioning of a Plural Society*, edited by Benjamin Braude and Bernard Lewis. The economic role of the Germans in Brazil is discussed in Chapter 2 of *Migrations and Cultures* by Thomas Sowell and the role of the Chinese in Malaysia and the Indians in Fiji are discussed in Chapters 5 and 7 of the same book. The role of the British in Argentina is discussed throughout *British-Owned Railways in Argentina: Their Effect on Economic Nationalism, 1854–1948* by Winthrop R. Wright. The role of the Belgians in Russia is discussed on page 35 of *Pioneers for Profit: Foreign Entrepreneurship and Russian Industrialization 1885–1913* by John P. McKay. Cambodian ownership of most doughnut shops in California is discussed in a front page story in the February 22, 1995 issue of the *Wall Street Journal* under the title "How Cambodians Came to Control California Doughnuts," by Jonathan Kaufman. Differences in the percentage of immigrants on welfare are from page 216 of *The Debate in the United States over Immigration*, edited by Peter Duignan and Lewis H. Gann. Data on American investments in the Netherlands and in Africa in 2001 are from page 20 of the February 2003 issue of *Survey of Current Business* and data on foreign earnings from assets owned in the United States in 2001 are from page 10 of the same issue. Page 68 of Myron Weiner's 1995 book, *The Migration Crisis* is the source of the statement that remittances from citizens living abroad exceed all the foreign aid from all the government agencies in the world. Professor P. T. Bauer's comment on foreign aid is from page 102 of his 1981 book *Equality, the Third World and Economic Delusion*, published by Harvard University Press. Peddlers who became founders of major companies like Levi Strauss, Macy's, etc. are discussed in Chapter 6 of my

Migrations and Cultures, where further specific citations of sources can be found in the end notes. The percentage of the world's land inhabited by Western Europeans and the additional percentage controlled by them in their overseas colonies is from page 87 of *The Dynamics of Global Dominance* by David B. Abernethy, published in 2000 by Yale University Press. The fact that foreigners took nearly $270 billion out of the American economy in 2001 is based on data on page 10 of the February 2003 issue of the *Survey of Current Business*. The estimate that only one person in ten works in a legally recognized enterprise in a typical African nation is from an article titled "Poverty and Property Rights," on pages 20 to 22 of the March 31, 2001 issue of *The Economist*. The estimate of the number of illegally built homes in Egypt is from page 20 of *The Mystery of Capital* by Hernando de Soto and the value of the illegally produced wealth in Peru is from pages 33 and 34. Robert Mundell's comment on the era of the gold standard is from his lecture at the Central Bank of Uruguay in May 20002 and J. P. Morgan's comment on gold was quoted on page 41 of *The New York Times Century of Business*. The varying exchange rates between the dollar and the euro have been discussed in many places, including two news stories beginning on page C1 of the *New York Times* of May 20, 2003. The quotation about the effect of Britain's pound sterling "weakening" against the Euro is from page 52 of the May 19, 2003 issue of *Businessweek* magazine, under the title "Beware the Super Euro." The effect of the "strong" Norwegian krona on purchases of groceries from Sweden was reported on page 42 of the August 31, 2002 issue of *The Economist*, under the title "Have Car-Boot, Will Travel." Data on Americans' overseas investments are from page 6 of a supplement titled "Globalisation and Its Critics" in *The Economist* of September 29, 2001. The fact that American multinational corporations employ more than 30 million people around the world is from page 112 of the December 2002 issue of the U.S. Department of Commerce publication, *Survey of Current Business*. Multinational companies' payment of double the wages received locally in poor countries is shown on page 13 of the same section.

CHAPTER 21: AN OVERVIEW

The public opinion poll on protectionism and free trade was mentioned on page 56 of *The Race to the Top: The Real Story of Globalization*, written by Tomas Larsson and published by the Cato Institute. The estimated costs of protectionism in the European Union countries are from page 62 of the same book. The statistics on the number of steel workers and the number of workers in steel-using industries is from page 229 of *Saving Capitalism from the Capitalism* by Rajan and Zingales. The respective costs of producing steel in the United States, Germany, Japan, Brazil, and South Korea were published on page 61 of *The Economist* magazine of March 9, 2000. Professor Jagdish Bhagwati's experience debating at Cornell is from pages 8 and 9 of his book *Free Trade Today*, published in 2002 by the Princeton University Press. Joseph Stiglitz's criticisms of the International Monetary Fund are found, among other places, in his book *Globalization and Its Discontents*. Data on the increasing role of international trade in the American economy is from page 76 of *Saving Capitalism from the Capitalists* by Rajan and Zingales. Information on the role of foreign investments in the economic development of the United States is from "U. S. Foreign Financial Relations in the Twentieth Century," by Barry Eichengreen in *The Cambridge Economic History of the United States*, Vol. III: *The Twentieth Century*, edited by Stanley L. Engerman and Robert E. Gallman and published in the year 2000 by the Cambridge University Press. The positive growth rates of poor countries that are more "globalized" and the negative growth rates of those that are not at from *The Economist* of December 8, 2001, under the title "Going Global." The report on failed development projects in Niger are from a front page story in the May 10, 2002 issue of the *Wall Street Journal*, under the titled "The Radio Offers Africans Rare Aid in Tune With Needs," by Roger Thurow.

CHAPTER 22: "NON-ECONOMIC" VALUES

BusinessWeek's survey of philanthropic entrepreneurs appeared in the December 2, 2002 issue, beginning on page 82. The complaint that the newspapers have to meet profit requirements determined by "faceless Wall Street analysts" is from a letter to the editor of *Editor & Publisher* magazine, published on page 4 of the October 8, 2001 issue.

CHAPTER 23: MYTHS ABOUT MARKETS

The role of the Indian software company Wipro in maintaining the computer systems for the American hardware chain Home Depot was mentioned on page W7 of the December 25, 2002 issue of the *New York Times*, in a story titled "India is Regaining Contacts With U.S.," written by Saritha Rai and beginning on page W1. The fact that phone calls to Harrod's department store in London are answered by people in India is noted on page 336 of *India Unbound* by Gurcharan Das. The fact that more than half the life insurance in the Philippines, Malaysia, and Singapore is provided by foreign insurance companies was reported on page 57 of *The Economist*, August 11, 2001 issue, in an article titled "Unprofitable Policies." The imported components used to produce Britain's Mini Cooper automobile are mentioned on page W7 of the May 16, 2003 issue of the *New York Times*, in a story beginning on page W1 titled "A Tale of 2 Carmakers and 2 Countries" by John Tiagliabue. The relationship between the Jews and the Jains in Antwerp was reported on page B6 of the May 27, 2003 issue of the *Wall Street Journal*, in a story that began on page B1 under the title, "A New Facet of the Diamond Industry: Indians" by Dan Bilefsky. "The comment that the marketplace was "amoral" and the mayor of Stockton's comment that "life-sustaining" water could not be entrusted to private enterprise are from page 11 of the February 2, 2003 issue of the *San Francisco Chronicle Magazine* in an article titled "Profit on Tap?" by Daffodil Altan, et al. The report on the privatization of municipal water supply in Argentina is from page 68 of the March 22, 2003 issue of *The Economist* under the title "Raise a Glass." Comparisons of the private water system in England with the government-owned water system in Scotland are from page 56 of the May 31, 2003 issue of *The Economist*, under the title "Frozen Taps." The exchange between an official in India and an Indian entrepreneur trying to get him to reduce excise taxes is from page 234 of *India Unbound* by Gurcharan Das. Information on prices at various California grocery stores is from page 47 of the Winter/Spring 2001 issue of *Bay Area Consumers' Checkbook*. The quote from India's Prime Minister Nehru about the number of brands of toothpaste is from page 153 of *India Unbound* by Gurcharan Das. The competition between Federal Express and United Parcel Service for earlier delivery times was discussed on page 41 of *50 Companies that Changed the World* by Howard Rothman, published in 2001 by Career Press. Josiah Wedgwood's pioneering in the use of brand names on consumer products was discussed on page 33 of *Brand New* by Nancy F. Koehn and Henry Heinz's pioneering in the use of brand names for processed foods on pages 59 and 60. The role of McDonald's in pioneering higher standards for French fries, hamburgers and milk shakes is from Chapter 6 of the revised 1996 edition of *McDonald's: Behind the Golden Arches* by John F. Love. The quotes from Adam Smith are from the Modern Library edition of *The Wealth of Nations*, pages 128 and 250. The quote from David Ricardo is from page 123 of Volume III of *The Works and Correspondence of David Ricardo*, edited by Piero Sraffa and published by Cambridge University Press. Business support for President Nixon's wage and price controls is mentioned on page 149 of *The Suicidal Corporation* by Paul Weaver. The fact that the bulk of agricultural subsidies go to big corporations, rather than to family farmers, can be verified from many sources, including *The Structure of American Industry* by Walter Adams and James Brock, 9th edition, page 29. The same book also has data on losses in the computer industry on pages 166–167. Data on air fares and better use of plane capacity after airline deregulation are from an article by Don Phillips titled "20 Days, 18 Flights," which appeared on page 8 of the *Washington Post National Weekly Edition* of July 5, 1999—and which probably appeared shortly before that in the regular daily edition. The estimate that airline fares were up to 50 percent higher under government regulation than they would have been in a free market is from page 248 of the Adams and Brock book mentioned above. For an example of the old federal "fair trade" laws in action, see Thomas O'Donnell and Janet Banford, "Jack Daniels, Meet Adam Smith" in the November 23, 1961 issue of *Forbes* magazine, page 163. Pre-World War II discrimination against blacks and Jews by non-profit organizations is discussed on pages 695 and 705 of "Through the Back Door, Academic Racism and the Negro Scholar" by Michael R. Winston in the Summer 1971 issue of *Daedalus*, on page 480 of *American Democracy* by Harold J. Laski and on page 323 of *An American Dilemma* by Gunnar Myrdal. Information on fees charged by non-profit organizations is from an interview with Peter Drucker that was published in the March/April 1999 issue of *Philanthropy* on page 11. The controversial practice of non-profit organizations selling the right to use their logos to commercial businesses is discussed in a *New York Times* story beginning on page A1 of their May 3, 1999 issue under the title, "Sales Pitches Tied to Charities Draw States' Scrutiny," written by Reed Abelson. The information about the number of American billionaires is from page 128 of the March 19, 2002 issue of *Forbes* magazine. The quote about a "trickle-down" theory is from page 288 of *Dalits in Modern India*, edited by S. M. Michael and published in 1999 by Vistaar Publications in New Delhi. The McDonald's chain's early brushes with bankruptcy are discussed on pages 175–181, and 199 of *McDonald's: Behind the Arches* by John F. Love.

CHAPTER 24: PARTING THOUGHTS

The quotation from Friedrich Hayek is from *The Road to Serfdom*, 1972 edition, published by the University of Chicago Press. The quotation from Paul Johnson is from page 138 of *The Quotable Paul Johnson* published in 1994 by Farrar, Straus and Giroux.

INDEX

A & P grocery chain, 63–64, 65, 66, 67, 77, 84,
    103, 110, 112, 117, 121, 125, 126, 137, 377,
    393
Absolute advantage (see also Comparative
    Advantage), 310–311, 312
Adams, John, 21
Advanced Micro Devices (AMD), 81
Advertising, 85–86, 88, 102, 113, 378–387
Aeroflot, 381
Africa, 51, 92–94, 128, 157, 166, 167, 168, 179,
    188, 194, 232, 258, 277, 314, 334, 336, 337,
    340, 344, 350, 351, 354, 355
Age, 145, 146, 150, 152, 153, 161, 162, 203, 224n,
    234, 236, 252
Agents, 130–131, 394
Aggregate Demand, 245, 247–249, 260
Agriculture, 22, 33–37, 58, 92–93, 127–129,
    297–298, 299, 348
Ahold, Royal, 315
Airlines, 88–89, 109, 383
Albania, 302–303
Alcoa, 100, 113
Alcohol, 57n, 291–292
Alexander the Great, 132, 223
Allocation of resources, 1, 3, 7, 10, 37, 42, 52, 74,
    75, 138, 176, 180–183, 198, 201, 236, 237,
    237, 298, 350, 395
Allstate, 132, 223
Amazon.com, 194, 197
American Cancer Society, 387
American Express, 259, 387
American Indians, 151, 321
American Medical Association, 387
Annheuser-Busch, 85
Annuities, 226
Antitrust laws, 104, 110–118, 377
Antwerp, 39–40, 284, 373
Argentina, 114, 195, 258, 315, 335, 336, 342, 373
Australia, 24, 26, 315, 335, 346, 350
Automobiles, 8–9, 20, 65–66, 72, 80–81, 85, 86,
    90–91, 119–120, 121, 122, 133, 185, 253,
    292, 314–315, 316–317, 373, 374
Avery, Sewell, 71, 124

Bhagwati, Jagdish, 347
Balance of Payments (see International Trade and
    Payments)
Balance of Trade (see International Trade and
    Payments)
Baltimore & Ohio Railroad, 332
Bank of America, 77, 395
Banks, 45, 77, 265, 266–270, 293, 299, 302–303,
    353
Barter, 257–258, 258–259
Baseball, 143, 300
Bauer, P.T., 167, 340
Beer, 85, 315
Berkeley, 26
Berlin, 136
Black Markets, 32–33, 50
Bloomingdale's, 71, 340
Bolivia, 273
Bonanza, 289
Bonds, 211–217, 222, 226
Bonior, David, 308
Brand Names, 378–381
Brazil, 114, 211, 227, 273, 277, 310, 315, 322,
    335, 336, 342,   248, 373
Bribes, 273–274, 286
Bridges, 90
Britain, 26, 27, 38, 135, 137, 145, 165, 181, 262,
    263, 271, 272, 276, 293, 303, 314, 315, 332,
    335, 336, 343, 346, 348, 356, 360, 374, 380
Burger King restaurants, 123, 381
Burma, 13, 232
Burns, Arthur F., 82, 230, 360
Buses, 237–238
Business and Industry, 63–138, 193–194,
    293–294, 299, 302, 381–384

Cadillacs, 97, 301
Cameras, 66–67, 135, 379–380
Canada, 37, 117, 145, 164, 165, 168, 275, 290,
    311, 312, 313,   315, 337, 344
Capacity, 88–90
Capital, 155–158, 319, 328–329, 354, 394
Capital Gains, 210, 213, 388, 389

Carnegie, Andrew, 82, 186, 187, 230, 360
Cartels, 99–105
Carter administration, 76, 207
Categorical Decisions (see Decisions)
Causation, 41, 43–49
    intentional: 45
    systemic: 43–46, 48
Cheese, 9–10
Chevrolets, 91, 97, 301, 314
Chile, 335
China, 13, 39, 42, 95, 142, 149, 164, 181, 192,
    194, 221, 271, 276, 283, 316, 318, 322, 327,
    334, 335
Chinese, 142, 151, 187, 232, 276, 277, 284, 297,
    318, 327, 334, 354, 355
Civil Aeronautics Board (CAB), 109
Communism and Communists, 7, 49–50, 127,
    137, 271, 272, 274, 278, 290, 302, 303, 350,
    363–364
Comparative Advantage, 311–314, 324
Competition, 53–60, 79, 100, 110–111, 123,
    137–138
Complexity, 47–48
Computers, 67, 81, 104, 113–114, 138, 152, 247,
    313, 324, 354–355, 373, 374, 383
Confiscation, 282, 328
Constraints (see Incentives and Constraints)
Consumer Price Index, 301
"Control" of markets, 112–117
Cooperation, 372–373
Corruption, 328, 353, 364
Costs, 10, 59–60, 79, 85, 105, 111, 177, 322, 368
    capacity: 88–90, 105–106
    capital costs: 319
    diseconomies of scale: 86–87, 105–106
    economies of scale: 85–86, 111–112, 267,
        314–316, 322
    specialization: 90–98
    wage rates vs. labor costs: 142, 178–179,
        318–319, 391
Credit and Creditors, 71, 201, 204, 209, 242, 260,
    299–300, 302–303, 352
Credit Suisse, 63
Cruise ships, 89–90
Cyrix, 81
Czech Republic, 302, 303, 373

DaimlerChrysler, 86, 96, 97
Debtor Nation (see International Debt)
Decisions,
    categorical: 10, 56–57, 290–291
    incremental: 55–57, 290–291, 292
    priorities: 38, 56–57
Deflation, 264–266

Dell Computers, 95, 137, 199
Demand (see Supply and Demand)
Department Stores, 68–71
Discrimination, 151–155, 187, 354, 386
Diseconomies of Scale,(see Costs)
Distribution of Income (see Income)
Dividends (see Stocks)
Dow Jones Industrial Average, 218, 219, 289
Dumping, 321–323

Economic Growth, 13, 150
Economics, 1–4, 13, 14, 41–42, 52, 360–361, 367,
    372, 388, 393, 395, 396
Economies of scale, (see Costs)
The Economist, 13, 20, 80, 123, 134, 142, 164, 181,
    182, 197, 227, 274, 283, 303, 328, 244, 346,
    352, 373
Economists, 11, 12, 28, 32, 249, 298, 301, 320,
    340, 347, 352, 388
Education, 185, 192–193, 290, 386, 387
Efficiency, 81, 82–83, 155–158, 289, 291, 299,
    370–371
Ehrlich, Paul, 207, 209
Electricity, 19, 105–107, 204, 215, 365–366
Employers (see Labor)
Engels, Friedrich, 15, 43
England (see Britain)
Enron, 64
Ethiopia, 52
Euro, 342, 343
Europe, 27, 51, 52, 74, 101, 127, 134, 156, 161,
    162, 164, 168,180, 181, 201, 259, 260, 276,
    322, 334, 335, 336, 339, 342, 344, 351, 355,
    356, 375
European Union, 36, 37, 227, 232, 322, 343, 346,
    350
Exploitation, 344–345
Exports (see International Trade and Payments)
External Costs and Benefits (see Social Costs and
    Social Benefits)

Fairness and Unfairness, 20, 138, 144, 223–224,
    383–384
Fallacy of Composition, 246–247, 297–298, 325
Far Eastern Economic Review, 35, 64, 956, 316
"Favorable" Balance of Trade, 308
Federal Communications Commission (FCC),
    105
Federal Deposit Insurance Corporation (FDIC),
    269
Federal Emergency Management Agency
    (FEMA), 132, 133
Federal Express, 95, 304, 380
Federal Reserve System, 265, 269, 270, 300

Fiji, 188, 221, 232, 277, 336, 354
Food, 19–20, 34–35, 51, 52–53, 299, 314, 374, 376
Forbes magazine, 119, 124, 146
Ford, Henry, 78, 82, 85, 133, 186, 187, 202, 230, 385, 394
Ford Motor Company, 72, 86, 119, 133, 315
Foreign Aid, 230, 338–341, 352–353, 354, 355
Foreign Investments (see International Trade and Payments)
Fortune magazine, 36, 63, 64, 71, 81, 84, 100
France, 26, 27, 164, 165, 257, 271, 335,, 341, 346, 393
Franchises, 121, 122, 125, 130–131, 394
Free Trade, 346–348
Friedman, Milton, 4, 265, 382
Fuji Film, 380

Gambling, 195, 235
Garden of Eden, 1
Gasoline, 30–32, 73, 75, 76, 91, 370–371, 378–379
Gates, Bill, 145, 383
General Motors, 63, 64, 86, 90, 97, 119, 133, 144, 162, 173, 245, 263, 314, 315, 365, 382
Germany, 13, 27, 135, 160, 165, 252, 335, 337, 349, 373
Ghana, 12–13, 52, 290, 350
Globalization, 347, 350
Goals, ix, 49–53, 282, 293, 392
Gold, 217, 218, 259, 260, 261, 267, 293, 308–309, 341–342
Goldsmiths, 267
Gorbachev, Mikhail, 7
Government, 99 118, 265, 266, 271–294, 298–301
  regulation: 104–110
  taxing and spending: 292, 374, 387
Graflex Corporation, 66–67, 112
Great Depression of the 1930s, 33, 34, 97, 120, 121–122, 245, 247, 248, 265, 266, 269, 270, 293, 300–301, 309, 330, 341, 349
Greed, 17, 18, 44, 46, 82, 361–367, 375, 387
Greenspan, Alan, 270
Groceries, 65–66, 110, 149, 376
Gross Domestic Product (GDP), 64, 249, 254, 331, 338
Gross National Product (GNP), 249, 251, 253, 254

Haiti, 340
Harvard, 234, 248, 289, 314, 385
Hayek, Friedrich A., 390
Heinz, Henry J., 135, 196, 197, 380

Hertz, 222
History, 13, 151, 236, 301, 392–393
Hitler, Adolf, 264, 392
Holmes, Oliver Wendell, Jr., 41, 308, 328
Homeless People, 28, 30
Honesty, 283–286, 328
Hong Kong, 164, 211, 281, 329
Hoover, Herbert, 266, 300
Hotels, 18–19, 89, 123, 379
Housing, 18, 22–31, 147, 279–281, 282, 392
  abandoned housing: 27–28, 393
  luxury housing: 29–30, 49, 392n
  rent control: 22–30, 49, 281, 282, 284–286, 392n
Huguenots, 335
Human Capital, 219–221, 350, 355
Hurricanes, 18

IBM, 81
Ice Cream, 9–10
Illinois Central Railroad, 332
Immigration, 334–336, 351
Imperialism, 327, 336–338
Imports (see International Trade and Payments)
Incentives and Constraints, 27, 30, 38, 49–53, 80–83, 281, 282, 288–294, 298, 299, 300, 388, 392, 393
Income,
  age: 145, 146, 150
  family income: 147
  household income: 147, 148
  income "distribution": 144–149, 184–188
  individual income: 147
  pay differentials: 141–142, 144, 149, 181–182, 183–184
  per capita income: 148, 149, 252, 298
  the poor: 145, 146, 149, 186, 187, 280, 390, 394, 396
  the rich: 36, 145, 146, 184–185, 186, 280, 390
  "unearned" income: 178, 200
Incremental Decisions (see Decisions)
India, 13, 35, 36, 37, 40, 51, 52, 79, 80, 81, 104, 112, 117, 118, 134, 138, 178, 182, 186, 187, 193, 201, 221, 226, 232, 240, 271, 274, 275, 276, 283, 284, 290, 298, 299, 300, 309, 318, 319, 322, 329, 338, 340, 350, 352, 354, 356, 364, 373, 378, 389
Infant Industries, 317, 320–321
Inflation, 213, 259–264
Infosys,
Insurance, 132, 204, 221–228, 373
Intel, 81
Intellectuals, ix–x, 14, 82, 394–395, 396
Intentions, 46, 102, 301

Interest rates, 46, 213, 229, 267, 392
International Debt, 309, 330–333, 390
International Monetary Fund, 339, 341, 347–348
International Trade and Payments, 307–326,
    348–356, 384
   balance of payments: 309, 330
   balance of trade: 329–330
   international Investment: 194, 327, 328–333,
    344–345, 348–351
   remittances: 327, 333—334
   transfers of wealth: 327–345
Interstate Commerce Commission (I.C.C.), 104,
    108, 109
Inventory, 198–199, 241, 376
Investment, 191–209, 226, 389
Ireland, 334
Italy, 39, 51, 77, 221, 252, 334, 346
Ivory Coast, 12–13

Jains, 284, 373
Japan, 3, 37, 39, 42, 64, 75, 76, 95, 96, 97, 142,
    173, 178, 253, 315, 318, 323, 328, 329, 335,
    336, 337, 341, 344, 349, 355, 356
J.C. Penney stores, 69, 70, 71, 82
Jews, 201, 151, 231, 232, 277, 283, 284, 355, 373,
    386–387
Job Security, 159–163
Jobs, 247, 324, 325, 346, 350, 391
Johnson, Howard, 88, 124, 131
Johnson, Lyndon B., 271
Johnson, Paul, 392
Jordan, 334
Jowett, Benjamin, 394

Kennedy, John F., 254
Kentucky Fried Chicken, 135
Keynes, John Maynard, 262, 266
Kibbutz, 16, 17
Knowledge, 14, 16, 68, 70, 72–77, 88, 126–131,
    198, 199, 218, 238, 298, 378–380, 393–395,
    396
Koch, Ed, 29
Kodak, 380
Kroc, Ray, 123, 136, 217–218, 394
Kroger's, 78, 79

Labor, 141–188
   employers: 170–172
   job security: 159–163
   maximum wage laws: 154
   minimum wage laws: 22, 154, 163–169, 394
   unions: 169–170, 172–175, 227, 299
   unemployment: 164–166, 181, 193, 245, 246,
    265

   wage rates vs. labor costs: 142, 178–179,
    318–319, 391
Lange, Oskar, 4
Latin America, 166, 179, 180, 260, 297, 327, 339,
    356
Law and order, 272–286, 290
Lenin, V. I., 126, 302, 337, 393
Lewis, John L., 172–173
Lloyd's of London, 63
Loans (see Credit and Creditors)
London, 13, 80, 128, 231, 303, 335, 373
Long Run versus Short Run, ix
Lombards, 231
Los Angeles, 44, 81, 91, 112
Losses (see Profits and Losses)
Luxuries, 185, 302, 374–375

Macy's, 71, 340
Malaysia, 193, 221, 322, 334, 336, 338, 350, 355,
    373
Management, 119–120, 124–126, 200–201, 384
Mantle, Mickey, 143
Maris, Roger, 143
Market Economies, (see also Non-Market
    Economies) 12–13, 53, 132–137, 300,
    372–389
Market Failure, 300
Marshall Plan, 339
Marx, Karl, 15, 79, 82, 177
Massachusetts, 28, 73
McDonald's restaurants, 77, 121, 122–124, 125,
    131, 135, 136, 137, 217, 279, 379, 380–381,
    390, 393, 395
Meat, 33
Media, ix, 186, 298, 396
Medical care, 38–39, 364
Mexico, 36, 89, 211, 319, 327, 341, 344
Microsoft, 63, 113, 114, 115, 330, 334, 377, 383
Middlemen, 91–94
Military, 4, 42, 287, 321
Minimum Wage Laws (see Labor)
Mizuho Bank, 64
Mohawk Indians, 151
Money, 245, 250, 257–270, 351–352, 393
   international monetary system: 341–343
   rate of circulation: 263–264, 265
Monitoring, 279
Monopoly, 99–105, 132
Montgomery Ward, 68–69, 103, 117, 121, 124,
    133
Moody's, 242, 352
Morality, 41, 283–286, 396
Morgan, J. P., 342
Mountain Bikes, 322

Mundell, Robert, 342
Mutual Funds, 218–219

Nader, Ralph, 347
Nationalization (see Confiscation)
Natural disasters, 18, 30, 132–133, 224, 225
Natural resources, 16, 50, 205–209, 229, 392
"Needs," 15–16, 300, 367–370
Nehru, Jawaharlal, 79, 82, 281, 378
Netherlands, 27, 145, 164, 315, 337, 348
New York Central Railroad, 332
New York City, 2, 24, 25, 26, 27–28, 29, 30, 32, 67, 71, 75, 108, 116, 191, 238, 261, 281, 283, 285, 360, 393
New York Herald-Tribune, 67
New York State, 18
New York Times, 2–3, 25, 35, 36, 67, 97, 116, 225, 307
New Zealand, 13, 64, 145, 153, 164, 168, 185, 227–228
Newspapers, 67, 91, 116, 362–363, 389
Niger, 353
Nigeria, 328, 330
Nikon, 67, 379
Nixon Administration, 52, 76, 289, 290
Non-Economic Values, 359–371
Non-Market Economies, 74–76, 132–137, 393–394
Non-Profit Organizations, 385–388
Norway, 254, 343

Ottoman Empire, 277, 336, 355

Pakistan, 334
Pan American Airlines, 67, 112
Pay (see Income)
Penney, James Cash, 69, 70, 186, 187, 394
Persian Gulf War, 236
Petroleum, 191, 194 , 389, 392
Politics, 28–30, 37 39–40, 108–110, 223–224, 225, 231, 235, 236, 261–262, 289, 292, 298–299, 300, 303–304, 351, 352–353, 396
Pollution, 290–292
The Poor (see Income)
Popov, Vladimir, 11, 281
"Predatory" Pricing, 323, 377–378
Present value (see Time)
Price control, 21–40, 52, 155, 289–290, 366–367, 391–392
   "ceiling" prices: 21, 22–33, 34
   "floor" prices: 21, 33–37
Prices, x, 7–60, 250, 375–378
Priorities (see Decisions)
Productivity, 142–143, 151, 178, 356

Profits and Losses (see also Non-Profit Organizations), 64–65, 78–98, 120, 179, 281, 381–388
   losses: 9, 20, 63, 64, 68, 81, 119, 123, 353–354, 383, 385
   profits on sales: 82, 83, 84
   profits on investment: 83
Property Rights, 231, 240–241, 277–282, 341, 394
Protectionism, 346–348
Purchasing Power, 252–253, 261, 262, 264–265, 266, 279, 280, 315, 341

Quality, 37–39, 81, 86, 133–136, 168, 301, 381

Railroads, 104, 108, 288, 332, 348, 350, 389
Rationing, 8, 17–19
Reagan, Ronald, 137
"Real" value, 17–18
Reconstruction Finance Corporation (RFC), 293–294
Rent control (see Housing)
Rhodes, Cecil, 336
Rhodesia, 128
Ricardo, David, 382
The Rich (see Income)
Risk, 194, 197, 200, 205–228
Robbins, Lionel, 1
Rockefeller Center, 329
Rockefellers, 36, 82, 136, 360, 385
Roman Empire, 51, 262, 290
Roosevelt, Franklin D., 266, 293, 300
Russia, 32, 51, 52–53, 127, 195, 209, 211, 263, 271, 274, 319, 323, 328, 336, 346, 350, 354, 393
Russian Roulette, 229, 235

Saccharin, 291
Safety, 291–293, 367
Safeway, 66, 100, 117, 121, 137, 376, 393
Sak's, 340
San Francisco, 25, 26, 29, 30, 73, 77, 116, 281, 282, 376
Sanders, Colonel, 135, 279
Sarnoff, David, 186
Scarcity, 1, 2, 3, 12, 24, 27, 30–32, 42, 51, 53–60, 138
Sears stores, 68, 69, 70, 82, 98, 121, 125, 133, 160, 395
Sears, Richard Warren, 97, 103, 117, 124, 186, 361
Sex, 149–150, 152
Shaw, George Bernard, 79, 82
Shmelev, Nikolai, 11, 281
Shortages, 16, 22, 23, 24, 30–32, 39, 51, 154–155

Simon, Julian, 207, 209
Singapore, 328, 349, 373
Small Business Administration (SBA), 294
Smith, Adam, 43, 177, 308, 317, 352, 362, 382, 386
Smith-Corona, 67–68, 112, 114, 137, 138
Social Costs and Social Benefits, 286–288, 292–293
Social Security, 226–227, 302
Socialism and Socialists, 79–80, 94–98, 179, 253, 272, 365, 372
Sonneborn, Harry, 124
Sony, 63, 64
South Korea, 13, 315, 356
Soviet Union, 7, 10, 11, 12, 15, 31, 48, 50, 74, 75, 76, 86–87, 94, 95, 96, 127, 128, 129, 151, 157, 158, 241, 263, 272, 278, 279, 281, 288, 290, 363–364, 381, 384
Spain, 39, 259, 327, 334, 335
Specialization, 90–98, 348–349
Speculation, 194–198, 304
Sri Lanka, 13, 241
Stalin, Josef, 48, 80
Standard & Poor's, 204, 219, 242, 352
Steel, 325, 347, 391
Stigler, George J., 360n
Stiglitz, Joseph, 348
Stocks, 210, 213–217, 220–221, 245
Subsidies, 57, 299, 385
Substitution, 56
Supermarkets, 44
Supply and Demand, 16, 141, 290
Surplus, 22, 33–37
Sweden, 23–24, 28, 138, 315, 343, 351
Switzerland, 3, 75, 164, 165, 331, 335

Taiwan, 109, 313, 315, 351, 356
Tariffs, 323, 349
Tata Industries, 193, 318
Taxes, 57, 76, 237, 239–240, 261, 292, 391
Thatcher, Margaret, 7, 137
Thailand, 13, 117, 275, 322, 344
Third World, 19–20, 36, 92–94, 156, 158, 166, 178, 193, 231, 240, 256, 273, 286, 337–341, 344–345, 350, 351, 353–356, 360, 367, 396
Thomas, Dave, 135
Thornton, Henry, 359
Time, 201, 202–203, 229, 232–242, 376, 384
    present value: 202–209, 229, 237, 290, 384
    risk: 217–218
    trends: 254–256
The Times of London, 27
Toronto, 27
Toyota, 96, 119, 120, 315, 329
"Trickle-Down" Theory, 388–389

Tsingtao Beer, 335
Turner, Ted, 36

Unemployment (see Labor)
Unfairness (see Fairness and Unfairness)
Uganda, 354
Union of Soviet Socialist Republics (USSR) (see Soviet Union)
Unions (see Labor)
UNISYS, 383
United Kingdom (see Britain)
United Parcel Service, 95, 304, 380
United States, 2, 11–12, 22, 23, 26, 31, 34, 35, 36, 55, 64, 65, 73, 74, 75, 76, 85, 90, 92, 95, 99, 100, 104, 108, 109, 110, 112, 113, 114, 121, 123, 132, 137, 145, 147, 151, 153, 156, 158–169, 173, 173, 178, 186, 188, 195, 205, 207, 211, 213, 222, 224, 226, 227, 234, 236, 240, 245, 246, 250–260, 264, 266, 269, 272, 274, 277, 278, 282, 286, 289, 293, 300, 301, 307–315, 317–327, 329–349, 351, 355, 360, 370, 373, 375, 386, 390–391

Venezuela, 236
Venture Capital, 214–215
Vietnam, 49

Wages and salaries (see Income)
Wales (see Ageitain)
Wall Street Journal, 36, 67, 79, 116, 162, 164, 218, 229, 325, 373
Wal-Mart, 66, 70, 79, 160, 362
Ward's Department Stores, 68, 69, 70, 71, 361
Washington, D.C., 26, 75, 108, 270, 325
Washington Post, 123, 148, 378
Waste, 157–158, 370–371
Water, 58, 366, 373–374
Wealth, 226, 227, 249–250, 304, 327–345, 364
Wendy's Restaurants, 135, 136, 381
Weyerhauser, Frederick, 186
White Castle Restaurants, 121–123, 131, 393
Williams, Ted, 143
Wilson, Woodrow, 265
Woolworth, Frank Winfield, 136, 394, 396
World Bank, 274, 339, 341, 347
World War I, 263, 293, 332, 341
World War II, 22, 33, 34, 42, 65, 71, 99, 120, 121, 122, 128, 151, 154, 155, 184, 250, 258, 337, 339, 386

Yogurt, 9–10

Zero-sum Activities, 109, 179, 295–297, 307, 344–345, 349, 350, 396